FUNDAMENTALS OF DISASTER MANAGEMENT

PRAVIN KHANDVE

ISBN 979-8-89186-436-8

Dedicated to

All My Friends and Students

Preface

When I was studying M. Tech in Environment Engineering in 2012 we have a subject "Hazardous Waste Management" for which as per the prescribed syllabus there are two units on topic Disaster Management. We are not getting any proper textbook covering given topics on Disaster Management. I started searching various references where I came to know that there are so many aspects related to Disaster management, and syllabus included is very vast hence studying many aspects will take long time. All the way, we could manage to collect the study material for all the topics and prepared brief notes for exam purpose. During this we have explored topics via Internet, books from library, handbook published by few agencies and studied the important topics related to Disaster Management. While writing book on Hazardous Waste Management, I came to know that Disaster Management is also one of the important areas to deal with. Hence I have decided to write this book. This book is the outcome of the various case studies done time to time. I got attracted towards this topic in 1993 after Latur Earthquake. Again in 2001 after Bhuj Earthquake occurs in India. Where I have prepared some of drawing sheets to explain about Earthquake – what, when, why, how where. The first case study I have started with Bhuj Earthquake where I have delivered my first technical presentation on earthquake organized by Institution of Engineers, India, Amravati Center at MJB Meeting Hall, Maltekadi, Amravati, for which my Professor A. P. Dange and Prof. P. S. Pajgade inspired me to prepare detailed presentation. In subsequent years I was engaged with few other NGOs and Government officers for Post Disaster works. Again in 2004 Tsunami Disaster occurred, where so many other aspects of post disaster management arrived as challenges for government agencies. The field visits to various villages & disaster sites, discussion held with officers & rescue team, observations thereof, challenges faced and solutions provided by experts given me lot of insights about disaster management. In 2019 again Corona Disaster strikes the world, and there are new challenges came across. During lockdown, I tried to evaluate the situation and written three long articles in Marathi about this new disaster and published them in local newspaper – Dainik Hindusthan. I received so many comments on these articles indicating for need of awareness on disaster management. This event triggered me to write a book on topic Disaster Management so that I can contribute for post disaster response as a social responsibility of every citizen.

In a world where the threat of natural and man-made disasters looms large, understanding and effectively managing these crises is of paramount importance. This book, "Fundamentals of Disaster Management" is a comprehensive exploration of the intricacies of disaster management in the Indian context. It delves deep into the multifaceted aspects of disasters, ranging from their causes, impacts, and response strategies to the pivotal role of technology in modern disaster management. This preface provides an overview of the book's contents and the importance of this knowledge in safeguarding our communities and environment.

The book begins with an introduction to disaster management, shedding light on various terms and concepts associated with it. It further explores the challenges India faces in managing disasters and the strategies employed to mitigate these challenges. The chapter underscores the significance of disaster management in a country as diverse and disaster-prone as India. It also discusses the various initiatives taken to enhance disaster preparedness and response at the national level.

Second chapter unravels the natural disasters that plague India, including floods, droughts, cyclones, earthquakes, tsunamis, and more. Each section provides in-depth insights into the nature and impact of these disasters, enabling readers to comprehend the complexity of disaster management in a country where nature's fury is a constant threat. While natural disasters garner significant attention, third chapter highlights the equally crucial realm of man-made disasters. From industrial pollution to terrorist strikes, this chapter dissects the various forms of man-made disasters, their implications, and the imperative need for efficient management.

Understanding the geographic and ecological vulnerabilities of India is crucial in the context of disaster management. Fourth chapter explores the unique hazard and vulnerability profiles of India's mountains, coastal areas, and fragile ecosystems, providing an essential backdrop for disaster risk reduction strategies. Disasters affect more than just physical infrastructure; they have far-reaching impacts on the environment, society, economics, and politics. Fifth chapter examines these multifaceted impacts, emphasizing the need for comprehensive impact assessments in disaster management.

Health and psycho-social well-being are often overlooked aspects of disaster management. Sixth chapter underscores the importance of addressing these issues, highlighting the roles of various government and non-governmental organizations, including the Ministry of Health and Family Welfare (MoHFW) and the National Disaster Management Authority (NDMA). Demographic factors play a significant role in determining a community's vulnerability to disasters. Seventh chapter explores the demographic aspects of disaster impact, gender considerations, age-specific vulnerabilities, and the need for an inclusive approach in disaster management.

Examining historical trends and case studies is essential for understanding the evolution of disaster management. Eighth chapter delves into global and national disaster trends, offering valuable insights into India's disaster management history. As climate change accelerates, urban areas become increasingly vulnerable to disasters. Ninth chapter elucidates the intricate relationship between climate change and urban disasters, emphasizing the importance of disaster-resilient urban planning.

Preventing disasters and reducing their impact is at the core of disaster management. Tenth chapter explores the principles, phases, and measures in disaster risk reduction, from mitigation to preparedness and recovery. Eleventh chapter outlines the institutional framework for disaster management in India, emphasizing the roles and responsibilities of government bodies, local authorities, NGOs, and civil society. It also discusses relevant legislation and policies.

Real-life case studies and best practices from India offer valuable insights into effective disaster management. Twelve chapter showcases national guidelines, disaster management practices, and the critical role of engineers and medical preparedness in disaster reduction. The final chapter dives into the modern technological advancements that are transforming disaster management. It explores how technologies like remote sensing, drones, AI, IoT, and more are enhancing disaster preparedness and response.

Thus "Fundamentals of Disaster Management" is a holistic guide that addresses the complexities of disaster management. This book is intended for a wide range of readers, from students and researchers to practitioners and policymakers, all of whom share a common goal: building resilience in the face of natural and man-made catastrophes. By understanding the challenges and learning from best practices, we hope to contribute to a safer and more disaster-resilient India and, by extension, a safer world.

– Prof. Er. Pravin V. Khandve

Contents

CHAPTER 1

Introduction to Disaster Management

1.1 Various terms related to "Disaster Management"

1.2 Disaster Risk in India: Challenges and Mitigation Strategies

1.3 Disaster management

    1.3.1 Disaster Management Framework in India

    1.3.2 Current Scenario of Disaster Management Cycle in India

    1.3.3 Importance of Disaster Management in India

    1.3.4 Statistics for Importance of Disaster Management

1.4 Disaster Management Initiatives in India

    1.4.1 Disaster Emergency Management Systems in India

    1.4.2 Initiatives and Success Stories

    1.4.3 Challenges and Way Forward

1.1 Various terms related to "Disaster Management"

1) **Capacity**: Capacity refers to the ability of individuals, communities, organizations, and systems to effectively anticipate, respond to, recover from, and adapt to the impacts of hazards or disasters. It includes resources, skills, knowledge, infrastructure, governance structures, and institutional frameworks. Building and strengthening capacity is crucial for effective disaster management and resilience building.

2) **Cascading Effects**: Cascading effects refer to the secondary or indirect impacts triggered by a disaster. These effects can include infrastructure failures, disruptions in critical services, economic losses, and social upheaval, which can further exacerbate the overall impact of the disaster.

3) **Community Engagement**: Community engagement involves actively involving community members in all stages

of disaster management, including planning, decision-making, and implementation. It recognizes the importance of local knowledge, perspectives, and capacities in effective disaster management.

4) **Community Resilience**: Community resilience refers to the ability of a community to withstand, adapt to, and recover from the impacts of disasters. It involves building social cohesion, enhancing local capacities, and fostering effective communication and collaboration among community members.

5) **Community-Based Disaster Management**: Community-based disaster management involves empowering local communities to actively participate in disaster risk reduction and response. It recognizes the knowledge, resources, and capacities within communities and promotes their involvement in planning, decision-making, and implementation of disaster management measures.

6) **Damage Assessment**: Damage assessment involves evaluating and documenting the extent of physical, infrastructure, and property damage caused by a disaster. It helps inform response and recovery efforts, resource allocation, and the prioritization of assistance.

7) **Disaster Preparedness Kits**: Disaster preparedness kits are packages of essential supplies and equipment that individuals and households should have readily available in case of a disaster. These kits typically include items such as non-perishable food, drinking water, first aid supplies, flashlights, batteries, a battery-powered radio, personal hygiene items, and important documents. Disaster preparedness kits help individuals and families meet their immediate needs during the initial phase of a disaster before further assistance becomes available.

8) **Disaster Recovery Funding**: Disaster recovery funding includes financial resources allocated by governments, international organizations, and donor agencies to support post-disaster recovery and reconstruction efforts. It

aims to cover the costs of infrastructure repair, housing reconstruction, livelihood restoration, and the provision of essential services. Disaster recovery funding sources can include government budgets, donor contributions, international aid, grants, loans, insurance claims, and public-private partnerships.

9) **Disaster Risk Financing**: Disaster risk financing refers to financial mechanisms and strategies put in place to manage and cover the costs of disaster response, recovery, and reconstruction. It involves methods to ensure the availability of financial resources during and after disasters, such as establishing contingency funds, insurance mechanisms, public-private partnerships, and risk transfer instruments. Disaster risk financing aims to enhance financial resilience, reduce fiscal burdens, and enable timely and effective disaster response and recovery.

10) **Disaster Simulation Exercises**: Disaster simulation exercises are practical drills, tabletop exercises, or simulations conducted to test and evaluate the preparedness and response capabilities of individuals, organizations, and communities. They help identify strengths, weaknesses, and areas for improvement.

11) **Disaster**: A disaster is an event or series of events that result in serious disruptions, destruction, and loss. It exceeds the capacity of affected communities to cope using their own resources and requires external assistance for recovery. Disasters can be natural (such as earthquakes, hurricanes, floods) or human-induced (such as industrial accidents, terrorist attacks).

12) **Early Warning Systems**: Early warning systems are designed to detect and provide timely information about impending hazards to at-risk populations. They involve monitoring and surveillance, data analysis, and dissemination of warnings to enable prompt action and evacuation if necessary.

13) **Emergency Operations Centre (EOC)**: The emergency operations center is a physical location where representatives

from various agencies, organizations, and disciplines come together to coordinate and manage emergency response operations during a disaster. It serves as a hub for information exchange, decision-making, and resource coordination.

14) **Emergency Response Plan**: An emergency response plan is a documented framework that outlines the specific actions, responsibilities, and procedures to be followed by individuals and organizations during a disaster or emergency. It provides a step-by-step guide for effective and coordinated response efforts. An emergency response plan typically includes protocols for emergency communication, evacuation procedures, resource allocation, incident management, and coordination with relevant stakeholders.

15) **Environmental Impact Assessment (EIA):** Environmental impact assessment is the process of evaluating and predicting the potential environmental consequences of a proposed development or project. It ensures that potential adverse environmental impacts are identified and mitigated.

16) **Evacuation Planning**: Evacuation planning involves the development of strategies, procedures, and routes for the safe and orderly movement of people from high-risk areas to designated safe locations during a disaster. It includes identifying evacuation zones, establishing evacuation routes, coordinating transportation resources, and ensuring the availability of shelter and essential services for evacuees. Evacuation plans aim to minimize casualties, reduce congestion, and facilitate the efficient evacuation of at-risk populations.

17) **Frequency**: Frequency refers to the rate of occurrence of a hazard or disaster within a specific time period. It measures how often similar events are likely to happen. Understanding the frequency helps in assessing the likelihood and recurrence of events and is important for planning, preparedness, and risk reduction efforts.

18) **Geographic Information System (GIS) Mapping**: GIS mapping refers to the use of computer-based tools and

technology to capture, analyse, manage, and visualize geospatial data related to hazards, vulnerabilities, resources, and infrastructure. It allows for the creation of maps and spatial analysis, aiding in the identification of high-risk areas, planning evacuation routes, assessing damage, and making informed decisions for disaster management.

19) **Hazard Communication**: Hazard communication involves the effective dissemination of information about hazards, risks, and safety measures to the public, stakeholders, and organizations. It ensures that individuals and communities are aware of potential threats and can take appropriate actions.

20) **Hazard Mapping**: Hazard mapping involves the identification, analysis, and visualization of areas that are prone to specific hazards. It helps in understanding the spatial distribution of risks and supports decision-making for land-use planning, infrastructure development, and emergency preparedness.

21) **Hazard Zonation**: Hazard zonation is the process of mapping and delineating areas based on the degree of vulnerability to specific hazards. It helps identify high-risk zones, which inform land-use planning, development regulations, and emergency response strategies.

22) **Hazard**: A hazard is a potential source of harm or adverse effect. It refers to the conditions or events with the potential to cause damage, destruction, or injury. Hazards can be classified as natural hazards (such as geological, hydrological, meteorological, and biological events) or human-induced hazards (such as technological accidents, environmental pollution, and conflicts).

23) **Hazardous Materials Management**: Hazardous materials management refers to the handling, storage, and disposal of hazardous substances or materials. It includes the implementation of safety protocols, regulations, and response plans to prevent or mitigate incidents involving hazardous materials.

24) **Hazard-Specific Planning:** Hazard-specific planning involves developing specific strategies and measures tailored to the unique characteristics and risks associated with a particular hazard, such as floods, earthquakes, or wildfires. It ensures targeted preparedness and response actions.

25) **Humanitarian Assistance:** Humanitarian assistance refers to the provision of aid, support, and relief services to affected populations during and after a disaster. It includes the delivery of food, water, shelter, healthcare, and other essential supplies to meet the immediate needs of those affected.

26) **Impact:** Impact refers to the consequences or effects of a hazard or disaster on various aspects such as human life, infrastructure, economy, environment, and social systems. It includes both immediate and long-term effects, such as injuries, fatalities, property damage, displacement, disruption of services, and environmental degradation. Assessing the impact helps in understanding the severity of the event and formulating appropriate response and recovery measures.

27) **Incident Command Post (ICP):** The incident command post is the designated location where the incident management team operates and coordinates the overall response to a disaster. It serves as the central command center for decision-making and information management.

28) **Incident Command System (ICS):** The Incident Command System is a standardized approach to the command, control, and coordination of emergency response efforts. It provides a hierarchical structure, roles, and responsibilities, and facilitates effective communication and coordination among responding agencies and organizations.

29) **Incident Management System:** An incident management system is a standardized approach and organizational structure used for managing emergencies and disasters. It provides a framework for effective command, control, coordination, and communication during response operations. Incident management systems typically follow

a hierarchical structure, with clearly defined roles and responsibilities for individuals and teams involved in incident response. They promote efficient decision-making, resource allocation, and information sharing among responding agencies and organizations.

30) **Incident Management Team**: An incident management team is a group of trained personnel responsible for coordinating and managing the response to a disaster or emergency. The team works together to assess the situation, allocate resources, and implement response plans.

31) **Incident Response Plan**: An incident response plan outlines the specific actions, responsibilities, and procedures to be followed in responding to a disaster or emergency. It includes protocols for activating the plan, mobilizing resources, coordinating response efforts, and communicating with stakeholders.

32) **International Humanitarian Assistance**: International humanitarian assistance involves support and aid provided by foreign countries, organizations, and agencies to assist a disaster-affected country. It includes financial assistance, technical expertise, relief supplies, and personnel.

33) **Mass Casualty Management**: Mass casualty management involves the coordination of emergency medical services and resources to provide timely and effective care for a large number of injured or affected individuals during a disaster. It includes triage, medical treatment, and transportation to appropriate healthcare facilities.

34) **Mitigation**: Mitigation refers to actions and measures taken to reduce or minimize the adverse impacts of hazards or disasters. It involves activities such as hazard mapping, structural measures (such as building retrofitting), ecosystem management, early warning systems, public education, and community preparedness. Mitigation aims to reduce vulnerability, enhance resilience, and lessen the impacts of future disasters.

35) **Multi-Hazard Approach:** The multi-hazard approach recognizes that communities and regions may face multiple hazards and addresses them collectively rather than individually. It involves integrated planning, risk assessments, and the development of comprehensive strategies and measures to address a range of potential hazards.

36) **Participatory Disaster Risk Assessment:** Participatory disaster risk assessment involves engaging community members, stakeholders, and experts in the assessment and analysis of disaster risks. It recognizes the local knowledge and expertise, ensuring a more inclusive and comprehensive understanding of hazards and vulnerabilities.

37) **Participatory Planning:** Participatory planning is an approach that involves engaging communities, stakeholders, and affected populations in the decision-making process of disaster management. It recognizes the importance of local knowledge, experiences, and perspectives in shaping effective and inclusive strategies. Participatory planning ensures that those most affected by disasters have a voice in the planning and decision-making processes, leading to more context-specific, sustainable, and community-centered disaster management approaches.

38) **Post-Disaster Needs Assessment (PDNA):** A post-disaster needs assessment is a comprehensive evaluation conducted after a disaster to assess the damages, losses, and recovery needs of affected areas. It helps inform recovery and reconstruction efforts and assists in resource allocation and planning.

39) **Post-Disaster Reconstruction:** Post-disaster reconstruction refers to the process of rebuilding and restoring affected infrastructure, housing, and communities after a disaster. It involves a comprehensive assessment, planning, and implementation of measures to facilitate long-term recovery and resilience.

40) **Preparedness:** Preparedness involves activities undertaken before a disaster to ensure effective response and recovery. It includes planning, organizing resources, training, and conducting drills or simulations.

41) **Prevention:** Prevention involves activities and measures aimed at eliminating or reducing the likelihood and occurrence of hazards or disasters. It focuses on addressing the root causes and underlying factors that contribute to the occurrence and severity of disasters. Prevention measures include land-use planning, building codes and regulations, early warning systems, public awareness, and policy interventions to reduce risks.

42) **Psychological First Aid:** Psychological first aid involves providing immediate support and assistance to individuals affected by a disaster to address their emotional and psychological needs. It aims to promote emotional well-being, reduce distress, and facilitate coping and resilience.

43) **Recovery Planning:** Recovery planning involves the development of strategies and actions to facilitate the long-term recovery and reconstruction of affected communities. It includes social, economic, and physical aspects, aiming to restore normalcy and enhance resilience.

44) **Recovery:** Recovery encompasses the long-term process of rebuilding and restoring affected communities and infrastructure following a disaster. It involves activities like reconstruction, rehabilitation, and the restoration of essential services and livelihoods.

45) **Relief:** Relief refers to the immediate assistance provided to affected populations during or immediately after a disaster. It includes activities like search and rescue, emergency medical care, and the provision of food, water, shelter, and basic necessities.

46) **Remote Sensing:** Remote sensing involves the use of satellite imagery, aerial photography, and other sensor technologies to gather information about the Earth's surface from a distance. In disaster management, remote sensing plays a crucial role in mapping and monitoring hazards, assessing damages, identifying changes in the environment, and supporting decision-making processes. It provides valuable data for hazard assessment, land-use

planning, and monitoring the impact of disasters over large areas.

47) **Resettlement and Rehabilitation:** Resettlement and rehabilitation involve the process of relocating and providing support to individuals or communities displaced or affected by a disaster. It includes finding suitable housing, ensuring access to basic services such as water, sanitation, and healthcare, and restoring livelihoods to help affected populations recover and rebuild their lives. Resettlement and rehabilitation efforts aim to minimize the social and economic impacts of displacement and promote long-term recovery and resilience.

48) **Resilience:** Resilience is the ability of a community or system to withstand, adapt to, and recover from the impacts of a disaster. It involves building capacities and implementing measures to reduce vulnerability and enhance preparedness.

49) **Risk Assessment:** Risk assessment is the process of evaluating the potential risks associated with a hazard. It involves analysing the probability of an event occurring, assessing the vulnerability of exposed elements, and estimating the potential impacts. Risk assessments inform decision-making and help prioritize mitigation and preparedness efforts.

50) **Risk Communication:** Risk communication is the process of sharing information about risks, hazards, and protective measures to individuals, communities, and stakeholders in a clear and effective manner. It involves conveying accurate and timely information to enhance understanding, raise awareness, and enable informed decision-making regarding potential hazards. Effective risk communication facilitates preparedness, response, and resilience-building efforts.

51) **Risk:** Risk is the likelihood or probability of an event occurring and the associated negative consequences or impacts. It involves assessing the potential for loss, damage, or harm resulting from exposure to a hazard. Risk is determined by considering the vulnerability of exposed

elements and the capacity to manage and respond to the hazard.

52) **Severity**: Severity refers to the extent and intensity of the impact or damage caused by a hazard or disaster. It measures the magnitude and scale of the event, including the degree of destruction, loss of life, economic losses, and environmental damage. Severity helps in understanding the intensity of the impact and the resources required for response and recovery.

53) **Shelter Management**: Shelter management involves the planning, coordination, and provision of adequate and safe shelter for displaced populations during and after a disaster. It includes site selection, construction or rehabilitation of shelters, and addressing the specific needs of vulnerable groups.

54) **Social Vulnerability**: Social vulnerability refers to the susceptibility of certain social groups or populations to the impacts of disasters due to underlying factors such as poverty, inequality, marginalization, and limited access to resources or services. It recognizes the differential impact of disasters on different segments of society.

55) **Stakeholder Engagement**: Stakeholder engagement involves actively involving relevant individuals, groups, organizations, and communities in the decision-making processes related to disaster management. It promotes collaboration, knowledge sharing, and inclusive decision-making to ensure that diverse perspectives and needs are considered.

56) **Technological Disasters**: Technological disasters refer to disasters caused by failures or accidents related to technology, infrastructure, or industrial processes. These can include incidents such as chemical spills, nuclear accidents, oil spills, industrial explosions, or collapses of infrastructure. Technological disasters often have unique characteristics and require specialized response strategies, including hazardous materials management,

decontamination procedures, and coordination with technical experts.

57) **Volunteer Management**: Volunteer management refers to the recruitment, training, coordination, and supervision of volunteers who contribute their time, skills, and resources to support disaster response and recovery operations. Effective volunteer management involves identifying volunteer needs, conducting volunteer training programs, establishing volunteer roles and responsibilities, and ensuring their safety and well-being during operations. It also includes recognizing and appreciating the contributions of volunteers.

58) **Vulnerability**: Vulnerability refers to the characteristics and circumstances of individuals, communities, systems, or assets that make them susceptible to the harmful effects of hazards or disasters. It encompasses various factors, including social, economic, environmental, and physical vulnerabilities. Vulnerability can be influenced by poverty, lack of access to resources, weak infrastructure, and limited coping capacities.

59) Understanding these terms related to disaster management will help in developing a comprehensive understanding of the field and its various dimensions. They encompass areas such as community engagement, business continuity, vulnerability assessment, and the integration of environmental considerations in disaster management practices.

1.2 Disaster Risk in India: Challenges and Mitigation Strategies

India is a country vulnerable to a wide range of natural and man-made disasters due to its diverse geographical, climatic, and geological characteristics. The frequency and intensity of disasters have increased over the years, posing significant challenges to the country's social, economic, and environmental well-being. Understanding and mitigating disaster risks in India is crucial to building resilience and safeguarding lives and assets.

Types of Disaster Risks in India: India faces various types of disaster risks, including:

i) Natural Disasters: These include floods, cyclones, earthquakes, droughts, landslides, heatwaves, and cold waves. India is particularly susceptible to cyclones along its coastal regions, earthquakes in seismic zones, and floods during monsoons.

ii) Man-Made Disasters: These disasters are often caused by human activities and include industrial accidents, chemical spills, nuclear accidents, and terrorist attacks.

iii) Environmental Degradation: Deforestation, soil erosion, and pollution can exacerbate the impact of natural disasters and contribute to long-term disaster risks.

Factors Contributing to Disaster Risk in India:

i) Geographical Vulnerability: India's vast coastline, presence in seismic zones, and diverse climatic regions make it prone to multiple hazards.

ii) Population Density: High population density in urban areas increases the vulnerability of communities to disasters.

iii) Urbanization: Rapid urbanization without adequate planning and infrastructure leads to increased disaster risks in cities.

iv) Climate Change: Changing climate patterns are resulting in more frequent and severe disasters, such as floods, droughts, and heatwaves.

v) Lack of Awareness: Limited awareness and preparedness among the population contribute to increased vulnerability during disasters.

vi) Inadequate Infrastructure: Weak infrastructure and inadequate enforcement of building codes can lead to higher casualties and damage during disasters.

Disaster Risk Mitigation Strategies in India:

i) Early Warning Systems: Implementing robust early warning systems for cyclones, floods, and earthquakes can save lives and enable timely evacuation.

ii) Disaster Preparedness and Training: Conducting regular drills and training programs for communities, first responders, and government agencies enhances preparedness.

iii) Infrastructure Development: Constructing disaster-resilient infrastructure and ensuring compliance with building codes can reduce damage during disasters.

iv) Ecosystem Conservation: Protecting and restoring ecosystems like wetlands and mangroves can act as natural buffers against disasters.

v) Climate Change Adaptation: Implementing measures to adapt to climate change, such as water conservation and drought-resistant agriculture, can reduce disaster risks.

vi) Community Participation: Involving local communities in disaster management planning and decision-making enhances resilience and effectiveness.

vii) Disaster Risk Financing: Creating disaster risk financing mechanisms ensures timely financial support for response and recovery efforts.

Government Initiatives for Disaster Risk Reduction:

i) National Disaster Management Plan (NDMP): The NDMP provides a comprehensive framework for disaster risk reduction and management in India.

ii) National Disaster Management Authority (NDMA): The NDMA coordinates disaster management efforts and provides policy guidance.

iii) National Disaster Response Force (NDRF): The NDRF is a specialized force trained for disaster response and rescue operations.

iv) National Cyclone Risk Mitigation Project (NCRMP): This project focuses on cyclone risk mitigation in coastal states.

v) National Disaster Database (NIDM): The NIDM maintains a comprehensive database of disasters in India.

Challenges in Disaster Risk Reduction (DRR) in India:

i) Resource Constraints: Limited resources, both financial and human, pose challenges in implementing comprehensive DRR initiatives across the vast and diverse country.

ii) Inter-Agency Coordination: Effective coordination among multiple government agencies and stakeholders is essential for successful disaster management. However, sometimes, there may be gaps in coordination and collaboration, hindering a cohesive response.

iii) Climate Change Impacts: India is experiencing the effects of climate change, including rising sea levels, increased frequency of extreme weather events, and changing monsoon patterns. These factors amplify the risk and complexity of managing disasters.

iv) Rural-Urban Divide: The difference in resources and infrastructure between rural and urban areas can lead to disparities in disaster preparedness and response capabilities.

v) Informal Settlements: Rapid urbanization has led to the growth of informal settlements with inadequate infrastructure, making these areas more vulnerable to disasters.

vi) Population Growth: India's large and growing population exacerbates the impact of disasters, especially in densely populated regions.

Innovations in Disaster Risk Reduction:

i) Use of Technology: Technology plays a significant role in disaster risk reduction. Remote sensing, GIS, satellite imagery, and drones are used for risk mapping, damage assessment, and early warning systems.

ii) Mobile Apps: Mobile applications have been developed for disseminating early warnings, collecting real-time data during disasters, and providing information to affected communities.

iii) Community-Based Approaches: Engaging local communities in disaster risk reduction efforts empowers them to take proactive measures and contributes to more sustainable and effective outcomes.

iv) Public-Private Partnerships: Collaboration between the government, private sector, and non-governmental organizations (NGOs) can enhance resources and expertise for disaster management.

v) Social Media: Social media platforms have emerged as valuable tools for disseminating information, coordinating relief efforts, and providing real-time updates during disasters.

vi) Climate-Resilient Agriculture: Promoting climate-resilient agricultural practices helps farmers adapt to changing weather patterns and reduces the impact of droughts and floods on food security.

Disaster risk in India is a complex and multifaceted issue that requires a comprehensive and integrated approach to address effectively. Addressing disaster risks requires a multi-faceted approach involving government agencies, communities, private sector, and civil society. By investing in disaster risk reduction strategies, early warning systems, infrastructure development, and community engagement, India can build resilience and reduce the impact of disasters on its people and economy. While India faces numerous challenges in disaster risk reduction, the country has made significant progress in implementing various initiatives and policies to build resilience. Embracing innovative technologies, fostering community participation, and strengthening inter-agency coordination are critical for enhancing disaster preparedness, response, and recovery. A proactive and coordinated approach to disaster risk reduction is essential to create a safer and more sustainable future for the country.

The government's commitment to disaster risk reduction, as evident through initiatives like the National Disaster Management Plan (NDMP) and National Disaster Management Authority

(NDMA), underscores the importance of disaster management in national development. By adopting proactive measures, integrating DRR in development plans, and investing in sustainable practices, India can continue to enhance its resilience to disasters and protect the well-being of its people and environment. Moreover, public awareness and education about disaster preparedness and mitigation play a vital role in empowering individuals and communities to actively contribute to disaster risk reduction efforts. In combination with government action and international cooperation, these efforts can lead to a safer and more disaster-resilient India.

1.3 Disaster management

Disaster management is the process of planning, organizing, coordinating, and implementing measures to prevent, prepare for, respond to, and recover from a disaster or emergency situation. It involves a systematic approach to reduce the impact of disasters on communities, infrastructure, and the environment. The disaster management framework provides a structured and comprehensive framework for managing disasters, while the disaster management cycle outlines the different phases of disaster management.

Disaster Management Framework:

The disaster management framework consists of four key components:

a) **Prevention and Mitigation:** This component focuses on activities and measures taken to prevent or reduce the occurrence of disasters and minimize their impact. It includes measures such as land-use planning, building codes and regulations, early warning systems, public awareness campaigns, and environmental protection initiatives.

b) **Preparedness:** Preparedness involves developing plans, procedures, and capabilities to respond effectively to a disaster. It includes activities such as creating emergency response plans, conducting drills and exercises, training personnel, stockpiling necessary supplies and equipment, and establishing communication systems.

c) **Response:** The response phase involves the immediate actions taken to address the effects of a disaster. It includes activities such as search and rescue operations, medical assistance, evacuation, providing emergency shelter, distributing food and water, and restoring essential services.

d) **Recovery:** The recovery phase focuses on restoring and rebuilding affected communities and infrastructure. It includes activities such as assessing damages, conducting post-disaster needs assessments, providing financial assistance and resources for reconstruction, facilitating community participation, and implementing long-term recovery plans.

Disaster Management Cycle:

The disaster management cycle represents the ongoing process of managing disasters and consists of four phases:

a) **Preparedness:** This phase involves activities undertaken in advance to ensure effective response to a disaster. It includes developing emergency response plans, conducting training and drills, establishing communication systems, identifying potential hazards and vulnerabilities, and stockpiling necessary resources.

b) **Response:** The response phase occurs when a disaster strikes or is imminent. It involves activating emergency plans, mobilizing resources, coordinating emergency services, conducting search and rescue operations, providing medical assistance, and implementing measures to protect lives and property.

c) **Recovery:** The recovery phase begins once the immediate threat has passed. It focuses on restoring essential services, repairing infrastructure, helping affected individuals and communities, and implementing measures to prevent similar disasters in the future.

d) **Mitigation:** The mitigation phase involves taking measures to minimize the impact of future disasters. It includes activities such as implementing building codes and regulations, improving infrastructure resilience, enhancing early warning systems, conducting public education campaigns, and promoting sustainable development practices.

It is important to note that the disaster management cycle is not a linear process but rather a continuous and iterative one. Lessons learned from previous disasters inform future planning and preparedness efforts, and each phase of the cycle contributes to building resilience and reducing the impact of future disasters.

Overall, the disaster management framework and cycle provide a comprehensive approach to managing disasters, from prevention and preparedness to response and recovery. By adopting this framework and following the cycle, governments, organizations, and communities can better prepare for, respond to, and recover from disasters, ultimately saving lives and reducing the impact on society.

1.3.1 Disaster Management Framework in India

In India, the disaster management framework is governed by the Disaster Management Act, 2005, which provides a legal framework for disaster management and lays down the roles and responsibilities of various stakeholders involved. The framework in India follows a multi-tiered approach, involving the central government, state governments, and local authorities, to effectively manage disasters. Here are the key components of the disaster management framework in India:

i) **National Disaster Management Authority (NDMA):** The NDMA is the apex body responsible for laying down policies, plans, and guidelines for disaster management in India. It is chaired by the Prime Minister and comprises representatives from various ministries, experts, and professionals. The NDMA provides overall direction and coordination for disaster management activities at the national level.

ii) **State Disaster Management Authority (SDMA):** Each state in India has a State Disaster Management Authority, headed by the Chief Minister, to coordinate and implement disaster management efforts within the state. The SDMA is responsible for formulating state-specific policies, plans, and guidelines, as well as coordinating with various departments and agencies to ensure effective disaster preparedness, response, and recovery.

iii) **District Disaster Management Authority (DDMA):** At the district level, the District Magistrate or Collector heads the District Disaster Management Authority. The DDMA is responsible for coordinating and implementing disaster management activities within the district, including preparedness, response, and recovery. It works closely with other government departments, local bodies, NGOs, and community-based organizations.

iv) **National Disaster Response Force (NDRF):** The NDRF is a specialized force constituted under the Disaster Management Act, 2005. It is responsible for specialized response tasks, such as search and rescue operations, medical assistance, evacuation, and providing immediate relief to affected communities. The NDRF teams are strategically stationed across the country for quick deployment during emergencies.

v) **Disaster Management Plans:** Under the disaster management framework, both national and state governments are required to prepare and regularly update disaster management plans. These plans outline the strategies, procedures, and resources needed to effectively respond to different types of disasters. They cover aspects such as early warning systems, evacuation plans, medical support, relief distribution, communication systems, and coordination mechanisms.

vi) **Information and Communication Technology (ICT):** The use of ICT plays a crucial role in disaster management in India. The National Disaster Management Authority has established a dedicated Emergency Operation Center (EOC) and set up the National Disaster Management Information System (NDMIS) to facilitate real-time information exchange, coordination, and decision-making during emergencies. ICT tools, such as mobile apps, websites, and social media platforms, are also utilized for public awareness, early warning dissemination, and reporting of incidents.

vii) **Capacity Building and Training**: The disaster management framework in India emphasizes capacity building and training at various levels. It includes training programs for government officials, emergency responders, community volunteers, and public awareness campaigns to enhance preparedness and response capabilities. Specialized training institutes, such as the National Institute of Disaster Management (NIDM), are responsible for conducting training programs and promoting research and knowledge dissemination in the field of disaster management.

viii) **Financial Mechanisms**: The Indian government has established the National Disaster Response Fund (NDRF) and State Disaster Response Funds (SDRF) to provide financial resources for immediate relief and response activities during disasters. These funds are used for rescue and relief operations, temporary shelters, medical support, and other emergency measures. The funds are supplemented by contributions from the corporate sector, public donations, and international assistance, if required.

ix) **Early Warning Systems**: India has established robust early warning systems to mitigate the impact of disasters. These systems include the Indian Meteorological Department (IMD) for weather-related warnings, the Indian National Centre for Ocean Information Services (INCOIS) for tsunami alerts, and the Central Water Commission (CWC) for flood forecasting. Early warning information is disseminated through various channels, including radio, television, SMS alerts, and mobile apps, to reach communities at risk.

x) **Community Participation and Capacity Building**: The disaster management framework in India recognizes the importance of community participation and local knowledge in disaster management. Efforts are made to involve local communities, NGOs, and voluntary organizations in disaster preparedness, response, and recovery activities. Community-based organizations, such as Village Disaster Management Committees (VDMCs), are formed to strengthen local resilience and facilitate community-led initiatives.

xi) **Sector-Specific Guidelines**: The disaster management framework in India includes sector-specific guidelines to address the unique challenges posed by various sectors. These guidelines cover sectors such as agriculture, health, education, infrastructure, and industry. They provide a framework for integrating disaster risk reduction measures into sectoral planning and implementation to minimize vulnerabilities and enhance resilience.

xii) **International Cooperation**: India actively participates in international cooperation and collaboration for disaster management. It engages with regional and international organizations such as the United Nations Office for Disaster Risk Reduction (UNDRR), the International Red Cross and Red Crescent Movement, and the South Asian Association for Regional Cooperation (SAARC). India also helps other countries during disasters and shares its expertise and best practices.

xiii) **Research and Development**: The disaster management framework in India promotes research and development in the field of disaster management. The National Institute of Disaster Management (NIDM) and other research institutions collaborate with academic institutions, experts, and practitioners to conduct research, develop innovative solutions, and promote knowledge exchange. This helps in improving disaster risk assessment, early warning systems, and response strategies.

xiv) **Policy and Legal Framework**: Apart from the Disaster Management Act, 2005, India has formulated several policies and guidelines to strengthen disaster management. The National Policy on Disaster Management, National Guidelines on School Safety, National Guidelines on Hospital Safety, and National Guidelines on Chemical Disasters are some of the key policy documents that provide a comprehensive framework for disaster risk reduction and management.

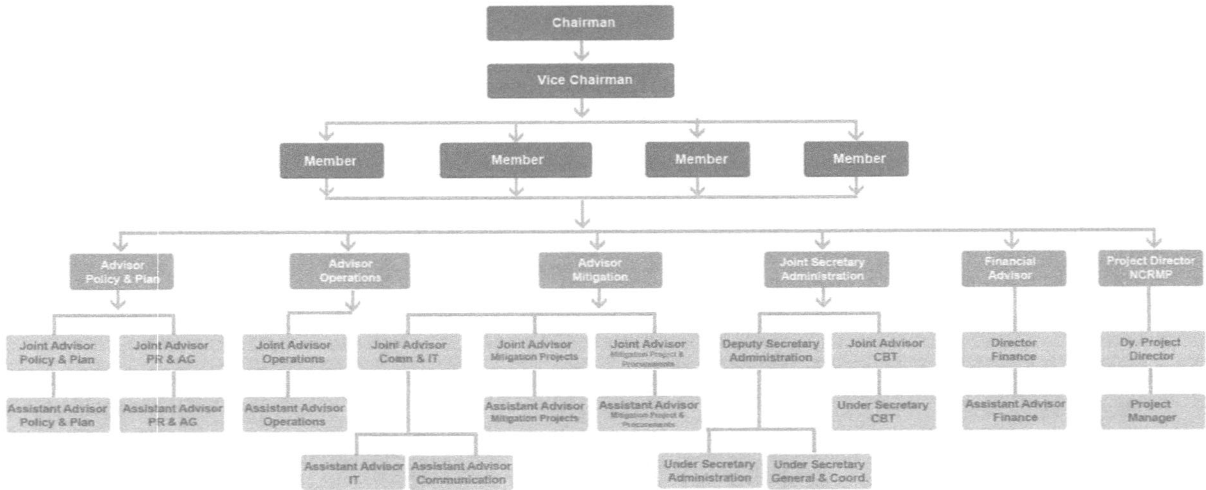

Figure 1.1 – NDMA Framework in India

xv) **Public Awareness and Education:** The disaster management framework in India places significant emphasis on public awareness and education. Awareness campaigns, training programs, workshops, and drills are conducted to educate the public about disaster risks, preparedness measures, and response actions. These efforts aim to empower individuals and communities to take timely and appropriate actions during emergencies.

The disaster management framework in India is an evolving process that continually learns from past experiences and incorporates new technologies and best practices. It strives to build a resilient nation that can effectively manage disasters, reduce risks, and protect lives, livelihoods, and infrastructure. By strengthening coordination, investing in preparedness, and promoting community participation, India aims to enhance its disaster management capabilities and minimize the impact of future disasters.

1.3.2 Current Scenario of Disaster Management Cycle in India

i) **Preparedness:** Preparedness is a crucial phase of the disaster management cycle in India. Efforts are made to enhance the preparedness of various stakeholders, including government agencies, communities, and individuals. This involves the development of disaster management plans, training programs, capacity building activities, and the establishment of early warning systems. Preparedness measures aim to improve the readiness of response agencies and the community to effectively handle disasters.

ii) **Response:** The response phase involves the immediate actions taken during and immediately after a disaster strikes. In India, response efforts are coordinated by the National Disaster Response Force (NDRF) along with state and local authorities. NDRF teams are strategically positioned across the country to ensure a prompt response. The response phase includes search and rescue operations, medical assistance, evacuation, relief distribution, and the restoration of essential services.

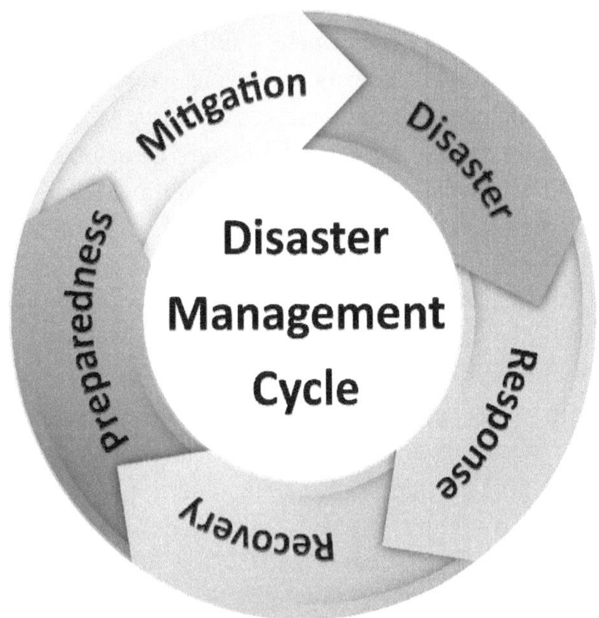

Figure 1.2 Disaster Management Cycle

iii) **Recovery:** The recovery phase focuses on the long-term rehabilitation and reconstruction of affected communities and infrastructure. It involves the assessment of damages, provision of financial assistance, reconstruction of homes and infrastructure, livelihood restoration, and psychosocial support for the affected population. Recovery efforts are led by state governments with support from central agencies, NGOs, and international organizations.

iv) **Mitigation:** Mitigation refers to measures taken to reduce the impact of future disasters. In India, mitigation efforts include the implementation of building codes and regulations, land-use planning, ecosystem restoration, strengthening infrastructure, and promoting resilient practices. The government emphasizes integrating disaster risk reduction into development plans and policies to minimize vulnerabilities and enhance resilience.

v) **Institutional Framework:** India has established an institutional framework to manage disasters effectively. This includes the National Disaster Management Authority (NDMA) at the national level, State Disaster Management Authorities (SDMAs) at the state level, and District Disaster Management Authorities (DDMAs) at the district level. These bodies are responsible for formulating policies, coordinating disaster management activities, and ensuring effective implementation of plans and guidelines.

vi) **Technology and Innovation:** India has been leveraging technology and innovation in disaster management. The use of early warning systems, satellite imagery, geospatial data, and communication technologies play a vital role in monitoring and responding to disasters. Mobile applications, social media platforms, and online portals are used for disseminating alerts, providing information to the public, and coordinating relief efforts.

vii) **Community Participation:** Community participation is increasingly recognized as a crucial aspect of disaster management in India. Efforts are made to involve local communities, non-governmental organizations, and volunteers in disaster preparedness, response, and recovery. Community-based organizations and platforms like Village Disaster Management Committees (VDMCs) are promoted to enhance local resilience and foster community-led initiatives.

It is important to note that the disaster management scenario in India is dynamic, and the country faces a range of natural and man-made disasters, including cyclones, floods, earthquakes, droughts, and industrial accidents. The government continues to strengthen its disaster management capabilities through policy reforms, capacity building initiatives, and collaborations with national and international partners.

For the most accurate and up-to-date information on the current scenario of the disaster management cycle in India, it is advisable to refer to the official websites of the National Disaster Management Authority (NDMA) and respective State Disaster Management Authorities (SDMAs).

1.3.3 Importance of Disaster Management in India

Disaster management is of paramount importance in India due to several factors:

i) **Vulnerability to Natural Disasters:** India is highly vulnerable to a wide range of natural disasters, including cyclones, floods, earthquakes, droughts, landslides, and heatwaves. The country's vast geographical diversity, coastal areas, and densely populated regions contribute to its susceptibility to such events. Effective disaster management is crucial to reduce the loss of life, protect infrastructure, and ensure the quick recovery of affected communities.

ii) **Population Density:** India is the second most populous country globally, with a large proportion of its population residing in urban areas. High population density increases the risk and impact of disasters, making disaster management essential for safeguarding lives and minimizing damage. Evacuation plans, early warning systems, and efficient emergency response mechanisms are crucial in densely populated areas.

iii) **Economic Impact:** Disasters have a significant economic impact in India. They can cause widespread damage to infrastructure, agriculture, industries, and livelihoods. Effective disaster management can help mitigate these economic losses by implementing preventive measures, ensuring rapid response and recovery, and promoting resilience in infrastructure and livelihood sectors.

iv) **Climate Change:** India is experiencing the effects of climate change, resulting in increased frequency and intensity of extreme weather events. Rising temperatures, changing rainfall patterns, and sea-level rise pose significant challenges. Disaster management plays a crucial role in adapting to climate change impacts, developing climate-resilient infrastructure, and implementing measures to reduce greenhouse gas emissions.

v) **Protecting Human Lives**: Disaster management in India places a primary focus on saving lives during emergencies. Rapid and well-coordinated response actions, such as search and rescue operations, medical assistance, and evacuation plans, are critical for protecting human lives. Pre-emptive measures like early warning systems and public awareness campaigns also contribute to ensuring the safety of individuals during disasters.

vi) **Sustainable Development:** Integrating disaster risk reduction into development planning is vital for sustainable development in India. By incorporating measures to reduce vulnerabilities and strengthen resilience, disaster management ensures that development gains are protected from potential hazards. This approach helps minimize setbacks caused by disasters and promotes sustainable growth and long-term well-being.

vii) **Humanitarian Considerations**: Disaster management in India upholds humanitarian principles, ensuring that affected populations receive timely assistance, protection, and support. It involves providing emergency relief, shelter, food, clean water, healthcare, and psychosocial support to affected communities. The focus on humanitarian considerations ensures the dignity and well-being of individuals and communities during and after disasters.

viii) **International Collaboration**: Effective disaster management in India also involves collaboration with the international community. Sharing best practices, knowledge, and resources with other countries and participating in international forums contributes to strengthening disaster management capabilities. It enables India to access global expertise, technologies, and financial assistance during large-scale disasters.

ix) **Effective Resource Allocation:** Disaster management helps in efficient resource allocation during emergencies. By having well-prepared plans and coordination mechanisms in place, resources such as manpower, equipment, relief supplies, and financial aid can be mobilized and distributed effectively to areas in need. This ensures that resources are utilized optimally, minimizing wastage and maximizing their impact in saving lives and aiding recovery.

x) **Minimizing Environmental Degradation:** Disasters often result in environmental degradation, such as pollution, destruction of ecosystems, and loss of biodiversity. Effective disaster management emphasizes environmentally sustainable approaches. It includes measures like promoting eco-friendly infrastructure, implementing waste management practices, restoring ecosystems, and incorporating climate adaptation strategies. By minimizing environmental impacts, disaster management contributes to long-term ecological sustainability.

xi) **Enhancing Public Confidence:** An efficient and well-executed disaster management system enhances public confidence and trust in the government's ability to protect and assist during emergencies. By demonstrating preparedness, responsiveness, and transparency, disaster management fosters a sense of security and reassurance among the population. This confidence encourages active participation from the public, facilitates cooperation, and strengthens community resilience.

xii) **Strengthening Infrastructure Resilience:** Disaster management plays a vital role in enhancing the resilience of critical infrastructure such as hospitals, schools, transportation networks, and utilities. By integrating risk reduction measures into infrastructure planning and design, structures can withstand potential hazards and continue functioning during and after disasters. This ensures the continuity of essential services, minimizes disruptions, and speeds up recovery processes.

xiii) **Promoting Research and Innovation:** Disaster management encourages research, innovation, and technological advancements in disaster preparedness, response, and recovery. This includes developing improved early warning systems, remote sensing techniques, data analytics, and predictive modelling to better understand and mitigate disaster risks. Investing in research and innovation enhances the effectiveness and efficiency of disaster management strategies and facilitates evidence-based decision-making.

xiv) **Strengthening International Relations:** Effective disaster management fosters international collaboration and cooperation. India actively engages with other countries, regional organizations, and international agencies in sharing experiences, knowledge, and best practices. This collaboration strengthens diplomatic ties, facilitates mutual assistance during emergencies, and enables the exchange of resources, expertise, and technological support.

xv) **Empowering Local Communities:** Disaster management recognizes the importance of empowering local communities to become active participants in their own safety and well-being. By involving communities in decision-making processes, raising awareness, and providing training, disaster management builds community capacity to prepare for, respond to, and recover from disasters. This grassroots involvement promotes self-reliance, resilience, and sustainable development at the local level.

Overall, the importance of disaster management in India cannot be overstated. It plays a crucial role in protecting lives, preserving infrastructure, reducing economic losses, promoting sustainable development, and ensuring the well-being of affected communities. By adopting proactive measures, investing in preparedness, and implementing effective response and recovery strategies, India can build resilience and minimize the impact of disasters. Thus, disaster management in India is crucial for protecting lives, minimizing economic losses, promoting sustainable development, and strengthening national resilience. By adopting a comprehensive and proactive approach, India can effectively address the increasing risks posed by natural and man-made disasters, safeguard communities, and ensure a safer and more sustainable future for its citizens.

1.3.4 Statistics for Importance of Disaster Management:

High Vulnerability: India is highly vulnerable to various types of disasters. According to the National Disaster Management Authority (NDMA), around 58.6% of India's landmass is prone to earthquakes of moderate to high intensity, over 12% of the country's area is flood-prone, and about 68% of the coastline is susceptible to cyclones and tsunamis.

Frequency and Impact of Disasters: India experiences a significant number of disasters annually, resulting in loss of life, property damage, and economic losses. For instance:

The India Meteorological Department (IMD) reported that between 2005 and 2015, India witnessed an average of 2,482 deaths per year due to floods alone.

According to the National Crime Records Bureau (NCRB), between 2010 and 2019, India witnessed an average of 2,605 deaths per year due to earthquakes.

The Annual Report 2019-2020 by the Ministry of Home Affairs states that during 2019, India experienced 21 cyclones, affecting over 7.2 million people.

Economic Impact: Disasters have significant economic implications in India. For instance:

The Economic Survey 2020-21 estimated that the average annual economic loss due to disasters in India between 2005 and 2019 was around 0.36% of GDP.

The World Bank's report "Acting Now: A Roadmap to Enhancing Disaster Preparedness Systems" highlighted that India's annual average disaster-related economic losses amount to approximately USD 9.8 billion.

Population Density: India's high population density magnifies the impact of disasters on human lives and infrastructure. For example:

The United Nations estimated that India's population would reach 1.64 billion by 2050, adding to the challenges of disaster management in terms of evacuation, shelter, and healthcare.

The National Institute of Disaster Management (NIDM) states that about 40% of India's population resides in vulnerable coastal areas, increasing the risk of cyclones, storm surges, and sea-level rise.

Climate Change Impact: India is vulnerable to the impacts of climate change, leading to increased frequency and intensity of extreme weather events. For example:

The Climate Risk Index 2021 by German watch ranked India as the seventh most affected country by climate change between 2000 and 2019, considering the number of deaths and economic losses.

According to the IMD, the frequency of heatwaves in India has increased over the past few decades, affecting human health, agriculture, and water resources.

These data and information highlight the urgency and significance of disaster management in India. Effective disaster management measures are essential to protect lives, mitigate economic losses, enhance resilience, and ensure sustainable development in the face of ongoing and future challenges posed by various disasters and climate change impacts.

Major Disasters in India: India has faced several major disasters that have underscored the need for robust disaster management measures. Some notable examples include:

The 2004 Indian Ocean Tsunami: It resulted in the loss of thousands of lives, widespread destruction along the coastal areas, and the displacement of a large population.

The 2013 Uttarakhand Floods: Flash floods and landslides caused extensive damage, resulting in thousands of deaths and significant infrastructure destruction.

The 2018 Kerala Floods: Heavy rainfall led to severe flooding in the state, affecting millions of people and causing substantial damage to infrastructure and agriculture.

1.4 Disaster Management Initiatives in India:

The Government of India has implemented various initiatives to strengthen disaster management capabilities. Some key initiatives include:

National Disaster Management Plan (NDMP): The NDMP outlines the strategies and actions for all phases of the disaster management cycle and serves as a guiding document for disaster management at all levels.

National Disaster Response Force (NDRF): The NDRF is a specialized force dedicated to disaster response operations. It comprises teams trained in various aspects of disaster response, including search and rescue, medical care, and chemical, biological, radiological, and nuclear (CBRN) emergencies.

Sendai Framework for Disaster Risk Reduction: India has adopted the Sendai Framework, a global framework for disaster risk reduction, and has aligned its national policies and plans accordingly.

National Cyclone Risk Mitigation Project (NCRMP): The NCRMP is aimed at enhancing the country's preparedness and response capacities for cyclones. It focuses on coastal states prone to cyclones and supports activities such as early warning systems, cyclone shelters, and capacity building.

Public Awareness and Education: Disaster management in India emphasizes public awareness and education. The National Disaster Management Authority (NDMA) conducts regular awareness campaigns, training programs, and drills to educate the public about disaster risks, preparedness measures, and response actions. These efforts aim to empower individuals and communities to make informed decisions and take appropriate actions during emergencies.

International Assistance and Collaboration: India actively collaborates with international organizations and countries to enhance its disaster management capabilities. It participates in regional forums like the South Asian Association for Regional Cooperation (SAARC) and engages in bilateral partnerships to share experiences, best practices, and technical expertise. International assistance is sought during large-scale disasters, further highlighting the importance of global collaboration in disaster management.

These data and information reinforce the critical importance of effective disaster management in India. By implementing comprehensive strategies, investing in preparedness, and fostering collaboration at all levels, India can reduce the impact of disasters, protect lives and livelihoods, and build a more resilient nation.

1.4.1 Disaster Emergency Management Systems in India:

Disasters are inevitable events that can cause significant disruptions to human life, infrastructure, and the environment. In India, with its diverse geography and climatic conditions, disasters are a recurring phenomenon. To effectively respond to and mitigate the impact of disasters, India has developed a comprehensive Disaster Emergency Management System (DEMS). The DEMS encompasses various institutions, policies, and strategies that work together to enhance preparedness, response, and recovery efforts.

Components of Disaster Emergency Management Systems in India:

National Disaster Management Authority (NDMA): The NDMA is the apex body responsible for formulating policies, plans, and guidelines for disaster management in India. It oversees disaster response and coordinates efforts between various ministries and agencies.

State Disaster Management Authorities (SDMAs): Each state in India has its own State Disaster Management Authority responsible for implementing disaster management plans and policies at the state level.

District Disaster Management Authorities (DDMAs): At the district level, DDMAs coordinate disaster management activities and liaise with various stakeholders within the district.

National Disaster Response Force (NDRF): NDRF is a specialized force that leads search and rescue operations during disasters. It plays a crucial role in providing immediate assistance in the aftermath of disasters.

Disaster Management Plans: India has a National Disaster Management Plan (NDMP) that outlines a comprehensive framework for disaster risk reduction and response. States and districts also have their respective disaster management plans tailored to their specific vulnerabilities and risks.

Early Warning Systems (EWS): India has developed early warning systems for cyclones, floods, earthquakes, and other hazards. These systems help in timely evacuation and preparedness.

National Disaster Database (NIDM): NIDM maintains a comprehensive database of disasters, their impacts, and response efforts. This database helps in analysing disaster trends and informing future policies.

Capacity Building and Training: Capacity building and training programs are conducted at various levels, including communities, first responders, and government officials, to enhance their preparedness and response skills.

Public Awareness and Education: The government conducts awareness campaigns to educate citizens about disaster preparedness, response measures, and safety protocols.

1.4.2 Initiatives and Success Stories:

Flood Early Warning Systems: India has made significant strides in developing flood early warning systems, particularly in flood-prone regions like Assam and Bihar. These systems provide timely alerts to communities and authorities, enabling them to take proactive measures.

Cyclone Preparedness: The successful evacuation of millions of people from coastal areas during cyclones like Cyclone Fani and Cyclone Amphan demonstrated India's improved cyclone preparedness and response.

Community-Based Disaster Management: Several states have adopted community-based disaster management approaches, where local communities actively participate in disaster preparedness and response efforts. This bottom-up approach has proven effective in reducing disaster risks.

National Cyclone Risk Mitigation Project (NCRMP): NCRMP focuses on cyclone risk mitigation, including the construction of cyclone shelters and strengthening coastal infrastructure.

National Disaster Communication Network (NDCN): The NDCN is a secure and reliable communication network that facilitates real-time communication during disasters, ensuring coordination among various agencies.

1.4.3 Challenges and Way Forward:

Despite the progress made in disaster emergency management, India still faces challenges that need to be addressed:

Urban Resilience: With increasing urbanization, there is a need to enhance the resilience of cities and urban areas to disasters.

Climate Change Adaptation: Climate change poses new challenges for disaster management. India needs to focus on climate change adaptation strategies and build resilience to extreme weather events.

Inter-Agency Coordination: Strengthening inter-agency coordination and collaboration is essential to ensure a cohesive and effective response during disasters.

Technology Integration: Utilizing emerging technologies such as AI, IoT, and big data analytics can enhance disaster management capabilities.

Community Participation: Further engaging communities in disaster management and decision-making processes can lead to more effective and sustainable outcomes.

Conclusion: India's Disaster Emergency Management System has evolved significantly over the years, and the country has made considerable progress in disaster preparedness, response, and mitigation. However, the complex and evolving nature of disasters requires continuous improvement and adaptation. By leveraging technology, enhancing inter-agency collaboration, and promoting community participation, India can build greater resilience and minimize the impact of disasters on its people and infrastructure. With a proactive and holistic approach, India can become a global leader in disaster risk reduction and emergency management, ensuring the safety and well-being of its citizens in the face of future challenges.

CHAPTER 2

Natural Disasters in India

2.1 Natural Disasters in India

India is blessed with a vast coastline spanning approximately 7,516 kilometres, encompassing several coastal states and Union territories. While the coastal regions offer immense economic and ecological benefits, they are also vulnerable to various natural hazards and disasters. The combination of geographical factors, climate patterns, and human activities in these regions makes them prone to a wide range of hazards, necessitating comprehensive disaster management strategies. This essay explores the natural hazards and disasters faced by coastal states of India, along with some notable examples.

1. **Cyclones:** Coastal states like Odisha, Andhra Pradesh, Tamil Nadu, and West Bengal frequently experience cyclones originating from the Bay of Bengal. These intense tropical storms bring strong winds, heavy rainfall, and storm surges,

causing widespread damage to infrastructure, agriculture, and livelihoods. Notable examples include Cyclone Phailin (2013) that affected Odisha and Cyclone Gaja (2018) that impacted Tamil Nadu.

2. **Tsunamis:** The Indian Ocean region is prone to tsunamis, which are triggered by undersea earthquakes or volcanic eruptions. The most devastating example in recent history is the Indian Ocean Tsunami of 2004, which struck the coastal areas of Tamil Nadu, Andhra Pradesh, and the Andaman and Nicobar Islands, causing widespread destruction and loss of life.

3. **Floods:** Coastal regions experience both riverine and coastal floods due to heavy rainfall and storm surges during cyclones. States like Kerala, Karnataka, and Maharashtra have witnessed severe floods, causing damage to homes, infrastructure, and agriculture.

4. **Erosion and Sea-Level Rise:** Coastal erosion is a significant hazard for states like Goa, Kerala, and West Bengal. Rising sea levels, driven by climate change, exacerbate erosion, leading to the loss of land and livelihoods for coastal communities.

Figure 2.1 Natural Disasters (Image by macrovector on Freepik)

5. **Storm Surges:** During cyclones, storm surges occur when strong winds push seawater onto the land, resulting in coastal inundation. States like Gujarat, Andhra Pradesh, and Odisha are vulnerable to storm surges, which can cause extensive damage to coastal settlements and infrastructure.

6. **Salinity Intrusion:** Coastal states like West Bengal and Odisha face the challenge of salinity intrusion into agricultural lands due to a rise in sea levels and reduced freshwater flow from rivers. This hampers agricultural productivity and affects livelihoods.

7. **Droughts:** While droughts are not limited to coastal areas, states like Gujarat and Andhra Pradesh have experienced drought conditions due to deficient monsoon rainfall and water scarcity.

Disaster Management in Coastal States: Given the susceptibility to natural hazards, disaster management in coastal states is of utmost importance. The Indian government, along with state governments, has implemented various measures to enhance preparedness, response, and recovery:

1. **Early Warning Systems:** Coastal states have established robust early warning systems for cyclones and tsunamis, enabling timely evacuation and preparedness.

2. **Cyclone Shelters:** Cyclone-prone states have built cyclone shelters to provide safe refuge to vulnerable populations during cyclones.

3. **Coastal Regulation Zone (CRZ) Rules:** The CRZ rules aim to protect coastal areas from haphazard development and ensure sustainable coastal management.

4. **Mangrove Conservation:** The preservation and restoration of mangroves act as natural barriers against storm surges and coastal erosion.

5. **Disaster Preparedness and Training:** Regular training and capacity building programs are conducted for communities, first responders, and local authorities to improve disaster preparedness and response.

The coastal states of India are blessed with abundant resources, but they are also vulnerable to a wide range of natural hazards and disasters. Cyclones, tsunamis, floods, erosion, and sea-level rise pose significant challenges to these regions. To effectively mitigate the impact of these hazards, disaster management efforts should focus on early warning systems, resilient infrastructure, mangrove conservation, and community engagement. By building resilience and implementing sustainable practices, India's coastal states can better cope with the challenges posed by natural hazards and create safer and more sustainable coastal communities.

2.2 Different Types of Natural Disasters

Floods: Floods refer to the overflow of water onto normally dry land due to heavy rainfall, river overflow, or dam failure. Floods can cause extensive damage to infrastructure, property, and crops, leading to displacement of people and loss of lives.

Drought: Drought is a prolonged period of abnormally low rainfall, resulting in a shortage of water resources. It leads to reduced crop yields, water scarcity, and adverse impacts on ecosystems, agriculture, and livelihoods.

Cyclones: Cyclones, also known as hurricanes or typhoons, are powerful rotating storms characterized by strong winds and heavy rainfall. In India, cyclones typically form in the Bay of Bengal and the Arabian Sea and can cause severe damage to coastal areas, including flooding, storm surges, and high-speed winds.

Volcanoes: Volcanoes are vents or openings in the Earth's crust through which molten lava, volcanic ash, and gases are ejected. While India does not have active volcanoes, it is important to study volcanoes' global impact due to their potential to cause ashfall, affect climate patterns, and disrupt air travel.

Earthquakes: Earthquakes are the shaking or trembling of the Earth's surface caused by the release of energy along fault lines. India is located in a seismically active zone, and earthquakes can lead to structural damage, landslides, and loss of life.

Tsunami: Tsunamis are large ocean waves generated by underwater disturbances, such as earthquakes, volcanic eruptions, or landslides. They can travel across long distances and cause devastating impacts when they reach coastal areas, including flooding, destruction of infrastructure, and loss of lives.

Landslides: Landslides occur when a mass of soil, rocks, or debris moves downhill due to factors like heavy rainfall, earthquakes, or human activities. Landslides can damage buildings, infrastructure, and transportation routes, posing risks to human lives and hindering access to affected areas.

Coastal Erosion: Coastal erosion refers to the gradual wearing a way of coastal land and beaches due to the action of waves, tides, and currents. It can lead to the loss of coastal habitats, infrastructure, and displacement of communities living in coastal areas.

Soil Erosion: Soil erosion is the process of the removal and displacement of topsoil due to factors like wind, water, and human activities. Soil erosion affects agricultural productivity, leads to loss of fertile land, and contributes to environmental degradation.

Forest Fires: Forest fires are uncontrolled fires that spread rapidly through forests, grasslands, and other vegetated areas. They can be caused by natural factors like lightning strikes or human activities. Forest fires pose risks to biodiversity, ecosystems, and human settlements near forested areas.

2.3 Natural Disasters – Floods

Floods: Floods refer to the overflow of water onto normally dry land due to heavy rainfall, river overflow, or dam failure. Floods can cause extensive damage to infrastructure, property, and crops, leading to displacement of people and loss of lives.

Floods are natural disasters characterized by the overflow of water onto normally dry land, leading to inundation and the disruption of normal life. They can occur due to various factors, including heavy rainfall, rapid snowmelt, dam failure, or the combination of these factors. Floods can affect both urban and rural areas, causing significant damage to infrastructure, property, and natural resources.

Floods have the potential to cause immense devastation and pose risks to human life and the environment. Here are some key aspects related to floods:

Causes of Floods:

Heavy Rainfall: Intense and prolonged rainfall can lead to the saturation of soil and overwhelm rivers, lakes, and drainage systems, causing them to overflow.

Snowmelt: Rapid melting of snow, especially during warm weather or due to rain, can result in excessive runoff and contribute to flooding.

Dam Failure: Failure or breach of dams or levees can result in the sudden release of large volumes of water, causing downstream flooding.

Types of Floods:

Riverine Floods: Riverine floods occur when rivers or streams overflow their banks, inundating nearby areas. They are often caused by heavy rainfall or a combination of heavy rain and snowmelt.

Flash Floods: Flash floods are rapid-onset floods that occur with little or no warning. They typically occur in low-lying areas or narrow channels and can be triggered by heavy rainfall, dam failure, or intense storms.

Impacts of Floods:

Infrastructure Damage: Floods can damage roads, bridges, buildings, and utilities, leading to disruptions in transportation, communication, and essential services.

Loss of Life and Displacement: Floods can result in the loss of human lives and cause the displacement of communities as people are forced to evacuate their homes.

Environmental Impact: Floodwaters can lead to erosion, sedimentation, and contamination of water bodies. They can also disrupt ecosystems, harm wildlife, and damage vegetation.

Health Risks: Floods can create health hazards such as waterborne diseases, contamination of water sources, and the spread of vector-borne illnesses.

Flood – Mitigation and Preparedness:

Floodplain Zoning: Identifying and mapping flood-prone areas to regulate land-use and development, ensuring that high-risk areas are avoided or appropriately protected.

Flood Forecasting and Early Warning Systems: Monitoring weather patterns, river levels, and rainfall to provide timely warnings and alerts to at-risk communities.

Infrastructure Planning: Designing infrastructure, such as drainage systems and embankments, to mitigate flood risks and minimize damage.

Emergency Response: Establishing efficient emergency response mechanisms, including search and rescue operations, evacuation plans, and the provision of relief supplies.

Community Awareness and Education: Promoting awareness among communities about flood risks, safety measures, and evacuation procedures.

In India, floods are a recurring natural disaster, particularly during the monsoon season when heavy rainfall is common. The country has faced devastating floods in various regions, causing significant loss of life and damage to infrastructure. Therefore, understanding the causes, impacts, and mitigation measures related to floods is crucial for effective disaster management and the protection of lives and livelihoods.

Flood Magnitude and Duration:

Flood Magnitude: The magnitude of a flood refers to the volume and flow rate of water involved. It is determined by factors such as the amount and intensity of rainfall, the size and slope of the watershed, and the capacity of river channels to convey water. High-magnitude floods can have a greater impact on infrastructure and communities.

Flood Duration: Flood duration refers to the length of time a particular area remains inundated. Floods can last for a few hours, several days, or even weeks, depending on the characteristics of the rainfall event and the capacity of the drainage system.

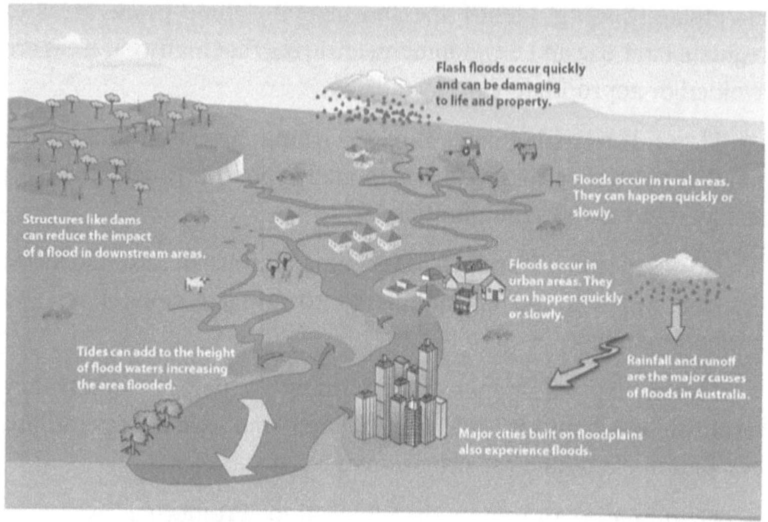

Figure 2.2 Characteristics of floods.

Factors Affecting Flood Severity:

Topography: The shape and slope of the land play a significant role in flood severity. Areas with steep slopes are more prone to flash floods, as water can quickly accumulate and flow downstream.

Soil Conditions: The soil's ability to absorb and retain water, known as its infiltration capacity, affects flood severity. Soils with high infiltration rates can absorb rainfall, reducing runoff and flood potential. However, saturated or compacted soils with low infiltration rates can increase runoff and exacerbate flooding.

Land-Use Changes: Alterations in land use, such as deforestation, urbanization, and the conversion of natural wetlands, can affect flood patterns. Changes in land cover can lead to increased surface runoff, decreased water infiltration, and altered drainage patterns, all of which influence flood severity.

Climate Change: Climate change can influence flood characteristics. Rising temperatures can increase the intensity of rainfall events, leading to more intense and frequent floods. Additionally, the melting of glaciers and ice caps can contribute to increased water flow in rivers and potential flood risks.

Flood Management Strategies:

Structural Measures: Structural measures involve the construction of physical infrastructure to manage floods, such as dams, levees, flood walls, and reservoirs. These structures help regulate water flow, store excess water, and protect communities and infrastructure from flood damage.

Non-Structural Measures: Non-structural measures focus on policies, regulations, and land-use planning to reduce vulnerability to floods. This includes implementing floodplain zoning regulations, preserving natural wetlands, and promoting sustainable land and water management practices.

Flood Insurance: Flood insurance programs provide financial protection to individuals and businesses against flood-related damages. Insurance coverage helps with post-flood recovery and reduces the economic burden on affected communities.

Community Preparedness: Community preparedness is vital in minimizing the impact of floods. It involves educating communities about flood risks, developing emergency response plans, establishing early warning systems, and promoting effective evacuation procedures. Additionally, community-based initiatives for flood monitoring, self-help groups, and local flood response teams can enhance community resilience.

In India, floods are a common occurrence, particularly during the monsoon season. The country experiences both riverine and flash floods, affecting various regions and causing significant loss and damage. Effective flood management strategies that incorporate structural and non-structural measures, along with community preparedness and early warning systems, are essential for mitigating flood risks and minimizing the impacts on human lives, infrastructure, and the environment.

Flood & Monsoon Season:

Monsoon Influence: India experiences a monsoon climate, characterized by a distinct rainy season. The Southwest Monsoon, which occurs from June to September, brings the majority of rainfall to the country. This monsoon period is responsible for a significant portion of annual precipitation and is a key driver of flood events.

Monsoon Dynamics: The monsoon rainfall in India is influenced by the seasonal reversal of wind patterns. Moisture-laden winds from the Indian Ocean converge over the subcontinent, resulting in widespread rainfall. The distribution of rainfall varies across different regions of India, with some areas receiving heavy and prolonged rainfall, increasing the likelihood of flooding.

Major Flood-Prone Regions:

Riverine Floods: India has several major rivers, including the Ganges, Brahmaputra, Yamuna, Krishna, Godavari, and Mahanadi, among others. These rivers, coupled with heavy monsoon rainfall, make many states susceptible to riverine floods. States such as Assam, Bihar, Uttar Pradesh, West Bengal, and parts of Maharashtra and Odisha are particularly prone to annual riverine floods.

Coastal Floods: The Indian coastline is vulnerable to flooding due to cyclones and storm surges. Coastal areas in states like Odisha, Andhra Pradesh, Tamil Nadu, and Kerala are at higher risk, as cyclones originating in the Bay of Bengal and the Arabian Sea can cause significant coastal flooding, leading to destruction and displacement.

Flash Floods: Hilly regions, such as the Himalayan states of Uttarakhand and Himachal Pradesh, are susceptible to flash floods caused by heavy rainfall, cloudbursts, or the rapid melting of snow. These flash floods occur due to the steep topography, which leads to rapid runoff, resulting in sudden and localized flooding.

Flood – Impacts and Challenges:

Loss of Lives and Property: Floods in India can cause significant loss of life and property. The densely populated regions along riverbanks and low-lying areas are particularly vulnerable. Thousands of people are affected, and damage to homes, infrastructure, agricultural fields, and livestock is widespread.

Displacement and Humanitarian Challenges: Floods often lead to the displacement of communities, forcing people to leave their homes and seek temporary shelter in relief camps. Providing immediate humanitarian assistance, including food, water, shelter, and medical aid, becomes a critical challenge during and after flood events.

Impact on Agriculture: Agriculture is a vital sector in India, and floods can have severe consequences for farmers. Crops are damaged or destroyed, leading to crop failure, loss of livelihoods, and disruptions in food production. The post-flood recovery of agricultural lands is often a long and challenging process.

Flood Management and Preparedness:

River Management: The Indian government, through agencies like the Central Water Commission, works on river management projects such as embankments, flood forecasting, and river training programs to control riverine floods.

Flood Forecasting and Warning Systems: The India Meteorological Department (IMD) operates a network of meteorological stations and provides timely weather forecasts and flood warnings. State-level agencies also play a crucial role in disseminating early warning information to vulnerable communities.

Infrastructure and Floodplain Zoning: Constructing embankments, reservoirs, and drainage systems, as well as implementing floodplain zoning regulations, helps mitigate flood risks and reduce the impact on communities and infrastructure.

Community Preparedness and Awareness: Community-level preparedness and awareness programs are essential to minimize the impact of floods. Educating communities about flood risks, promoting early warning systems, conducting mock drills, and establishing community-based flood response teams contribute to effective disaster management.

India faces significant challenges in managing and mitigating the impacts of floods due to its vast geographical extent, high population density, and climatic variability. However, through improved infrastructure, enhanced early warning systems, community participation, and coordinated efforts among government agencies, NGOs, and community organizations, progress is being made in reducing the vulnerability of communities to flood events and building resilience in flood-prone areas.

Regions in India Prone to Floods

India is prone to floods in various regions due to its diverse geographical and climatic conditions. The major regions prone to floods in the country are as follows:

North India: The states in northern India, particularly the Indo-Gangetic plains, are highly vulnerable to floods. States like Uttar Pradesh, Bihar, and West Bengal experience frequent flooding due to heavy rainfall and overflowing rivers like Ganga, Yamuna, and Brahmaputra.

North-East India: The North-Eastern states of Assam, Meghalaya, Arunachal Pradesh, and Manipur are prone to severe floods during the monsoon season. The Brahmaputra River and its tributaries cause extensive flooding in the region.

Eastern India: The states of Odisha and Chhattisgarh in eastern India witness floods due to heavy rainfall and the Mahanadi and Godavari River systems overflowing their banks.

Western India: Gujarat, Maharashtra, and parts of Rajasthan are susceptible to floods caused by cyclonic storms and heavy monsoon rains. Rivers like Sabarmati, Narmada, and Tapi are prone to flooding in this region.

Central India: Madhya Pradesh, parts of Uttar Pradesh, and Jharkhand face flooding due to excessive rainfall during the monsoon season.

South India: Kerala, Karnataka, Tamil Nadu, Andhra Pradesh, and Telangana experience floods during the southwest monsoon. Rivers like Krishna, Godavari, Cauvery, and Tungabhadra overflow during heavy rains.

Himalayan Region: The Himalayan states of Uttarakhand, Himachal Pradesh, and Jammu and Kashmir are prone to flash floods and glacial lake outburst floods (GLOFs) due to rapid snowmelt and cloudbursts.

Coastal Areas: Coastal regions, especially in states like Goa, Kerala, and West Bengal, face floods due to heavy rains during cyclonic storms and tidal surges.

It is important to note that flood-prone areas can change over time due to factors like urbanization, deforestation, and climate change. Effective flood management strategies, including early warning systems, floodplain zoning, and improved drainage systems, are crucial to reducing the impact of floods on communities and infrastructure.

Methods of Flood Forecasting

Flood forecasting is a critical aspect of disaster management, helping to predict and mitigate the impact of potential floods. Various methods and technologies are used to forecast floods. Some of the prominent methods of flood forecasting include:

a. Rainfall-Runoff Models:
b. Hydrological Models:
c. Satellite Remote Sensing:
d. Radar-Based Rainfall Estimation:
e. Numerical Weather Prediction (NWP):
f. Ensemble Forecasting:
g. Data Assimilation Techniques:
h. Flood Warning Systems:
i. Historical Data and Statistical Analysis:
j. Decision Support Systems (DSS):

1. **Rainfall-Runoff Models:** These models simulate the process of rainfall converting into runoff and flowing into rivers and streams. They use data on precipitation, soil type, land use, and topography to estimate the amount of runoff that will enter river systems during a rainfall event. Example: A rainfall-runoff model is used to predict the runoff generated from a heavy rainfall event in a small catchment area. The model considers factors such as the intensity and duration of rainfall, soil type, land use, and topography. Based on these inputs, it estimates the amount of water that will flow into nearby rivers and streams, helping authorities issue flood warnings to downstream communities.

2. **Hydrological Models:** Hydrological models are more comprehensive than rainfall-runoff models and consider various hydrological processes, including evapotranspiration, infiltration, and surface runoff. These models are valuable for predicting river discharge and water levels during flood events. Example: A hydrological model is employed to forecast river discharge and water levels in a large river basin. The model considers various hydrological processes, including rainfall, evapotranspiration, soil moisture, and snowmelt. By analysing these factors, the model can predict the volume and timing of water flow in the river during a flood event, aiding in flood preparedness and response planning.

3. **Satellite Remote Sensing:** Satellite data, especially from weather satellites, can provide real-time information on rainfall patterns and cloud cover. This data is essential for flood forecasting, as it helps in monitoring rainfall trends and identifying potential flood-prone areas. Example: During the monsoon season, weather satellites capture data on cloud cover and rainfall patterns over a specific region. For instance, data from weather satellites can reveal heavy rainfall and cloud formation over a river basin. By analysing this information, meteorologists and hydrologists can anticipate potential flood risks in the area.

4. **Radar-Based Rainfall Estimation**: Weather radars can estimate rainfall intensity and distribution in real-time, offering valuable input for flood forecasting models. Radar-based systems provide high-resolution rainfall data, enhancing the accuracy of flood predictions. Example: In the event of a severe thunderstorm, weather radars can estimate the intensity and spatial distribution of rainfall. For instance, a weather radar detects heavy rainfall over a particular city or town. This information is immediately relayed to flood forecasting agencies, allowing them to issue timely warnings and advisories to residents in flood-prone areas.

5. **Numerical Weather Prediction (NWP)**: NWP models use mathematical equations to simulate atmospheric processes and predict weather conditions. These models can forecast the onset, duration, and intensity of rainfall, aiding in flood forecasting. Example: Numerical weather prediction models are used to forecast upcoming weather conditions. For instance, a weather forecasting agency uses NWP to predict a significant rainfall event in a coastal state. Based on the model's output, authorities can anticipate potential flooding in low-lying areas and coastal regions.

6. **Ensemble Forecasting**: Ensemble forecasting involves running multiple simulations with slight variations in initial conditions and model parameters. It helps to account for uncertainties in weather predictions and provides a range of possible flood scenarios. Example: Meteorologists use ensemble forecasting to predict a range of possible flood scenarios during a tropical cyclone. The model generates multiple simulations with slight variations in initial conditions and parameters, providing a probabilistic forecast. This helps authorities prepare for different flood intensity scenarios and allocate resources accordingly.

7. **Data Assimilation Techniques**: Data assimilation involves integrating observed data, such as rainfall and river discharge measurements, into forecasting models. This process helps

improve the accuracy of flood forecasts by incorporating real-time data. Example: A river basin is equipped with monitoring stations that measure river discharge and rainfall in real-time. Data assimilation techniques are applied to integrate this observed data into hydrological models. This process improves the accuracy of the model's flood forecasts by incorporating real-time information.

8. **Flood Warning Systems:** Flood warning systems use sensors and monitoring stations to collect real-time data on rainfall, river levels, and other parameters. This data is relayed to a central control room, which issues flood warnings to authorities and the public. Example: A city has an advanced flood warning system that includes rainfall and river level sensors. During heavy rainfall, the sensors detect rising river levels and increased rainfall intensity. The data is transmitted to a central control room, which activates flood warning sirens and sends alert messages to residents in flood-prone areas.

9. **Historical Data and Statistical Analysis:** Historical flood data and statistical methods are used to assess flood risk and analyse trends in flood occurrences. This information can help in predicting the likelihood of floods in the future. Example: A coastal state analyses historical flood data from the past few decades. Statistical analysis of this data reveals patterns of flood occurrences during the monsoon season. By understanding these trends, authorities can better anticipate flood risks and implement suitable mitigation measures.

10. **Decision Support Systems (DSS):** DSS are computer-based tools that integrate data and models to assist decision-makers in making informed choices during flood events. DSS can provide real-time flood updates, flood impact assessments, and recommended response actions. Example: A coastal city has a DSS that integrates data from various sources, such as weather forecasts, river gauges, and urban drainage systems. During a cyclone, the DSS provides real-time flood updates, estimates flood impacts on critical

infrastructure, and recommends evacuation routes for affected communities. This aids authorities in making informed decisions to safeguard lives and property.

Thus, Flood forecasting is a complex process that requires the integration of various data sources, models, and technologies. Advances in meteorology, hydrology, remote sensing, and computing have significantly improved the accuracy and lead time of flood forecasts. Timely and reliable flood forecasts play a crucial role in disaster preparedness and response, enabling authorities and communities to take proactive measures to protect lives and property during flood events.

2.4 Natural Disasters – Draughts

Drought is a prolonged period of abnormally low rainfall or precipitation in a particular region, resulting in a deficiency of water resources. It is a natural disaster that can have severe impacts on agriculture, ecosystems, water supplies, and human livelihoods. Droughts can occur due to various factors, including climatic patterns, shifts in weather systems, and geographical characteristics. Here are key aspects related to droughts:

Causes of Draughts:

Meteorological Factors: Droughts can be caused by changes in large-scale weather patterns, such as the El Niño-Southern Oscillation (ENSO) phenomenon. During El Niño events, the warming of sea surface temperatures in the Pacific Ocean can disrupt global weather patterns, leading to reduced rainfall in certain regions.

Climate Change: Climate change can influence the frequency and intensity of droughts. Rising temperatures can increase evaporation rates, alter precipitation patterns, and exacerbate water scarcity in some regions.

Natural Climate Variability: Some regions are naturally prone to periodic droughts due to their geographical location, such as arid or semi-arid areas. These regions may experience cyclical patterns of wet and dry periods.

Types of Droughts:

Meteorological Drought: Meteorological drought refers to a deficiency in precipitation relative to the long-term average for a specific region. It is determined by analysing rainfall data over a specified period and comparing it to historical averages.

Agricultural Drought: Agricultural drought occurs when the lack of rainfall or soil moisture negatively affects crop growth and agricultural productivity. It can lead to crop failure, reduced yields, and food insecurity.

Hydrological Drought: Hydrological drought relates to a deficit in water availability in rivers, reservoirs, and groundwater systems. It occurs when the water levels in water bodies drop below normal, impacting water supplies for drinking, irrigation, and industrial purposes.

Socioeconomic Drought: Socioeconomic drought encompasses the broader impacts of drought on society, including economic losses, impacts on livelihoods, and societal well-being. It considers factors such as water scarcity, food security, and the ability of communities to cope with the effects of drought.

Impacts of Draughts:

Agricultural Losses: Droughts can cause crop failures, reduced yields, and livestock losses. This has significant implications for farmers, rural communities, and food production, leading to food shortages and economic hardships.

Water Scarcity: Droughts result in reduced water availability for domestic, industrial, and agricultural use. Water scarcity affects households, industries, and ecosystems, impacting daily life, hygiene, and economic activities.

Ecosystem Stress: Droughts can negatively impact ecosystems, leading to the degradation of forests, wetlands, and other natural habitats. This affects biodiversity, disrupts ecological balance, and threatens the survival of plant and animal species.

Health and Socioeconomic Impacts: Droughts can lead to health issues such as waterborne diseases, malnutrition, and migration of affected populations in search of water and livelihood opportunities. Economic sectors dependent on water, such as tourism and hydropower generation, may also suffer.

Draughts – Mitigation and Preparedness:

Water Conservation: Implementing water conservation measures, such as efficient irrigation techniques, rainwater harvesting, and water recycling, helps reduce water demand and preserve water resources during droughts.

Drought Monitoring and Early Warning Systems: Regular monitoring of meteorological and hydrological indicators enables the timely identification and prediction of drought conditions. Early warning systems help inform stakeholders and trigger proactive response measures.

Drought Resistant Crops and Agricultural Practices: Promoting the use of drought-resistant crop varieties and implementing sustainable agricultural practices, such as crop rotation and soil conservation methods, can enhance agricultural resilience to drought.

Water Resource Management: Implementing integrated water resource management approaches, including the sustainable use of groundwater, efficient water allocation, and the development of alternative water sources, helps cope with water scarcity during droughts.

Drought Contingency Planning: Developing and implementing drought contingency plans at regional and national levels helps coordinate response efforts, manage water allocation, and provide support to affected communities.

In India, droughts are a recurring natural disaster that affect various regions, particularly those dependent on monsoon rains. States like Maharashtra, Rajasthan, Gujarat, and parts of South India are prone to drought conditions. The Indian government, along with state agencies and community organizations, implements measures to mitigate the impacts of drought, including drought monitoring, water conservation, and support for affected farmers and communities. Building resilience to droughts through sustainable water management practices, agricultural diversification, and preparedness measures is crucial for reducing vulnerability and ensuring the well-being of communities affected by droughts.

Characteristics of Drought:

Duration and Severity: Droughts can vary in duration and severity, ranging from short-term dry spells to long-lasting and severe drought events that persist for months or even years. The severity of a drought is determined by factors such as the extent of water deficit, impacts on ecosystems, and socioeconomic consequences.

Figure 2.3 Characteristics of Draughts (Source: naturalenergyhub.com)

Spatial Variability: Droughts can affect different regions within a country in varying degrees. While one region may experience severe drought conditions, nearby areas may have relatively normal or even above-average rainfall. This spatial variability of drought can pose challenges in terms of resource allocation and drought management.

Compound Events: Droughts can coincide with other natural hazards, such as heatwaves, wildfires, and insect infestations.

These compound events can exacerbate the impacts of droughts and lead to cascading effects on ecosystems, agriculture, and water resources.

Draughts – Impacts and Challenges in India:

Agriculture and Food Security: India's economy heavily relies on agriculture, and droughts have a significant impact on agricultural productivity. Crop failures, reduced yields, and livestock losses can lead to food shortages, income decline, and food price inflation, affecting the food security of vulnerable populations.

Water Scarcity and Depletion: Droughts cause water scarcity, leading to reduced availability of drinking water, irrigation water for agriculture, and industrial water supply. Groundwater levels can decline, surface water sources can dry up, and reservoirs can reach critically low levels, further exacerbating water scarcity issues.

Socioeconomic and Livelihood Challenges: Droughts can result in economic losses, job insecurity, and migration as people seek alternative livelihoods. The livelihoods of farmers, especially small-scale and rain-fed agriculture-dependent communities, are particularly vulnerable to drought impacts.

Environmental and Ecosystem Impacts: Droughts have far-reaching consequences on ecosystems, including the degradation of forests, wetlands, and aquatic habitats. Reduced water availability and prolonged dry conditions can lead to the loss of biodiversity, damage to ecosystems, and disruptions in ecosystem services.

Drought Management and Preparedness:

Drought Monitoring and Early Warning Systems: Regular monitoring of meteorological conditions, hydrological indicators, and soil moisture levels helps in assessing drought severity and providing early warnings to farmers, communities, and decision-makers.

Drought Contingency Planning: Developing and implementing drought contingency plans at regional and national levels helps in anticipating, preparing for, and responding to drought events. These plans outline strategies for water allocation, crop diversification, water conservation, and social support mechanisms.

Water Management and Efficiency: Efficient water management practices, such as water conservation, water-use efficiency measures, and promoting efficient irrigation techniques, help in optimizing water resources during droughts.

Rainwater Harvesting: Promoting rainwater harvesting systems, both at individual and community levels, helps in capturing and storing rainwater during periods of rainfall, which can be used during droughts for domestic purposes and agriculture.

Diversification of Agriculture: Encouraging the cultivation of drought-tolerant crop varieties and promoting diversified farming practices, such as agroforestry and mixed cropping, can enhance agricultural resilience to drought and reduce dependency on water-intensive crops.

Public Awareness and Education: Conducting public awareness campaigns to educate communities about water conservation, sustainable farming practices, and the importance of preparedness can enhance community resilience to drought events.

In India, drought management efforts are carried out at the national, state, and local levels through government initiatives, research institutions, NGOs, and community-based organizations. The implementation of drought monitoring systems, contingency plans, water conservation measures, and support mechanisms for affected communities contributes to mitigating the impacts of droughts and building resilience in the face of this natural disaster.

Droughts Scenario in India:

Geographic Vulnerability: India is highly vulnerable to drought due to its diverse climate and geographical characteristics. Several regions, particularly the semi-arid and arid zones, face recurrent drought conditions. States such as Rajasthan, Gujarat, Maharashtra, Karnataka, Andhra Pradesh, and Tamil Nadu are particularly prone to drought events.

Dependence on Monsoon: India relies heavily on the monsoon rains for agricultural activities and water resources. Droughts occur when the monsoon rainfall is significantly below average or when there is a prolonged dry spell during the monsoon season. Insufficient or erratic monsoon rains can lead to severe droughts, affecting agriculture, water availability, and livelihoods.

Types of Droughts:

Meteorological Drought: Meteorological drought refers to a prolonged period of below-average precipitation. It is determined by comparing the current rainfall or precipitation levels with long-term averages for a specific region. A sustained deficit in rainfall indicates meteorological drought conditions.

Agricultural Drought: Agricultural drought occurs when the deficiency of water affects crop growth and agricultural productivity. It is characterized by insufficient soil moisture, reduced groundwater levels, and inadequate irrigation water. Crop failures, reduced yields, and economic losses are common consequences of agricultural drought.

Hydrological Drought: Hydrological drought relates to the impacts of water scarcity on surface water and groundwater resources. It occurs when water availability in rivers, lakes, reservoirs, and aquifers declines below normal levels. Hydrological droughts affect water supplies for drinking, irrigation, industry, and ecosystems.

Characteristics of droughts include:

Duration: Droughts can persist for an extended period, ranging from months to years. Unlike short-term dry spells, droughts involve prolonged periods of inadequate precipitation.

Lack of Moisture: Droughts are characterized by a significant deficiency in rainfall and a lack of moisture in the atmosphere. This leads to reduced soil moisture, depleted surface water sources, and declining groundwater levels.

Water Deficit: Droughts result in a shortage of water resources, affecting various sectors such as agriculture, industry, and domestic water supply. The imbalance between water demand and supply is a key characteristic of drought conditions.

Dry Spells: Droughts are associated with prolonged dry spells, where rainfall is significantly below average for an extended period. These dry spells can lead to desiccated vegetation, reduced stream flows, and drying up of water bodies.

Spatial Variability: Droughts can exhibit spatial variability, meaning they affect different regions to varying degrees. While one area may experience severe drought conditions, adjacent regions may have relatively better moisture levels. This spatial variation poses challenges in terms of resource allocation and drought management.

Impact on Agriculture: Droughts have a profound impact on agriculture, resulting in reduced crop yields, crop failures, and loss of livestock. The lack of water for irrigation and inadequate soil moisture adversely affects plant growth and agricultural productivity.

Economic Consequences: Droughts have significant economic implications. The agricultural sector, which relies heavily on water availability, faces reduced income, loss of jobs, and increased food prices during drought periods. Other sectors, such as hydropower generation and tourism, may also experience negative impacts.

Environmental Consequences: Droughts can lead to ecological imbalances and environmental degradation. Reduced water availability affects ecosystems, leading to the loss of biodiversity, habitat degradation, and the drying up of wetlands and rivers. The long-term effects can be detrimental to the overall health of ecosystems.

Social and Health Impacts: Droughts can have social and health consequences. Water scarcity can result in limited access to clean drinking water, leading to health issues such as waterborne diseases. Drought-related economic hardships and food insecurity can also impact the well-being of communities, particularly vulnerable populations.

Cumulative Effects: Droughts can have cumulative effects, meaning their impacts can worsen over time. As drought conditions persist, the lack of water availability intensifies, leading to more severe consequences for ecosystems, agriculture, and human livelihoods.

Managing droughts involves implementing measures for water conservation, promoting efficient water use, implementing drought monitoring and early warning systems, and implementing policies and practices that enhance drought resilience in various sectors.

Draughts Impacts and Challenges:

Agriculture and Food Security: Droughts have significant impacts on agriculture, which is a crucial sector in India's economy. Crop failures, reduced yields, and livestock losses can result in food shortages, price fluctuations, and economic hardships for farming communities. Drought-induced food insecurity affects vulnerable populations, particularly in rural areas.

Water Scarcity and Depletion: Droughts lead to water scarcity, affecting both surface water and groundwater resources. Reduced rainfall and prolonged dry periods deplete water reserves, causing wells to dry up, lakes and rivers to shrink, and water tables to decline. Water scarcity affects drinking water supplies, irrigation, industrial operations, and ecosystems.

Socioeconomic and Livelihood Challenges: Droughts can result in economic losses, job insecurity, and migration as people seek alternative livelihoods. Farming communities, small-scale farmers, and marginalized groups are particularly vulnerable to drought impacts. Drought-induced economic stress can lead to poverty, indebtedness, and social challenges.

Environmental and Ecosystem Impacts: Droughts have significant ecological consequences. They result in the drying up of wetlands, reduced stream flows, and loss of habitat for plants and wildlife. Biodiversity loss, soil erosion, deforestation, and degradation of ecosystems are common effects of prolonged drought conditions.

Drought Management and Preparedness:

Drought Monitoring and Early Warning Systems: Regular monitoring of meteorological data, hydrological indicators, and groundwater levels helps in identifying drought conditions and providing early warnings. Timely information and forecasts enable stakeholders to initiate appropriate mitigation measures.

Water Management and Efficiency: Promoting water management practices such as water conservation, efficient irrigation techniques, and rainwater harvesting helps optimize water resources during droughts. Implementing water-use efficiency measures in industries and households also contributes to mitigating water scarcity.

Crop Diversification and Sustainable Agriculture: Encouraging crop diversification, promoting drought-tolerant crop varieties, and implementing sustainable farming practices like agroforestry and conservation agriculture enhance agricultural resilience to drought. These practices conserve soil moisture, improve water retention, and reduce dependence on water-intensive crops.

Social Safety Nets and Support Systems: Establishing social safety nets, including insurance schemes, financial support mechanisms, and social welfare programs, helps vulnerable populations cope with the economic and social impacts of drought. These safety nets provide relief and support during periods of agricultural distress.

Public Awareness and Education: Conducting awareness campaigns about drought risks, water conservation, and sustainable land and water management practices is crucial for building community resilience. Educating farmers, stakeholders, and communities about drought mitigation strategies and early response measures enhances preparedness.

In India, drought management efforts are carried out at the national, state, and local levels. Government agencies, research institutions, NGOs, and community-based organizations work together to implement drought monitoring systems, contingency plans, water conservation programs, and support mechanisms for affected communities. Building resilience, promoting sustainable practices, and ensuring water security are key goals in managing and mitigating the impacts of droughts in India.

2.5 Natural Disaster – Cyclones

Cyclones, also known as hurricanes or typhoons, are powerful tropical storms characterized by low-pressure systems with organized rotating winds. They form over warm ocean waters near the equator and are accompanied by heavy rain, strong winds, and storm surges. Cyclones can cause extensive damage to coastal areas and have a significant impact on human lives, infrastructure, and the environment.

Key aspects related to Cyclones Formation:

Favourable Conditions: Cyclones typically form over warm ocean waters with surface temperatures of at least 26.5°C (80°F). The presence of moist air, low vertical wind shear, and a convergence of winds near the surface creates a conducive environment for their development.

Tropical Depression to Cyclone: The formation of a cyclone begins with a tropical disturbance, which may evolve into a tropical depression when sustained winds reach 38 kilometres per hour (24 miles per hour). As the system intensifies, it progresses to a tropical storm (winds of 63 kilometres per hour or 39 miles per hour) and eventually becomes a cyclone when winds exceed 119 kilometres per hour (74 miles per hour).

Cyclone Structure and Hazards:

Eye and Eyewall: Cyclones have a central area called the "eye," which is a relatively calm region characterized by clear skies. Surrounding the eye is the "eyewall," where the strongest winds and heaviest rainfall occur. The eyewall is the most dangerous part of the cyclone.

Heavy Rainfall: Cyclones produce intense rainfall, leading to flash floods, landslides, and waterlogging. The combination of heavy rain and the slow movement of cyclones can result in prolonged periods of rainfall, exacerbating the flood risk.

Strong Winds: Cyclones are known for their strong winds, often exceeding 200 kilometres per hour (124 miles per hour) or more in severe cases. These high-speed winds can cause significant damage to buildings, infrastructure, and vegetation.

Storm Surges: The low-pressure center of cyclones can cause a rise in sea levels known as a storm surge. Storm surges can lead to coastal inundation, flooding, and erosion, posing a significant threat to coastal communities and infrastructure.

Cyclone Classification:

Tropical Cyclones: These are cyclones that form over warm tropical oceans and are classified based on their maximum sustained wind speed. In the Indian Ocean region, tropical cyclones are categorized as tropical depressions, deep depressions, cyclonic storms, severe cyclonic storms, and very severe cyclonic storms.

Extratropical Cyclones: These cyclones form outside the tropics, typically in the mid-latitude regions. They are associated with the interaction of warm and cold air masses, often resulting in severe weather conditions, including strong winds and heavy rainfall.

Cyclone Impacts and Challenges:

Human Lives and Infrastructure: Cyclones pose a significant threat to human lives, especially in coastal areas. The strong winds can cause structural damage to buildings, infrastructure, and utilities, leading to power outages and disruptions in communication and transportation networks.

Coastal Flooding and Erosion: Storm surges associated with cyclones can cause coastal flooding, leading to the submergence of low-lying areas and the destruction of homes and infrastructure. The erosion of beaches and coastlines can also occur, further exacerbating the vulnerability of coastal communities.

Displacement and Humanitarian Concerns: Cyclones can result in the displacement of communities, forcing people to evacuate their homes and seek temporary shelter in relief camps or with relatives. Providing immediate humanitarian assistance, including food, water, healthcare, and sanitation, is crucial to address the needs of affected populations.

Environmental Impact: Cyclones can have significant environmental impacts, including damage to coral reefs, destruction of coastal ecosystems, and the loss of biodiversity. The destruction of forests and vegetation can lead to soil erosion, landslides, and long-term ecological disturbances.

Cyclone Preparedness and Management:

Early Warning Systems: Effective cyclone preparedness involves the establishment of robust early warning systems. Meteorological agencies monitor cyclone formation and track their movement, issuing timely alerts and advisories to authorities, communities, and the public.

Evacuation Planning: Evacuation plans are crucial for vulnerable coastal communities. Identifying evacuation routes, establishing shelters, and conducting drills to ensure preparedness and efficient evacuation during cyclone events are essential.

Infrastructure Resilience: Designing and constructing buildings and infrastructure with cyclone-resistant features can minimize damage. Implementing building codes, reinforcing structures, and using resilient materials are key aspects of infrastructure resilience.

Community Awareness and Education: Educating communities about cyclones, their impacts, and preparedness measures is vital. Awareness programs, training sessions, and dissemination of information through various media channels help increase community resilience and response capabilities.

In India, cyclones commonly affect the coastal regions, particularly along the Bay of Bengal and the Arabian Sea. The Indian Meteorological Department (IMD) closely monitors cyclone activity and issues warnings, allowing for preparedness and timely evacuation. Government agencies, disaster management authorities, and local communities work together to minimize the impacts of cyclones through effective early warning systems, infrastructure resilience, and community engagement.

Cyclone Tracks and Regional Variations:

Bay of Bengal and Arabian Sea: India's coastal regions are prone to cyclones due to their proximity to the Bay of Bengal and the Arabian Sea. Cyclones originating in these regions can affect the eastern and western coasts of India, respectively. The Bay of Bengal is more active in terms of cyclone frequency, with the majority of cyclones affecting the eastern coastal states of Odisha, West Bengal, Andhra Pradesh, and Tamil Nadu. Cyclones in the Arabian Sea generally impact the western coast, particularly the states of Gujarat, Maharashtra, and Karnataka.

Cyclone Tracks: The tracks of cyclones can vary, with some moving along a west-northwest trajectory towards the Indian subcontinent, while others recurve towards the northeast, heading towards Bangladesh or Myanmar. The path and intensity of cyclones depend on various factors, including atmospheric conditions, steering currents, and interaction with land masses.

Cyclone Naming:

Naming Systems: Cyclones are named to facilitate easy identification and communication. The Indian Meteorological Department (IMD) uses a naming system for cyclones in the North Indian Ocean, alternating between male and female names sourced from different countries in the region.

Impacts and Challenges in India:

Vulnerable Coastal Populations: Coastal communities are particularly vulnerable to the impacts of cyclones. These areas often have dense populations, inadequate infrastructure, and limited access to resources, making them more susceptible to damage and disruptions caused by cyclones.

Coastal Flooding and Saline Inundation: Cyclones can result in significant coastal flooding, which leads to the submergence of low-lying areas and damage to homes, agriculture, and infrastructure. In some cases, saltwater intrusion due to storm surges can contaminate freshwater sources, affecting drinking water supplies and agricultural land.

Disruption of Livelihoods: Cyclones can disrupt livelihoods, particularly in coastal areas dependent on fishing, agriculture, and tourism. Damage to boats, loss of fishing gear, destruction of crops, and disruptions to tourism activities can have long-lasting economic consequences for affected communities.

Post-Cyclone Recovery: Following a cyclone, the process of recovery and rehabilitation is essential. This involves clearing debris, restoring infrastructure, providing support for affected populations, and rebuilding homes and livelihoods. Timely and effective post-cyclone recovery efforts are crucial for the well-being and resilience of affected communities.

Cyclone Preparedness and Management:

Early Warning Systems: The Indian Meteorological Department (IMD) operates a sophisticated cyclone tracking and warning system. This includes monitoring weather patterns, using weather satellites, and issuing cyclone alerts and advisories to authorities, communities, and the public. Timely warnings help in preparedness and evacuation efforts.

Evacuation and Shelter Management: Evacuation plans and the establishment of cyclone shelters are critical for ensuring the safety of coastal populations. Identifying vulnerable areas, preparing evacuation routes, and coordinating with local authorities to organize shelter facilities are key components of cyclone preparedness.

Communication and Awareness: Effective communication and raising awareness among communities are crucial in ensuring preparedness and response to cyclones. This involves disseminating information about cyclones, their impacts, and evacuation procedures through various channels, including mass media, community meetings, and educational campaigns.

Infrastructure Resilience: Building resilient infrastructure in coastal areas helps reduce the damage caused by cyclones. This includes constructing cyclone-resistant buildings, strengthening coastal embankments, and implementing measures to mitigate coastal erosion and flooding.

Community Participation and Engagement: Engaging communities in preparedness efforts empowers them to take proactive measures. This includes conducting drills, organizing community-based early warning systems, and training volunteers to support emergency response activities.

Cyclone management in India involves the coordinated efforts of multiple stakeholders, including government agencies, disaster management authorities, research institutions, NGOs, and local communities. By enhancing early warning systems, improving infrastructure resilience, raising awareness, and building community resilience, India aims to mitigate the impacts of cyclones and reduce the vulnerability of coastal populations.

Cyclones in India:

Cyclone Seasons: India experiences two main cyclone seasons. The pre-monsoon season from April to June is characterized by cyclones in the Bay of Bengal, while the post-monsoon season from October to December sees cyclones in the Arabian Sea.

Cyclone Frequency: The eastern coast of India, particularly the states of Odisha, West Bengal, Andhra Pradesh, and Tamil Nadu, is more prone to cyclones originating in the Bay of Bengal. The western coast, including the states of Gujarat, Maharashtra, and Karnataka, is susceptible to cyclones from the Arabian Sea.

Historical Impact: India has faced severe cyclones in the past that have caused significant damage and loss of life. Notable cyclones include the Super Cyclone of 1999 (Odisha), Cyclone Phailin in 2013 (Odisha), Cyclone Hudhud in 2014 (Andhra Pradesh), Cyclone Fani in 2019 (Odisha), and Cyclone Amphan in 2020 (West Bengal).

Impacts and Challenges in India:

Coastal Flooding and Storm Surge: Cyclones bring intense rainfall and storm surges that can lead to coastal flooding. Low-lying areas, particularly in delta regions, are at high risk of inundation, which results in damage to infrastructure, displacement of communities, and contamination of freshwater sources.

High Wind Speeds: Cyclones are characterized by strong winds, often exceeding 200 kilometres per hour (124 miles per hour) or more. These high-speed winds can cause widespread destruction of buildings, uproot trees, damage power lines, and disrupt communication and transportation networks.

Agriculture and Livelihoods: Cyclones can have devastating effects on agriculture, particularly in coastal areas. Crop damage, loss of livestock, and destruction of agricultural infrastructure can result in significant economic losses and impact the livelihoods of farming communities.

Evacuation and Humanitarian Concerns: Cyclones require timely and well-coordinated evacuation efforts to ensure the safety of coastal populations. Providing temporary shelters, emergency supplies, and healthcare facilities for evacuated communities is crucial in addressing humanitarian concerns during cyclone events.

Post-Cyclone Recovery and Rehabilitation: After a cyclone, the process of recovery and rehabilitation is essential. This includes clearing debris, restoring infrastructure, providing support for affected populations, and rebuilding homes and livelihoods. Long-term efforts are required to restore normalcy and enhance the resilience of communities.

Cyclone Preparedness and Management in India:

Cyclone Warning Systems: The Indian Meteorological Department (IMD) operates a sophisticated cyclone tracking and warning system. It issues cyclone advisories and alerts to authorities, communities, and the public, providing timely information on cyclone development, intensity, and projected path.

Evacuation Planning: Evacuation plans are crucial to ensure the safety of coastal populations. Identifying vulnerable areas, preparing evacuation routes, and establishing cyclone shelters are key components of cyclone preparedness. Local authorities, along with state and national disaster management agencies, coordinate evacuation efforts.

Infrastructure Resilience: Constructing cyclone-resistant buildings, strengthening coastal embankments, and implementing measures to mitigate coastal erosion and flooding help reduce the damage caused by cyclones. Building codes and guidelines for cyclone-resistant construction practices are developed and enforced.

Community Awareness and Engagement: Raising awareness among communities about cyclones, their impacts, and preparedness measures is essential. Conducting drills, organizing community-based early warning systems, and training volunteers to support emergency response activities contribute to community resilience.

Coordination and Capacity Building: Collaboration among government agencies, disaster management authorities, research institutions, NGOs, and local communities is crucial for effective cyclone management. Capacity building programs, training sessions, and knowledge sharing platforms help enhance preparedness and response capabilities.

In India, the National Disaster Management Authority (NDMA) and State Disaster Management Authorities (SDMAs) play a vital role in cyclone preparedness, response, and recovery efforts. The focus is on improving early warning systems, strengthening infrastructure resilience, raising community awareness, and building the capacity of stakeholders to mitigate the impacts of cyclones and protect vulnerable coastal populations.

Factors affecting Cyclone Severity

Several factors contribute to the severity of cyclones. These factors influence the development, intensity, and potential impacts of cyclones. Here are the key factors affecting cyclone severity:

Sea Surface Temperature: Warm Ocean waters provide the primary source of energy for cyclone formation and intensification. When sea surface temperatures exceed a threshold of around 26.5°C (80°F), they facilitate the transfer of heat and moisture from the ocean into the atmosphere, providing the necessary conditions for cyclone development. Higher sea surface temperatures can lead to increased cyclone intensity.

Ocean Heat Content: In addition to sea surface temperature, the total heat content of the upper ocean layer is crucial for sustaining and intensifying cyclones. A deep layer of warm water allows for greater heat transfer and energy exchange with the atmosphere, fuelling the cyclone's growth. Higher ocean heat content can contribute to more intense and longer-lasting cyclones.

Atmospheric Instability: Cyclones thrive in atmospheres with significant vertical instability. This occurs when there is a rapid decrease in temperature with height, which encourages the upward movement of warm, moist air. Such instability promotes the development of thunderstorms and convective activity, essential for cyclone formation and intensification.

Low Vertical Wind Shear: Wind shear refers to the change in wind speed and direction with height. Low vertical wind shear allows cyclones to maintain their structure and intensify. When wind shear is weak, cyclones can vertically stack their warm core and maintain their organization, allowing them to strengthen and persist.

Atmospheric Moisture: The presence of abundant moisture in the lower atmosphere is crucial for cyclone development. Moist air provides the necessary fuel for condensation and cloud formation, releasing latent heat that further powers the cyclone. Higher moisture content can contribute to the intensification of cyclones and increase the potential for heavy rainfall.

Upper-Level Steering Currents: Cyclones are steered by the prevailing winds at higher altitudes, typically in the upper levels of the troposphere. The direction and strength of these steering currents influence the path a cyclone follows. Factors such as the position and intensity of the subtropical high-pressure systems and the interaction with mid-latitude weather systems determine the path and potential landfall of a cyclone.

Interaction with Landmasses: When cyclones make landfall or interact with landmasses, their intensity can be influenced by various factors. The frictional effect of land can weaken cyclones by disrupting their low-level circulation and reducing the inflow of warm, moist air from the ocean. However, the presence of favourable topography or warm land surfaces can sustain or even enhance cyclone intensity in some cases.

Vertical Structure and Organization: The vertical structure and organization of a cyclone play a role in its intensity and potential impacts. A well-organized cyclone with a consolidated core, a distinct eye, and a tightly wrapped eyewall is more likely to be intense. The presence of a strong eyewall with deep convection and spiral rainbands indicates a well-developed and potentially severe cyclone.

It is important to note that while these factors contribute to cyclone severity, predicting the exact behaviour and intensity of cyclones remains challenging. Sophisticated modelling techniques, data analysis, and ongoing research help improve our understanding of cyclone dynamics and enhance forecasting capabilities, enabling better preparedness and response to these natural hazards.

2.6 Natural Disaster – Volcanoes

Volcanoes: Volcanoes are vents or openings in the Earth's crust through which molten lava, volcanic ash, and gases are ejected. While India does not have active volcanoes, it is important to study volcanoes' global impact due to their potential to cause ashfall, affect climate patterns, and disrupt air travel. Volcanoes are geological features that occur when molten rock (magma), gases, and other materials rise to the Earth's surface. Volcanic eruptions can have significant impacts on human lives, infrastructure, and the environment.

Causes of Volcanoes:

Plate Tectonics: Volcanic activity is primarily associated with the movement and interaction of Earth's tectonic plates. Most volcanoes occur at plate boundaries, including divergent boundaries (where plates move apart), convergent boundaries (where plates collide), and transform boundaries (where plates slide past each other).

Subduction Zones: The majority of explosive volcanoes occur at subduction zones, where an oceanic plate subducts beneath a continental plate. The subducting plate melts, generating magma that rises through the overriding plate, eventually leading to volcanic eruptions.

Characteristics:

Magma Chamber: Volcanoes have a magma chamber beneath their surface where molten rock accumulates. Pressure builds up within the magma chamber over time, leading to eventual eruptions.

Vent: A vent is the opening through which volcanic materials, including magma, gases, and ash, are expelled during an eruption. Vents can vary in size and shape, ranging from fissures to craters or calderas.

Lava Flows: Lava, the molten rock that reaches the Earth's surface during an eruption, can flow down the sides of a volcano. The type and viscosity of the lava determine the flow characteristics, which can range from slow-moving to highly fluid or explosive.

Types of Volcanoes:

Shield Volcanoes: Shield volcanoes have gentle slopes and broad, shield-like profiles. They are typically formed by low-viscosity lava flows, resulting in wide, flat, and broad-shaped volcanoes. The Hawaiian Islands are examples of shield volcanoes.

Stratovolcanoes (Composite Volcanoes): Stratovolcanoes are steep-sided and cone-shaped. They are characterized by alternating layers of solidified lava flows, volcanic ash, and pyroclastic materials. Stratovolcanoes are often associated with explosive eruptions and are found in subduction zone regions, such as the Pacific Ring of Fire.

Cinder Cones: Cinder cones are small, steep-sided volcanoes that form from explosive eruptions of gas-rich magma. They are composed of fragmented volcanic material called cinders or scoria. Cinder cones are typically formed over a short period and can be found on the flanks of larger volcanoes.

Calderas: Calderas are large, basin-shaped depressions that form after a volcanic eruption. They result from the collapse of the volcano's summit or the emptying of the underlying magma chamber. Calderas can be several kilometres in diameter and are often associated with explosive eruptions.

Volcanoes – Impact and Challenges:

Primary Hazards: The primary hazards associated with volcanic eruptions include pyroclastic flows (fast-moving, superheated currents of gas and volcanic material), lava flows, ashfall, and volcanic gases. These hazards can cause direct damage to structures, infrastructure, and human health.

Secondary Hazards: Volcanic eruptions can trigger secondary hazards such as lahars (mudflows or debris flows), landslides, tsunamis (if the volcano is near a body of water), and volcanic ash clouds. These hazards can have far-reaching impacts on nearby communities and regions.

Environmental Impact: Volcanic eruptions can have both short-term and long-term environmental consequences. They can result in the destruction of ecosystems, including forests and habitats, and contaminate water sources with volcanic ash and chemicals. The deposition of ash can also affect air quality and agricultural productivity.

Displacement and Resettlement: Eruptions can lead to the displacement of populations, forcing communities to evacuate and seek temporary shelter. Resettlement and recovery efforts can be challenging, as volcanic eruptions may render certain areas uninhabitable due to ongoing volcanic activity or environmental degradation.

Volcano Mitigation and Preparedness:

Volcano Monitoring: Continuous monitoring of volcanoes is essential to detect signs of volcanic unrest, such as ground deformation, gas emissions, and seismic activity. This helps in issuing timely warnings and advisories to at-risk communities.

Hazard Zoning: Hazard zoning involves mapping and delineating areas at risk from volcanic hazards. This information is used for land-use planning, restricting development in high-risk areas, and implementing appropriate mitigation measures.

Emergency Response and Evacuation Plans: Developing emergency response plans and evacuation procedures is crucial for ensuring the safety of communities near active volcanoes. Establishing evacuation routes, designating evacuation centers, and conducting regular drills help improve preparedness and response.

Volcanic Ash Monitoring and Air Traffic Management: Monitoring volcanic ash clouds is critical for aviation safety. Volcanic ash can severely damage aircraft engines, leading to potential accidents. Effective communication and coordination between volcano observatories, meteorological agencies, and aviation authorities are vital in managing airspace during volcanic eruptions.

Public Awareness and Education: Raising public awareness about volcanic hazards, their impacts, and appropriate safety measures is essential. Community education programs, dissemination of information through various media channels, and engaging with local communities help improve preparedness and enhance resilience.

Scientific Research and Cooperation: Continuous scientific research, data collection, and collaboration among volcanologists, geologists, and disaster management agencies contribute to understanding volcanic processes, improving hazard assessment, and enhancing response capabilities.

Managing the impacts of volcanic eruptions requires a comprehensive approach involving monitoring, hazard assessment, preparedness, and response measures. By implementing effective mitigation strategies, early warning systems, and community engagement, the risks associated with volcanic activity can be minimized, and the resilience of affected communities can be enhanced.

Volcano Magnitude and Duration:

Magnitude: The magnitude of a volcanic eruption refers to the amount of volcanic material and energy released during the event. It is often measured using the Volcanic Explosivity Index (VEI), which categorizes eruptions on a scale from 0 to 8 based on factors such as the volume of erupted material, eruption column height, and duration of the eruption. Higher VEI values indicate larger and more explosive eruptions.

Duration: The duration of a volcanic eruption can vary significantly, ranging from short-lived explosive eruptions that last hours to effusive eruptions that can continue for months or even years. The duration of an eruption depends on factors such as the volume and viscosity of the erupted magma, the supply of magma from the subsurface, and the dynamics of the volcanic system.

Factors Affecting Severity of Volcano:

Volcanic Explosivity: The explosivity of a volcano is influenced by the composition and gas content of the magma. High gas content, particularly high levels of dissolved water vapor and carbon dioxide, can contribute to more explosive eruptions. The viscosity of the magma, which affects its ability to release gases, also plays a role.

Vent Structure: The structure of the volcanic vent, including its size, shape, and condition, can impact the severity of an eruption. Narrow vents can lead to more explosive eruptions, as they restrict the release of volcanic gases, resulting in pressure buildup. A collapsed or blocked vent can also contribute to explosive events.

Volcanic Ash and Pyroclastic Flows: Volcanic ash and pyroclastic flows pose significant hazards during eruptions. The size, composition, and dispersal of volcanic ash can affect its impact on aviation, infrastructure, and human health. Pyroclastic flows, fast-moving currents of hot gas and volcanic fragments, can cause widespread destruction in the vicinity of the volcano.

Volcano Management Strategies:

Volcano Monitoring: Continuous monitoring of volcanoes using seismometers, gas analysers, ground deformation measurements, and thermal imaging helps detect signs of volcanic unrest. Monitoring data can provide early warning of potential eruptions, enabling authorities to issue timely advisories and evacuate at-risk populations.

Hazard Zoning and Land-use Planning: Mapping and zoning volcanic hazards allows for informed land-use planning and the restriction of development in high-risk areas. This involves identifying zones based on the potential impact of volcanic hazards, such as pyroclastic flows, lava flows, lahars (mudflows), and ashfall.

Emergency Preparedness and Response: Developing emergency response plans, establishing communication networks, and conducting regular drills are essential for effective emergency management. Evacuation routes, designated shelters, and coordination with local communities and relevant agencies are key components of preparedness and response efforts.

Public Awareness and Education: Raising public awareness about volcanic hazards, safety measures, and evacuation protocols is crucial. Educational campaigns, community engagement programs, and information dissemination through various media channels help enhance preparedness and facilitate informed decision-making during volcanic events.

Major Volcano Prone Regions:

Pacific Ring of Fire: The Pacific Ring of Fire is the most geologically active region in the world, hosting a significant number of active volcanoes. It spans the coasts of the Pacific Ocean, including countries such as Japan, Indonesia, the Philippines, and the western coast of the Americas.

Mediterranean: The Mediterranean region, including countries like Italy, Greece, and Iceland, is another area prone to volcanic activity. The presence of subduction zones, volcanic arcs, and rift systems contribute to volcanic activity in this region.

East Africa Rift System: The East Africa Rift System, extending from Mozambique to Ethiopia, is known for its volcanic activity. Countries such as Tanzania, Kenya, and Ethiopia have active volcanoes along this rift system.

Volcano – Management and Preparedness:

Volcano Observatories: Establishing volcano observatories equipped with monitoring instruments and staffed by volcanologists helps gather data, analyse volcanic activity, and issue timely alerts and advisories.

International Cooperation: Collaboration and information sharing among countries and scientific institutions play a crucial role in volcanic hazard assessment, research, and preparedness. International organizations such as the International Association of Volcanology and Chemistry of the Earth's Interior (IAVCEI) facilitate cooperation and knowledge exchange.

Volcanic Ash Monitoring and Aviation Safety: Volcanic ash poses a significant risk to aviation. Collaboration between volcano observatories, meteorological agencies, and aviation authorities is necessary to monitor ash clouds, issue advisories, and manage airspace during volcanic eruptions.

Resilience and Recovery: Developing strategies for post-eruption recovery and long-term resilience building is essential. This includes assisting affected communities in rebuilding infrastructure, restoring livelihoods, and addressing the environmental and social impacts of volcanic eruptions.

Effective management and preparedness for volcanic hazards require a multidisciplinary approach, involving scientific research, monitoring, hazard assessment, community engagement, and coordination among government agencies, disaster management authorities, and international organizations. By implementing proactive measures and educating communities, the impacts of volcanic eruptions can be minimized, and the resilience of affected regions can be enhanced.

2.7 Natural Disasters – Earthquakes

Earthquakes: Earthquakes are the shaking or trembling of the Earth's surface caused by the release of energy along fault lines. India is located in a seismically active zone, and earthquakes can lead to structural damage, landslides, and loss of life.

Causes of Earthquakes:

Earthquakes occur due to the sudden release of energy in the Earth's crust, resulting in seismic waves. The primary causes of earthquakes include:

Tectonic Plate Movements: The majority of earthquakes are associated with the movement of tectonic plates. The Earth's lithosphere is divided into several large plates that float on the semi-fluid asthenosphere. When these plates interact, they can collide, move apart, or slide past each other, resulting in stress and deformation along plate boundaries. This stress eventually exceeds the strength of rocks, causing them to fracture and release stored energy in the form of an earthquake.

Faulting: Earthquakes commonly occur along faults, which are fractures in the Earth's crust where rocks on either side have moved relative to each other. Different types of faults, such as strike-slip faults, normal faults, and thrust faults, are associated with specific plate boundary interactions and have distinct motion characteristics.

Other Causes: Earthquakes can also be triggered by volcanic activity, such as the movement of magma beneath the surface, or by human activities like mining, reservoir-induced seismicity (due to the filling of large reservoirs), and hydraulic fracturing (fracking) for oil and gas extraction.

Characteristics of Earthquake:

Focus and Epicentre: The focus (hypocentre) of an earthquake is the actual point where the energy is released below the Earth's surface. The epicenter is the point on the Earth's surface directly above the focus. The depth and location of the focus, along with the energy release, determine the characteristics and impact of the earthquake.

Seismic Waves: Earthquakes generate different types of seismic waves that propagate through the Earth. Primary waves (P-waves) are the fastest and compressional waves that travel through solids, liquids, and gases. Secondary waves (S-waves) are slower and shear waves that can only pass through solids. Surface waves are slower and generate the shaking felt at the Earth's surface, causing the most damage.

Types of Earthquakes:

Tectonic Earthquakes: These are the most common type of earthquakes and occur along plate boundaries. Subcategories include interplate earthquakes (between different plates) and intraplate earthquakes (within a single tectonic plate).

Volcanic Earthquakes: These earthquakes are associated with volcanic activity and occur due to the movement of magma beneath a volcano. They can be indicators of an impending volcanic eruption.

Induced Earthquakes: These earthquakes are triggered by human activities, such as mining, hydraulic fracturing (fracking), reservoir impoundment, and underground nuclear testing.

Earthquake Impact and Challenges:

Ground Shaking: The primary impact of earthquakes is ground shaking, which can cause buildings, infrastructure, and the ground itself to move. The severity of shaking depends on the magnitude of the earthquake, distance from the epicenter, depth of the focus, local soil conditions, and building construction standards.

Surface Rupture: Large earthquakes can result in surface rupture, where the Earth's surface is displaced along the fault line. This can lead to visible cracks, displacement of structures, and damage to infrastructure.

Landslides and Tsunamis: Earthquakes can trigger landslides in hilly or mountainous regions, posing risks to communities and infrastructure. Underwater earthquakes can also generate tsunamis, which are large ocean waves that can cause devastating coastal flooding.

Secondary Hazards: Earthquakes can trigger secondary hazards such as aftershocks, which are smaller earthquakes that occur after the main shock. Aftershocks can cause additional damage and hinder rescue and recovery efforts. Other secondary hazards include liquefaction (when saturated soil temporarily loses strength and behaves like a liquid) and soil amplification (where certain soil types amplify ground shaking).

Earthquake Mitigation and Preparedness:

Building Codes and Regulations: Implementing and enforcing seismic building codes and regulations is crucial for constructing structures that can withstand seismic forces. This includes incorporating proper structural design, materials, and reinforcement techniques to reduce the vulnerability of buildings and infrastructure.

Seismic Hazard Assessment: Conducting detailed seismic hazard assessments helps identify areas at higher risk and guides land-use planning and development decisions. This involves mapping active faults, determining soil liquefaction potential, and assessing the vulnerability of critical infrastructure.

Early Warning Systems: Developing and implementing earthquake early warning systems can provide seconds to minutes of advance warning before shaking reaches populated areas. These systems use seismic monitoring networks to detect earthquake waves and rapidly issue alerts.

Public Education and Preparedness: Raising public awareness about earthquakes, their impacts, and safety measures is essential. This includes educating communities on proper response actions during an earthquake, conducting drills, and promoting the use of emergency kits and communication plans.

Seismic Monitoring and Research: Maintaining and expanding seismic monitoring networks, along with ongoing research on earthquake processes, helps in improving understanding, early detection, and forecasting capabilities. This enables better preparedness and response to earthquakes.

International Cooperation: Collaboration among countries, scientific institutions, and international organizations plays a crucial role in sharing data, research, and expertise. This promotes best practices in earthquake monitoring, hazard assessment, and disaster management.

Earthquakes are complex natural phenomena, and mitigating their impact requires a multi-faceted approach that includes understanding the causes, implementing building codes, enhancing preparedness, and fostering public education. By adopting measures to reduce vulnerability, enhance resilience, and improve response capabilities, the impacts of earthquakes can be minimized, and the safety of communities can be enhanced.

Earthquake Magnitude and Duration:

Magnitude: Earthquakes in India vary in magnitude, ranging from minor tremors to significant seismic events. The magnitude of an earthquake is measured using the Richter scale or moment magnitude scale (Mw). Notable earthquakes in India have ranged from moderate magnitudes (around 5.0) to major events exceeding magnitude 7.0.

Duration: The duration of an earthquake can vary depending on various factors, including the magnitude and depth of the earthquake, as well as the geological characteristics of the region. Most earthquakes last for a few seconds to a minute, but larger earthquakes with prolonged aftershock sequences can have a duration of several minutes or more.

Factors Affecting Severity of Earthquake:

Magnitude: The magnitude of an earthquake directly influences its severity. Larger magnitude earthquakes tend to cause more significant ground shaking and can result in greater damage to buildings, infrastructure, and the environment.

Depth of the Focus: The depth at which an earthquake occurs affects the severity of ground shaking. Shallow earthquakes, which occur closer to the Earth's surface, tend to generate stronger shaking and cause more immediate damage. Deeper earthquakes, although capable of transmitting seismic waves over larger distances, may cause less severe shaking at the surface.

Distance from the Epicenter: The proximity of populated areas to the epicenter of an earthquake impacts the level of shaking experienced. Areas closer to the epicenter generally experience more intense ground shaking and are at higher risk of damage.

Site Conditions: The geology and soil composition of an area influence the severity of ground shaking during an earthquake. Soft or loose soil amplifies seismic waves, increasing the potential for damage to structures. Areas with rock or stiffer soil generally experience less ground shaking.

Earthquake – Management Strategies:

Seismic Monitoring and Early Warning Systems: Maintaining a network of seismic monitoring stations helps detect earthquakes, monitor activity, and issue timely warnings. Early warning systems provide alerts to communities, allowing them to take immediate actions to protect themselves and mitigate potential damage.

Building Codes and Regulations: Implementing and enforcing seismic building codes and regulations is crucial for constructing earthquake-resistant structures. These codes specify design standards, materials, and construction techniques that can withstand seismic forces and reduce the vulnerability of buildings and infrastructure.

Land-use Planning and Zoning: Identifying and mapping areas prone to higher seismic hazards allows for appropriate land-use planning and zoning regulations. This helps guide development away from high-risk zones and ensures that critical infrastructure is located in safer areas.

Public Awareness and Education: Educating the public about earthquake risks, safety measures, and response protocols is vital. This includes conducting public awareness campaigns, organizing drills and exercises, and disseminating information through various media channels.

Major Earthquake Prone Regions:

Himalayan Region: The Himalayan region, including states such as Jammu and Kashmir, Himachal Pradesh, Uttarakhand, Sikkim, and Arunachal Pradesh, is highly seismically active due to the ongoing collision between the Indian and Eurasian tectonic plates. The region is prone to both shallow and deep earthquakes, including major ones.

Northeastern Region: The northeastern states of India, including Assam, Meghalaya, Manipur, Mizoram, and Nagaland, are situated in a seismically active zone due to the convergence of the Indian and Eurasian plates. The region experiences frequent earthquakes, including some significant events.

Earthquake Management and Preparedness:

National Seismological Network: The India Meteorological Department (IMD) operates a national seismological network that monitors earthquake activity across the country. The network provides real-time data on earthquake occurrences and enables prompt analysis and dissemination of information.

National Disaster Management Authority (NDMA): The NDMA plays a crucial role in formulating policies, coordinating efforts, and promoting best practices in disaster management, including earthquakes. The NDMA works in collaboration with state disaster management authorities to enhance preparedness and response capabilities.

Earthquake Preparedness and Response Plans: Developing and implementing earthquake preparedness and response plans at the national, state, and local levels is essential. These plans include actions for early warning dissemination, evacuation procedures, medical assistance, search and rescue operations, and post-earthquake recovery efforts.

Community Engagement and Capacity Building: Engaging local communities through awareness campaigns, training programs, and capacity-building initiatives helps empower individuals to respond effectively during earthquakes. This includes educating communities on response actions, establishing community-based early warning systems, and promoting self-help measures.

International Cooperation: Collaboration with international organizations and neighbouring countries on seismic monitoring, research, and knowledge sharing strengthens earthquake preparedness and response efforts. Cooperation facilitates access to advanced technologies, expertise, and resources in managing earthquake risks.

Managing earthquakes requires a comprehensive approach that includes monitoring and early warning systems, implementing building codes, enhancing public awareness and education, and promoting effective coordination among government agencies, scientific institutions, and communities. By implementing proactive measures and fostering a culture of preparedness, the impacts of earthquakes can be minimized, and the resilience of affected regions can be enhanced.

Measurement of Seismic Waves of Earthquake

Earthquakes can be recorded using seismometers, which are instruments designed to detect and measure seismic waves generated by earthquakes. Seismometers are crucial tools for monitoring and studying earthquakes, as they provide valuable data for understanding the earthquake's magnitude, location, and depth. Let us discuss the components of a seismometer and how they measure seismic waves:

1. Mass and Frame: The primary component of a seismometer is a massive weight, often referred to as the "mass," suspended within a frame or housing. The frame is firmly anchored to the ground, while the mass is free to move in response to ground motion.
2. Restoring Spring: To maintain stability, the mass is attached to the frame by a restoring spring. The spring allows the mass to return to its equilibrium position after being displaced by seismic waves.
3. Seismic Sensor: The seismic sensor is a key element that detects ground motion and converts it into an electrical signal. There are various types of seismic sensors used in seismometers, including:

Mechanical Sensors: These sensors rely on the relative motion between the mass and frame to generate electrical signals. They are based on the principle of relative displacement caused by ground motion.

Piezoelectric Sensors: These sensors utilize piezoelectric materials that generate an electrical charge when subjected to mechanical stress. The ground motion causes the piezoelectric sensor to generate voltage, which is then recorded.

Optical Sensors: Some modern seismometers use optical sensors, such as interferometers, to detect ground motion. These sensors measure the changes in the interference pattern of laser light caused by seismic waves.

4. Data Recorder: The electrical signal from the seismic sensor is transmitted to a data recorder, which records the seismic wave data. In modern seismometers, the data is often digitized and stored digitally for further analysis.

Working Principle: When an earthquake occurs, seismic waves propagate through the Earth's crust and reach the seismometer. The ground motion causes the frame to move, but due to its mass, the seismic sensor resists this motion. As a result, the mass moves relative to the frame, creating a relative displacement.

This relative displacement generates a force within the restoring spring, which acts to bring the mass back to its equilibrium position. The force in the spring is proportional to the ground motion, and it generates an electrical signal in the seismic sensor. This electrical signal is then recorded by the data recorder.

Types of Seismometers:

There are several types of seismometers used for different applications:

Short Period Seismometers: These seismometers are sensitive to higher frequency seismic waves and are used to study local earthquakes.

Broadband Seismometers: These seismometers have a wide frequency response and can detect seismic waves from distant earthquakes.

Strong Motion Seismometers: These specialized seismometers are designed to measure strong ground motion during large earthquakes.

Thus, Seismometers play a vital role in recording earthquakes and studying their characteristics. By detecting and measuring seismic waves, seismometers provide essential data for earthquake monitoring, hazard assessment, and scientific research, helping us better understand and prepare for seismic events.

2.8 Natural Disaster – Tsunami

Tsunami: Tsunamis are large ocean waves generated by underwater disturbances, such as earthquakes, volcanic eruptions, or landslides. They can travel across long distances and cause devastating impacts when they reach coastal areas, including flooding, destruction of infrastructure, and loss of lives.

Causes of Tsunami:

A tsunami is a series of large ocean waves triggered by an underwater disturbance, typically associated with seismic activity. The primary causes of tsunamis include:

Underwater Earthquakes: The most common cause of tsunamis is the vertical displacement of the seafloor due to underwater earthquakes. When tectonic plates move, particularly along subduction zones, the sudden release of energy can generate powerful seismic waves that propagate through the ocean, creating a tsunami.

Submarine Landslides: Massive underwater landslides, often triggered by earthquakes, volcanic eruptions, or slope instability, can displace large volumes of water and generate tsunamis. These landslides can occur along continental slopes, volcanic island flanks, or even the collapse of volcanic edifices.

Volcanic Eruptions: Certain volcanic eruptions, especially those that occur in or near bodies of water, can generate tsunamis. These tsunamis result from the explosive release of volcanic material into the water, the collapse of volcanic edifices, or the interaction of magma with water.

Impacts from Asteroids or Meteorites: In rare cases, large impacts from asteroids or meteorites in bodies of water can generate tsunamis. The energy released from the impact can displace water and create powerful waves.

Characteristics of Tsunami:

Wave Formation: Tsunamis are characterized by long-wavelength waves that travel across the ocean at high speeds, typically hundreds of kilometres per hour. In deep ocean waters, tsunamis may go unnoticed as the waves have low amplitudes and are widely spaced.

Shoaling: As a tsunami approaches shallow coastal waters, the wave height increases due to the decrease in water depth. This shoaling effect causes the tsunami waves to slow down, compress, and stack up, resulting in a higher amplitude when they reach the shore.

Wave Energy: Tsunamis carry a significant amount of energy across vast distances. The energy is distributed throughout the water column, from the surface to the seafloor, making them capable of causing widespread destruction and inundation when they reach the coast.

Wave Period: Tsunami waves have longer periods, typically ranging from a few minutes to several hours, compared to wind-generated waves. This means that the time between successive wave crests is much longer, resulting in a slower and more sustained flooding of coastal areas.

Types of Tsunamis:

Local Tsunamis: Local tsunamis are generated by earthquakes near the coastline. They typically have a short travel time, reaching nearby coastal areas within minutes to an hour after the earthquake. These tsunamis pose a significant threat to coastal communities due to their rapid onset.

Distant Tsunamis: Distant tsunamis originate from far-off earthquakes or other triggering events. They can travel across ocean basins, taking several hours or even a day to reach distant coastlines. While the amplitude of distant tsunamis may be reduced, they can still cause significant damage when they reach the shore.

Tsunami Impact and Challenges:

Coastal Inundation: Tsunamis can cause rapid and extensive flooding of coastal areas, leading to the destruction of buildings, infrastructure, and ecosystems. The force of the waves and the associated currents can erode coastlines, deposit sediment, and cause significant changes to the nearshore environment.

Loss of Life and Injury: Tsunamis can result in the loss of human life and cause injuries due to the force of the waves, drowning, and impact with debris. The sudden onset and rapid inundation leave little time for evacuation, making it challenging to ensure the safety of coastal populations.

Infrastructure Damage: Tsunamis can cause severe damage to coastal infrastructure, including buildings, roads, bridges, ports, and utilities. The force of the waves and the inundation of saltwater can lead to the collapse of structures and render critical facilities inoperable.

Environmental Impact: Tsunamis can have long-term environmental consequences. The deposition of sediment and debris can smother ecosystems and disrupt habitats, while the introduction of saltwater into freshwater ecosystems can harm flora and fauna. Coastal ecosystems, including coral reefs and mangroves, can be severely impacted.

Tsunami Mitigation and Preparedness:

Tsunami Warning Systems: Implementing robust tsunami warning systems helps detect and alert coastal communities of impending tsunamis. These systems rely on seismic monitoring, ocean sensors, and communication networks to detect earthquakes and disseminate timely warnings.

Land-use Planning and Zoning: Mapping and zoning coastal areas based on tsunami hazards helps guide land-use planning decisions and ensures that critical infrastructure is located in safer areas. This includes identifying evacuation routes, establishing safe zones, and restricting development in high-risk areas.

Public Awareness and Education: Educating the public about tsunamis, their warning signs, and appropriate response measures is essential. Public awareness campaigns, community drills, and educational programs contribute to better preparedness and response.

Coastal Engineering: Implementing coastal engineering measures, such as seawalls, breakwaters, and elevated structures, can help mitigate the impact of tsunamis. These structures are designed to dissipate wave energy and protect coastal communities and infrastructure.

International Cooperation: Collaborating with neighbouring countries and international organizations in sharing data, expertise, and resources strengthens regional tsunami preparedness and response capabilities. This includes coordination on monitoring systems, early warning dissemination, and capacity building.

Managing the impacts of tsunamis requires a comprehensive approach that includes early warning systems, land-use planning, public awareness, coastal engineering, and international cooperation. By implementing effective mitigation measures and fostering a culture of preparedness, the impacts of tsunamis can be minimized, and the safety and resilience of coastal communities can be enhanced.

Magnitude and Duration of Tsunami:

Magnitude: The magnitude of a tsunami is not directly measured like earthquakes. Instead, it is often associated with the magnitude of the earthquake or underwater event that triggered the tsunami. Magnitude values for earthquakes are measured using the Richter scale or moment magnitude scale. The larger the magnitude of the triggering event, the more significant the potential tsunami.

Duration: The duration of a tsunami event can vary depending on factors such as the size and energy of the triggering event, the distance the tsunami travels, and the coastal geography. Tsunamis can last from a few minutes to several hours, including multiple waves or surges.

Factors Affecting Severity of Tsunami:

Magnitude of the Underwater Event: The magnitude and energy released by the underwater event, such as an earthquake or submarine landslide, directly influence the severity of the resulting tsunami. Larger magnitudes and more significant displacements of water can generate more powerful and destructive tsunamis.

Distance from the Epicenter: The distance between the epicenter of the underwater event and the affected coastline plays a role in the severity of the tsunami. The closer the coastal area is to the epicenter, the less time there is for warning and preparation, potentially increasing the impact.

Coastal Topography: The shape and slope of the coastline can affect the severity of the tsunami. Narrow bays or inlets can amplify the height and power of the waves, causing more significant damage to coastal areas.

Tsunami – Management Strategies:

Tsunami Warning Systems: Implementing a robust tsunami warning system is crucial for early detection and rapid dissemination of alerts to potentially affected areas. In India, the Indian National Centre for Ocean Information Services (INCOIS) operates the Indian Tsunami Early Warning System (ITEWS), which includes a network of tide gauges, seismometers, and deep-sea buoys for detecting and monitoring tsunamigenic events.

Evacuation Plans and Preparedness: Developing evacuation plans and preparedness measures is essential for coastal communities at risk of tsunamis. This includes identifying safe zones, establishing evacuation routes, conducting drills, and raising public awareness about the signs of a tsunami and appropriate response actions.

Land-use Planning and Zoning: Mapping and zoning coastal areas based on tsunami hazards help guide land-use planning decisions and ensure that critical infrastructure and settlements are located in safer areas. This involves identifying high-risk zones and implementing regulations to restrict development in those areas.

Major Tsunami Prone Regions in India:

East Coast: The eastern coast of India, including the states of Andhra Pradesh, Odisha, Tamil Nadu, and Puducherry, is prone to tsunamis. The Bay of Bengal is susceptible to underwater seismic activity and potential tsunamis.

Andaman and Nicobar Islands: The Andaman and Nicobar Islands, situated in the Bay of Bengal, are vulnerable to tsunamis due to their location near the active tectonic boundary between the Indian and Burma plates.

Tsunami Management and Preparedness in India:

National Disaster Management Authority (NDMA): The NDMA, in coordination with the coastal states, plays a crucial role in formulating policies, guidelines, and coordination mechanisms for disaster management, including tsunamis. It provides overall guidance and support in developing preparedness and response plans.

Public Awareness and Education: Raising public awareness about tsunamis and disseminating information on preparedness and response measures is essential. The NDMA, along with state-level disaster management authorities, conducts awareness campaigns, educational programs, and community drills to enhance public understanding and readiness.

Capacity Building: Building the capacity of coastal communities, government agencies, and first responders is crucial. This involves providing training on early warning systems, evacuation procedures, search and rescue techniques, and post-tsunami recovery and rehabilitation.

International Cooperation: India collaborates with regional and international organizations to enhance its tsunami preparedness and response capabilities. This includes sharing data, expertise, and resources, as well as participating in joint exercises, workshops, and knowledge exchange programs.

By implementing effective management strategies, raising public awareness, and enhancing preparedness and response capabilities, India aims to minimize the impacts of tsunamis and protect coastal communities. Collaboration with international partners and continuous efforts to strengthen the tsunami warning system contribute to a more resilient coastal region.

2.9 Natural Disasters – Landslides

Landslides: Landslides occur when a mass of soil, rocks, or debris moves downhill due to factors like heavy rainfall, earthquakes, or human activities. Landslides can damage buildings, infrastructure, and transportation routes, posing risks to human lives and hindering access to affected areas.

Causes of Landslides:

Landslides are geological events in which a mass of soil, rock, or debris moves down a slope. The primary causes of landslides include:

Slope Stability: The stability of a slope can be affected by various factors, including the angle of the slope, the type and characteristics of the soil or rock, and the presence of water. Excessive slope steepness, weak soil or rock layers, and increased water content can all contribute to slope instability and trigger landslides.

Earthquakes: Seismic activity can induce landslides by shaking the ground and destabilizing slopes. The strong ground motions generated during an earthquake can cause the failure of already unstable slopes or trigger new landslides.

Rainfall and Water Saturation: Heavy or prolonged rainfall can saturate the soil, reducing its strength and increasing pore water pressure. This weakened state can lead to landslides, especially in areas with steep slopes or when the soil is already at its capacity to hold water.

Geological and Geological Activities: Geological processes such as erosion, weathering, and changes in groundwater levels can contribute to slope instability. Human activities such as excavation, mining, and construction can also disturb slopes and increase the likelihood of landslides.

Characteristics of Landslides:

Types of Landslides: Landslides can occur in various forms depending on the movement and materials involved. Common types include:

Rockfalls: Sudden falling or rolling of individual rocks or boulders down a slope.

Slides: Downslope movement of a mass of soil or rock along a well-defined surface.

Flows: Rapid movement of saturated or semi-fluid material down a slope, such as debris flows or mudflows.

Slumps: Rotation and downward movement of a mass of soil or rock along a curved failure surface.

Creep: Slow, gradual movement of soil or rock over time.

Velocity and Impact: The velocity of a landslide can vary widely, ranging from slow creeping movements to rapid, destructive slides. The impact of landslides can be devastating, resulting in loss of life, damage to infrastructure, disruption of transportation routes, and environmental degradation.

Landslides – Impact and Challenges:

Loss of Life and Infrastructure: Landslides can cause significant loss of life and injuries, particularly when they occur in populated areas or affect transportation routes. They can damage or destroy buildings, roads, bridges, and other infrastructure, leading to economic losses and hindering access to essential services.

Environmental Consequences: Landslides can disrupt ecosystems, damage vegetation, and alter watercourses. They can lead to the deposition of debris in rivers, resulting in blockages and potential flooding. The displacement of soil and rock can also have long-term impacts on soil fertility and stability.

Rapid Onset and Lack of Warning: Landslides can occur suddenly and without much warning, making it challenging to evacuate people or take preventive measures. The rapid onset and lack of early warning systems pose significant challenges for disaster preparedness and response.

Landslides – Mitigation and Preparedness:

Hazard Mapping and Risk Assessment: Identifying landslide-prone areas through hazard mapping and risk assessment helps in land-use planning and zoning. This information guides the development of regulations and building codes that restrict construction in high-risk areas and promote safer practices.

Early Warning Systems: Developing and implementing early warning systems specific to landslides can provide advance notice to communities at risk. These systems utilize monitoring techniques such as ground deformation measurements, rainfall monitoring, and seismic sensors to detect potential landslide activity and issue timely warnings.

Stabilization Measures: Implementing engineering solutions to stabilize slopes and mitigate landslide risks is crucial. Techniques such as slope grading, terracing, retaining walls, and drainage systems help improve slope stability and reduce the likelihood of landslides.

Education and Awareness: Educating communities about landslide risks, early warning signs, and appropriate response actions is vital. Public awareness campaigns, community training, and dissemination of information through various channels enhance preparedness and empower individuals to take preventive measures.

Land-use Planning and Building Codes: Incorporating landslide considerations into land-use planning and building codes ensures that infrastructure and settlements are designed and located in safer areas. This includes considering slope stability, drainage systems, and appropriate building materials and techniques.

Emergency Response and Recovery: Developing emergency response plans specific to landslides is essential. These plans should include protocols for search and rescue operations, evacuation procedures, medical assistance, and coordination among relevant agencies. Post-landslide recovery efforts focus on restoring infrastructure, assisting affected communities, and implementing measures to mitigate future risks.

Landslide management requires a multi-faceted approach that involves understanding the causes and characteristics of landslides, implementing mitigation measures, raising public awareness, and developing early warning systems. By integrating these strategies into land-use planning, engineering practices, and disaster management efforts, the impacts of landslides can be minimized, and the safety and resilience of communities can be enhanced.

Magnitude and Duration of Landslides:

Magnitude: Landslides are not typically measured in terms of magnitude like earthquakes. The size and magnitude of a landslide are usually described based on the volume of material involved and the extent of the affected area. Larger landslides can have a more significant impact on the environment and infrastructure.

Duration: The duration of a landslide event can vary widely. Some landslides occur suddenly and last only for a few seconds or minutes, while others may develop gradually over days or even months. The speed at which a landslide progresses depends on factors such as the type of movement, slope angle, and geological conditions.

Factors Affecting Severity of Landslides:

Slope Angle and Stability: Steeper slopes are generally more prone to landslides as they are more susceptible to gravitational forces. The stability of a slope is influenced by factors such as soil or rock strength, geological structure, and the presence of water. Weaker or saturated materials are more likely to fail and trigger landslides.

Geological and Soil Conditions: The type of soil or rock and its properties play a crucial role in landslide occurrence and severity. For example, loose, unconsolidated soils like clay and silt are more prone to landslides than cohesive soils like clay or hard rock formations. Geological features like weak bedding planes or fractures can also contribute to instability.

Water Content and Saturation: Water plays a significant role in landslide occurrence. Excessive rainfall, melting snow, or high groundwater levels can increase the pore pressure within soils or rocks, reducing their strength and triggering landslides. Saturation of slopes due to prolonged precipitation is a common cause of landslides in hilly regions.

Human Activities: Human-induced factors, such as deforestation, improper land-use practices, excavation, and construction activities, can destabilize slopes and increase the likelihood of landslides. Altering the natural drainage patterns, removing vegetation cover, and modifying slopes can significantly affect slope stability.

Landsides – Management Strategies:

Hazard Mapping and Risk Assessment: Identifying landslide-prone areas through geological and geomorphological studies, remote sensing, and field surveys helps in land-use planning and zoning. This information is crucial for implementing regulations and building codes that minimize exposure to landslide hazards.

Early Warning Systems: Developing and implementing early warning systems specific to landslides can provide advance notice to communities at risk. These systems use monitoring techniques such as inclinometers, ground-based radar, and rainfall gauges to detect ground movements or changes in slope conditions and issue timely warnings.

Slope Stabilization and Engineering Measures: Implementing engineering solutions to stabilize slopes and mitigate landslide risks is essential. Techniques include slope grading, terracing, retaining walls, erosion control measures, drainage systems, and slope reinforcement using geotextiles or soil nails.

Land-use Planning and Regulations: Incorporating landslide considerations into land-use planning and regulations helps ensure that infrastructure and settlements are designed and located in safer areas. This involves considering slope stability, avoiding high-risk zones, and implementing appropriate building codes and regulations.

Major Landslides Prone Regions in India:

Himalayan Region: The Himalayan region, including states such as Jammu and Kashmir, Himachal Pradesh, Uttarakhand, Sikkim, and Arunachal Pradesh, is highly susceptible to landslides due to its complex geology, steep slopes, and high rainfall. The hilly terrain and fragile geological formations make these areas prone to landslides.

Western Ghats: The Western Ghats, stretching along the western coast of India through states like Maharashtra, Karnataka, Kerala, and Tamil Nadu, experience significant rainfall and have hilly terrain, making them prone to landslides. The combination of intense rainfall and steep slopes contributes to landslide hazards in this region.

Landslides Management and Preparedness in India:

Geological Surveys and Research Institutions: Organizations such as the Geological Survey of India (GSI) and research institutions play a crucial role in conducting geological and geotechnical studies, hazard assessments, and providing technical expertise in landslide management.

Disaster Management Authorities: The National Disaster Management Authority (NDMA) and state-level disaster management authorities in India work towards formulating policies, guidelines, and coordination mechanisms for disaster management, including landslides. They focus on preparedness, response, and recovery efforts.

Public Awareness and Education: Educating communities about landslide risks, early warning signs, and appropriate response measures is essential. Public awareness campaigns, community training programs, and dissemination of information through various media channels enhance preparedness and empower individuals to take preventive measures.

Capacity Building: Building the capacity of local communities, government agencies, and first responders is crucial. This involves providing training on landslide monitoring and early warning systems, evacuation procedures, search and rescue techniques, and post-landslide recovery and rehabilitation.

Sustainable Land Management: Promoting sustainable land-use practices, afforestation, and soil conservation measures helps minimize the vulnerability of slopes to landslides. Encouraging responsible construction practices, adherence to building codes, and proper drainage systems also contribute to reducing landslide risks.

By integrating scientific knowledge, implementing mitigation measures, raising public awareness, and developing early warning systems, the impacts of landslides can be reduced. Continuous monitoring, research, and collaboration among government agencies, scientific institutions, and communities are essential for effective landslide management and enhancing the resilience of landslide-prone regions.

2.10 Natural Disasters – Coastal Erosions

Coastal Erosion: Coastal erosion refers to the gradual wearing a way of coastal land and beaches due to the action of waves, tides, and currents. It can lead to the loss of coastal habitats, infrastructure, and displacement of communities living in coastal areas.

Causes of Coastal Erosions:

Coastal erosion refers to the gradual or rapid removal of land or sediment from the coastline. It occurs due to a combination of natural processes and human activities. The primary causes of coastal erosion include:

Wave Action: Waves are a significant driver of coastal erosion. The energy carried by waves, especially during storms, can directly impact the shoreline, eroding and removing sediment from the coast.

Currents and Tides: Ocean currents and tides also contribute to coastal erosion. Longshore currents, which run parallel to the shoreline, can transport sediment away from the coast, causing erosion. Tidal movements can introduce additional energy that erodes the coastline.

Sea Level Rise: Rising sea levels due to climate change are a significant factor in coastal erosion. As sea levels rise, the shoreline recedes, leading to increased erosion along vulnerable coastlines.

Storms and Extreme Weather Events: Intense storms, hurricanes, and cyclones can generate powerful waves and storm surges that erode coastal areas. These events can cause significant erosion in a short period, leading to rapid land loss.

Human Activities: Human interventions, such as construction of coastal structures, dredging, sand mining, and alteration of natural coastal processes, can accelerate coastal erosion. These activities disrupt sediment transport, alter wave patterns, and remove natural protective barriers, exacerbating erosion.

Characteristics of Costal erosion:

Shoreline Retreat: Coastal erosion often results in the retreat of the shoreline landward. As sediment is eroded and carried away, the coastline recedes, reducing the width of beaches, cliffs, or dunes.

Loss of Coastal Features: Erosion can lead to the loss of natural coastal features such as sand dunes, cliffs, and vegetation. These features act as protective buffers, absorbing wave energy and preventing erosion. Their loss leaves the coastline more vulnerable.

Sediment Transport: Erosion involves the removal and transport of sediment along the coast. Sediment can be carried away and deposited elsewhere, impacting neighbouring areas or changing the dynamics of coastal ecosystems.

Types of Erosions:

Beach Erosion: Beaches are susceptible to erosion as waves remove sand and sediment from the shoreline. Beach erosion often leads to the loss of recreational areas, impacts tourism, and reduces natural coastal defences.

Cliff Erosion: Erosion of cliffs occurs when waves and weathering processes undermine and erode the base of coastal cliffs. This can result in landslides, rockfalls, and the collapse of cliff faces.

Dune Erosion: Sand dunes, which provide protection from coastal erosion and storm surges, can erode when wave action or human activities disturb the dune system. Dune erosion leads to the loss of natural barriers and increased vulnerability of coastal areas.

Erosion – Impact and Challenges:

Loss of Land and Property: Coastal erosion can result in the loss of valuable land and property near the coast. This includes residential and commercial areas, infrastructure, and critical facilities such as hospitals and schools.

Coastal Flooding and Increased Vulnerability: Erosion reduces the natural protection offered by coastal features, leaving communities more exposed to flooding and storm surges. This increased vulnerability can lead to property damage, displacement of communities, and loss of livelihoods.

Habitat Loss and Environmental Impacts: Coastal erosion can lead to the loss of vital habitats, including coastal wetlands, dunes, and mangroves. These ecosystems provide essential services, such as coastal protection, wildlife habitat, and water filtration. Their loss can disrupt ecological balance and impact biodiversity.

Erosion – Mitigation and Preparedness:

Shoreline Stabilization: Implementing shoreline stabilization measures can help mitigate erosion. This includes constructing seawalls, breakwaters, groins, and revetments to absorb wave energy and reduce erosion. However, these measures should be carefully designed to minimize negative impacts on neighbouring areas.

Beach Nourishment: Beach nourishment involves replenishing eroded beaches with sediment. This can be done through the placement of sand or sediment dredged from offshore or nearby sources. Beach nourishment helps maintain recreational areas and provides a buffer against erosion.

Dune Restoration: Restoring or creating sand dunes helps protect the coast from erosion and storm impacts. Planting dune vegetation helps stabilize the sand and encourages the natural accretion of sand, providing a barrier against wave action.

Land-use Planning and Zoning: Effective land-use planning and zoning regulations play a crucial role in managing coastal erosion. Identifying vulnerable areas, implementing setback regulations, and restricting development in high-risk zones can help reduce exposure to erosion hazards.

Coastal Monitoring and Early Warning Systems: Monitoring coastal erosion through geophysical surveys, remote sensing, and regular assessments helps identify erosion hotspots and monitor changes over time. Early warning systems can provide alerts for impending erosion events and support timely evacuation or response actions.

Public Awareness and Education: Educating coastal communities about erosion risks, appropriate land-use practices, and response measures is essential. Public awareness campaigns, community engagement, and educational programs enhance preparedness, promote sustainable practices, and encourage community involvement in erosion management.

Coastal erosion management requires a multi-faceted approach that considers natural processes, human interventions, and long-term planning. By implementing appropriate mitigation measures, raising public awareness, and incorporating erosion considerations into coastal development, the impacts of coastal erosion can be minimized, and the resilience of coastal communities can be enhanced.

Erosion Magnitude and Duration:

Magnitude: Coastal erosion is not typically measured in terms of magnitude like earthquakes. The severity of erosion is often described based on the rate of shoreline retreat, the volume of sediment loss, and the impact on coastal features and infrastructure.

Duration: Coastal erosion can occur over both short and long timeframes. Some erosion events may happen rapidly during storms or extreme weather events, resulting in significant damage within a short period. Long-term erosion can occur gradually over years or even decades, causing a gradual retreat of the shoreline.

Factors Affecting Severity of Erosion:

Wave Energy: The energy carried by waves is a significant factor affecting the severity of coastal erosion. More energetic waves, especially during storms, have a higher capacity to erode the coastline and remove sediment.

Sediment Supply: The availability of sediment along the coast plays a crucial role in coastal erosion. A decrease in sediment supply, such as due to dam construction or sediment trapping by human activities, can lead to erosion as the natural replenishment of sediment is hindered.

Sea Level Rise: Rising sea levels exacerbate coastal erosion by causing the shoreline to recede. As sea levels rise, the erosive forces of waves and tidal currents reach higher up the coast, leading to increased erosion and land loss.

Coastal Geology: The geological characteristics of the coast, including the type of rock or sediment, can influence erosion severity. Soft or unconsolidated sediments are more susceptible to erosion than harder rock formations.

Erosion Management Strategies:

Shoreline Protection: Implementing measures to protect the shoreline is crucial in managing coastal erosion. Strategies include constructing seawalls, revetments, breakwaters, and groynes to absorb wave energy, reduce erosion, and protect vulnerable areas. However, these measures should consider potential impacts on neighbouring areas and long-term coastal processes.

Beach Nourishment: Beach nourishment involves adding sediment to eroded beaches to restore their width and volume. Sand or sediment can be dredged from offshore or nearby sources and placed on eroded beaches to replenish the sand supply, maintain recreational areas, and provide a natural buffer against erosion.

Dune Restoration: Restoring or creating sand dunes helps stabilize the coastline and reduce erosion. Planting dune vegetation helps bind the sand, promote natural accretion, and provide a protective barrier against wave action.

Managed Retreat: In areas experiencing severe and ongoing erosion, managed retreat may be a viable option. This involves relocating structures and infrastructure away from the eroding coastline, allowing natural coastal processes to occur without the need for extensive shoreline protection.

Major Erosion Prone Regions in India:

Coastal States: Several coastal states in India are prone to coastal erosion. These include states such as Kerala, Tamil Nadu, Andhra Pradesh, Odisha, West Bengal, Maharashtra, and Gujarat.

Vulnerability varies across regions due to differences in coastal geomorphology, sediment supply, and wave climate.

Erosion – Management and Preparedness in India:

Coastal Regulation Zone (CRZ): The Coastal Regulation Zone (CRZ) notification by the Ministry of Environment, Forest and Climate Change in India regulates activities in coastal areas to protect sensitive ecosystems and manage coastal erosion. It delineates different zones based on vulnerability and restricts certain activities in high-risk areas.

Coastal Monitoring and Research: Monitoring coastal erosion through surveys, remote sensing, and geophysical techniques helps identify vulnerable areas, assess erosion rates, and track changes over time. Research institutions and organizations like the National Centre for Coastal Research (NCCR) contribute to scientific understanding and provide valuable data for management and planning.

Integrated Coastal Zone Management (ICZM): Integrated Coastal Zone Management plans aim to balance development activities with conservation and sustainable coastal management. These plans consider erosion hazards, ecological sensitivity, and social and economic aspects to guide coastal development in a sustainable and resilient manner.

Public Awareness and Education: Raising public awareness about coastal erosion risks, sustainable land-use practices, and appropriate response measures is crucial. Public awareness campaigns, community engagement programs, and educational initiatives enhance preparedness and promote community involvement in coastal erosion management.

Early Warning Systems: Implementing early warning systems specific to coastal erosion can provide timely alerts to communities at risk. These systems rely on monitoring coastal processes, erosion rates, and sediment transport to issue warnings and support preventive actions.

Managing and mitigating coastal erosion in India requires a combination of strategic planning, effective regulations, and sustainable coastal management practices. By implementing appropriate management strategies, raising public awareness, and integrating erosion considerations into coastal development, the impacts of coastal erosion can be minimized, and the resilience of coastal communities can be enhanced.

2.11 Natural Disasters – Soil Erosions

Soil Erosion: Soil erosion is the process of the removal and displacement of topsoil due to factors like wind, water, and human activities. Soil erosion affects agricultural productivity, leads to loss of fertile land, and contributes to environmental degradation.

Causes of Soil Erosion:

Soil erosion refers to the process of detachment, transport, and deposition of soil particles by wind, water, or human activities. It occurs due to a combination of natural factors and human practices. The primary causes of soil erosion include:

Water Erosion: Rainfall and surface runoff are major contributors to water erosion. The impact of raindrops, along with the force of flowing water, dislodges soil particles and carries them away. The intensity and duration of rainfall, slope gradient, and land cover affect the severity of water erosion.

Wind Erosion: Wind erosion occurs in areas with dry and loose soils that are susceptible to wind transport. Strong winds can lift and transport fine soil particles, causing soil erosion. Factors such as soil texture, wind speed, and land cover influence the extent of wind erosion.

Slope and Topography: Steep slopes increase the vulnerability to soil erosion as water or wind has more force to dislodge and transport soil particles. The length, shape, and orientation of slopes can also affect the direction and magnitude of erosion.

Vegetation and Land Cover: Vegetation plays a crucial role in reducing soil erosion. Plant roots bind soil particles, and the canopy intercepts rainfall, reducing its erosive impact. Deforestation, improper land management, and removal of vegetation cover increase the risk of soil erosion.

Human Activities: Unsustainable agricultural practices, improper land-use management, overgrazing, mining, and construction activities contribute to soil erosion. Removing natural vegetation, improper irrigation techniques, and inadequate soil conservation measures intensify erosion risks.

Characteristics of Soil Erosion:

Soil Loss: Soil erosion leads to the loss of topsoil, which is the most fertile layer of soil that supports plant growth. The erosion process removes the nutrient-rich topsoil, leaving behind less fertile and compacted soil.

Sedimentation: Eroded soil particles are transported by water or wind and eventually deposited elsewhere, leading to sedimentation in water bodies, rivers, lakes, and reservoirs. Excessive sedimentation affects water quality, disrupts aquatic ecosystems, and reduces water storage capacity.

Gully Erosion: In areas with concentrated water flow, gullies may form, which are deep channels eroded into the soil. Gully erosion intensifies the erosion process and results in severe soil loss and landscape degradation.

Sheet Erosion: Sheet erosion occurs when a thin layer of soil is removed uniformly from the surface, resembling a sheet. It is often caused by raindrop impact and runoff, resulting in the loss of valuable topsoil.

Soil Erosion – Impact and Challenges:

Reduced Agricultural Productivity: Soil erosion affects agricultural lands by depleting the nutrient-rich topsoil necessary for crop growth. It reduces soil fertility, limits water-holding capacity, and hampers crop productivity, leading to food security concerns.

Environmental Degradation: Soil erosion can result in the degradation of ecosystems. It contributes to loss of biodiversity, changes in soil structure and composition, and the release of sediment and pollutants into water bodies, affecting aquatic habitats and water quality.

Increased Flooding and Sedimentation: Eroded soil particles can accumulate in water bodies, obstructing water flow and increasing the risk of flooding. Sedimentation reduces water storage capacity in reservoirs, impairs irrigation systems, and damages infrastructure.

Soil Degradation and Desertification: Continuous soil erosion leads to soil degradation, making the land less productive and more susceptible to desertification. Desertification is the process by which fertile land becomes increasingly arid and unable to support vegetation or agriculture.

Soil Erosion – Mitigation and Preparedness:

Soil Conservation Practices: Implementing soil conservation measures is vital in mitigating soil erosion. These include contour plowing, terracing, strip cropping, agroforestry, cover cropping, and conservation tillage techniques. Such practices help slow down water flow, enhance infiltration, and reduce erosion rates.

Reforestation and Afforestation: Planting trees and vegetation in eroded areas helps stabilize the soil, reduce wind speed, and prevent water erosion. Reforestation of degraded lands and afforestation in vulnerable areas contribute to soil conservation efforts.

Soil and Water Management: Proper irrigation techniques, such as drip irrigation or controlled flooding, prevent excessive water runoff and soil erosion. Managing water flow, implementing appropriate drainage systems, and preserving wetlands also help mitigate erosion.

Sediment Control Measures: Constructing sediment basins, retention ponds, check dams, and vegetative buffer strips can trap and control sediment runoff, reducing downstream erosion and sedimentation.

Land-use Planning and Regulations: Implementing land-use planning measures that consider soil erosion risks helps ensure appropriate land management practices. Enforcing regulations to prevent deforestation, unsustainable agricultural practices, and improper land development minimizes erosion hazards.

Education and Training: Educating farmers, landowners, and communities about soil conservation practices, sustainable land management, and erosion prevention techniques is crucial. Training programs and extension services help promote adoption of best practices and increase awareness.

Soil Erosion Monitoring: Regular monitoring of erosion rates, soil quality, and land cover changes helps identify erosion-prone areas and assess the effectiveness of mitigation measures. Remote sensing, geographic information systems (GIS), and field surveys are used for erosion monitoring.

In India, initiatives such as the National Mission for Sustainable Agriculture and programs under the National Soil Conservation Project focus on soil erosion management. Promoting sustainable agricultural practices, raising awareness, and integrating soil conservation measures into land-use planning contribute to reducing soil erosion risks and enhancing the resilience of agricultural systems and ecosystems.

Soil Erosion – Magnitude and Duration:

Magnitude: Soil erosion is typically measured in terms of the amount of soil lost per unit area over a specific period. Magnitude can be described as the volume or thickness of the eroded soil layer. It is usually measured in tons per hectare or millimeters of soil depth lost.

Duration: Soil erosion can occur over both short-term and long-term durations. Short-term erosion events may happen during heavy rainfall or high-intensity wind events, resulting in immediate soil loss. Long-term erosion occurs gradually over years or decades due to continuous erosive forces.

Factors Affecting Severity of Soil Erosion:

Rainfall Intensity and Distribution: The intensity and duration of rainfall influence soil erosion rates. Heavy rainfall events with high-intensity downpours and inadequate vegetation cover can lead to more runoff and soil detachment, causing severe erosion.

Slope Gradient and Length: Steep slopes are more prone to erosion as gravity assists the movement of water and soil particles. Longer slopes allow more time for runoff to accumulate and carry soil particles downslope, increasing erosion severity.

Soil Properties: Soil characteristics, such as texture, structure, organic matter content, and permeability, affect erosion severity. Soils with fine particles (e.g., clay) are more prone to detachment and transport. Soils with poor structure or low organic matter content are less resistant to erosion.

Land Cover and Vegetation: Vegetation cover plays a vital role in mitigating soil erosion. Dense vegetation, including grasses, shrubs, and trees, protects the soil surface, reduces the impact of raindrops, enhances infiltration, and binds soil particles together, reducing erosion severity.

Land Management Practices: Unsustainable land management practices, such as excessive tilling, improper crop rotation, overgrazing, and improper irrigation techniques, can contribute to erosion. Inadequate conservation practices and improper soil and water management increase erosion risks.

Soil Erosion Management Strategies:

Conservation Tillage: Implementing conservation tillage practices, such as minimum tillage or no-till farming, helps reduce soil disturbance and erosion. These techniques leave crop residues on the field, protecting the soil from erosive forces and enhancing water infiltration.

Terracing and Contouring: Constructing terraces and contour plowing helps reduce slope gradient, control runoff, and enhance water infiltration. These practices help slow down water flow, minimize erosion, and conserve soil moisture.

Agroforestry and Windbreaks: Planting trees, shrubs, and grasses in agricultural fields can provide windbreaks, reduce wind speed, and protect the soil from wind erosion. Agroforestry systems with a combination of crops and trees improve soil stability and contribute to erosion control.

Cover Crops and Crop Rotation: Planting cover crops, such as legumes or grasses, during fallow periods helps protect the soil surface, reduce erosion, and enhance nutrient retention. Crop rotation practices diversify plant species, improve soil health, and reduce erosion risks.

Watershed Management: Implementing watershed management approaches focuses on the holistic management of water resources and land use. It involves coordinated efforts to address erosion at the watershed level, including soil conservation, afforestation, and integrated water management practices.

Soil Erosion – Major Prone Regions in India:

Western Himalayas: The hilly regions of Uttarakhand, Himachal Pradesh, and Jammu and Kashmir are prone to soil erosion due to steep slopes, high rainfall, and intensive agricultural practices.

North-Eastern States: States like Meghalaya, Mizoram, and Nagaland experience significant soil erosion due to heavy rainfall, deforestation, and shifting cultivation practices.

Central Indian Plateau: Parts of Madhya Pradesh, Chhattisgarh, and Maharashtra are prone to soil erosion due to undulating topography, intensive agriculture, and unsustainable land management practices.

Soil Erosion Management and Preparedness in India:

National Soil Conservation Program (NSCP): The Government of India initiated the NSCP to promote soil and water conservation practices, including terracing, contour bunding, and watershed management. The program aims to reduce soil erosion, improve soil health, and enhance sustainable agricultural practices.

Land Use Planning and Regulations: Integrating soil erosion considerations into land use planning and zoning regulations helps ensure sustainable land management practices. This includes promoting conservation practices, limiting deforestation, and encouraging proper land management techniques.

Capacity Building and Training: Providing training and capacity-building programs for farmers, landowners, and local communities is essential to promote awareness about soil erosion, its causes, and effective conservation measures. These programs facilitate the adoption of sustainable land management practices.

Soil Health Cards: The Soil Health Card scheme in India aims to assess soil fertility and provide farmers with recommendations for appropriate nutrient management practices. By improving soil health, the scheme indirectly contributes to erosion control and sustainable land management.

Research and Development: Ongoing research and development efforts focus on soil conservation techniques, erosion modelling, and innovative approaches to address soil erosion challenges. Collaborations between research institutions, agricultural universities, and government agencies contribute to knowledge sharing and effective erosion management.

Managing soil erosion requires a combination of sustainable land management practices, conservation techniques, and awareness-building efforts. By implementing appropriate erosion control measures, promoting sustainable agriculture, and integrating soil erosion considerations into land use planning, the impacts of soil erosion can be minimized, soil health can be improved, and agricultural productivity can be sustained.

2.12 Natural Disasters – Forest Fires

Forest Fires: Forest fires are uncontrolled fires that spread rapidly through forests, grasslands, and other vegetated areas. They can be caused by natural factors like lightning strikes or human activities. Forest fires pose risks to biodiversity, ecosystems, and human settlements near forested areas.

Causes of Forest Fires:

Forest fires, also known as wildfires or bushfires, are typically caused by a combination of natural factors and human activities. The primary causes of forest fires include:

Natural Causes: Lightning strikes are a common natural cause of forest fires. Electrical discharges during thunderstorms can ignite vegetation and start fires. Volcanic eruptions can also lead to forest fires by emitting hot materials that ignite surrounding vegetation.

Human Activities: The majority of forest fires are caused by human activities. These can include:

a. Unattended Campfires: Negligence in managing campfires or leaving them unattended can spark forest fires.

b. Arson: Deliberate setting of fires by individuals with malicious intent can lead to large-scale forest fires.

c. Careless Discarding of Cigarettes: Improper disposal of cigarettes or smoking materials can ignite dry vegetation and start fires.

d. Agricultural Activities: Poorly managed agricultural practices such as slash-and-burn agriculture or burning of crop residues can unintentionally lead to forest fires.

e. Equipment Malfunction: Malfunctioning or improper use of equipment, such as machinery or power tools, can cause sparks that ignite vegetation.

Characteristics Forest Fires:

Rapid Spread: Forest fires can spread quickly, especially under favourable weather conditions such as high temperatures, low humidity, and strong winds. The combination of dry vegetation and wind can enable fires to advance rapidly.

Intensity and Heat: Forest fires generate intense heat due to the combustion of vegetation and flammable materials. The high temperatures can cause the release of toxic gases and create a hostile environment for both wildlife and firefighting personnel.

Fire Behaviour: Forest fires can exhibit different behaviours based on factors such as fuel types, topography, weather conditions, and the presence of natural or man-made barriers. Fire behaviour can range from slow-moving ground fires to fast-spreading crown fires that consume the tops of trees.

Types of Forest Fires:

Ground Fires: Ground fires burn surface fuels, such as leaf litter and organic material, on or near the forest floor. They typically move slowly but can smoulder underground, burning tree roots and organic matter.

Surface Fires: Surface fires occur on the forest floor and burn low-lying vegetation, including grasses, shrubs, and small plants. These fires can spread rapidly and can be more destructive if they reach the tree canopy.

Crown Fires: Crown fires burn through the upper portions of trees, spreading rapidly from treetop to treetop. They can be the most dangerous and destructive type of forest fire, as they consume the entire tree and can generate intense heat and embers.

Forest Fires – Impact and Challenges:

Ecological Impact: Forest fires can have both short-term and long-term ecological impacts. They can destroy vegetation, disrupt ecosystems, and cause habitat loss for wildlife. Some plant and animal species may struggle to recover, affecting biodiversity.

Air Quality and Health: Forest fires emit smoke, particulate matter, and hazardous gases, which can reduce air quality and pose health risks to both humans and animals. Smoke inhalation can lead to respiratory problems and other health issues.

Carbon Emissions and Climate Change: Forest fires release significant amounts of carbon dioxide (CO_2) and other greenhouse gases into the atmosphere. The increased carbon emissions contribute to climate change and further exacerbate the warming of the planet.

Economic Losses: Forest fires can cause substantial economic losses. They can destroy timber resources, agricultural land, infrastructure, and property. The costs associated with firefighting efforts, rehabilitation, and recovery can be significant.

Forest Fires – Mitigation and Preparedness:

Fire Prevention: Implementing fire prevention measures such as public awareness campaigns, education, and regulations on activities that can spark fires. This includes promoting responsible behaviour in fire-prone areas, enforcing fire bans during dry periods, and regulating land-use practices.

Firefighting and Suppression: Developing firefighting capabilities, including well-trained personnel, equipment, and infrastructure, is crucial. Establishing fire stations, firebreaks, and water sources in fire-prone areas aids in rapid response and effective suppression.

Early Warning Systems: Implementing early warning systems that utilize weather forecasting, remote sensing, and fire behaviour modelling can provide advance notice of fire risk and allow for timely evacuation or deployment of firefighting resources.

Fuel Management: Conducting fuel management activities, such as controlled burns, selective tree thinning, and creating fuel breaks, helps reduce the accumulation of flammable vegetation. This can help prevent the rapid spread of wildfires and reduce their intensity.

Community Engagement and Preparedness: Educating communities about fire safety, evacuation plans, and emergency preparedness is essential. Engaging local communities in fire management efforts, establishing community fire response teams, and conducting drills enhances preparedness and response capabilities.

Reforestation and Ecosystem Restoration: After a forest fire, reforestation efforts help restore ecosystems, enhance vegetation cover, and promote ecological recovery. Planting native species and employing appropriate land management practices aid in the long-term restoration of fire-affected areas.

Forest Fires – Major Prone Regions in India:

Western Ghats: The Western Ghats region, spanning states like Kerala, Karnataka, Tamil Nadu, and Maharashtra, is prone to forest fires due to the presence of dry deciduous forests and favourable fire-prone weather conditions.

Himalayan Region: The forests in the Himalayan region, including Uttarakhand, Himachal Pradesh, and Arunachal Pradesh,

Forest Fires – Magnitude and Duration:

Magnitude: Forest fires can vary in magnitude depending on the size of the affected area, intensity of the fire, and the amount of vegetation and biomass involved. The magnitude of a forest fire can be measured by the area burned, the volume of biomass consumed, or the severity of the ecological impact.

Duration: The duration of a forest fire can range from a few hours to several weeks, depending on various factors such as the size of the fire, fuel availability, weather conditions, and firefighting efforts. Large-scale forest fires often require extended periods to fully extinguish and cool down.

Factors Affecting Severity of Forest Fires:

Weather Conditions: Weather plays a crucial role in determining the severity of forest fires. Factors such as temperature, humidity, wind speed, and precipitation influence the rate of fire spread, fire behaviour, and the availability of fuel. Hot, dry, and windy conditions increase the risk of severe wildfires.

Fuel Availability and Condition: The amount and condition of fuel, including vegetation, dead biomass, and forest litter, affect the severity of forest fires. Dry and highly combustible fuel increases the intensity and spread of fires.

Topography: The topography of the region, including slope gradient and aspect, can affect the severity of forest fires. Steep slopes can facilitate the rapid spread of fires, while flat or gentle terrain may slow down the rate of fire spread.

Vegetation Type: Different vegetation types have varying fuel characteristics, including moisture content and flammability. Forests with dense, resinous, or highly flammable vegetation, such as pine forests, are more prone to severe fires.

Human Activities: Human activities, including accidental or intentional ignition, can significantly affect the severity of forest fires. Negligence in fire safety practices, improper land management, and arson contribute to the occurrence and severity of wildfires.

Forest Fires Management Strategies:

Fire Prevention: Fire prevention strategies focus on reducing the risk of forest fires. These include public awareness campaigns, educating communities about fire safety, enforcing fire bans during dry periods, regulating activities that can spark fires, and promoting responsible behaviour in fire-prone areas.

Fire Suppression: Fire suppression involves actively fighting and extinguishing forest fires. Strategies include developing well-equipped firefighting forces, establishing fire stations in strategic locations, utilizing aerial firefighting resources (such as helicopters and airplanes), and coordinating efforts with local communities and other agencies.

Controlled Burning: Controlled or prescribed burning involves intentionally setting fires under controlled conditions. This practice reduces the accumulation of flammable vegetation, removes excess fuel, and promotes ecosystem health. Controlled burning is typically done during favourable weather conditions and under trained supervision.

Forest Management Practices: Implementing Forest management practices that reduce the risk of severe fires is essential. This includes thinning dense vegetation, creating fuel breaks or firebreaks, and promoting forest diversity to decrease fire continuity and intensity.

Early Warning Systems: Developing and utilizing early warning systems that utilize weather monitoring, fire behaviour modelling, and remote sensing technologies helps detect and predict fire risks. Timely information and alerts allow for early response, evacuation planning, and effective allocation of firefighting resources.

Forest Fires – Major Prone Regions in India:

Western Ghats: The Western Ghats region, encompassing states like Kerala, Karnataka, Tamil Nadu, and Maharashtra, is prone to forest fires. These fires are often fuelled by dry deciduous forests, favourable fire-prone weather conditions, and the presence of flammable vegetation.

Himalayan Region: The forests in the Himalayan region, including Uttarakhand, Himachal Pradesh, and Arunachal Pradesh, are susceptible to forest fires. Factors such as the presence of pine forests, dry undergrowth, and rugged terrain contribute to the fire risk.

Forest Fires Management and Preparedness in India:

Forest Fire Management: Forest departments, along with local communities, play a crucial role in managing forest fires. They engage in active fire monitoring, training personnel in firefighting techniques, and maintaining firefighting infrastructure.

National Afforestation Program: The National Afforestation Program in India aims to increase forest cover, restore degraded forests, and promote sustainable forest management. The program includes initiatives to prevent and manage forest fires through community participation and awareness.

Research and Technology: Continuous research and development efforts focus on improving fire detection and monitoring systems, developing fire-resistant tree species, and enhancing fire behaviour modelling. Technology plays a vital role in supporting early warning systems and firefighting strategies.

Community Participation and Awareness: Engaging local communities and raising awareness about fire prevention, responsible land management, and fire safety practices is crucial. Community-based fire management programs empower local residents to actively participate in fire prevention, detection, and suppression.

Mutual Aid Agreements: Mutual aid agreements between forest departments, local communities, and other agencies facilitate coordinated response and resource sharing during large-scale forest fires. These agreements enhance firefighting capabilities and support timely response efforts.

Managing and mitigating forest fires requires a combination of preventive measures, suppression strategies, community involvement, and advanced technologies. By promoting responsible land management, raising awareness, and implementing effective fire management practices, the impacts of forest fires can be minimized, ecosystems can be preserved, and communities

CHAPTER 3

Manmade Disasters in India

3.1 Manmade Disaster – Definition:

3.2 Manmade Disaster – Industrial Pollution

3.3 Manmade Disaster – Artificial Flooding

3.4 Manmade Disaster – Nuclear Radiation

3.5 Manmade Disaster – Chemical Spills

3.6 Manmade Disasters – Transportation Accidents

3.7 Manmade Disaster – Terrorists Strikes

3.1 Manmade Disaster – Definition:

Man-made disasters, also known as anthropogenic disasters, are disasters caused by human activities. Unlike natural disasters that result from natural processes, man-made disasters arise from human actions, negligence, or failures. These disasters can have severe consequences for human life, infrastructure, the environment, and the economy. Here are some key aspects of man-made disasters:

Cause of Man-made Disasters:

Man-made disasters can occur due to a variety of factors, including:

Technological Accidents: These disasters result from failures or accidents in industrial processes, transportation systems, nuclear facilities, or chemical plants. Examples include chemical spills, industrial explosions, nuclear accidents, and oil spills.

Environmental Pollution: Pollution caused by human activities, such as improper waste disposal, air and water pollution, and toxic contamination, can have long-term negative impacts on human health, ecosystems, and natural resources.

Human Conflicts: Disasters can arise from armed conflicts, wars, terrorism, or civil unrest. These events can result in widespread destruction, displacement of populations, loss of lives, and social disruptions.

Infrastructure Failures: Failures in critical infrastructure systems, such as dam collapses, bridge failures, or power grid disruptions, can lead to significant disasters and subsequent impacts.

Figure 3.1 Man Made Disasters (Source: Spectrum, Mumbai)

Characteristics of Man-made Disasters:

Man-made disasters share several characteristics:

Human-Caused: Man-made disasters are directly or indirectly caused by human activities, whether intentional or unintentional.

Predictability: Unlike natural disasters, man-made disasters often have a higher degree of predictability since they are influenced by human behaviour and technological systems. This predictability offers opportunities for prevention and mitigation measures.

Complexity: Man-made disasters are often more complex and challenging to manage due to the involvement of multiple stakeholders, technical aspects, and the potential for long-lasting impacts.

Types of Man-made Disasters:

Man-made disasters can be categorized into various types based on their causes and impacts. Some common types include:

Industrial Disasters: These disasters result from accidents or failures in industrial operations, such as chemical leaks, explosions, or structural collapses.

Environmental Disasters: These disasters occur due to human activities that lead to environmental degradation, such as pollution, deforestation, or degradation of ecosystems.

Transportation Accidents: Disasters in this category include plane crashes, train derailments, maritime accidents, or major road accidents that result in significant loss of life and property.

Terrorism and Conflicts: Man-made disasters can result from acts of terrorism, such as bombings, hijackings, or cyber-attacks, as well as armed conflicts that cause widespread destruction and displacement.

Man-made Disasters – Impact and Challenges:

Man-made disasters have far-reaching consequences:

Loss of Life and Injuries: Man-made disasters can result in significant loss of life, injuries, and long-term health effects for individuals and communities affected by the event.

Environmental Damage: These disasters can cause severe damage to the environment, including pollution of air, water, and soil, destruction of habitats, and loss of biodiversity.

Economic Losses: Man-made disasters can lead to substantial economic losses, including damage to infrastructure, businesses, and disruptions to economic activities.

Social Disruption: These disasters often disrupt communities, causing displacement, loss of livelihoods, and social disintegration.

Man-made Disasters – Mitigation and Preparedness:

To mitigate the impact of man-made disasters and enhance preparedness, various measures can be taken:

Risk Assessment: Conducting risk assessments to identify potential hazards, vulnerabilities, and areas of concern can inform targeted mitigation and preparedness efforts.

Regulations and Safety Measures: Implementing and enforcing regulations, codes, and safety measures to ensure the proper operation of industries, transportation systems, and infrastructure can help prevent or minimize disasters.

Emergency Response Planning: Developing comprehensive emergency response plans, including evacuation procedures, communication systems, and coordination mechanisms, is crucial to effectively respond to man-made disasters.

Public Awareness and Education: Promoting public awareness and education about potential hazards, safety measures, and emergency preparedness can enhance community resilience and response capabilities.

International Cooperation: Collaborating with international organizations, sharing best practices, and promoting knowledge exchange can strengthen preparedness and response to man-made disasters.

Man-made disasters pose unique challenges due to their human-caused nature. By implementing appropriate preventive measures, improving safety standards, and enhancing emergency response capabilities, the impacts of man-made disasters can be reduced, and societies can become more resilient to these events.

Table 3.1 Difference Between Natural Disasters & Man-made Disasters

Parameters	Natural Disasters	Man-Made Disasters
Cause	Result from natural processes	Caused by human activities

Parameters	Natural Disasters	Man-Made Disasters
Examples	Earthquakes, floods, hurricanes, wildfires, volcanic eruptions, etc.	Industrial accidents, oil spills, terrorist attacks, wars, etc.
Occurrence	Naturally and unpredictably	Can be predicted and influenced by human actions
Severity	Severity varies based on the magnitude of the event and environmental conditions	Severity varies based on the magnitude of the event and human factors involved
Predictability	Often challenging to predict, although forecasting and early warning systems are improving	More predictable as they are influenced by human behaviour and technological systems
Impact	Widespread damage to infrastructure, loss of life, displacement of communities, ecological disruption	Environmental damage, loss of life, economic losses, social disruption
Mitigation	Focus on preparedness, response, and recovery measures	Focus on prevention, regulations, safety measures, and emergency response planning
Examples of Mitigation Measures	Earthquakes in fault zones, building codes, earthquake-resistant structures, early warning systems	Industrial accidents like the Bhopal gas tragedy, regulations to prevent pollution, safety protocols in transportation, etc.

3.2 Manmade Disaster – Industrial Pollution

Industrial pollution refers to the contamination and degradation of the environment, including air, water, and soil, as a result of industrial activities.

Causes of Industrial Pollution:

Industrial Pollution arises from various causes, such as:

Emission of Harmful Substances: Industries release pollutants into the air through smokestacks and chimneys. These emissions can include greenhouse gases, particulate matter, sulphur dioxide, nitrogen oxides, volatile organic compounds (VOCs), and heavy metals.

Improper Waste Disposal: Inadequate management of industrial waste, including hazardous substances, chemicals, and by-products, can lead to their improper disposal into water bodies, landfills, or through illegal dumping. This contaminates water sources and soils.

Chemical Spills and Accidents: Industrial accidents, such as chemical spills or leaks, can occur due to equipment failures, human errors, or inadequate safety measures. These incidents can result in the release of toxic substances into the environment.

Characteristics of Industrial Pollution:

Scale and Intensity: Industrial pollution can occur on a large scale and with high intensity, especially in heavily industrialized areas. The concentration of pollutants can be significantly higher in these regions, leading to severe environmental and health impacts.

Persistent and Cumulative Effects: Industrial pollutants can persist in the environment for long periods, leading to cumulative effects over time. They can bioaccumulate in ecosystems and food chains, causing long-term damage to human and ecological health.

Types of Industrial Pollution:

Air Pollution: Industries release various pollutants into the atmosphere, contributing to air pollution. This includes emissions from combustion processes, chemical reactions, and the release of industrial gases and particulate matter.

Water Pollution: Industrial activities discharge untreated or inadequately treated wastewater containing pollutants into water bodies. This contamination affects aquatic ecosystems, drinking water sources, and agricultural water supplies.

Soil and Land Pollution: Improper disposal of industrial waste, including hazardous materials and heavy metals, can contaminate soils and adversely impact land quality and agricultural productivity.

Industrial Pollution – Impact & Challenges:

Environmental Impact: Industrial pollution has detrimental effects on ecosystems, biodiversity, and natural resources. It can lead to the degradation of air quality, contamination of water bodies, destruction of habitats, and soil erosion. It disrupts ecological balance and affects the health of flora and fauna.

Health Impacts: Exposure to industrial pollutants can have severe health consequences for nearby communities. Airborne pollutants contribute to respiratory diseases, cardiovascular problems, and increased cancer risks. Water and soil contamination can lead to waterborne diseases, poisoning, and long-term health issues.

Economic Costs: Industrial pollution poses economic challenges, including the costs associated with environmental cleanup, healthcare expenses for affected populations, and the loss of productivity due to environmental damage.

Industrial Pollution – Mitigation & Preparedness:

Regulatory Measures: Governments need to enforce strict regulations and standards on industrial emissions, waste management, and pollution control measures. This includes setting emission limits, monitoring and reporting requirements, and penalties for non-compliance.

Pollution Prevention: Industries should adopt cleaner production techniques, resource efficiency, and waste reduction measures to minimize pollution at the source. This includes the use of cleaner technologies, recycling, and proper waste management practices.

Treatment and Control Systems: Industries should install effective pollution control systems, such as air scrubbers, wastewater treatment plants, and containment measures, to minimize the release of pollutants into the environment.

Environmental Impact Assessments: Conducting comprehensive environmental impact assessments before establishing or expanding industrial operations can help identify potential pollution risks and develop appropriate mitigation measures.

Public Awareness and Participation: Raising public awareness about the impacts of industrial pollution, encouraging responsible consumption, and promoting public participation in decision-making processes can strengthen environmental protection efforts.

Technological Advancements: Continued research and development of cleaner technologies, alternative energy sources, and sustainable industrial practices can contribute to reducing industrial pollution.

Addressing industrial pollution requires a multi-faceted approach involving effective regulations, technological advancements, and responsible industrial practices. By implementing stringent pollution control measures, promoting sustainable production, and fostering collaboration among industries, governments, and communities, the impacts of industrial pollution can be mitigated, and a cleaner and healthier environment can be achieved.

Industrial Pollution – Magnitude and Duration:

Magnitude: The magnitude of industrial pollution can vary depending on factors such as the size and type of industries, the volume and toxicity of pollutants released, and the proximity to human settlements and sensitive ecosystems. Industries with high emissions or improper waste management practices can contribute significantly to the magnitude of pollution.

Duration: Industrial pollution can persist for long periods, especially if appropriate pollution control measures are not in place. The duration of pollution can be influenced by the continuous operation of industries, the release of persistent pollutants, and the accumulation and dispersion characteristics of pollutants in the environment.

Factors Affecting Severity of Industrial Pollution:

Types and Concentration of Pollutants: The types of pollutants emitted by industries, including toxic gases, particulate matter, heavy metals, and chemicals, influence the severity of industrial pollution. The concentration and persistence of these pollutants in the environment determine their potential impacts on human health and ecosystems.

Proximity to Human Settlements and Sensitive Areas: The proximity of industrial sites to densely populated areas, residential neighbourhoods, and ecologically sensitive regions can affect the severity of pollution. The closer the industries are too vulnerable populations and ecosystems, the higher the potential risks and impacts.

Industrial Practices and Compliance: The extent to which industries adhere to pollution control measures, environmental regulations, and best practices significantly affects the severity of industrial pollution. Compliance with emission standards, proper waste management, and adoption of cleaner production technologies are essential in reducing pollution levels.

Industrial Pollution – Management Strategies:

Regulatory Framework: Implementing and enforcing robust environmental regulations, emission standards, and pollution control norms is crucial in managing industrial pollution. Governments establish legal frameworks that mandate industries to comply with pollution limits, undertake regular monitoring, and adhere to pollution control guidelines.

Pollution Prevention and Control: Adopting pollution prevention strategies and implementing control measures within industrial processes can minimize pollution at the source. This includes cleaner production techniques, efficient use of resources, waste reduction, and implementing technologies to capture and treat pollutants before their release.

Monitoring and Enforcement: Regular monitoring of industrial emissions, effluents, and waste disposal practices is necessary to ensure compliance with pollution control standards. Effective enforcement mechanisms, including inspections, penalties for non-compliance, and incentives for pollution reduction, can help deter pollution and encourage responsible practices.

Industrial Pollution – Major Prone Regions in India:

Industrialized States: States with significant industrial activity, such as Maharashtra, Gujarat, Tamil Nadu, Uttar Pradesh, and Andhra Pradesh, are prone to industrial pollution. These regions have a concentration of industries across sectors like manufacturing, petrochemicals, textiles, and mining.

Urban and Industrial Clusters: Urban areas with dense industrial clusters, such as Delhi-NCR, Kolkata, Mumbai Metropolitan Region, Chennai, and Ahmedabad, are particularly susceptible to industrial pollution due to the presence of numerous industries in close proximity to residential areas.

Industrial Pollution – Management and Preparedness in India:

Environmental Regulations: India has implemented various environmental laws and regulations to address industrial pollution, including the Water (Prevention and Control of Pollution) Act, Air (Prevention and Control of Pollution) Act, and the Hazardous Waste Management Rules. These regulations set emission standards, prescribe pollution control measures, and establish regulatory bodies for monitoring and enforcement.

Pollution Control Boards: State Pollution Control Boards (SPCBs) play a crucial role in managing industrial pollution. They issue licenses, conduct monitoring, and enforce compliance with pollution control norms. SPCBs also work to create awareness, provide technical assistance, and promote pollution prevention measures.

Environmental Impact Assessments: Industrial projects in India undergo environmental impact assessments (EIAs) to evaluate potential environmental and social impacts. EIAs help identify mitigation measures, ensure compliance with pollution control standards, and involve public consultation to address concerns.

Technology Upgradation and Cleaner Production: The government encourages industries to adopt cleaner production technologies, such as improved emission control systems, waste minimization, and energy efficiency measures. Financial incentives and subsidies are provided to industries that invest in pollution control and clean technologies.

Public Awareness and Citizen Initiatives: Increasing public awareness about the impacts of industrial pollution, promoting citizen participation in monitoring and reporting pollution incidents, and encouraging community-led initiatives play a crucial role in managing and addressing industrial pollution.

The management and preparedness for industrial pollution in India involve a combination of regulatory measures, pollution control technologies, monitoring and enforcement mechanisms, public awareness, and community involvement. Continuous efforts are being made to enhance pollution control practices, reduce emissions, and ensure sustainable industrial development while safeguarding human health and the environment.

3.3 Manmade Disaster – Artificial Flooding

Artificial flooding refers to the intentional or unintentional manipulation of water systems that leads to flooding in certain areas.

Causes of Artificial Flooding:

It is typically caused by human activities and can result from various factors, including:

Poor Urban Planning: Improper urban planning, including inadequate drainage systems, encroachments on natural waterways, and excessive urbanization without proper water management, can contribute to artificial flooding.

Dam or Reservoir Releases: Improper management of dams, reservoirs, or other water control structures can result in excessive water releases, overwhelming downstream areas and causing flooding.

Deforestation and Land Use Changes: Deforestation, land clearing, and changes in land use patterns can lead to reduced infiltration, increased surface runoff, and altered hydrological patterns, increasing the risk of artificial flooding.

Infrastructure Development: Construction of infrastructure, such as roads, buildings, and parking lots, can lead to increased impervious surfaces, reducing natural water absorption and exacerbating runoff, which can contribute to artificial flooding.

Characteristics of Artificial Flooding:

Deliberate or Unintended: Artificial flooding can be either intentional, as in controlled releases from dams for water management purposes, or unintended, resulting from poor water management practices or inadequate infrastructure.

Localized or Widespread: Artificial flooding can occur in specific areas or affect larger regions depending on the scale and nature of the activities causing the flooding.

Timing and Duration: Artificial flooding events can occur during specific periods, such as heavy rainfall, dam releases, or periods of intense land development. The duration of the flooding depends on the factors causing it and the effectiveness of mitigation measures.

Types of Artificial Flooding:

Dam Releases: Controlled or uncontrolled releases of water from dams or reservoirs can cause downstream flooding if not properly managed.

Urban Runoff: Poorly designed or inadequate drainage systems in urban areas can result in localized flooding during heavy rainfall events or improper stormwater management.

Channel Alterations: Modifications to natural river channels, such as straightening or narrowing, can disrupt natural flow patterns and increase the risk of flooding downstream.

Artificial Flooding – Impact & Challenges:

Property Damage and Loss: Artificial flooding can cause significant damage to buildings, infrastructure, and personal property, leading to financial losses for individuals, businesses, and communities.

Displacement of People: Flooding can force people to evacuate their homes and communities, leading to temporary or long-term displacement.

Environmental Impacts: Artificial flooding can disrupt ecosystems, destroy habitats, and harm aquatic life due to changes in water levels, sedimentation, and pollution.

Socioeconomic Consequences: The disruption caused by artificial flooding can result in social and economic challenges, including loss of livelihoods, reduced economic activities, and increased social vulnerabilities.

Artificial Flooding – Mitigation & Preparedness:

Improved Urban Planning: Implementing effective urban planning measures, including proper stormwater management, green infrastructure, and preserving natural waterways, can help mitigate the risk of artificial flooding.

Enhanced Drainage Systems: Developing and maintaining adequate drainage systems, including the construction of stormwater detention basins, retention ponds, and flood control channels, can help manage and mitigate the impacts of artificial flooding.

Water Management Practices: Implementing responsible water management practices, including controlled releases from dams and reservoirs, can help regulate water flows and reduce the risk of artificial flooding.

Early Warning Systems: Establishing early warning systems to monitor water levels, rainfall patterns, and potential flood risks can help alert communities and authorities in advance, allowing for timely response and evacuation if necessary.

Community Education and Preparedness: Educating communities about the risks of artificial flooding, promoting flood preparedness measures, and developing community-based response plans can enhance resilience and reduce the impacts of artificial flooding.

Addressing artificial flooding requires a combination of effective water management practices, urban planning strategies, and community involvement. By implementing proper drainage systems, regulating water releases, and raising awareness about flood risks, the impacts of artificial flooding can be mitigated, and communities can be better prepared to cope with such events.

Artificial Flooding – Magnitude and Duration:

Magnitude: The magnitude of artificial flooding can vary depending on factors such as the volume and velocity of water released, the topography of the area, and the capacity of drainage systems. The magnitude can range from localized flooding in specific areas to widespread flooding affecting larger regions.

Duration: The duration of artificial flooding events can vary based on the factors causing the flooding and the effectiveness of mitigation measures. It can range from short-term flooding events triggered by heavy rainfall or dam releases to prolonged flooding in cases of inadequate drainage systems or persistent water releases.

Factors Affecting Severity of Artificial Flooding:

Water Management Practices: The management of water resources, including dam operations, water releases, and reservoir management, significantly affects the severity of artificial flooding. Inadequate planning or mismanagement of water systems can lead to uncontrolled releases and increased flood risks.

Urbanization and Infrastructure Development: Rapid urbanization without proper water management measures, such as inadequate drainage systems or the conversion of natural waterways into concrete channels, can contribute to the severity of artificial flooding. Increased impervious surfaces and the alteration of natural drainage patterns amplify the risk of flooding.

Climate Change: Climate change can influence the severity of artificial flooding by altering rainfall patterns, increasing the frequency and intensity of extreme weather events, and affecting hydrological systems. Changing climate conditions can exacerbate flood risks and contribute to more severe flooding events.

Artificial Flooding – Management Strategies:

Integrated Water Management: Implementing integrated water management practices that consider the entire water cycle, including rainfall, surface water, groundwater, and runoff, can help mitigate the risk of artificial flooding. This includes the proper design and maintenance of drainage systems, retention ponds, and flood control measures.

Infrastructure Development: Constructing and maintaining adequate infrastructure, such as robust drainage systems, flood control channels, and stormwater management facilities, can help manage and mitigate the impacts of artificial flooding. Upgrading and expanding existing infrastructure can enhance flood resilience.

Land Use Planning: Integrating water-sensitive land use planning strategies, such as preserving natural waterways, implementing green infrastructure, and avoiding construction in flood-prone areas, can reduce the risk of artificial flooding and minimize potential damage.

Artificial Flooding – Major Prone Regions in India:

Urban Areas: Rapidly urbanizing regions in India, such as major cities and towns, are prone to artificial flooding due to increased impervious surfaces, inadequate drainage systems, and improper urban planning practices.

Coastal Areas: Low-lying coastal regions, especially those affected by urbanization and land use changes, can be susceptible to artificial flooding, particularly during high tides or storm surges.

Artificial Flooding – Management and Preparedness in India:

Flood Management Authorities: In India, flood management falls under the purview of various agencies at the national, state, and local levels. The Central Water Commission (CWC) and the State Water Resources Departments play significant roles in flood management, including the management of dam releases and reservoir operations.

Flood Forecasting and Warning Systems: The India Meteorological Department (IMD) provides flood forecasting services to predict and issue warnings about potential flooding events. These warnings help in evacuation and emergency response planning.

Drainage Infrastructure Development: The National Urban Sanitation Policy and programs like the Atal Mission for Rejuvenation and Urban Transformation (AMRUT) emphasize the development and improvement of urban drainage infrastructure to address issues related to urban flooding.

Community Engagement and Awareness: Engaging communities and raising awareness about flood risks, preparedness measures, and the importance of responsible water management can help build community resilience and facilitate timely response during artificial flooding events.

Research and Innovation: Ongoing research and innovation in flood modelling, forecasting technologies, and sustainable water management practices can contribute to better flood management strategies and preparedness in India.

Addressing artificial flooding requires a combination of effective water management practices, proper infrastructure development, and community participation. By implementing comprehensive flood management strategies, enhancing infrastructure, improving urban planning, and raising awareness, India can mitigate the impacts of artificial flooding and build resilience in vulnerable regions.

3.4 Manmade Disaster – Nuclear Radiation

Nuclear radiation refers to the release of harmful ionizing radiation from nuclear materials, such as radioactive isotopes, during nuclear accidents, nuclear weapon detonations, or improper handling and disposal of radioactive waste.

Causes of Nuclear Radiation:

The causes of nuclear radiation disasters include:

Nuclear Accidents: Accidents or failures in nuclear power plants, research reactors, or nuclear facilities can result in the release of radioactive materials into the environment. Examples include the Chernobyl disaster in 1986 and the Fukushima Daiichi nuclear disaster in 2011.

Nuclear Weapons: Nuclear weapon detonations release massive amounts of radiation, causing immediate and long-term impacts on the environment and human health.

Improper Waste Management: Inadequate handling, storage, or disposal of radioactive waste materials from nuclear power plants, medical facilities, or research institutions can lead to radiation leaks and contamination.

Characteristics of Nuclear Radiation:

Ionizing Radiation: Nuclear radiation consists of ionizing radiation, which includes alpha particles, beta particles, gamma rays, and neutron radiation. These forms of radiation have high energy and can ionize atoms, causing damage to living organisms and the environment.

Radioactive Decay: Radioactive materials emit radiation during the process of radioactive decay, where unstable atomic nuclei release energy and transform into more stable forms. This decay process can continue for extended periods, leading to long-lasting radiation hazards.

Types of Nuclear Radiation:

Alpha Radiation: Alpha particles consist of two protons and two neutrons and have low penetration power. They can be harmful if ingested or inhaled but can be stopped by a sheet of paper or a few centimeters of air.

Beta Radiation: Beta particles are fast-moving electrons or positrons. They can penetrate deeper into materials than alpha particles and can be shielded by a few millimeters of aluminium or plastic.

Gamma Radiation: Gamma rays are high-energy electromagnetic waves and can penetrate through most materials. They require denser shielding, such as thick concrete or lead, to reduce exposure.

Nuclear Radiation – Impact & Challenges:

Health Effects: Exposure to high levels of nuclear radiation can cause severe health effects, including radiation sickness, acute radiation syndrome, increased cancer risks, genetic mutations, and long-term chronic health problems.

Environmental Contamination: Nuclear radiation can contaminate air, soil, water, and ecosystems. It can lead to long-term ecological disruption, genetic mutations in plants and animals, and bioaccumulation in the food chain.

Societal Disruption: Nuclear radiation disasters can result in the displacement of populations, social and economic disruptions, loss of infrastructure and resources, and psychological and sociocultural impacts on affected communities.

Nuclear Radiation – Mitigation & Preparedness:

Nuclear Safety Measures: Stringent safety regulations, robust design standards, and effective management practices for nuclear facilities are essential to prevent accidents and mitigate the risk of radiation releases.

Emergency Response Plans: Developing comprehensive emergency response plans, including evacuation procedures, radiation monitoring, medical facilities, and communication systems, is crucial to minimize the impact of nuclear radiation disasters.

Radiation Monitoring and Detection: Establishing radiation monitoring networks and early warning systems can aid in the early detection of radiation leaks and the prompt implementation of protective measures.

Public Awareness and Education: Educating the public about the risks associated with nuclear radiation, promoting radiation safety practices, and providing information on emergency preparedness can enhance public understanding and response capabilities.

International Cooperation: Collaboration between countries, sharing of information, and adherence to international agreements and guidelines, such as those by the International Atomic Energy Agency (IAEA), contribute to improved nuclear safety and preparedness.

Addressing the risks of nuclear radiation requires a combination of stringent safety measures, effective emergency response plans, and ongoing research and development of safer nuclear technologies. By emphasizing safety, promoting international cooperation, and ensuring proper handling and disposal of radioactive materials, the risks associated with nuclear radiation disasters can be mitigated, and their impact on human health and the environment can be minimized.

Nuclear Radiation – Magnitude and Duration:

Magnitude: The magnitude of a nuclear radiation disaster depends on factors such as the amount and type of radioactive materials released, the proximity to populated areas, and the effectiveness of containment and mitigation measures. Nuclear radiation disasters can range from localized incidents to large-scale events with significant environmental and human health impacts.

Duration: The duration of a nuclear radiation event depends on several factors, including the type of radioactive materials released, the half-life of those materials (the time it takes for half of the radioactive atoms to decay), and the effectiveness of containment and cleanup efforts. The effects of nuclear radiation can persist for varying periods, ranging from days to years or even longer.

Factors Affecting Severity of Nuclear Radiation:

Type and Quantity of Radioactive Materials: The type of radioactive materials released during a nuclear radiation event, such as cesium-137, iodine-131, or plutonium-239, can affect the severity of the disaster. Some radioactive isotopes have longer half-lives and can pose risks for extended periods.

Proximity to Populated Areas: The proximity of the incident to populated areas determines the potential for human exposure and health risks. The closer the event occurs to densely populated regions, the higher the potential for widespread health impacts and the need for evacuation and protective measures.

Release Mechanism: The method of release, such as a nuclear power plant accident, a nuclear weapon detonation, or improper handling and disposal of radioactive waste, can affect the severity of the nuclear radiation event.

Nuclear Radiation – Management Strategies:

Safety Measures and Regulations: Implementing stringent safety measures and regulations for nuclear facilities, including proper design, operation, and maintenance, is essential to prevent accidents and minimize the risk of radiation releases.

Emergency Preparedness and Response: Developing comprehensive emergency preparedness plans, including early warning systems, evacuation procedures, radiation monitoring, and medical response capabilities, is crucial to mitigate the impact of nuclear radiation disasters.

Containment and Cleanup: Effective containment and cleanup strategies are necessary to minimize the spread of radioactive materials and mitigate their long-term impacts. This includes decontamination of affected areas, proper disposal of radioactive waste, and the use of protective barriers.

International Cooperation and Standards: Collaboration with international organizations, such as the International Atomic Energy Agency (IAEA), and adherence to international safety standards and guidelines contribute to better management and preparedness for nuclear radiation disasters.

Nuclear Radiation – Major Prone Regions in India:

Nuclear Power Plants: India has several nuclear power plants located in different regions, including Tarapur (Maharashtra), Kalpakkam (Tamil Nadu), Rawatbhata (Rajasthan), and Narora (Uttar Pradesh). These regions are prone to potential nuclear radiation incidents due to the presence of nuclear facilities.

Nuclear Radiation – Management and Preparedness in India:

Atomic Energy Regulatory Board (AERB): The AERB is responsible for regulating nuclear and radiation safety in India. It sets safety standards, conducts inspections, and ensures compliance with safety measures at nuclear facilities.

Emergency Response: India has established emergency response organizations, including the Nuclear Power Corporation of India Limited (NPCIL) and the National Disaster Management Authority (NDMA), to handle nuclear emergencies and coordinate response efforts.

Nuclear Liability Act: The Civil Liability for Nuclear Damage Act, 2010, outlines the liability of operators in the event of a nuclear incident and provides a legal framework for compensating victims.

Training and Capacity Building: India focuses on training and capacity building of personnel involved in nuclear operations, emergency response, and radiation monitoring. This includes regular drills, simulations, and exercises to test and enhance preparedness.

Public Awareness: India emphasizes public awareness programs to educate the population about nuclear safety, radiation risks, and emergency preparedness. These programs aim to enhance public understanding and participation in nuclear safety measures.

Efforts in India are directed towards ensuring the safety of nuclear facilities, establishing effective emergency response mechanisms, and promoting awareness and preparedness among the population. Regular safety reviews, adherence to international standards, and continuous training and capacity building contribute to better management and preparedness for nuclear radiation events.

3.5 Manmade Disaster – Chemical Spills

Chemical spills occur when hazardous chemicals are released into the environment due to accidents, leaks, transportation incidents, or improper handling and storage practices.

Causes of Chemical spills:

Causes of chemical spills include:

Industrial Accidents: Accidents in industrial facilities, such as chemical plants, refineries, or storage facilities, can lead to chemical spills. Equipment failures, human errors, or process malfunctions can result in the release of hazardous substances.

Transportation Incidents: Spills can occur during the transportation of chemicals via road, rail, air, or water. Accidents, collisions, derailments, or leaks from containers or tankers can lead to chemical releases.

Improper Handling and Storage: Inadequate handling, storage, or disposal practices in laboratories, factories, or other facilities can result in chemical spills. Improper containment, lack of safety protocols, or inadequate training can contribute to incidents.

Characteristics of Chemical spills:

Variety of Chemicals: Chemical spills can involve a wide range of hazardous substances, including toxic chemicals, flammable materials, corrosive agents, or radioactive substances. Each type of chemical has its own characteristics and risks.

Immediate and Long-term Effects: Chemical spills can have immediate effects on human health, the environment, and surrounding communities. Additionally, long-term impacts can occur due to contamination of soil, water sources, and ecosystems.

Types of Chemical Spills:

Industrial Chemical Spills: Spills that occur within industrial facilities, such as chemical plants or manufacturing units, involving hazardous chemicals used in production processes.

Transportation Chemical Spills: Spills that occur during the transportation of chemicals via trucks, trains, ships, or airplanes. Accidents or leaks during transit can lead to chemical releases.

Chemical spills – Impact & Challenges:

Human Health Risks: Chemical spills can pose immediate risks to human health through inhalation, ingestion, or skin contact with toxic substances. Exposure to hazardous chemicals can cause respiratory problems, skin irritation, burns, poisoning, or long-term health effects.

Environmental Contamination: Chemical spills can contaminate soil, water bodies, and ecosystems, causing damage to plants, animals, and aquatic life. Contamination can persist for an extended period, affecting the environment and natural resources.

Fire and Explosion Hazards: Spills of flammable or combustible chemicals can lead to fire or explosion risks, endangering lives, property, and the surrounding environment.

Cleanup and Remediation Challenges: Managing and cleaning up chemical spills can be challenging due to the complexity of hazardous substances involved, the need for specialized equipment and expertise, and the potential for long-term environmental impacts.

Chemical spills – Mitigation & Preparedness:

Risk Assessment and Prevention: Conducting risk assessments, implementing proper storage and handling procedures, and adopting preventive measures, such as safety training, regular equipment maintenance, and inspections, can reduce the likelihood of chemical spills.

Emergency Response Plans: Developing and practicing emergency response plans specific to chemical spills, including spill containment, evacuation procedures, and coordination with emergency services, is crucial for effective response and mitigation.

Spill Response Teams: Establishing trained spill response teams or hazardous material response units can ensure a swift and efficient response to chemical spills, minimizing their impact and implementing proper containment and cleanup measures.

Spill Containment and Cleanup: Using appropriate containment measures, such as barriers, booms, or absorbent materials, can help limit the spread of spilled chemicals. Proper cleanup and disposal of hazardous materials should be conducted following established protocols and regulations.

Public Awareness and Education: Raising awareness among industries, workers, and the general public about the risks of chemical spills, safety protocols, and proper handling practices can help prevent incidents and facilitate timely response during emergencies.

Efforts in mitigating and preparing for chemical spills involve a combination of preventive measures, emergency response planning, proper training, and public awareness. Implementing strict safety regulations, enhancing monitoring and inspection practices, and promoting responsible handling and storage of hazardous chemicals contribute to reducing the risks and impacts associated with chemical spills.

Chemical spills – Magnitude and Duration:

Magnitude: The magnitude of a chemical spill can vary depending on factors such as the type and quantity of chemicals involved, the location and extent of the spill, and the effectiveness of containment measures. Chemical spills can range from small-scale incidents with minimal impact to large-scale disasters that pose significant risks to human health and the environment.

Duration: The duration of a chemical spill event depends on factors such as the time taken to contain and clean up the spill, the persistence of the chemicals in the environment, and the potential for long-term impacts. The duration can vary from hours to days or even longer, depending on the nature of the spill and the effectiveness of response efforts.

Chemical spills – Factors Affecting Severity:

Chemical Properties: The properties of the spilled chemicals, such as toxicity, flammability, reactivity, and volatility, play a crucial role in determining the severity of the incident. Highly toxic or corrosive substances pose greater risks to human health and the environment.

Spill Location: The location of the spill, including proximity to population centers, water bodies, sensitive ecosystems, or critical infrastructure, can affect the severity of the incident. Spills near densely populated areas or ecologically sensitive regions pose higher risks and challenges for response and mitigation.

Spill Volume and Rate: The volume and rate at which the chemicals are released during a spill can impact its severity. Larger spills or rapid releases can lead to more significant impacts and challenges in containment and cleanup.

Chemical spills – Management Strategies:

Prevention and Preparedness: Implementing preventive measures, such as risk assessments, safety protocols, training programs, and regular equipment maintenance, can help prevent chemical spills. Developing and practicing emergency response plans specific to chemical spills is crucial for effective management.

Spill Containment and Cleanup: Swift containment of the spilled chemicals using barriers, booms, or absorbent materials is essential to prevent further spread and minimize the impact. Cleanup and decontamination should be conducted using proper procedures and equipment to mitigate risks to human health and the environment.

Stakeholder Collaboration: Effective management of chemical spills requires coordination among various stakeholders, including government agencies, industry operators, emergency response teams, and local communities. Collaborative efforts in planning, response, and recovery can enhance the overall effectiveness of spill management.

Chemical spills – Major Prone Regions in India:

Industrial Zones: Regions with significant industrial activities, such as chemical manufacturing plants, refineries, and storage facilities, are prone to chemical spills. Examples include industrial areas in Gujarat, Maharashtra, Tamil Nadu, and Andhra Pradesh.

Transportation Corridors: Areas along major transportation routes, including highways, railways, and ports, are prone to chemical spills from accidents involving the transportation of hazardous materials.

Chemical spills – Management and Preparedness in India:

Regulatory Framework: India has established regulatory bodies such as the Central Pollution Control Board (CPCB) and State Pollution Control Boards (SPCBs) to enforce environmental regulations and ensure compliance with safety measures related to chemical handling, storage, and transport.

Hazardous Waste Management: The Hazardous Waste (Management, Handling, and Transboundary Movement) Rules, 2016, provide guidelines for the safe management, handling, and disposal of hazardous waste, including measures to prevent chemical spills.

Emergency Response Infrastructure: India has developed dedicated emergency response teams, such as the National Disaster Response Force (NDRF), State Disaster Response Forces (SDRFs), and Fire Services, which play a crucial role in responding to chemical spills and coordinating with other agencies.

Industrial Safety Practices: Industries in India are encouraged to adopt safety measures, conduct regular safety audits, and train personnel on proper handling and emergency response procedures to prevent and mitigate chemical spills.

Awareness and Capacity Building: Public awareness campaigns, training programs, and workshops are conducted to educate industries, workers, emergency responders, and the general public about chemical safety, spill response, and preparedness measures.

Efforts in India focus on implementing strict regulations, enhancing safety practices, building response capabilities, and promoting awareness to prevent and mitigate chemical spills. Continuous monitoring, periodic safety inspections, and adherence to international standards contribute to effective management and preparedness for chemical spill incidents.

3.6 Manmade Disasters – Transportation Accidents

Transportation accidents refer to incidents involving the transportation of goods, people, or vehicles that result in significant damage, injuries, or loss of life.

Causes of Transportation accidents:

Causes of transportation accidents can include:

Human Error: Errors made by drivers, pilots, train operators, or other transportation personnel, such as distracted driving, fatigue, speeding, or impaired operation, can lead to accidents.

Equipment Failure: Malfunctions or failures in vehicle components, such as brakes, tires, engines, or navigation systems, can contribute to transportation accidents.

Infrastructure Issues: Poorly maintained roads, inadequate signage, faulty traffic control systems, or infrastructure-related failures can increase the risk of transportation accidents.

Weather Conditions: Adverse weather conditions, such as heavy rain, fog, snow, ice, or strong winds, can impair visibility, reduce traction, and increase the likelihood of accidents.

Characteristics of Transportation accidents:

Multiple Modes of Transportation: Transportation accidents can involve various modes of transportation, including road vehicles, trains, airplanes, ships, or pipelines.

Potential for Mass Casualties: Transportation accidents often involve multiple individuals or large groups, which can lead to significant injuries, fatalities, and property damage.

Sudden and Unpredictable: Transportation accidents typically occur suddenly and unexpectedly, leaving little time for preventive measures or mitigation.

Types of Transportation Accidents:

Road Accidents: Collisions, rollovers, or incidents involving motor vehicles, motorcycles, bicycles, or pedestrians on roads and highways.

Rail Accidents: Train derailments, collisions, or other incidents related to railway transportation.

Aviation Accidents: Plane crashes, runway incidents, or other accidents involving aircraft.

Maritime Accidents: Ship collisions, groundings, sinkings, or oil spills related to maritime transportation.

Transportation accidents – Impact & Challenges:

Loss of Life and Injuries: Transportation accidents can result in significant loss of life, injuries, and long-term health consequences for individuals involved in the accidents.

Property Damage: Accidents can cause extensive damage to vehicles, infrastructure, and surrounding property, leading to financial losses.

Disruption of Services: Transportation accidents can cause disruptions to transportation services, leading to delays, rerouting, or suspension of services, impacting commerce, trade, and daily life.

Environmental Consequences: Accidents involving hazardous materials, such as chemical spills or oil leaks, can result in environmental pollution and long-term ecological damage.

Transportation accidents – Mitigation & Preparedness:

Safety Regulations and Standards: Implementing and enforcing safety regulations and standards specific to each mode of transportation can help prevent accidents. This includes driver training and licensing requirements, vehicle inspections, and maintenance protocols.

Infrastructure Maintenance: Regular maintenance and inspection of transportation infrastructure, including roads, bridges, railway tracks, and airport runways, are essential to minimize the risk of accidents.

Emergency Response Planning: Developing comprehensive emergency response plans specific to transportation accidents, including coordinated efforts between emergency services, transportation authorities, and local authorities, can enhance preparedness and response capabilities.

Technology and Safety Systems: Utilizing advanced safety technologies, such as collision avoidance systems, lane departure warnings, and automatic emergency braking, can help mitigate the risk of transportation accidents.

Public Awareness and Education: Educating the public about safe driving, following traffic rules, understanding transportation safety measures, and promoting responsible behaviour can contribute to accident prevention.

Efforts in mitigating transportation accidents involve a combination of regulations, infrastructure improvements, emergency response planning, and public education. Emphasizing safety, implementing effective maintenance practices, and promoting responsible driving behaviours contribute to reducing the risks and impacts associated with transportation accidents.

Transportation accidents – Magnitude and Duration:

Magnitude: The magnitude of transportation accidents can vary depending on factors such as the number of vehicles involved, the type of transportation mode, the severity of the collision, and the number of casualties or injuries. Accidents can range from minor incidents involving a single vehicle to major incidents with multiple vehicles and significant impact.

Duration: The duration of a transportation accident refers to the time taken for the accident response, rescue operations, and recovery efforts. The duration can vary depending on the complexity of the accident, the number of casualties, the extent of damage, and the efficiency of emergency response and recovery procedures.

Factors Affecting Severity of Transportation accidents:

Vehicle Speed and Impact: The speed at which vehicles are traveling during an accident and the resulting impact can greatly affect the severity of the incident. Higher speeds generally lead to more severe accidents with a greater risk of injuries or fatalities.

Vehicle Occupancy: The number of occupants in the vehicles involved in the accident can influence the severity. Accidents involving larger vehicles, such as buses or trucks, or vehicles carrying a higher number of passengers can have a more significant impact on casualties.

Infrastructure and Road Conditions: The condition of roads, including design, maintenance, and signage, can affect the severity of transportation accidents. Poorly designed roads, inadequate maintenance, or lack of proper signage can contribute to accidents and their severity.

Transportation accidents – Management Strategies:

Safety Regulations and Standards: Implementing and enforcing strict safety regulations and standards for vehicles, drivers, and transportation infrastructure is crucial to prevent accidents. This includes setting speed limits, enforcing traffic rules, conducting regular vehicle inspections, and ensuring proper maintenance.

Driver Training and Licensing: Providing comprehensive driver training programs and ensuring strict licensing procedures help promote safe driving practices. Ongoing driver education and awareness campaigns contribute to accident prevention.

Infrastructure Improvements: Regular maintenance, repair, and improvement of transportation infrastructure, including roads, bridges, railway tracks, and airports, can enhance safety and reduce accident risks.

Emergency Response Planning: Developing and practicing emergency response plans specific to transportation accidents, including coordination between emergency services, transportation authorities, and local authorities, is crucial for effective management and response.

Transportation accidents – Major Prone Regions in India:

Highways and Road Networks: Major highways and road networks in India, particularly those with high traffic volume and inadequate infrastructure, can be prone to transportation accidents. Examples include the Mumbai-Pune Expressway, the Golden Quadrilateral, and national highways connecting major cities.

Urban Areas: Dense urban areas with heavy traffic, such as metropolitan cities and congested commercial zones, have a higher risk of transportation accidents due to factors like increased vehicle density, traffic congestion, and complex road networks.

Transportation accidents – Management and Preparedness in India:

Road Safety Initiatives: The Government of India has implemented road safety initiatives, such as the National Road Safety Policy, to improve road infrastructure, promote safe driving behaviour, and reduce transportation accidents.

Traffic Management Systems: Installing and improving traffic management systems, including traffic signals, signage, and intelligent transportation systems, helps regulate traffic flow and reduce the risk of accidents.

Emergency Services and Response: India has established emergency services, including ambulance services, police, and fire departments, which play a crucial role in accident response, rescue operations, and medical assistance.

Road Safety Education and Awareness: Promoting road safety education and awareness among the public, schools, and communities helps cultivate responsible behaviour, increase awareness of traffic rules, and reduce the risk of transportation accidents.

National Highways Authority of India (NHAI): The NHAI is responsible for the development, maintenance, and management of national highways in India. They focus on improving road infrastructure, including widening roads, constructing bypasses, and implementing safety measures to reduce accidents.

Efforts in India are directed towards improving road safety, implementing stricter regulations, enhancing emergency response capabilities, and promoting public awareness to prevent and manage transportation accidents. Ongoing infrastructure development, driver training programs, and technology-driven initiatives contribute to reducing the risks and impacts associated with transportation accidents.

3.7 Manmade Disaster – Terrorists Strikes

Terrorist strikes refer to intentional acts of violence carried out by individuals or organized groups with the aim of instilling fear, causing harm, and achieving ideological, political, or religious objectives.

Causes of Terrorists Strikes:

The causes of terrorist strikes can include:

Ideological Motivations: Terrorist groups may carry out strikes to advance their ideological or political agenda, promote a particular religious belief, or challenge the established political or social order.

Grievances and Conflict: Socio-political grievances, unresolved conflicts, or perceived injustices can fuel terrorist activities, as individuals or groups seek to address their grievances through acts of violence.

Characteristics of Terrorists Strikes:

Deliberate Intent: Terrorist strikes are premeditated and planned with the specific intention of causing fear, panic, and harm to innocent civilians, infrastructure, or symbolic targets.

Targeting Civilians: Terrorist strikes often target civilian populations, public spaces, transportation systems, religious sites, government institutions, or symbolic landmarks to maximize impact and generate fear.

Types of Terrorist Strikes:

Bombings: Explosive devices, such as improvised explosive devices (IEDs), car bombs, or suicide bombings, are commonly used by terrorists to inflict casualties and damage property.

Armed Attacks: Terrorists may carry out armed attacks using firearms, grenades, or other weapons, targeting specific locations, such as schools, shopping malls, or transportation hubs.

Kidnappings and Hostage Situations: Terrorists may seize individuals or groups as hostages to exert pressure, gain attention, or secure concessions from governments or organizations.

Terrorists Strikes – Impact & Challenges:

Loss of Life and Injuries: Terrorist strikes can result in significant loss of life, injuries, and long-lasting physical and psychological trauma for victims and their families.

Societal Disruption: Terrorist strikes disrupt social cohesion, instill fear, and create a sense of insecurity among the population. They can lead to economic disruption, damage infrastructure, and hinder normal daily activities.

Political and Social Consequences: Terrorist strikes often have far-reaching political and social consequences, including changes in government policies, increased security measures, erosion of civil liberties, and societal divisions.

Terrorists Strikes – Mitigation & Preparedness:

Intelligence and Surveillance: Strengthening intelligence capabilities, information sharing, and surveillance systems is crucial to identify and prevent terrorist activities before they are executed.

Counterterrorism Measures: Governments implement measures to detect, deter, and disrupt terrorist networks, including law enforcement operations, border security, intelligence cooperation, and financial tracking.

Public Awareness and Vigilance: Promoting public awareness, encouraging citizen reporting, and educating communities about recognizing suspicious activities contribute to early detection and prevention of terrorist strikes.

Crisis Management and Response: Developing robust crisis management and emergency response plans, including coordination among law enforcement agencies, emergency services, and community organizations, helps minimize the impact of terrorist strikes.

International Cooperation: Collaborating with international partners and organizations to share intelligence, exchange best practices, and coordinate efforts enhances global counterterrorism strategies.

Efforts in mitigating and preparing for terrorist strikes involve a combination of preventive measures, intelligence gathering, law enforcement operations, public awareness, and international cooperation. Strengthening security infrastructure, promoting community engagement, and addressing underlying grievances and conflicts contribute to reducing the risks and impacts associated with terrorist strikes.

Terrorists Strikes – Magnitude and Duration:

Magnitude: The magnitude of terrorist strikes can vary significantly depending on factors such as the nature of the attack, the number of attackers, the target location, the type of weaponry used, and the number of casualties. Terrorist strikes can range from small-scale attacks with localized impact to large-scale incidents causing widespread devastation and loss of life.

Duration: The duration of a terrorist strike refers to the time taken for the attack to unfold, including the planning, execution, and aftermath. The duration can vary from a few minutes for a single attack to several hours or even days for more complex and prolonged incidents.

Factors Affecting Severity of Terrorists Strikes:

Scale and Intensity: The scale and intensity of a terrorist strike depend on factors such as the number of attackers, the type and quantity of weapons or explosives used, and the level of coordination among the perpetrators. Multiple coordinated attacks can have a more severe impact than isolated incidents.

Target Selection: The choice of target can influence the severity of a terrorist strike. Attacks on crowded public spaces, critical infrastructure, government buildings, transportation hubs, or iconic landmarks can have a higher impact and result in greater casualties.

Response and Preparedness: The effectiveness and swiftness of the response by law enforcement agencies and emergency services can influence the severity of a terrorist strike. Prompt response, effective communication, and coordinated efforts can help mitigate the impact and reduce casualties.

Terrorists Strikes – Management Strategies:

Intelligence and Surveillance: Strengthening intelligence networks, gathering actionable intelligence, and maintaining robust surveillance capabilities are essential for detecting and preventing terrorist activities before they occur.

Counterterrorism Operations: Governments implement counterterrorism strategies that include law enforcement operations, targeted strikes against terrorist networks, disruption of financing channels, and dismantling recruitment and radicalization pathways.

Security Measures: Enhancing security measures at public spaces, transportation systems, critical infrastructure, and sensitive facilities through the deployment of security personnel, surveillance technologies, access control mechanisms, and security protocols helps deter and mitigate terrorist strikes.

Crisis Management and Emergency Response: Developing comprehensive crisis management plans, including coordination among law enforcement agencies, emergency services, and other stakeholders, is crucial for effective response during and after a terrorist strike.

Public Awareness and Vigilance: Promoting public awareness about the signs of suspicious activities, encouraging citizens to report any unusual behaviour, and fostering a sense of vigilance among the population contribute to early detection and prevention of terrorist strikes.

Terrorists Strikes – Major Prone Regions in India:

Jammu and Kashmir: The region has experienced a significant history of terrorist strikes due to ongoing conflicts and cross-border infiltration.

North-Eastern States: Insurgent groups in certain states, such as Manipur, Nagaland, and Assam, have carried out sporadic terrorist activities.

Major Cities: Metropolitan cities like Mumbai, Delhi, Chennai, and Kolkata have been targeted in the past due to their high population density, economic importance, and symbolic value.

Terrorists Strikes – Management and Preparedness in India:

National Counterterrorism Agencies: India has specialized agencies such as the National Investigation Agency (NIA), the Intelligence Bureau (IB), and state-level Special Task Forces (STFs) that focus on counterterrorism operations, intelligence gathering, and coordination.

Security Forces and Law Enforcement: The Central Reserve Police Force (CRPF), National Security Guard (NSG), and state police forces play a crucial role in responding to terrorist strikes and maintaining law and order.

International Cooperation: India engages in international cooperation and intelligence sharing with various countries and organizations to combat terrorism effectively.

Public-Private Partnerships: Collaboration between government agencies, private sector entities, and the public in enhancing security measures, sharing information, and promoting awareness is essential for effective management and preparedness.

Efforts in India focus on strengthening intelligence networks, implementing counterterrorism measures, enhancing security infrastructure, promoting public awareness, and fostering international cooperation to prevent and respond to terrorist strikes. Continuous training of security forces, community engagement, and intelligence-driven operations contribute to the management and preparedness for potential terrorist threats.

Do's and Don'ts for Pre, During, and Post Atomic Explosion:

Pre-Explosion:

Seek Shelter: Identify and construct a sturdy shelter, preferably underground, to increase chances of survival during an atomic explosion. Structures made of thick concrete or reinforced materials provide better protection.

Stay Informed: Stay informed about the situation through official channels. Follow updates from emergency services and authorities for evacuation instructions and safety guidelines.

Prepare an Emergency Kit: Assemble an emergency kit containing essential supplies such as food, water, first aid supplies, flashlight, and a battery-operated radio.

Create a Family Emergency Plan: Develop a family emergency plan, including designated meeting places and communication methods in case family members are separated during the explosion.

Identify Safe Zones: Know the locations of designated fallout shelters or safe zones in your area. Familiarize yourself with evacuation routes to reach these areas quickly.

Avoid Crowded Places: Minimize visits to crowded places or areas near potential targets during times of heightened tension.

During the Explosion:

Get Indoors Immediately: If caught outside during an atomic explosion, seek shelter indoors as quickly as possible. If no shelter is nearby, lie flat on the ground and protect your head and neck.

Stay Away from Windows: Avoid windows, glass doors, and exterior walls, as they may shatter due to the force of the blast.

Cover Exposed Skin: If possible, cover exposed skin to reduce exposure to radioactive fallout. Use clothing, a mask, or any available materials for protection.

Stay Low: If sheltering in place, stay as low as possible to reduce exposure to radiation. The earth or concrete offers better protection against radiation.

Keep Listening to Updates: Continue to listen to updates from emergency services and follow their instructions for further actions.

Do not Look at the Explosion: Never look directly at the explosion, as it can cause temporary or permanent eye damage.

Post-Explosion:

Wait for Instructions: Stay in the shelter until you receive instructions from authorities that it is safe to leave. It might take hours or days for radioactive fallout to decrease to safer levels.

Avoid Contaminated Areas: Avoid areas with visible signs of damage or contamination, as they might be hazardous due to radiation, fires, or structural instability.

Use Protective Clothing: When venturing outside, use protective clothing, masks, and gloves to minimize contact with radioactive particles.

Keep Children and Pets Indoors: Keep children and pets indoors until authorities declare it safe to go outside.

Do not Spread Contamination: Be cautious not to spread radioactive contamination to other areas. Remove contaminated clothing and shoes before entering a shelter.

Monitor News and Updates: Continue monitoring news and updates from reliable sources to stay informed about developments and further instructions.

Conclusion: In the event of an atomic explosion, following the do's and don'ts can significantly increase your chances of survival and reduce the risk of exposure to radiation and other hazards. Preparedness, quick action, and adherence to official guidelines are crucial for personal safety and the well-being of others during and after such a catastrophic event. It is essential to stay informed and remain calm to make informed decisions in such critical situations.

CHAPTER 4

Hazard and Vulnerability Profile of India

4.1 Hazard and Vulnerability Profile of India

The hazard and vulnerability profile of India refers to an assessment of the potential hazards and vulnerabilities faced by the country. It involves identifying the types of hazards that occur in different regions of India and understanding the factors that contribute to the vulnerability of the population, infrastructure, and environment.

Hazards in India: India is prone to a wide range of natural and man-made hazards, including:

a. **Natural Hazards:**

Earthquakes: India is located in a seismically active region, making it vulnerable to earthquakes. The Himalayan region, northeastern states, and areas along the western and central parts of the country are particularly susceptible.

Cyclones: Coastal regions, especially the Bay of Bengal and the Arabian Sea, experience cyclones, which can cause extensive damage through strong winds, heavy rainfall, storm surges, and flooding.

Floods: Several river basins, including the Ganges, Brahmaputra, and their tributaries, are prone to floods during the monsoon season. Flash floods can also occur in hilly regions.

Droughts: Certain parts of India, particularly the arid and semi-arid regions, face recurring droughts, resulting in water scarcity, agricultural losses, and socio-economic impacts.

Landslides: Hilly regions, including the Himalayas and the Western Ghats, are susceptible to landslides, especially during heavy rainfall.

Heatwaves: Heatwaves are becoming increasingly frequent and intense in India, particularly in the central and northern regions, leading to health risks and economic impacts.

b. **Man-made Hazards:**

Industrial Accidents: India's industrial sectors, including chemical plants, refineries, and manufacturing units, face the risk of accidents, such as chemical spills, explosions, or fires.

Terrorism: Certain regions in India, such as Jammu and Kashmir and some northeastern states, have faced acts of terrorism, including bombings, armed attacks, and hostage situations.

Transportation Accidents: India's extensive transportation networks, including road, rail, and air, can be susceptible to accidents, resulting in casualties and disruptions.

Vulnerability Factors: Several factors contribute to the vulnerability of India to these hazards:

a. Population Density: India's large population, coupled with high population density in many regions, increases the vulnerability to hazards due to the potential for greater exposure and impacts.

b. Urbanization: Rapid urbanization in cities and towns often leads to inadequate infrastructure, overcrowding, informal settlements, and inadequate services, making urban areas more vulnerable to hazards.

c. Poverty and Socio-economic Disparities: Poverty, inequality, and lack of access to basic services, including healthcare, education, and infrastructure, contribute to the vulnerability of marginalized communities.

d. Environmental Degradation: Deforestation, land degradation, loss of wetlands, and improper land-use practices increase the vulnerability to hazards, such as floods, landslides, and soil erosion.

e. Climate Change: India is highly susceptible to the impacts of climate change, including increased frequency and intensity of extreme weather events, sea-level rise, and changes in rainfall patterns, which exacerbate vulnerability to hazards.

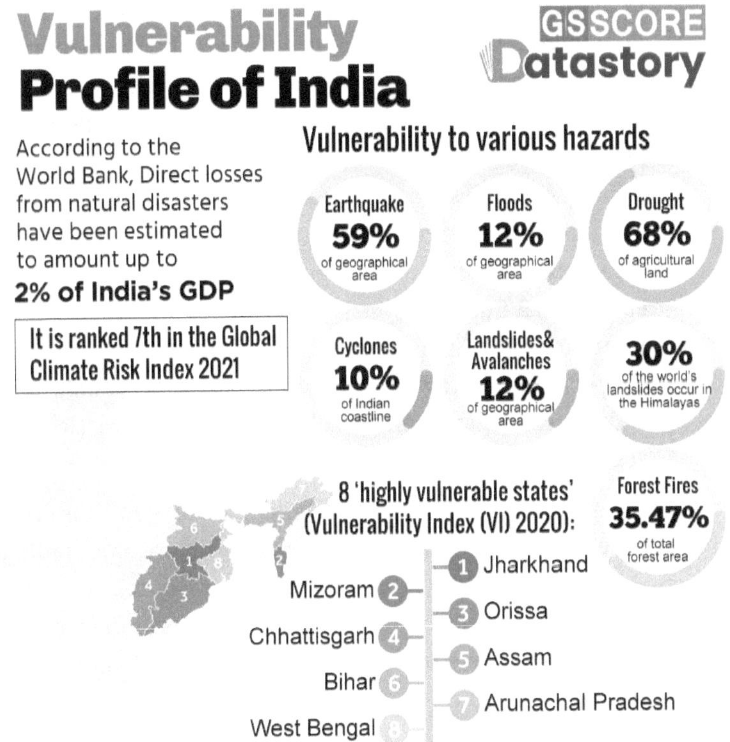

Figure 4.1 Hazard and Vulnerability Profile of India (Source: GS Score)

Management and Preparedness: Efforts to address the hazard and vulnerability profile of India involve various strategies and measures:

a. Disaster Risk Reduction: Implementing comprehensive disaster risk reduction measures, including early warning systems, infrastructure resilience, land-use planning, and community-based preparedness initiatives.

b. Infrastructure Development: Investing in robust and resilient infrastructure, such as flood control systems, cyclone shelters, earthquake-resistant buildings, and improved transportation networks.

c. Capacity Building: Enhancing the capacity of government agencies, local communities, and civil society organizations in disaster management, response, and recovery.

d. Policy and Governance: Formulating and implementing policies, regulations, and guidelines related to hazard mitigation, urban planning, land-use management, and building codes.

e. Public Awareness and Education: Promoting awareness among the public about hazards, risks, and preparedness measures through campaigns, training programs, and educational initiatives.

f. International Cooperation: Engaging in international cooperation, knowledge-sharing, and partnerships to address common challenges, learn from best practices, and access resources for disaster management.

Understanding the hazard and vulnerability profile of India is crucial for effective disaster management, risk reduction, and building resilience. It helps guide policy decisions, resource allocation, and targeted interventions to mitigate the impacts of hazards and enhance the preparedness of communities and infrastructure.

Impact and Challenges of Hazards:

The hazard and vulnerability profile of India presents several significant impacts and challenges:

a. Human Casualties: Hazards in India, such as earthquakes, cyclones, floods, and droughts, can result in the loss of human lives and injuries, particularly among vulnerable populations living in high-risk areas.

b. Infrastructure Damage: Hazards can cause substantial damage to infrastructure, including buildings, roads, bridges, power lines, and communication networks. This leads to disruptions in services, transportation, and utilities, affecting the overall socio-economic fabric of the affected regions.

c. Economic Losses: Hazards and their impacts often result in significant economic losses, including damage to agriculture, industries, businesses, and tourism. The reconstruction and recovery process can place a strain on the national economy.

d. Displacement and Migration: Hazard events can force communities to flee their homes, resulting in temporary or long-term displacement. Migration to safer areas in search of livelihoods and basic necessities can lead to social and economic challenges.

e. Health and Sanitation: Hazards can adversely affect public health, leading to the spread of diseases, inadequate access to clean water and sanitation facilities, and the loss of healthcare infrastructure, increasing vulnerability and health risks.

f. Climate Change Resilience: India's vulnerability to climate change exacerbates the challenges related to hazards. Adapting to changing climate patterns and building resilience against climate-related risks is critical for long-term hazard management.

Major Hazard Prone Regions in India:

Different regions in India face varying levels of susceptibility to specific hazards:

a. Earthquakes: The Himalayan region, including Jammu and Kashmir, Himachal Pradesh, Uttarakhand, and parts of northeastern states, are prone to earthquakes.

b.   Cyclones: Coastal areas along the Bay of Bengal, including Odisha, West Bengal, Andhra Pradesh, and Tamil Nadu, experience cyclonic events.

c.   Floods: River basins like the Ganges-Brahmaputra-Meghna, the Indus, and major rivers in northeastern states are prone to floods.

d.   Droughts: Arid and semi-arid regions, such as Rajasthan, Gujarat, and parts of central India, often face drought conditions.

e.   Landslides: Hilly regions, including the Himalayas, the Western Ghats, and northeastern states, are susceptible to landslides.

Hazard Management and Preparedness in India:

India has undertaken various measures to address the hazard and vulnerability profile, including:

a.   National and State-Level Policies: India has formulated policies and frameworks such as the National Disaster Management Plan, State Disaster Management Plans, and Building Codes to guide disaster management and preparedness.

b.   Early Warning Systems: Implementing advanced early warning systems for cyclones, floods, and other hazards to provide timely alerts and enable evacuation and preparedness measures.

c.   Capacity Building: Enhancing the capacity of government institutions, first responders, and community-based organizations through training programs, drills, and exercises.

d.   Risk Assessment and Mapping: Conducting hazard and vulnerability assessments, risk mapping, and data collection to identify high-risk areas and prioritize interventions.

e.   Community Engagement: Encouraging community participation and strengthening community-based organizations to enhance resilience, preparedness, and response.

f. International Cooperation: Collaborating with international organizations, neighbouring countries, and partners to share best practices, technical expertise, and resources for disaster management.

Efforts in India aim to improve disaster preparedness, response, and recovery by integrating risk reduction into development planning, strengthening institutional frameworks, and promoting community resilience. Strengthening infrastructure, improving early warning systems, enhancing public awareness, and mainstreaming disaster risk reduction into various sectors contribute to effective management and preparedness for hazards in India.

Hazard Data and Research:

Continuous data collection, research, and analysis are essential for understanding the hazard and vulnerability profile of India. This includes:

a. Hazard Mapping and Modelling: Conducting hazard mapping exercises to identify high-risk areas and assess the potential impact of various hazards. This involves analysing historical data, geological surveys, climate patterns, and other relevant factors.

b. Vulnerability Assessments: Assessing the vulnerability of communities, infrastructure, and ecosystems to different hazards. This involves considering factors such as socio-economic conditions, access to services, quality of infrastructure, and environmental factors.

c. Climate Change Assessments: Integrating climate change projections and scenarios into hazard and vulnerability assessments to understand the potential impacts of climate change on hazard frequency, intensity, and distribution.

Hazard Challenges and Future Outlook:

Despite ongoing efforts, several challenges exist in addressing the hazard and vulnerability profile of India:

a. Limited Resources: Allocating sufficient financial and human resources for disaster risk reduction, infrastructure development, and community resilience remains a challenge, particularly in resource-constrained regions.

b. Rapid Urbanization: The rapid growth of cities and urban areas poses challenges in terms of managing increasing population density, informal settlements, and the need for resilient infrastructure.

c. Climate Change Adaptation: Adapting to the impacts of climate change requires integrating climate resilience into development planning, policy frameworks, and infrastructure projects.

d. Multi-hazard Approach: India faces multiple hazards, and adopting a multi-hazard approach in disaster management and preparedness is crucial to effectively address the range of risks.

e. Inclusive Approach: Ensuring inclusivity and addressing the vulnerabilities of marginalized communities, including women, children, the elderly, and people with disabilities, is important to achieve equitable resilience.

f. Public-Private Partnerships: Enhancing collaboration between the public and private sectors, civil society organizations, academia, and communities can strengthen the effectiveness of hazard management strategies.

Moving forward, India aims to strengthen disaster risk reduction measures, improve early warning systems, enhance emergency response capabilities, and mainstream resilience in development planning. The integration of hazard and vulnerability considerations into policy frameworks, investments in infrastructure, and capacity-building efforts will play a crucial role in reducing the impacts of hazards and building a resilient nation.

Continued research, data collection, and knowledge sharing, both nationally and internationally, will contribute to a deeper understanding of India's hazard and vulnerability profile and enable more targeted and effective risk reduction strategies.

4.2 Hazard and Vulnerability Profile of Mountain in India

The hazard and vulnerability profile of mountainous regions in India refers to the assessment of potential hazards and vulnerabilities specific to these areas. Mountain regions in India are characterized by their unique geographical features, diverse ecosystems, and socio-economic factors that contribute to their specific hazard and vulnerability profiles.

Hazards in Mountainous Regions:

Mountainous regions in India are susceptible to various hazards, including:

a. Landslides: Steep slopes, geological instability, heavy rainfall, and seismic activity make mountainous areas prone to landslides. Slope failures and rockfalls can result in loss of life, damage to infrastructure, and disruption of transport networks.

b. Flash Floods: Mountainous regions experience intense rainfall, which can lead to flash floods due to the rapid runoff of water along steep gradients. These floods can be highly destructive, causing significant damage to settlements, roads, and agricultural lands.

c. Glacial Lake Outburst Floods (GLOFs): The presence of glaciers in mountainous regions can give rise to glacial lakes. If these lakes experience a sudden breach or overflow, it can result in glacial lake outburst floods, posing a significant threat downstream to settlements, infrastructure, and livelihoods.

d. Avalanches: Snow-covered Mountain slopes are prone to avalanches, which can be triggered by heavy snowfall, temperature variations, or seismic activity. Avalanches can be highly destructive, endangering lives and damaging infrastructure.

e. Earthquakes: Mountainous regions, especially those located along tectonic plate boundaries like the Himalayas, are susceptible to earthquakes. Seismic activity in these regions can lead to significant ground shaking, landslides, and other secondary hazards.

Vulnerability Factors in Mountainous Regions:

Several factors contribute to the vulnerability of mountainous regions in India:

a. Population Density and Settlement Patterns: Despite the challenging terrain, mountainous regions often have significant population settlements. The concentration of people in vulnerable areas, such as steep slopes or near riverbanks, increases their exposure to hazards.

b. Fragile Ecosystems: Mountain ecosystems are characterized by diverse flora and fauna, but they are also fragile and sensitive to disturbances. Deforestation, improper land-use practices, and climate change impacts can weaken these ecosystems, making them more vulnerable to hazards.

c. Limited Infrastructure: Mountainous regions may have limited infrastructure, including roads, bridges, and communication networks. This can hinder emergency response and access to affected areas during and after a hazard event.

d. Inadequate Early Warning Systems: Some mountainous regions may lack robust early warning systems for hazards such as landslides, flash floods, and avalanches. This limits the ability to provide timely alerts and evacuation measures.

e. Socio-economic Conditions: Mountain communities often face socio-economic challenges such as poverty, limited access to healthcare and education, and dependence on agriculture or tourism. These factors can amplify vulnerability and reduce resilience to hazards.

Management and Preparedness in Mountainous Regions:

Addressing the hazard and vulnerability profile of mountainous regions requires specific management and preparedness strategies:

a. Hazard Mapping and Risk Assessment: Conducting detailed hazard mapping and risk assessments specific to mountainous regions helps identify high-risk areas, vulnerable communities, and critical infrastructure that require targeted interventions.

b. Slope Stabilization and Engineering Measures: Implementing slope stabilization measures, such as terracing, retaining walls, and erosion control techniques, helps mitigate landslide risks. Proper road construction and slope management can reduce the impact of landslides and avalanches.

c. Early Warning Systems: Installing and maintaining early warning systems for flash floods, landslides, and avalanches in mountainous regions enables timely evacuation and preparedness measures.

d. Community-Based Disaster Risk Reduction: Engaging Mountain communities in disaster risk reduction initiatives, including training, awareness programs, and capacity building, enhances their resilience and enables them to respond effectively during hazards.

e. Infrastructure Development: Investing in robust infrastructure, including roads, bridges, and communication networks, improves accessibility, facilitates emergency response, and enables quick recovery in mountainous regions.

f. Sustainable Development Practices: Promoting sustainable development practices, including responsible tourism, ecosystem conservation, and climate change adaptation, contributes to the long-term resilience of mountainous regions.

g. Strengthening Local Institutions: Building the capacity of local institutions, such as local governments, community-based organizations, and civil society groups, to plan, manage, and respond to hazards in mountainous areas is crucial for effective disaster management.

It is important to adopt an integrated approach that considers the unique hazards and vulnerabilities in mountainous regions, while also addressing socio-economic, ecological, and governance aspects. This involves collaboration between various stakeholders, including government agencies, local communities, research institutions, and non-governmental organizations, to develop and implement context-specific strategies for hazard management and preparedness in mountainous regions.

Environmental Factors in Mountainous Regions:

Mountainous regions have distinct environmental factors that contribute to their hazard and vulnerability profile:

a. Steep Topography: The rugged and steep topography of mountainous regions increases the susceptibility to hazards such as landslides, avalanches, and erosion. The steep slopes make it challenging to construct infrastructure and settlements in a stable manner.

b. High Precipitation: Mountainous areas often receive higher precipitation due to orographic effects, resulting in intense rainfall and snowfall. This increased precipitation contributes to hazards like flash floods, landslides, and glacial lake outburst floods.

c. Glaciers and Glacial Lakes: Mountain regions may have glaciers and glacial lakes, which are highly vulnerable to climate change. The melting of glaciers can lead to the formation of glacial lakes, and the subsequent release of water can trigger devastating glacial lake outburst floods downstream.

d. Biodiversity and Ecosystem Services: Mountain ecosystems are known for their rich biodiversity and ecosystem services. Hazards can negatively impact these ecosystems, leading to the loss of biodiversity, disruption of ecological processes, and the loss of essential ecosystem services.

Major Hazard Prone Mountainous Regions in India:

India has several mountainous regions that are prone to various hazards:

a. Himalayan Region: The Himalayan region, including states like Jammu and Kashmir, Himachal Pradesh, Uttarakhand, Sikkim, and Arunachal Pradesh, is highly prone to landslides, flash floods, earthquakes, and glacial lake outburst floods.

b. Western Ghats: The Western Ghats, spanning states like Maharashtra, Karnataka, Kerala, and Tamil Nadu, are susceptible to landslides, flash floods, and biodiversity-related hazards.

c. Northeastern States: States in the northeastern region, including Assam, Meghalaya, Nagaland, and Manipur, face hazards such as landslides, flash floods, earthquakes, and riverbank erosion.

Management and Preparedness in India's Mountainous Regions:

Addressing the hazard and vulnerability profile of mountainous regions in India requires specific management and preparedness approaches:

a. Integrated Land Use Planning: Implementing land-use planning that considers the unique characteristics of mountainous regions, including slope stability, soil erosion, and the preservation of natural ecosystems.

b. Early Warning Systems: Establishing and maintaining early warning systems for various hazards specific to mountainous areas, such as landslides, flash floods, and glacial lake outburst floods.

c. Infrastructure Resilience: Ensuring that infrastructure development in mountainous regions incorporates resilience measures to withstand hazards, such as proper slope stabilization, bridge design, and road construction techniques.

d. Community-Based Adaptation: Encouraging community involvement in disaster risk reduction and adaptation strategies by raising awareness, providing training, and promoting indigenous knowledge and practices.

e. Ecosystem Conservation and Restoration: Protecting and restoring mountain ecosystems, including forests, wetlands, and biodiversity hotspots, contributes to the resilience of these regions and their ability to cope with hazards.

f. Climate Change Adaptation: Integrating climate change adaptation measures into hazard management and preparedness strategies, considering long-term climate projections and their impacts on mountain regions.

g. Cross-Sectoral Collaboration: Promoting collaboration among various sectors, including government agencies, local communities, researchers, and non-governmental organizations, to ensure a comprehensive approach to hazard management and preparedness.

Efforts to address the hazard and vulnerability profile of mountainous regions in India aim to minimize the impacts of hazards on communities, infrastructure, and ecosystems. By integrating scientific knowledge, local expertise, and community participation, effective management strategies can be implemented to enhance resilience and reduce vulnerability in these regions.

Socio-Economic Factors in Mountainous Regions:

Socio-economic factors play a significant role in shaping the hazard and vulnerability profile of mountainous regions:

a. Rural Livelihoods: Mountainous regions often have a significant rural population engaged in agriculture, pastoralism, and forestry. Hazards can disrupt these livelihoods, leading to economic losses and increased vulnerability.

b. Limited Access to Services: Mountainous regions may face challenges in accessing basic services such as healthcare, education, and infrastructure due to difficult terrain and remote locations. This can hinder the response and recovery efforts during and after hazard events.

c. Indigenous and Tribal Communities: Mountainous regions are home to many indigenous and tribal communities with unique cultural practices and traditional knowledge. These communities often have specific vulnerabilities that need to be addressed, including their socio-economic marginalization and limited access to resources.

d. Tourism and Recreation: Mountainous regions attract tourists and adventure enthusiasts, contributing to local economies. However, tourism activities can also increase vulnerability to hazards, such as overburdening infrastructure and exacerbating environmental degradation.

Management and Preparedness Challenges in mountainous regions:

Addressing the hazard and vulnerability profile of mountainous regions comes with specific challenges:

a. Difficult Terrain and Inaccessibility: The challenging topography and remote locations of mountainous regions pose logistical challenges for effective hazard management, emergency response, and access to affected areas.

b. Limited Resources and Capacity: Some mountainous regions may have limited resources and institutional capacity for disaster management and preparedness. This can hinder timely response, coordination, and implementation of mitigation measures.

c. Communication and Connectivity: Communication networks can be weak or unreliable in mountainous regions, making it difficult to disseminate timely information, warnings, and emergency messages during hazard events.

d. Sustainable Development Balancing: Balancing the need for development with sustainable practices in mountainous regions is crucial. Ensuring that development initiatives prioritize environmental conservation, community well-being, and disaster resilience is a challenge that needs to be addressed.

e. Climate Change Impacts: Mountainous regions are particularly vulnerable to the impacts of climate change, such as glacier retreat, altered precipitation patterns, and increased frequency of extreme weather events. Adapting to these changes and integrating climate resilience into hazard management is essential.

Best Practices and Initiatives to address Hazards:

Several initiatives and best practices are being implemented to address the hazard and vulnerability profile of mountainous regions in India:

a. Community-Based Early Warning Systems: Engaging local communities in the development and operation of early warning systems helps ensure the effective dissemination of warnings and community response during hazard events.

b. Nature-Based Solutions: Implementing nature-based solutions, such as afforestation, watershed management, and soil conservation measures, helps mitigate the impacts of hazards and enhance ecosystem resilience.

c. Capacity Building and Training: Strengthening the capacity of local communities, government agencies, and non-governmental organizations through training programs, workshops, and knowledge-sharing initiatives improves preparedness and response.

d. Disaster Risk Financing: Developing risk financing mechanisms, including insurance schemes and contingency funds, helps enhance financial resilience and enables faster recovery in mountainous regions.

e. Cross-Border Cooperation: Promoting cross-border cooperation and knowledge exchange among neighbouring countries facing similar hazards in mountainous regions facilitates collaborative efforts in hazard management and preparedness.

As the hazard and vulnerability profile of mountainous regions in India continues to evolve, there is a need for ongoing research, monitoring, and adaptation to effectively address the challenges. Strengthening early warning systems, improving infrastructure resilience, promoting sustainable development practices, and integrating climate resilience into planning are key focus areas for future interventions.

By fostering community participation, promoting interagency collaboration, and ensuring the inclusion of marginalized groups, mountainous regions in India can become more resilient to hazards and achieve sustainable development that balances socio-economic progress with environmental conservation.

4.3 Hazard and Vulnerability Profile of Coastal Areas in India

The hazard and vulnerability profile of coastal areas in India refers to the assessment of potential hazards and vulnerabilities specific to these regions. India has a vast coastline along the Arabian Sea and the Bay of Bengal, making its coastal areas prone to various hazards. Understanding the hazard and vulnerability profile helps in developing effective strategies for hazard management, risk reduction, and enhancing the resilience of coastal communities. :

Hazards in Coastal Areas:

Coastal areas in India are susceptible to several hazards, including:

a. Cyclones: Coastal regions are prone to cyclones originating from the Bay of Bengal and the Arabian Sea. Cyclones bring strong winds, heavy rainfall, storm surges, and coastal flooding, causing significant damage to infrastructure, coastal ecosystems, and communities.

b. Coastal Erosion: Continuous wave action, tidal currents, and sea-level rise contribute to coastal erosion, leading to the loss of land, erosion of beaches, and vulnerability of coastal infrastructure.

c. Tsunamis: Undersea earthquakes or other disturbances can generate tsunamis, which are large oceanic waves that can devastate coastal areas. Coastal communities need to be prepared for potential tsunamis in vulnerable regions.

d. Saltwater Intrusion: Rising sea levels and excessive groundwater extraction can lead to the intrusion of saltwater into coastal aquifers, compromising freshwater sources and affecting agriculture and drinking water supplies.

e. Storm Surges: Intense cyclones and severe weather events can cause storm surges, which are abnormal rises in sea level. Storm surges can result in coastal flooding, damage to infrastructure, and displacement of coastal communities.

Vulnerability Factors in Coastal Areas:

Several factors contribute to the vulnerability of coastal areas in India:

a. Population Density: Coastal areas often have high population densities due to their favourable living conditions and economic opportunities. This increases the exposure and vulnerability of communities to coastal hazards.

b. Infrastructure and Development: Coastal regions witness rapid urbanization and infrastructure development, including ports, industries, and tourism. Poorly planned and constructed infrastructure can exacerbate vulnerability and increase the risk of damage during hazards.

c. Ecosystem Degradation: Coastal ecosystems, such as mangroves, coral reefs, and coastal wetlands, act as natural buffers against hazards. However, ecosystem degradation due to human activities, pollution, and coastal development reduces their protective capacity and increases vulnerability.

d. Climate Change Impacts: Coastal areas are highly vulnerable to climate change, including rising sea levels, changing rainfall patterns, and increased frequency of extreme weather events. Climate change exacerbates existing vulnerabilities and poses additional challenges for coastal communities.

e. Socio-Economic Disparities: Coastal communities often face socio-economic disparities, including poverty, inadequate access to basic services, and limited livelihood opportunities. These disparities increase vulnerability and hinder resilience-building efforts.

Management and Preparedness in Coastal Areas:

Addressing the hazard and vulnerability profile of coastal areas requires specific management and preparedness strategies:

a. Early Warning Systems: Implementing effective early warning systems for cyclones, storm surges, and tsunamis is critical to providing timely alerts to coastal communities and enabling evacuation and preparedness measures.

b. Coastal Protection and Infrastructure: Implementing coastal protection measures such as seawalls, dikes, and beach nourishment can help mitigate the impacts of coastal erosion, storm surges, and sea-level rise. Constructing resilient infrastructure in coastal areas is crucial.

c. Ecosystem-Based Approaches: Conserving and restoring coastal ecosystems, such as mangroves and coral reefs, helps enhance natural coastal protection, reduce erosion, and provide habitat for biodiversity.

d. Land-Use Planning: Ensuring proper land-use planning and zoning regulations in coastal areas to prevent encroachment in hazard-prone zones and preserve natural buffers.

e. Community Engagement: Involving coastal communities in disaster risk reduction initiatives, raising awareness, conducting capacity-building programs, and promoting participatory approaches for decision-making.

f. Integrated Coastal Zone Management: Implementing Integrated Coastal Zone Management (ICZM) approaches that consider the entire coastal ecosystem and address the interconnected nature of coastal hazards, development, and conservation.

g. Climate Change Adaptation: Integrating climate change adaptation measures into coastal planning, such as considering sea-level rise projections, promoting sustainable coastal development, and implementing adaptive land-use practices.

Major Costal Hazard Prone Regions in India:

Several regions in India are prone to coastal hazards:

a. Bay of Bengal: Coastal areas of West Bengal, Odisha, Andhra Pradesh, and Tamil Nadu are susceptible to cyclones, storm surges, and coastal erosion.

b. Arabian Sea: Coastal areas of Gujarat, Maharashtra, Karnataka, Kerala, and Tamil Nadu along the Arabian Sea face the risks of cyclones, coastal erosion, and sea-level rise.

c. Research and Monitoring: Continuous research, monitoring, and data collection are essential for understanding and managing coastal hazards. This includes:

d. Coastal Monitoring Systems: Establishing robust coastal monitoring systems to track sea-level rise, shoreline changes, and erosion rates, which provide critical data for effective planning and decision-making.

e. Hazard Modelling and Mapping: Conducting hazard modelling and mapping exercises to identify high-risk areas and assess the potential impact of coastal hazards on communities and infrastructure.

f. Climate Change Research: Studying the impacts of climate change on coastal areas, including projections of sea-level rise, changes in storm patterns, and their implications for coastal vulnerability.

g. Socio-Economic Assessments: Conducting socio-economic assessments to understand the vulnerabilities and needs of coastal communities, including their capacity to cope with hazards and adapt to climate change.

Addressing the hazard and vulnerability profile of coastal areas requires a comprehensive and multi-dimensional approach that integrates scientific knowledge

Challenges in Coastal Areas:

Coastal areas face specific challenges in managing their hazard and vulnerability profile:

a. Land-Use Conflicts: Coastal regions often experience conflicts between development activities, such as tourism, ports, and industries, and the need to preserve natural ecosystems and coastal resilience. Balancing development needs with environmental conservation is a challenge.

b. Multi-Hazard Environment: Coastal areas are prone to multiple hazards, such as cyclones, storm surges, coastal erosion, and tsunamis. Managing and preparing for multiple hazards requires comprehensive planning and coordination among various stakeholders.

c. Limited Resources: Coastal areas may have limited financial and human resources for hazard management and resilience-building initiatives. Mobilizing adequate resources and funding for coastal protection and infrastructure development is crucial.

d. Population Growth and Urbanization: Rapid population growth and urbanization in coastal areas can increase vulnerability due to unplanned settlements, inadequate infrastructure, and the strain on natural resources.

e. Climate Change Uncertainty: Uncertainties associated with climate change, such as the rate of sea-level rise and changes in storm patterns, pose challenges in developing accurate projections and planning for future coastal hazards.

f. Inadequate Policy Frameworks: The absence of comprehensive policies and regulations specific to coastal areas may hinder effective hazard management and adaptive measures. Strengthening policy frameworks and implementing coastal management plans are crucial.

Coastal Resilience and Adaptation Strategies:

Building resilience and adapting to the hazard and vulnerability profile of coastal areas involves several strategies:

a. Community-Based Adaptation: Engaging coastal communities in adaptation planning and implementation, considering their local knowledge, needs, and priorities. This involves raising awareness, providing training, and promoting participatory approaches.

b. Nature-Based Solutions: Implementing nature-based solutions, such as mangrove restoration, dune stabilization, and beach nourishment, to enhance natural coastal protection, reduce erosion, and preserve biodiversity.

c. Integrated Coastal Zone Management (ICZM): Adopting an ICZM approach that integrates various sectors, including environment, fisheries, tourism, and urban planning, to ensure sustainable development while addressing coastal hazards and ecosystem conservation.

d. Coastal Regulation Zone (CRZ) Guidelines: Implementing and enforcing the CRZ guidelines that regulate developmental activities and prevent encroachment in hazard-prone areas along the coast.

e. Capacity Building and Knowledge Sharing: Enhancing the capacity of coastal communities, local institutions, and government agencies through training programs, workshops, and knowledge-sharing initiatives on hazard management, early warning systems, and resilience-building.

f. International Cooperation: Promoting international cooperation and collaboration in addressing coastal hazards, sharing best practices, and developing joint initiatives for coastal resilience.

Future Outlook: The hazard and vulnerability profile of coastal areas in India is expected to evolve due to climate change, population growth, and urbanization. Key areas of focus for the future include:

a. Climate Change Adaptation: Strengthening adaptive capacities and integrating climate change considerations into coastal planning, including sea-level rise projections, storm surge modelling, and climate-resilient infrastructure.

b. Integrated Approaches: Adopting integrated approaches that consider the interconnected nature of coastal hazards, ecosystem conservation, and sustainable development to achieve long-term resilience.

c. Stakeholder Engagement: Encouraging the active involvement of coastal communities, local governments, researchers, and non-governmental organizations in decision-making processes and the implementation of coastal management strategies.

d. Monitoring and Research: Continuously monitoring and researching coastal hazards, vulnerabilities, and ecosystem dynamics to improve understanding, develop accurate projections, and inform evidence-based policies and strategies.

e. Policy and Governance: Strengthening policy frameworks, regulatory mechanisms, and governance structures to address the specific needs and challenges of coastal areas in hazard management and resilience-building.

By implementing effective management strategies, fostering community participation, and integrating scientific knowledge with local expertise, coastal areas in India can enhance their resilience, reduce vulnerability, and promote sustainable development in the face of coastal hazards.

Major Costal Hazard Prone Regions in India:

Coastal areas across India face varying degrees of vulnerability to hazards. Some of the major prone regions include:

a. East Coast: The east coast of India, particularly the states of Odisha, Andhra Pradesh, and Tamil Nadu, is highly susceptible to cyclones, storm surges, and coastal erosion. The low-lying regions along the Bay of Bengal are particularly vulnerable.

b. West Coast: The west coast of India, encompassing states such as Gujarat, Maharashtra, Karnataka, Kerala, and Tamil Nadu, is prone to cyclones, coastal erosion, and sea-level rise. The regions along the Arabian Sea experience varying degrees of vulnerability.

c.   Andaman and Nicobar Islands: Located in the Bay of Bengal, the Andaman and Nicobar Islands are exposed to cyclones, tsunamis, and coastal erosion. The island chain's low-lying areas are particularly vulnerable to storm surges.

Management and Preparedness in Coastal Areas of India:

To address the hazard and vulnerability profile of coastal areas, specific management and preparedness strategies are crucial:

a.   Coastal Planning and Regulation: Implementing effective coastal planning and regulation, including Coastal Regulation Zone (CRZ) guidelines, to manage development activities, prevent encroachment in hazard-prone areas, and safeguard ecosystems.

b.   Early Warning Systems: Establishing robust early warning systems for cyclones, storm surges, and tsunamis to provide timely alerts and enable evacuation and preparedness measures.

c.   Coastal Protection Measures: Implementing coastal protection measures such as seawalls, revetments, and beach nourishment to reduce the impact of coastal erosion, storm surges, and sea-level rise on infrastructure and communities.

d.   Ecosystem Conservation: Protecting and restoring coastal ecosystems such as mangroves, coral reefs, and sand dunes, which act as natural buffers against coastal hazards and support biodiversity.

e.   Infrastructure Resilience: Incorporating resilience measures into the design and construction of coastal infrastructure, including buildings, ports, and transportation networks, to withstand the impacts of hazards.

f.   Community Engagement and Capacity Building: Engaging coastal communities in disaster risk reduction initiatives, raising awareness, providing training on evacuation procedures, and promoting community-led resilience-building activities.

g. Multi-Sectoral Collaboration: Promoting collaboration among various sectors, including government agencies, local communities, researchers, and non-governmental organizations, to ensure a comprehensive and coordinated approach to coastal hazard management.

h. Climate Change Adaptation: Integrating climate change adaptation measures into coastal planning and management, considering future sea-level rise projections, changing storm patterns, and the potential impact on vulnerable coastal areas.

Research and Monitoring in Costal Hazard Zone:

Continuous research, monitoring, and data collection are essential for improving the understanding of coastal hazards and vulnerabilities. This includes:

a. Coastal Monitoring: Implementing robust coastal monitoring systems to track shoreline changes, erosion rates, sea-level rise, and coastal water quality. This data aids in assessing vulnerability and informing management decisions.

b. Hazard Mapping and Modelling: Conducting hazard mapping and modelling exercises to identify high-risk areas, understand the extent of potential hazards, and evaluate the impact on coastal communities and ecosystems.

c. Socio-Economic Assessments: Conducting socio-economic assessments to understand the vulnerabilities and needs of coastal communities, including their capacity to cope with hazards and adapt to changing conditions.

d. Climate Change Impact Studies: Studying the specific impacts of climate change on coastal areas, including projections of sea-level rise, changes in storm intensity, and the potential influence on coastal hazards.

International Cooperation and Knowledge Exchange:

Promoting international cooperation and knowledge exchange is essential for addressing the hazard and vulnerability profile of coastal areas. This includes sharing best practices, experiences, and lessons learned from coastal management initiatives in other countries facing similar challenges.

By adopting a multi-dimensional approach that integrates scientific knowledge, community participation, and effective governance, the hazard and vulnerability profile of coastal areas in India can be effectively managed. This will enhance resilience, reduce the impacts of hazards, and promote sustainable development in these regions.

4.4 Ecological Fragility in Manmade Disasters

Ecological fragility refers to the vulnerability and sensitivity of ecosystems to disturbances and disruptions caused by human activities or manmade disasters. In the context of manmade disasters in India, ecological fragility highlights the susceptibility of ecosystems to degradation, pollution, habitat loss, and other adverse impacts resulting from human actions. Ecological fragility in the context of manmade disasters in India is discussed here:

Fragile Ecosystems in India: India is home to diverse ecosystems, including forests, wetlands, grasslands, coastal areas, and mountains, each with its unique ecological characteristics and biodiversity. However, many of these ecosystems are inherently fragile and susceptible to disturbances due to their complex ecological interactions and limited resilience.

Impact of Manmade Disasters on Ecosystems: Manmade disasters, such as industrial pollution, chemical spills, deforestation, urbanization, and improper waste management, can have severe consequences for ecosystems and their functioning. These disasters can disrupt ecological balance, degrade habitats, contaminate water bodies, and lead to the loss of biodiversity. The ecological fragility of ecosystems exacerbates their vulnerability to such disasters.

Causes and Characteristics of Ecological Fragility:

a. Habitat Destruction: Human activities, such as deforestation, urbanization, and infrastructure development, result in the destruction and fragmentation of natural habitats. This disrupts ecological processes, reduces biodiversity, and weakens ecosystem resilience.

b. Pollution and Contamination: Industries, improper waste disposal, chemical spills, and excessive use of agrochemicals contribute to pollution and contamination of air, water bodies, and soil. Ecological fragility increases the susceptibility of ecosystems to the harmful effects of pollutants, affecting the health of plants, animals, and microorganisms.

c. Invasive Species: Introduction of invasive alien species, either intentionally or unintentionally, disrupts native ecosystems by outcompeting native species for resources, altering habitats, and reducing biodiversity.

d. Overexploitation of Resources: Unsustainable practices such as overfishing, illegal wildlife trade, and excessive extraction of natural resources deplete ecosystem resources, leading to imbalances and ecological fragility.

e. Climate Change: The impacts of climate change, including rising temperatures, altered rainfall patterns, and sea-level rise, exacerbate ecological fragility by disrupting ecosystems' ability to adapt and affecting the distribution and abundance of species.

Impacts of Ecological Fragility:

a. Biodiversity Loss: Ecological fragility contributes to the loss of biodiversity as ecosystems experience habitat degradation, fragmentation, and species decline or extinction.

b. Ecosystem Services Decline: Fragile ecosystems struggle to provide essential ecosystem services such as water purification, climate regulation, pollination, and soil fertility. This has adverse consequences for human well-being and livelihoods.

c. Disruption of Ecological Processes: Ecological fragility disrupts vital ecological processes, including nutrient cycling, seed dispersal, and predation, which are essential for the functioning and resilience of ecosystems.

d. Increased Vulnerability to Disasters: Fragile ecosystems are less resilient to manmade disasters, such as chemical spills or industrial accidents. They struggle to recover and restore their ecological balance, exacerbating the impacts and prolonging the recovery period.

Mitigation and Restoration Strategies:

a. Sustainable Resource Management: Implementing sustainable practices in resource extraction, agriculture, fisheries, and forestry to minimize ecological degradation and promote the long-term health and resilience of ecosystems.

b. Pollution Control and Remediation: Implementing strict pollution control measures, promoting cleaner technologies, and developing effective mechanisms for pollution monitoring, enforcement, and remediation.

c. Habitat Restoration: Initiating efforts to restore degraded habitats, including reforestation, wetland conservation, and coral reef restoration, to enhance ecosystem functioning and biodiversity.

d. Conservation and Protected Areas: Expanding the network of protected areas, national parks, and wildlife sanctuaries to safeguard vulnerable ecosystems and species.

e. Education and Awareness: Increasing public awareness about ecological fragility, the importance of biodiversity conservation, and sustainable practices to foster a sense of responsibility towards ecosystem protection.

f. Policy and Regulatory Measures: Developing and enforcing stringent environmental regulations, sustainable land-use policies, and laws that promote ecosystem conservation and restoration.

g. Research and Monitoring: Conducting research and monitoring programs to understand ecological fragility, assess the impacts of manmade disasters, and develop evidence-based strategies for mitigation and restoration.

Addressing ecological fragility in the context of manmade disasters in India requires a multi-faceted approach that combines scientific knowledge, community engagement, and effective governance. By promoting sustainable practices, conserving ecosystems, and integrating ecological considerations into development plans, the country can work towards minimizing the impacts of manmade disasters on fragile ecosystems and fostering long-term ecological resilience.

Major Ecological Fragility Prone Regions in India:

Ecological fragility and the vulnerability of ecosystems to manmade disasters can vary across different regions of India. Some of the major prone regions include:

a. Industrial and Urban Centers: Industrial and urban centers with high population densities and intensive industrial activities are particularly prone to environmental pollution and degradation. Regions with a concentration of industries, such as the industrial belts in Gujarat, Maharashtra, Tamil Nadu, and West Bengal, face significant ecological fragility.

b. River Basins and Water Bodies: River basins and water bodies, such as the Ganges-Brahmaputra-Meghna delta, the Yamuna River basin, and the lakes in urban areas, are susceptible to pollution from industrial effluents, sewage discharge, and solid waste dumping, leading to ecological fragility.

c. Coastal Areas: Coastal areas, including the mangrove ecosystems along the Bay of Bengal and the Arabian Sea, face threats from industrial pollution, coastal development, and unsustainable fishing practices, which contribute to ecological fragility.

d. Forested Regions: Forested regions, such as the Western Ghats, Eastern Ghats, and the Himalayan foothills, are prone to ecological fragility due to deforestation, illegal logging, encroachment, and habitat destruction.

Management and Preparedness to Address Ecological Fragility in India:

To address ecological fragility and mitigate the impacts of manmade disasters, various management and preparedness strategies are employed in India:

a. Environmental Impact Assessment (EIA): Conducting thorough EIA studies for proposed industrial projects, infrastructure development, and urban expansion to assess potential environmental impacts and ensure necessary mitigation measures are in place.

b. Pollution Control Measures: Implementing pollution control measures, such as the enforcement of emission standards, wastewater treatment regulations, and solid waste management practices, to minimize pollution levels and mitigate the impacts on ecosystems.

c. Waste Management: Developing robust waste management systems that include proper waste segregation, recycling, and disposal mechanisms to prevent environmental contamination and promote resource conservation.

d. Conservation Initiatives: Promoting conservation initiatives and programs to protect ecologically sensitive areas, biodiversity hotspots, and endangered species through the establishment of protected areas, wildlife reserves, and conservation projects.

e. Sustainable Agriculture and Forestry: Encouraging sustainable agricultural practices, such as organic farming and agroforestry, to reduce the use of chemical inputs and minimize soil erosion. Implementing sustainable forestry practices, including afforestation, reforestation, and community-based forest management, to prevent deforestation and habitat loss.

f. Public Awareness and Education: Conducting awareness campaigns and educational programs to enhance public understanding of the importance of ecological conservation, sustainable practices, and the impacts of manmade disasters on ecosystems.

g. Collaboration and Partnerships: Facilitating collaboration among government agencies, non-governmental organizations, local communities, and other stakeholders to jointly address ecological fragility, share knowledge, and coordinate efforts in disaster management and environmental conservation.

h. Research and Innovation: Supporting research and innovation in environmental sciences, sustainable technologies, and ecosystem management to develop effective solutions and strategies for mitigating ecological fragility.

Policy and Legal Framework to address Ecological Fragility:

India has a policy and legal framework in place to address ecological fragility and promote sustainable development. The key legislations and policies include:

a. Environment Protection Act, 1986: Provides the legal framework for environmental protection and conservation, including the regulation of pollution and the prevention and control of environmental hazards.

b. Forest Conservation Act, 1980: Regulates the diversion of forestland for non-forest purposes and promotes sustainable forest management practices.

c. Coastal Regulation Zone (CRZ) Notification, 2011: Sets guidelines for coastal development activities, preventing encroachment and ensuring the protection of fragile coastal ecosystems.

d. National Green Tribunal (NGT) Act, 2010: Establishes the NGT as a specialized forum for adjudicating environmental disputes and ensuring the effective enforcement of environmental laws.

e. National Environment Policy, 2006: Provides a framework for sustainable development, biodiversity conservation, and pollution control, with an emphasis on integrating environmental concerns into various sectors.

Ecological Fragility – Future Outlook:

The management of ecological fragility in the context of manmade disasters in India requires a continued focus on:

a. Strengthening Policy Implementation: Ensuring effective implementation and enforcement of existing environmental policies and regulations, along with periodic revisions to address emerging challenges.

b. Integrated Planning and Sustainable Development: Integrating environmental considerations into development planning at all levels to balance economic growth with ecological sustainability.

c. Technological Innovations: Promoting research and innovation in eco-friendly technologies, waste management, pollution control, and sustainable practices to minimize environmental impacts.

d. Stakeholder Engagement: Enhancing collaboration and partnership among government agencies, local communities, NGOs, and industry stakeholders to foster a participatory approach in environmental management and disaster preparedness.

e. Climate Change Adaptation: Incorporating climate change adaptation measures into environmental planning and disaster management to enhance ecosystem resilience and reduce vulnerability to climate-related impacts.

By adopting a comprehensive and holistic approach that combines regulatory frameworks, community participation, scientific research, and sustainable practices, India can effectively address ecological fragility, mitigate the impacts of manmade disasters, and promote a more environmentally sustainable future.

Ecological Fragility and Sustainable Development:

Ecological fragility highlights the need for sustainable development practices that prioritize the protection and conservation of ecosystems. By recognizing the interconnectedness of ecological health, human well-being, and economic growth, sustainable development aims to strike a balance between meeting present needs and preserving resources for future generations.

Promoting Ecosystem Resilience:

Enhancing ecosystem resilience is a crucial aspect of mitigating ecological fragility. This involves:

a. Ecosystem Restoration: Implementing measures to restore degraded ecosystems, such as reforestation, wetland rehabilitation, and coral reef restoration, to rebuild their ecological functions and enhance their ability to withstand disturbances.

b. Conservation of Biodiversity: Protecting and conserving biodiversity through the establishment of protected areas, wildlife corridors, and conservation programs. Preserving species diversity is essential for maintaining ecosystem resilience and ensuring the provision of ecosystem services.

c. Sustainable Land Use Practices: Promoting sustainable land use practices, including land zoning, agroforestry, and sustainable agriculture, to minimize habitat loss, soil erosion, and the use of harmful chemicals.

d. Water Resource Management: Implementing integrated water resource management strategies that focus on sustainable water use, watershed conservation, and protection of water bodies to ensure the availability of clean water for both ecosystems and human populations.

e. Green Infrastructure: Incorporating green infrastructure, such as green spaces, urban forests, and vegetative buffers, into urban planning and development projects to enhance ecosystem services, mitigate pollution, and reduce the impacts of manmade disasters.

Ecological Fragility – Challenges and Way Forward:

Despite efforts to address ecological fragility, several challenges persist:

a. Policy Implementation Gaps: Ensuring effective implementation of environmental policies and regulations at all levels of governance remains a challenge. Strengthening enforcement mechanisms and improving compliance are essential.

b. Public Participation: Enhancing public awareness and engagement in environmental issues is crucial. Encouraging public participation, especially among local communities, helps foster a sense of ownership and responsibility towards ecosystem conservation.

c. Coordination and Collaboration: Enhancing coordination among different government departments, agencies, and stakeholders is necessary to ensure integrated planning, effective management, and disaster preparedness.

d. Capacity Building: Building the capacity of government institutions, NGOs, and local communities in environmental management, disaster risk reduction, and sustainable practices is vital for long-term success.

e. Research and Innovation: Continued research and innovation in environmental sciences, sustainable technologies, and ecosystem management are essential for developing effective solutions and strategies to address ecological fragility.

To move forward, it is crucial to strengthen policies, promote sustainable practices, engage stakeholders, and invest in research and capacity-building initiatives. By adopting a holistic approach that integrates environmental considerations into decision-making processes, India can effectively address ecological fragility, mitigate the impacts of manmade disasters, and foster a sustainable future for both ecosystems and human populations.

Disaster Impacts

5.1 Disaster Impact

Disaster impact refers to the consequences or effects of a disaster on various aspects of society, the environment, and the economy. It encompasses the immediate and long-term effects of a disaster event and can have significant implications for individuals, communities, and nations.

Types of Impact:

Disaster impact can be categorized into several dimensions:

a. Physical Impact: This includes the direct physical damage caused by the disaster, such as the destruction of infrastructure, buildings, roads, and other physical assets. Physical impact also involves changes in the landscape, erosion, or alteration of natural features.

b. Economic Impact: The economic impact refers to the consequences of a disaster on the economy. This includes direct losses incurred due to damage to infrastructure, businesses, agriculture, and industries, as well as indirect losses resulting from disrupted supply chains, reduced economic activities, and the cost of recovery and reconstruction.

c. Social Impact: Social impact refers to the effects of a disaster on human well-being, communities, and social systems. It includes casualties, injuries, displacement of people, psychological trauma, social disruption, and changes in social structures and community dynamics.

d. Environmental Impact: The environmental impact refers to the effects of a disaster on the natural environment. This includes damage to ecosystems, loss of biodiversity, contamination of water bodies, soil erosion, and degradation of natural resources.

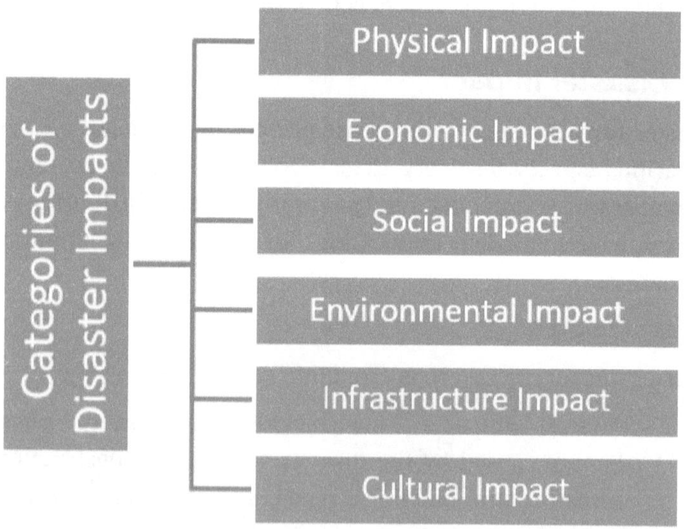

Figure 5.1 Categories of Disaster Impact

e. Infrastructure Impact: Infrastructure impact encompasses the consequences of a disaster on critical infrastructure, such as transportation networks, power grids, water supply systems, communication systems, and healthcare facilities. Damage to infrastructure can hamper relief and recovery efforts and impact the functioning of society.

f. Cultural Impact: Cultural impact refers to the effects of a disaster on cultural heritage, historical sites, traditions, and cultural practices. Disasters can lead to the loss or damage of cultural assets, disrupt cultural events, and impact the identity and social cohesion of communities.

Immediate and Long-Term Impact:

Disaster impact can be categorized into immediate and long-term effects:

a. Immediate Impact: The immediate impact refers to the initial consequences of a disaster. These include casualties, injuries, displacement of people, damage to infrastructure, disruption of services, and the immediate response efforts. Immediate impact is typically observed in the immediate aftermath of a disaster.

b. Long-Term Impact: The long-term impact refers to the enduring effects of a disaster that persist beyond the initial response phase. This includes the long-term economic, social, environmental, and infrastructure consequences that can shape the trajectory of affected communities and regions for years to come. Long-term impacts may include long-term displacement, changes in livelihood patterns, altered social dynamics, economic recovery, and the rebuilding of infrastructure.

Factors Affecting Impact Severity:

Several factors influence the severity of disaster impact:

a. Magnitude and Intensity: The magnitude and intensity of a disaster event, such as the strength of an earthquake or the size of a flood, can significantly influence the severity of impact. Greater magnitude and intensity generally lead to more severe consequences.

b. Vulnerability and Resilience: The vulnerability of the affected population and the resilience of communities and systems play a critical role in determining the impact severity. Higher vulnerability and lower resilience can amplify the impact, while lower vulnerability and higher resilience can help mitigate the consequences.

c. Population Density: The density of the population in the affected area can influence the impact severity. Higher population density often leads to a greater number of casualties, displacement, and challenges in providing relief and recovery services.

d. Preparedness and Response Capacity: The level of preparedness and response capacity of the affected region and the effectiveness of disaster management systems can impact the severity of the consequences. Adequate preparedness and timely response can help mitigate the impact.

e. Socioeconomic Conditions: The socioeconomic conditions of the affected area, such as poverty levels, access to healthcare, education, and resources, can influence the resilience of communities and their ability to recover from the disaster.

Mitigation and Preparedness to Reduce Impact:

Mitigation and preparedness measures aim to reduce the impact of disasters. These include:

a. Risk Reduction Measures: Implementing measures to reduce the vulnerability and exposure of communities and infrastructure to hazards. This can involve land-use planning, building codes, early warning systems, and infrastructure resilience measures.

b. Preparedness Planning: Developing emergency response plans, conducting drills and exercises, and enhancing the capacity of emergency services and community-based organizations to effectively respond to disasters.

c. Public Awareness and Education: Promoting public awareness and education on disaster risks, preparedness measures, and the importance of early warning systems. This helps individuals and communities make informed decisions and take appropriate actions during a disaster event.

d. Infrastructure Resilience: Designing and constructing infrastructure with resilience in mind, considering the potential hazards and their impact. This includes building resilient housing, critical infrastructure, and lifeline systems.

e. Community Engagement: Engaging communities in disaster risk reduction initiatives, encouraging community participation, and involving local knowledge and practices in preparedness and response efforts.

5.2 Disaster Impact Assessment:

Conducting impact assessments is crucial for understanding the extent and nature of disaster impact. Impact assessments involve evaluating the physical, economic, social, and environmental consequences of a disaster, identifying affected populations, and assessing the needs for relief, recovery, and reconstruction.

Impact assessments provide essential information for decision-making, resource allocation, and the formulation of strategies and policies to address the short-term and long-term effects of a disaster.

Thus, disaster impact encompasses the wide-ranging consequences of a disaster event on various aspects of society, the environment, and the economy. Understanding the different dimensions of impact is crucial for effective disaster management, including mitigation, preparedness, response, and recovery efforts. By reducing vulnerability, enhancing resilience, and implementing appropriate measures, the severity and duration of disaster impact can be minimized, leading to more resilient and sustainable communities.

Disaster Impact on Human Lives and Health:

Disasters can have significant impacts on human lives and health. These include:

a. Casualties and Injuries: Disasters can result in the loss of human lives and cause injuries to individuals. The severity of casualties and injuries depends on the type and magnitude of the disaster, the population density in the affected area, and the vulnerability of the affected population.

b. Physical and Mental Health Effects: Disasters can lead to physical health issues such as injuries, waterborne diseases, respiratory problems due to air pollution, and exposure to hazardous materials. They can also have psychological impacts, including post-traumatic stress disorder (PTSD), anxiety, depression, and grief.

c. Displacement and Homelessness: Disasters can force people to leave their homes and become internally displaced or homeless. Displacement can disrupt livelihoods, social networks, and access to essential services, creating challenges for the affected population.

d. Public Health Risks: Disasters can lead to increased public health risks, including the spread of infectious diseases, inadequate access to healthcare facilities, and limited availability of clean water, sanitation, and hygiene facilities.

Impact on Infrastructure and Essential Services:

Disasters can cause significant damage to infrastructure and disrupt essential services. This includes:

a. Damage to Buildings and Structures: Disasters such as earthquakes, cyclones, and floods can cause extensive damage to buildings, bridges, roads, and other infrastructure, rendering them unsafe or unusable.

b. Disruption of Lifeline Services: Lifeline services, including electricity, water supply, communication networks, transportation, and healthcare facilities, can be severely affected during and after a disaster. This can hamper rescue and relief efforts and make it challenging for affected communities to access essential services.

c. Economic Losses: The damage to infrastructure and disruption of economic activities can lead to significant economic losses. Businesses may suffer financial losses, and communities may experience reduced income, unemployment, and decreased economic growth.

d. Impact on Utilities: Disasters can disrupt utility services, such as power grids, water treatment plants, and sewage systems, leading to interruptions in electricity supply, water scarcity, and sanitation issues.

Social and Community Impact:

Disasters can have social and community-level impacts, including:

a. Social Disruption: Disasters can disrupt social structures and community cohesion. Displacement, loss of homes, separation of families, and changes in community dynamics can affect social relationships and support systems.

b. Disruption of Education: Disasters can interrupt educational activities, damage school infrastructure, and result in the temporary or long-term closure of schools. This can impact children's access to education and hinder their long-term development.

c. Economic Disparity: Disasters can exacerbate existing economic disparities and inequalities. Vulnerable populations, such as the poor, marginalized communities, and informal workers, are often disproportionately affected and may face more significant challenges in recovering from the disaster's impact.

d. Community Resilience: Despite the challenges, disasters can also foster community resilience and solidarity. Communities may come together to support each other, mobilize resources, and engage in collective efforts for recovery and rebuilding.

Environmental Impact:

Disasters can have adverse effects on the environment, including:

a. Habitat Destruction and Biodiversity Loss: Disasters can lead to the destruction and degradation of natural habitats, causing the loss of biodiversity and disruption of ecological balance. This can have long-term implications for ecosystems and the services they provide.

b. Water and Soil Contamination: Disasters such as chemical spills, industrial accidents, or oil spills can contaminate water bodies and soil, affecting aquatic life, agriculture, and the overall ecosystem health.

c. Deforestation and Land Degradation: Disasters, such as wildfires or unsustainable logging practices, can contribute to deforestation and land degradation, leading to the loss of forest cover, soil erosion, and increased vulnerability to future disasters.

d. Climate Change Feedback: Disasters, particularly those related to extreme weather events, can be influenced by climate change. The impacts of disasters contribute to the feedback loop of climate change, further exacerbating the frequency and intensity of future disasters.

Challenges in Assessing and Managing Impact:

Assessing and managing the impact of disasters poses several challenges:

a. Data Availability and Quality: Obtaining accurate and timely data on the extent and nature of the impact can be challenging, especially in resource-constrained settings. Lack of comprehensive data can hinder effective planning and decision-making.

b. Interconnectedness of Impacts: Disasters often result in multi-dimensional impacts that are interconnected and can affect various sectors simultaneously. Understanding and addressing these interconnected impacts require a comprehensive and interdisciplinary approach.

c. Recovery and Reconstruction: The process of recovery and reconstruction following a disaster is complex and requires careful planning, resource mobilization, and coordination among various stakeholders. Rebuilding infrastructure, restoring essential services, and supporting affected communities pose significant challenges.

d. Long-Term Effects: Disasters can have long-term effects on communities and regions, including socio-economic, health, and environmental consequences. Addressing these long-term effects requires sustained efforts and a focus on sustainable development.

Impact Mitigation and Preparedness:

Mitigating the impact of disasters and enhancing preparedness can help reduce the severity of the consequences. This includes:

a. Risk Assessment and Mapping: Conducting risk assessments to identify hazards, vulnerabilities, and exposure patterns, and developing hazard maps to inform land-use planning and disaster management strategies.

b. Early Warning Systems: Establishing robust early warning systems to provide timely and accurate information about impending disasters, allowing communities to take appropriate actions and evacuate if necessary.

c. Community Education and Capacity Building: Enhancing public awareness and understanding of disaster risks, promoting knowledge and skills for preparedness and response, and building the capacity of individuals and communities to effectively cope with disasters.

d. Infrastructure Resilience: Designing and constructing infrastructure with resilience in mind, considering the potential hazards and their impact. This includes incorporating measures such as flood-resistant building techniques, reinforced structures, and protective infrastructure.

e. Emergency Response Planning: Developing and implementing comprehensive emergency response plans, including coordination mechanisms, resource mobilization strategies, and protocols for rapid response and relief distribution.

f. Post-Disaster Recovery and Rehabilitation: Implementing effective post-disaster recovery and rehabilitation strategies, which focus on building back better, restoring essential services, and supporting the social and economic recovery of affected communities.

In conclusion, understanding the various dimensions of disaster impact is crucial for effective disaster management. By implementing mitigation measures, enhancing preparedness, and adopting a multi-sectoral approach, the severity of the impact can be minimized, and communities can become more resilient in the face of disasters.

5.3 Environmental Impact of Disasters

The environmental impact of disasters refers to the effects that natural or man-made disasters have on the natural environment. Disasters can cause significant damage to ecosystems, biodiversity, land, water, air, and other environmental components.

Habitat Destruction and Biodiversity Loss: Disasters can lead to the destruction and degradation of natural habitats, resulting in the loss of biodiversity. Fires, floods, hurricanes, and other catastrophic events can directly destroy habitats, including forests, wetlands, coral reefs, and grasslands. This loss of habitat can have far-reaching ecological consequences, including the displacement or extinction of plant and animal species.

Soil Erosion and Land Degradation: Disasters such as floods, landslides, and windstorms can cause soil erosion and land degradation. The force of water, wind, or the displacement of landmasses can strip away topsoil, leading to decreased soil fertility, reduced agricultural productivity, and increased vulnerability to future erosion events. Soil erosion can also contribute to sedimentation in rivers, lakes, and coastal areas, negatively impacting aquatic ecosystems.

Water Contamination: Disasters can result in water contamination, posing risks to both human health and the environment. Chemical spills, industrial accidents, and flooding can introduce pollutants into water bodies, leading to water pollution. Contaminated water can harm aquatic life, disrupt ecosystems, and contaminate drinking water sources, creating public health concerns.

Air Pollution: Certain disasters, such as wildfires or industrial accidents, can generate significant air pollution. These events release harmful pollutants into the atmosphere, including particulate matter, smoke, ash, and toxic gases. Air pollution can have adverse effects on human health, vegetation, and the overall air quality of an area, leading to respiratory issues, damage to crops, and ecological imbalances.

Damage to Ecosystem Services: Ecosystem services are the benefits that humans derive from the natural environment, including the provision of clean water, regulation of climate, pollination, and nutrient cycling. Disasters can disrupt or damage these services, impacting human well-being and the functioning of ecosystems. For example, the destruction of forests can lead to decreased water regulation, soil erosion, and reduced carbon sequestration capacity.

Impact on Wildlife and Biodiversity: Disasters can have severe consequences for wildlife and biodiversity. They can directly cause injury, displacement, or death of animal populations. Habitat destruction and fragmentation can result in the loss of critical habitats and disrupt migration patterns. Disasters can also disrupt breeding cycles, affect food availability, and introduce invasive species, leading to shifts in ecosystems and declines in biodiversity.

Contamination and Spills: Man-made disasters such as oil spills, chemical leaks, or nuclear accidents can have severe environmental consequences. Oil spills can result in the contamination of marine and coastal ecosystems, leading to the death of marine life, damage to coral reefs, and long-term ecological impacts. Chemical spills can have similar effects, causing water and soil contamination and posing risks to human and ecosystem health.

Long-Term Environmental Changes: Some disasters, particularly those related to climate change, can lead to long-term environmental changes. For instance, rising temperatures, changes in precipitation patterns, and sea-level rise can result in shifts in ecosystems, altered habitats, and the loss of vulnerable coastal areas. These changes can have cascading effects on biodiversity, water resources, and overall ecosystem functioning.

Ecological Resilience: The environmental impact of disasters highlights the importance of ecological resilience. Resilient ecosystems have the ability to absorb and recover from disturbances, minimizing long-term environmental damage. Protecting and restoring ecosystems, implementing conservation measures, and promoting sustainable land and resource management practices can enhance ecological resilience and reduce the environmental impact of disasters.

Environment Impact Mitigation and Preparedness:

Mitigating the environmental impact of disasters involves various strategies:

a. Sustainable Development Practices: Adopting sustainable development practices that balance economic growth with environmental conservation can reduce the vulnerability of ecosystems to disasters.

b. Land-Use Planning: Implementing effective land-use planning strategies, including zoning regulations and hazard mapping, to minimize development in high-risk areas and protect sensitive ecosystems.

c. Environmental Impact Assessments: Conducting comprehensive environmental impact assessments for development projects to identify potential environmental risks and implement appropriate mitigation measures.

d. Environmental Management Systems: Developing and implementing environmental management systems that ensure compliance with environmental regulations, promote pollution prevention, and enhance environmental stewardship.

e. Conservation and Restoration: Prioritizing the conservation and restoration of ecosystems and biodiversity to enhance their resilience and reduce vulnerability to disasters.

f. Emergency Response Planning: Integrating environmental considerations into emergency response plans, including strategies for environmental cleanup, waste management, and restoration of affected areas.

g. Public Awareness and Education: Raising public awareness about the environmental impact of disasters and the importance of sustainable practices. Promoting environmental education and engagement to encourage responsible behaviour and informed decision-making.

Thus, the environmental impact of disasters encompasses the damage and disruption caused to the natural environment by catastrophic events. Mitigating the environmental impact requires a combination of sustainable development practices, effective land-use planning, conservation efforts, and environmental management strategies. By prioritizing environmental considerations in disaster management, we can reduce the negative consequences on ecosystems, biodiversity, and the overall well-being of the planet.

Government Agencies for Assessing Environment Impact

a. Ministry of Environment, Forest and Climate Change (MoEFCC): MoEFCC is responsible for formulating and implementing policies and programs for environmental protection and conservation. The ministry collects data on various environmental indicators, including those related to disasters.

b. National Disaster Management Authority (NDMA): NDMA is responsible for disaster management in India. It collects and analyses data on the impacts of disasters, including environmental consequences, and coordinates response and recovery efforts.

c. Central Pollution Control Board (CPCB): CPCB monitors and assesses environmental pollution levels across the country. It provides data on air quality, water pollution, and other environmental parameters that may be influenced by disasters.

Research Institutions and Academic Studies for Environment Impact Assessment:

Various research institutions and academic studies contribute to data collection and statistical analysis of the environmental impact of disasters in India. These institutions conduct research, surveys, and assessments to understand the extent of environmental damage caused by disasters. They often collaborate with government agencies, NGOs, and international organizations to gather data and conduct studies.

National and State-Level Disaster Management Plans: National and state-level disaster management plans often include data and statistical information on the environmental impact of disasters. These plans provide guidelines and strategies for disaster management and incorporate data on the environmental consequences of different types of disasters.

Environmental Impact Assessments (EIAs): Environmental Impact Assessments are conducted for various development projects in India. These assessments evaluate the potential environmental impacts of a project, including its vulnerability to natural disasters. EIAs often include data on the environmental baseline, potential risks, and proposed mitigation measures.

Disaster-Specific Reports: Government agencies, research institutions, and NGOs publish reports on specific disasters and their environmental impacts. These reports provide detailed information on the extent of environmental damage, the loss of biodiversity, the contamination of water bodies, and other relevant parameters.

Data Analysis and Statistical Tools: Data collected on the environmental impact of disasters is often subjected to statistical analysis to identify trends, patterns, and correlations. Statistical tools and software are used to analyse and interpret the data, enabling researchers and policymakers to make informed decisions.

Challenges in Data Collection and Analysis:

While efforts are made to collect and analyse data on the environmental impact of disasters in India, several challenges exist:

a. Data Availability: Data collection on environmental impact can be challenging due to limited resources, lack of standardized methodologies, and the vast geographic expanse of the country. Data availability may vary across regions and types of disasters.

b. Data Consistency and Quality: Ensuring consistency and quality of data across different sources and time periods is important for meaningful analysis. Data collection processes and methodologies need to be standardized and regularly updated to maintain data quality.

c. Integration of Data: Integrating data from various sources, including government agencies, research institutions, and NGOs, can be complex. Developing data sharing mechanisms and platforms can enhance collaboration and integration of data for better analysis.

d. Access to Remote and Vulnerable Areas: Collecting data from remote and vulnerable areas, especially in the aftermath of a disaster, can be challenging due to logistical constraints and accessibility issues. Efforts are required to ensure data collection in such areas.

e. Long-Term Monitoring: Long-term monitoring and data collection are essential to understand the ongoing environmental impacts and track changes over time. Establishing robust monitoring systems can provide valuable insights into the long-term consequences of disasters.

5.4 Physical Impact of Disasters

The physical impact of disasters refers to the direct physical damage caused by a disaster event. It encompasses the destruction or alteration of infrastructure, buildings, natural features, and the physical environment.

Infrastructure Damage: Disasters can cause significant damage to infrastructure, including buildings, roads, bridges, power lines, water and sanitation systems, and communication networks. The severity of infrastructure damage depends on the type and magnitude of the disaster. For example:

a. Earthquakes can result in the collapse of buildings and infrastructure due to ground shaking, leading to casualties and destruction.

b. Cyclones and hurricanes can cause severe damage to buildings, roofs, and infrastructure due to high-speed winds and storm surge.

c. Floods can damage roads, bridges, and other transportation infrastructure, disrupt water and sanitation systems, and impact electrical networks.

d. Wildfires can destroy vegetation, damage power lines, and pose risks to infrastructure in affected areas.

Destruction of Buildings and Structures: Disasters can cause the destruction or severe damage of buildings and structures. This can include residential houses, commercial buildings, hospitals, schools, and other critical infrastructure. The collapse or partial collapse of structures can lead to casualties and injuries.

Landscape Changes and Alterations: Disasters can result in significant changes to the landscape and natural features. This can include:

a. Erosion: Floods, landslides, and windstorms can cause soil erosion, leading to the loss of topsoil and changes in land topography. Erosion can impact agricultural lands, contribute to sedimentation in water bodies, and lead to long-term environmental degradation.

b. Land Subsidence: Some disasters, such as earthquakes or mining-related activities, can cause land subsidence, where the ground sinks or settles. Land subsidence can damage infrastructure, disrupt drainage systems, and impact the stability of buildings and structures.

c. Changes in Water Bodies: Disasters like floods or tsunamis can alter the course of rivers, change the shape of coastlines, and cause sedimentation or deposition of debris in water bodies. These changes can affect aquatic ecosystems, navigation routes, and water supply systems.

Loss of Natural Features: Disasters can result in the loss or alteration of natural features, including forests, wetlands, coral reefs, and other ecosystems. These natural features provide essential services such as habitat for biodiversity, water regulation, and carbon sequestration. The destruction of natural features can have long-term ecological consequences.

Impact on Critical Facilities: Disasters can impact critical facilities that provide essential services to communities. This includes:

a. Healthcare Facilities: Hospitals and medical centers can be damaged or rendered inoperable during a disaster, limiting access to medical care for affected populations.

b. Educational Institutions: Schools and educational facilities can suffer damage, disrupting educational activities and impacting the learning environment for students.

c. Emergency Services: Fire stations, police stations, and other emergency response facilities can be affected by disasters, reducing their capacity to provide immediate assistance.

d. Power and Water Supply: Disasters can disrupt power generation and distribution systems, causing power outages. They can also damage water supply infrastructure, leading to water scarcity or contamination.

Environmental Contamination: Some disasters, particularly man-made ones, can result in environmental contamination. This can include:

a. Chemical Spills: Industrial accidents or transportation incidents can lead to chemical spills, contaminating soil, water bodies, and air. Chemical spills pose risks to human health, wildlife, and ecosystems.

b. Oil Spills: Accidental or intentional oil spills in marine or coastal areas can contaminate water, affect marine life, and damage ecosystems. Oil spills can have long-lasting ecological impacts.

c. Nuclear Accidents: Nuclear accidents can release radioactive materials, leading to contamination of the environment and posing risks to human health and the ecosystem.

Challenges in Assessing Physical Impact:

Assessing the physical impact of disasters poses several challenges:

a. Rapid Assessment: Conducting rapid assessments immediately after a disaster to determine the extent of physical damage can be challenging due to access constraints, safety concerns, and the need for comprehensive coverage.

b. Infrastructure Vulnerability: Assessing the vulnerability of infrastructure and buildings to disasters requires detailed knowledge of structural design, construction standards, and maintenance practices.

c. Data Availability: Obtaining accurate and comprehensive data on the physical impact of disasters can be difficult, especially in resource-constrained areas or during ongoing emergency response efforts.

d. Long-Term Monitoring: Monitoring the long-term physical impact, such as the stability of structures or landscape changes, requires sustained efforts over an extended period.

e. Cost Estimation: Estimating the cost of physical damage caused by disasters is complex and involves considering various factors, including the type of infrastructure, replacement or repair costs, and indirect economic losses.

Economic Losses: The physical impact of disasters often results in significant economic losses. The destruction of infrastructure, buildings, and productive assets can disrupt economic activities and lead to financial setbacks. Industries may experience disruptions in production, trade routes may be affected, and businesses may face challenges in resuming operations. These economic losses can have long-term implications for the affected region's development and growth.

Impacts on Critical Lifeline Services: Disasters can disrupt critical lifeline services, which are essential for the functioning of society. These services include electricity, water supply, transportation, communication networks, and healthcare facilities. The damage to infrastructure and systems supporting these services can result in prolonged power outages, water scarcity, disrupted transportation networks, limited communication, and compromised healthcare delivery. Restoring and maintaining these lifeline services is crucial for effective disaster response and recovery.

Social Disruption and Displacement: The physical impact of disasters often leads to social disruption and displacement of populations. Communities may be forced to evacuate their homes due to immediate threats or the destruction of their living environment. Displacement can disrupt social networks, separate families, and create challenges in accessing basic needs such as shelter, food, and healthcare. Displaced individuals may also face psychological and emotional challenges as they cope with the loss of their homes and familiar surroundings.

Challenges in Reconstruction and Recovery:

Rebuilding and recovering from the physical impact of disasters pose several challenges. These include:

a. Resource Constraints: The financial and material resources required for reconstruction can be substantial, especially in low-income regions. Securing funding and resources for rebuilding efforts can be a significant challenge.

b. Infrastructure Planning and Design: The reconstruction phase provides an opportunity to incorporate disaster-resilient infrastructure. However, planning and designing infrastructure that can withstand future disasters while considering environmental sustainability and community needs require careful consideration.

c. Time Constraints: Communities affected by disasters often face time constraints in rebuilding their lives. Balancing the need for quick recovery with long-term resilience and sustainable development can be a complex task.

d. Community Engagement and Participation: Involving affected communities in the decision-making process and ensuring their participation in the reconstruction efforts is vital. Community engagement promotes ownership, fosters resilience, and ensures that the reconstruction addresses the specific needs and priorities of the affected population.

e. Integrated Planning: Effective reconstruction and recovery require integrated planning, involving multiple sectors such as housing, infrastructure, environment, and social services. Coordination among various stakeholders, including government agencies, NGOs, and the private sector, is essential for successful post-disaster reconstruction.

Building Resilience:

Mitigating the physical impact of disasters and building resilience involves various strategies:

a. Risk Reduction Measures: Implementing measures to reduce vulnerability and enhance the resilience of infrastructure, such as incorporating hazard-resistant building codes, strengthening critical infrastructure, and implementing early warning systems.

b. Land-Use Planning: Adopting land-use planning strategies that consider the vulnerability of different areas to hazards and restrict development in high-risk zones.

c. Retrofitting and Upgrading: Retrofitting existing buildings and infrastructure to make them more resilient to disasters, incorporating measures such as seismic strengthening, flood-proofing, and wind-resistant design.

d. Nature-Based Solutions: Utilizing nature-based solutions, such as restoring natural ecosystems, constructing green infrastructure, and implementing sustainable land management practices to reduce the physical impact of disasters and enhance resilience.

e. Public Awareness and Education: Promoting public awareness and education on disaster risk reduction, including educating communities on preparedness, response, and the importance of resilient infrastructure.

f. International Cooperation: Collaborating with international organizations, sharing best practices, and learning from experiences of other countries in mitigating the physical impact of disasters.

Lifespan and Intensity of Physical Impact:

The physical impact of disasters can vary in terms of the lifespan and intensity of the event. Some disasters, such as earthquakes or hurricanes, can occur suddenly and have a relatively short duration but cause rapid and severe damage. Others, like floods or wildfires, can develop slowly or persist for an extended period, leading to prolonged physical impacts.

Infrastructure Disruptions: Disasters can disrupt critical infrastructure networks, including transportation, communication, and utilities. Roads and bridges may become impassable, communication systems may be damaged or overloaded, and water and power supply may be disrupted. These infrastructure disruptions can hinder emergency response efforts, delay recovery, and impact the functioning of communities.

Public and Private Property Damage: Disasters can result in significant damage to public and private properties. Homes, businesses, and public facilities may experience structural damage, collapse, or become uninhabitable. The physical impact on property can lead to financial losses for individuals, businesses, and governments, requiring extensive repair or reconstruction efforts.

Impacts on Natural Resources: Disasters can have adverse effects on natural resources, including forests, water bodies, and agricultural land. Forest fires can result in the destruction of vast forested areas, leading to ecological imbalances and loss of biodiversity. Floods can contaminate water sources, impacting aquatic ecosystems and disrupting water availability for various uses. Soil erosion caused by disasters can degrade agricultural land and reduce its productivity.

Disruption of Critical Services: The physical impact of disasters can disrupt critical services that are essential for daily life. These services include healthcare, education, transportation, and emergency response. Hospitals and medical facilities may be damaged, schools may be forced to close, transportation systems may be disrupted, and emergency services may face challenges in providing timely assistance. These disruptions can have severe implications for the affected population's well-being and safety.

Impact on Cultural Heritage: Disasters can also impact cultural heritage sites and structures. Historical buildings, monuments, archaeological sites, and cultural artifacts may suffer damage or destruction. This loss can have significant cultural, historical, and tourism-related implications for the affected region. Preserving and restoring cultural heritage is an important aspect of post-disaster recovery and resilience.

Secondary Hazards: In addition to the direct physical impact of the initial disaster event, secondary hazards can also pose risks. For example, aftershocks following an earthquake, landslides triggered by heavy rainfall, or disease outbreaks due to compromised sanitation and hygiene conditions can exacerbate the physical impact and further hinder recovery efforts.

Role of Structural and Non-Structural Measures: Mitigation and preparedness strategies involve both structural and non-structural measures to minimize the physical impact of disasters. Structural measures include building resilient infrastructure, such as reinforced buildings, flood control structures, and seawalls. Non-structural measures encompass early warning systems, emergency response planning, community preparedness, and public awareness campaigns.

Geographic Variations: The physical impact of disasters can vary based on geographic locations. Coastal areas may be more susceptible to the impact of hurricanes and storm surges, while mountainous regions may face risks such as landslides or avalanches. Understanding the specific vulnerabilities and physical risks associated with different geographical contexts is essential for effective disaster management and preparedness.

Physical Impact Data Collection and Sources:

Data on the physical impact of disasters in India is collected from various sources, including government agencies, research institutions, academic studies, and field surveys. These sources provide information on infrastructure damage, property loss, casualties, and other physical impacts. Some key data sources include:

a. National Disaster Management Authority (NDMA): NDMA collects data on disasters, including the physical impact, through its various divisions and departments. This data helps in analysing trends, patterns, and severity of disasters across different regions.

b. Central and State Government Agencies: Government agencies such as the Central Public Works Department (CPWD), State Disaster Management Authorities (SDMAs), and other departments involved in disaster management collect data on infrastructure damage, property loss, and casualties caused by disasters.

c. Academic Institutions and Research Organizations: Research institutions and academic studies contribute valuable data and statistical analysis on the physical impact of disasters. These studies often focus on specific disaster events or geographical regions and provide detailed insights into the extent of physical damage.

d. Field Surveys and Assessments: Field surveys conducted by government agencies, NGOs, and research organizations collect on-ground data related to infrastructure damage, property loss, and other physical impacts. These surveys provide real-time and localized information for immediate response and recovery efforts.

Data Analysis and Statistical Tools: Data collected on the physical impact of disasters in India is analysed using statistical tools and techniques to identify trends, patterns, and correlations. Statistical analysis helps in understanding the severity of disasters, their spatial distribution, and the impact on different sectors. It also facilitates the comparison of data across different time periods, regions, and disaster types.

National and State-Level Disaster Management Plans: National and state-level disaster management plans incorporate data and statistical information on the physical impact of disasters. These plans outline strategies and guidelines for response, recovery, and risk reduction efforts. Data on infrastructure damage, property loss, and casualties are used to identify high-risk areas, prioritize resource allocation, and formulate effective mitigation measures.

Cost Estimation and Economic Analysis: Data and statistical information are utilized to estimate the economic losses caused by the physical impact of disasters. Economic analysis helps in quantifying the direct and indirect costs of infrastructure damage, property loss, and disruptions to critical services. This information is essential for resource allocation, insurance claims, and planning for post-disaster recovery and reconstruction.

Long-Term Monitoring and Impact Assessment: Data and statistical information are used for long-term monitoring and impact assessment of the physical impact of disasters. It helps in evaluating the effectiveness of mitigation measures, monitoring changes in vulnerability, and assessing the progress made in building resilience. Long-term monitoring and impact assessment contribute to evidence-based decision-making and continuous improvement of disaster management strategies.

Physical Impact – Challenges in Data Collection and Analysis:

There are several challenges in data collection and analysis in the Indian context:

a. Data Availability and Accessibility: Availability and accessibility of data can vary across regions and disaster types. Some areas may have limited data coverage, especially in remote and vulnerable regions.

b. Data Standardization: Standardizing data collection methodologies and formats is essential to ensure consistency and comparability. Lack of standardized data collection practices can hinder data analysis and integration.

c. Data Quality and Reliability: Ensuring the quality and reliability of data is crucial for accurate analysis. Challenges such as underreporting, data gaps, and inconsistencies can impact the reliability of the data.

d. Integrating Data from Multiple Sources: Integrating data from various sources can be challenging due to differences in data formats, collection methodologies, and reporting systems. Harmonizing and integrating data from different sources is necessary for comprehensive analysis.

e. Capacity Building: Building the capacity of government agencies, research institutions, and data collection entities in data management and analysis is essential for improving the quality and usability of data.

Thus, data and statistical information play a vital role in understanding the physical impact of disasters in the Indian context. They assist in assessing infrastructure damage, property loss, casualties, and economic impacts. Data analysis and statistical tools aid in identifying trends, patterns, and vulnerabilities. However, challenges related to data availability, standardization, quality, and integration need to be addressed to improve data-driven decision-making and enhance disaster management strategies in India.

5.5 Social Impact of Disasters

The social impact of disasters refers to the consequences and effects that disasters have on individuals, communities, and society as a whole. It encompasses various aspects of human life, including physical and mental health, social cohesion, community dynamics, and cultural heritage.

Loss of Lives and Injuries: Disasters often result in the loss of lives and injuries, causing immense emotional and social distress. The sudden loss of family members, friends, or neighbours can have long-lasting impacts on the affected individuals and communities. Injuries may lead to disabilities or impairments, affecting the well-being and functioning of individuals.

Disruption of Social Structures: Disasters can disrupt social structures and community dynamics. Communities may face displacement, separation of families, and disruption of social networks. Social cohesion and community bonds may be strained as individuals and families cope with the aftermath of the disaster.

Psychological and Emotional Impact: Disasters can have profound psychological and emotional impacts on individuals. Survivors may experience trauma, post-traumatic stress disorder (PTSD), anxiety, depression, and other mental health issues. The fear, uncertainty, and loss experienced during and after a disaster can significantly affect the well-being and mental health of individuals and communities.

Displacement and Homelessness: Disasters often result in the displacement of individuals and families from their homes. People may be forced to seek temporary shelter in evacuation centers, camps, or with relatives and friends. The loss of homes and belongings can lead to homelessness and create challenges in finding suitable and safe housing.

Access to Basic Services: Disasters can disrupt access to basic services such as healthcare, education, water, sanitation, and food. Healthcare facilities may be damaged or overwhelmed, schools may be closed, and water and sanitation systems may be compromised. Access to clean water, nutritious food, and adequate healthcare becomes a challenge, particularly in the immediate aftermath of a disaster.

Vulnerable Populations: Disasters often exacerbate the vulnerabilities of certain populations, including children, elderly individuals, persons with disabilities, women, and marginalized communities. These groups may face additional challenges in accessing resources, receiving appropriate support, and recovering from the social impact of the disaster.

Social Inequalities and Marginalization: Disasters can expose and amplify existing social inequalities and marginalization within society. Vulnerable and marginalized communities may face disproportionate impacts and limited access to resources and support. Gender inequalities, caste-based discrimination, and socio-economic disparities can be heightened during and after a disaster.

Disruption of Education: Disasters disrupt educational systems, leading to the closure of schools, colleges, and universities. This interruption in education can have long-term effects on the learning and development of children and youth. The loss of education opportunities can hinder their future prospects and contribute to social and economic inequalities.

Cultural Heritage Loss: Disasters can result in the loss or damage to cultural heritage sites, monuments, artifacts, and intangible cultural practices. This loss has significant cultural, historical, and social implications, impacting a community's identity, sense of belonging, and tourism-related activities. Efforts to preserve and restore cultural heritage are crucial for post-disaster recovery and resilience.

Community Resilience and Social Capital: While disasters can have adverse social impacts, they can also foster community resilience and strengthen social capital. Communities come together to support and help each other during challenging times. Social networks, community organizations, and local leadership play a vital role in helping, organizing response efforts, and facilitating recovery and reconstruction.

Role of Social Support Systems: Social support systems, including family, friends, neighbours, and community organizations, are instrumental in providing emotional support, material assistance, and resources during and after a disaster. These support systems help individuals and communities cope with the social impact of disasters and facilitate recovery.

Challenges in Social Recovery: Addressing the social impact of disasters and facilitating social recovery pose several challenges:

a. Mental Health and Psychosocial Support: Ensuring access to mental health services, psychosocial support, and counselling is crucial for individuals and communities affected by disasters. Building capacity in mental health and psychosocial support services is essential for effective response and recovery.

b. Social Protection and Safety Nets: Establishing social protection mechanisms and safety nets is important to address the immediate and long-term needs of vulnerable populations. These mechanisms provide social and financial support to individuals and families affected by disasters.

c. Community Participation and Engagement: Engaging affected communities in decision-making processes, including planning, implementation, and evaluation of recovery programs, fosters ownership, empowerment, and resilience.

d. Gender and Social Inclusion: Ensuring gender equality and social inclusion in disaster management and recovery efforts is critical. Recognizing the specific needs and vulnerabilities of different groups, addressing gender disparities, and promoting inclusive practices are essential for equitable and effective social recovery.

e. Long-Term Social Resilience: Building long-term social resilience involves investing in community capacity building, social networks, and social cohesion. Strengthening local institutions, promoting community-based initiatives, and fostering social solidarity contribute to sustainable recovery and resilience.

Community Disruption and Social Dislocation: Disasters can lead to the disruption and dislocation of communities, causing changes in social structures and dynamics. Communities may be physically dispersed due to evacuation or relocation, resulting in the loss of a sense of community and a breakdown of social connections. Disasters can also lead to the displacement of communities from their traditional lands or neighbourhoods, impacting their cultural identity and social cohesion.

Social Vulnerability and Inequities: Disasters tend to highlight and exacerbate existing social vulnerabilities and inequities within society. Certain groups, such as the poor, marginalized communities, minorities, and those with limited access to resources and services, may be disproportionately affected by the social impact of disasters. Socio-economic disparities can deepen, and marginalized groups may face additional challenges in accessing relief, resources, and support.

Social Disruption in Daily Life: Disasters disrupt the normal routines and activities of daily life, leading to social disarray. Schools and workplaces may be closed, transportation systems may be disrupted, and access to essential services may be limited. These disruptions can have a ripple effect on social interactions, relationships, and the overall functioning of society.

Social Cohesion and Solidarity: While disasters can disrupt social structures, they can also foster a sense of social cohesion and solidarity. In times of crisis, communities often come together to support and help one another. Acts of kindness, mutual aid, and community resilience are witnessed as people rally together to overcome the challenges posed by the disaster. This social cohesion can contribute to the recovery and rebuilding process.

Disruption of Social Services: Disasters can disrupt the delivery of social services, such as healthcare, education, and social welfare programs. Healthcare facilities may be damaged or overwhelmed, educational institutions may be temporarily closed, and social support programs may face challenges in meeting the increased demand. The disruption of these services can have long-term implications for the well-being and social development of individuals and communities.

Impacts on Social Networks and Relationships: Disasters can strain social networks and relationships. Families and friends may be separated during evacuations or in the aftermath of the disaster, leading to emotional distress and uncertainty about the well-being of loved ones. Disasters can also disrupt community networks and relationships, impacting social support systems and the ability to mobilize resources for recovery.

Impact on Livelihoods and Economic Stability: The social impact of disasters extends to livelihoods and economic stability. Disruptions to economic activities, business closures, and job losses can result in financial hardships, unemployment, and increased poverty rates. This can have far-reaching social consequences, including increased inequality, social unrest, and a loss of livelihood options for individuals and families.

Changes in Social Norms and Values: Disasters can bring about changes in social norms, values, and behaviours. Community members may adopt new practices, modify traditional customs, or prioritize different values in response to the disaster and its aftermath. These changes can be both positive and negative, reflecting the resilience and adaptability of communities.

Role of Social Institutions and Civil Society: Social institutions, including government agencies, NGOs, and civil society organizations, play a crucial role in addressing the social impact of disasters. They provide support, resources, and services to affected communities, facilitate community engagement and participation, and advocate for the needs and rights of vulnerable populations. The collaboration between social institutions and community members is essential for effective social recovery.

Long-Term Social Resilience and Preparedness: Building long-term social resilience and preparedness is key to mitigating the social impact of disasters. This involves promoting community engagement and participation, strengthening social networks and support systems, enhancing social capital, and investing in social infrastructure. Empowering communities to actively participate in disaster management and recovery efforts contributes to their ability to withstand future shocks and stresses.

Social Impact Data Collection and Sources:

Data on the social impact of disasters in India is collected from various sources, including government agencies, research institutions, surveys, and field assessments. These sources provide information on various aspects of the social impact, such as population displacement, social vulnerabilities, health indicators, education disruptions, and community dynamics. Some key data sources include:

National Sample Survey (NSS): The NSS collects data on various socio-economic aspects, including household and individual-level information that can be useful for understanding the social impact of disasters.

Census of India: The decennial Census provides comprehensive demographic data, including population characteristics, housing conditions, and socio-economic indicators, which can help assess the social impact of disasters on different population groups.

National Family Health Survey (NFHS): The NFHS collects data on various health indicators, including maternal and child health, nutrition, and healthcare access, which can contribute to understanding the health-related social impact of disasters.

Field Surveys and Assessments: Surveys and assessments conducted by government agencies, research institutions, and NGOs provide on-ground data on social vulnerabilities, community dynamics, social cohesion, and other social impact indicators specific to disaster-affected areas.

Data Analysis and Statistical Tools: Data collected on the social impact of disasters in India is analysed using statistical tools and techniques to identify trends, patterns, and correlations. Statistical analysis helps in understanding the demographic characteristics of affected populations, identifying vulnerable groups, assessing changes in social indicators, and evaluating the effectiveness of response and recovery efforts. Analysis of data enables evidence-based decision-making for policy formulation and resource allocation.

Social Vulnerability Mapping: Data and statistical information are used to create social vulnerability maps, which identify areas and populations that are more susceptible to the social impact of disasters. These maps consider socio-economic indicators, such as poverty rates, access to basic services, education levels, and social networks. Social vulnerability maps help prioritize resources and interventions for the most vulnerable communities.

Socio-economic Impact Assessment: Data and statistics are used to assess the socio-economic impact of disasters. This involves estimating the loss of livelihoods, income disparities, changes in poverty levels, and disruptions to social services. Such assessments help identify the needs of affected populations and inform policy decisions for recovery and reconstruction.

Monitoring Social Indicators: Data and statistical information are used to monitor social indicators in disaster-affected areas over time. This includes tracking changes in health outcomes, education enrolment rates, access to basic services, and social cohesion indicators. Monitoring social indicators helps evaluate the progress of recovery efforts and identify areas that require additional support or interventions.

Targeted Interventions and Resource Allocation: Data and statistics assist in targeting interventions and resource allocation to address the social impact of disasters. By identifying vulnerable populations, understanding their needs, and mapping available resources, policymakers can direct assistance, support, and services to those most affected. This ensures that resources are utilized efficiently and effectively in mitigating the social impact.

Policy Formulation and Advocacy: Data and statistical information contribute to evidence-based policy formulation and advocacy efforts related to the social impact of disasters. Robust data and analysis help in highlighting social vulnerabilities, identifying gaps in service delivery, and advocating for policies that promote social resilience, inclusive recovery, and equitable access to resources and services.

Enhancing Data Collection and Integration: Efforts are made to enhance data collection and integration systems to improve the availability, quality, and accessibility of data on the social impact of disasters. This includes strengthening data collection mechanisms, promoting standardized data collection practices, and improving data sharing and integration among various stakeholders.

Building Data Management Capacity: Capacity building initiatives focus on enhancing data management skills and knowledge among government agencies, research institutions, and data collection entities. This ensures better data collection, analysis, interpretation, and utilization for decision-making and policy formulation.

Data Dissemination and Public Awareness: Dissemination of data and statistical information on the social impact of disasters is essential for raising public awareness, promoting transparency, and facilitating evidence-based decision-making. Efforts are made to make data publicly accessible, user-friendly, and easily understandable to various stakeholders, including policymakers, researchers, communities, and the general public.

Long-term Data Monitoring and Evaluation: Data monitoring and evaluation systems are established to track the long-term social impact of disasters and the effectiveness of interventions. These systems help assess the outcomes and impacts of disaster management efforts, identify areas for improvement, and inform future planning and policy formulation.

In conclusion, data and statistical information play a crucial role in understanding the social impact of disasters in the Indian context. They inform policy decisions, resource allocation, and targeted interventions. By utilizing data-driven approaches, policymakers, researchers, and communities can effectively address the social impact of disasters, promote social resilience, and work towards building more inclusive and sustainable societies.

5.6 Ecological Impact of Disasters

The ecological impact of disasters refers to the consequences and effects that disasters have on the natural environment and ecosystems. It encompasses the disruption or alteration of ecological processes, damage to biodiversity, and the loss of ecosystems and their services.

Disruption of Ecological Processes: Disasters can disrupt ecological processes that are essential for the functioning and balance of ecosystems. For example, floods can alter the flow patterns of rivers, disrupt sediment transport, and impact aquatic habitats. Forest fires can interrupt the natural regeneration cycle, affect nutrient cycling, and alter the composition of plant and animal communities. Such disruptions can have cascading effects on the entire ecosystem.

Habitat Loss and Fragmentation: Disasters often result in the loss and fragmentation of habitats. Floods, landslides, and hurricanes can cause extensive damage to forests, wetlands, coral reefs, and other ecosystems. This loss of habitat can lead to the displacement and endangerment of wildlife species, affecting biodiversity and ecological balance.

Biodiversity Loss and Species Extinction: Disasters can cause significant biodiversity loss and even lead to the extinction of species. Habitat destruction, pollution, and disturbances caused by disasters can directly harm and kill organisms. They can also disrupt the food chain and ecological interactions, leading to population declines and, in extreme cases, local extinctions. The loss of biodiversity has long-term ecological consequences and impacts ecosystem resilience.

Soil Erosion and Degradation: Certain disasters, such as floods and landslides, can result in soil erosion and degradation. Excessive rainfall or intense runoff can wash away topsoil, nutrients, and organic matter, reducing soil fertility and compromising the ability of ecosystems to support plant and animal life. Soil erosion can also contribute to sedimentation in water bodies, impacting water quality and aquatic ecosystems.

Water and Air Pollution: Disasters, particularly industrial accidents and chemical spills, can lead to water and air pollution. Chemicals, hazardous substances, and pollutants released during disasters can contaminate water bodies, soil, and the atmosphere. This pollution can have detrimental effects on aquatic life, soil fertility, and the health of both humans and wildlife.

Loss of Ecosystem Services: Disasters can disrupt or completely destroy the services provided by ecosystems, known as ecosystem services. These services include the provision of clean water, regulation of climate, pollination of crops, nutrient cycling, and flood regulation. When ecosystems are damaged or destroyed, these services are compromised, leading to significant ecological and socio-economic impacts.

Impacts on Marine and Coastal Ecosystems: Coastal regions are particularly vulnerable to the ecological impacts of disasters. Coastal disasters like hurricanes, cyclones, and tsunamis can cause severe damage to coral reefs, mangrove forests, and seagrass beds. These ecosystems provide critical habitats for marine species, protect shorelines from erosion, and contribute to coastal resilience. Disruptions to these ecosystems can have far-reaching consequences for both marine and human communities.

Long-term Ecological Recovery: The ecological recovery of affected areas following a disaster can take a considerable amount of time. Natural processes such as regeneration, succession, and recolonization are crucial for ecological recovery. However, the presence of human-induced stressors and ongoing environmental degradation can hinder the natural recovery process and necessitate active restoration efforts.

Mitigation and Restoration: Efforts to mitigate the ecological impact of disasters and restore affected ecosystems are vital. Mitigation measures include implementing disaster risk reduction strategies, conserving natural habitats, and adopting sustainable land and water management practices. Restoration activities involve rehabilitating damaged ecosystems, reestablishing native vegetation, and reintroducing key species. These efforts aid in the recovery and resilience of ecosystems.

Environmental Planning and Management: Environmental planning and management are essential components of disaster management. Integrating environmental considerations into land-use planning, infrastructure development, and disaster response can help reduce the ecological impact of disasters. This includes promoting ecosystem-based approaches, implementing green infrastructure, and adopting sustainable practices that minimize the vulnerability of ecosystems to disasters.

Monitoring and Research: Monitoring the ecological impact of disasters is crucial for understanding the extent of damage, identifying vulnerable ecosystems, and evaluating the effectiveness of mitigation and restoration efforts. Research plays a vital role in expanding knowledge of ecosystem dynamics, developing innovative solutions, and informing evidence-based decision-making in disaster management.

International Cooperation and Conservation: Given that many ecological systems extend beyond national borders, international cooperation is essential in conserving and protecting ecosystems. Collaborative efforts among countries can facilitate the exchange of knowledge, resources, and expertise in disaster management and conservation. International frameworks, such as the Sendai Framework for Disaster Risk Reduction and the Convention on Biological Diversity, promote cooperation and collaboration in addressing the ecological impact of disasters at a global scale.

Ecological Interactions and Species Interdependence: Disasters can disrupt ecological interactions and the delicate balance between species within ecosystems. For example, the loss of pollinators due to a disaster can affect plant reproduction and the availability of food resources for other species. Disruptions to predator-prey relationships or symbiotic partnerships can have cascading effects throughout the ecosystem.

Alteration of Ecosystem Dynamics: Disasters can alter the natural dynamics and functioning of ecosystems. For instance, a wildfire can result in the loss of vegetation cover, changing nutrient cycling patterns and leading to soil erosion. These alterations can impact the availability of resources, such as food and shelter, for various organisms within the ecosystem.

Impact on Keystone Species: Disasters can have a significant impact on keystone species, which play a crucial role in maintaining the structure and stability of ecosystems. The loss of keystone species can disrupt ecological balance and cascade throughout the food chain. For instance, the decline of a predator species can lead to an overabundance of prey species, impacting vegetation growth and other ecosystem components.

Effects on Migration Patterns and Animal Behaviour: Disasters can influence the migration patterns and behaviour of animals. For instance, a natural disaster may disrupt the normal migratory routes of birds or alter the spawning behaviour of fish. These disruptions can have consequences for the population dynamics and genetic diversity of species, as well as impact ecosystem processes such as seed dispersal or nutrient transfer.

Disruption of Aquatic Ecosystems: Disasters such as oil spills or chemical leaks can have severe consequences for aquatic ecosystems. These incidents can result in the contamination of water bodies, killing aquatic organisms and disrupting the delicate balance of the ecosystem. Aquatic species, including fish, amphibians, and invertebrates, are particularly vulnerable to such disruptions.

Impact on Forests and Biodiversity Hotspots: Disasters can significantly impact forests and biodiversity hotspots, which are home to a wide range of species. Forest fires, logging accidents, or invasive species introductions can lead to deforestation, habitat degradation, and loss of biodiversity. Protecting and restoring these areas are crucial for conserving unique species and maintaining ecological resilience.

Effects on Ecosystem Resilience: Disasters can challenge the resilience of ecosystems, affecting their ability to recover and adapt to changing conditions. Factors such as the frequency and severity of disasters, the resilience of individual species, and the availability of intact habitats all play a role in determining the long-term resilience of ecosystems. Strengthening ecosystem resilience involves preserving intact habitats, managing human activities, and addressing underlying drivers of environmental degradation.

Link to Climate Change: Disasters and their ecological impacts are often interconnected with climate change. The increasing frequency and intensity of certain disasters, such as hurricanes or droughts, can be attributed to climate change. These events further exacerbate ecological challenges, such as habitat loss, species decline, and ecosystem disruptions. Addressing the ecological impact of disasters requires addressing climate change through mitigation and adaptation strategies.

Community Engagement and Conservation Efforts: Communities play a crucial role in conserving ecosystems and mitigating the ecological impact of disasters. Engaging local communities in conservation efforts, promoting sustainable land and resource management practices, and fostering environmental education and awareness are essential for building resilience and protecting ecosystems.

Integration of Indigenous Knowledge: Indigenous knowledge and traditional ecological practices can contribute to understanding the ecological impact of disasters and developing appropriate management strategies. Indigenous communities often possess valuable knowledge about ecosystem dynamics, adaptation strategies, and sustainable practices that can inform disaster management and ecological conservation efforts.

Thus, the ecological impact of disasters encompasses a range of effects on ecosystems, including habitat loss, biodiversity decline, disruption of ecological processes, and altered species interactions. Recognizing and addressing these impacts is crucial for promoting ecosystem resilience, conserving biodiversity, and ensuring the sustainable management of natural resources. By implementing conservation measures, restoring degraded habitats, and incorporating ecological considerations into disaster management, it is possible to mitigate the ecological impact of disasters and foster a more sustainable coexistence between humans and the natural environment.

Ecological Impact Data Collection and Sources:

Data on the ecological impact of disasters in India is collected from various sources, including government agencies, research institutions, environmental surveys, remote sensing, and field studies. These sources provide information on ecological indicators such as habitat loss, species diversity, forest cover, water quality, and climate variables. Key data sources include:

Ministry of Environment, Forest and Climate Change (MoEFCC): The MoEFCC collects and maintains data on various ecological parameters, including forest cover, protected areas, and biodiversity hotspots.

Indian Council of Forestry Research and Education (ICFRE): The ICFRE conducts extensive research and monitoring on forest ecosystems, biodiversity, and forest health across the country.

Indian Space Research Organisation (ISRO): ISRO utilizes remote sensing data to assess changes in land cover, vegetation, and ecological parameters before and after disasters.

State Forest Departments and Environmental Agencies: State-level Forest departments and environmental agencies contribute to data collection efforts by conducting surveys, research, and monitoring activities within their respective jurisdictions.

Data Analysis and Interpretation: Data collected on the ecological impact of disasters in India undergoes analysis and interpretation using statistical techniques and modelling approaches. This analysis helps identify trends, patterns, and spatial distributions of ecological parameters, such as habitat loss, species composition, and ecosystem services. Statistical tools allow for the identification of significant changes, correlations, and the quantification of the impact of disasters on specific ecological indicators.

Ecological Mapping and Spatial Analysis: Data and statistical information are used to create ecological maps and conduct spatial analysis. These maps help visualize the distribution of ecosystems, biodiversity hotspots, protected areas, and areas prone to ecological risks. Spatial analysis techniques, such as Geographic Information Systems (GIS), allow for the integration of multiple data layers and aid in identifying vulnerable ecological zones and priority areas for conservation and restoration efforts.

Long-term Monitoring and Trends: Data and statistical information contribute to long-term monitoring and trend analysis of ecological parameters. By comparing data collected over time, researchers and policymakers can assess changes in habitat quality, species abundance, forest cover, water quality, and other ecological indicators. Long-term monitoring helps identify ecological trends, evaluate the effectiveness of conservation measures, and guide adaptive management strategies.

Ecosystem Services Valuation: Data and statistical information are utilized to assess and value ecosystem services, which provide important benefits to human well-being. Economic valuation techniques help quantify the contribution of ecosystems to areas such as carbon sequestration, water regulation, pollination, and soil fertility. Such assessments enable policymakers to incorporate the value of ecosystem services in decision-making processes, ensuring their conservation and sustainable management.

5.6.1 Environmental Impact Assessments (EIAs):

EIAs play a crucial role in evaluating the potential ecological impacts of development projects and disasters. Data and statistical information are utilized in conducting baseline assessments, impact predictions, and environmental modelling. These assessments help identify potential ecological risks, suggest mitigation measures, and ensure that development activities are carried out in an environmentally sustainable manner.

Policy Formulation and Conservation Strategies: Data and statistical information on the ecological impact of disasters support evidence-based policy formulation and the development of conservation strategies. Robust data analysis aids in identifying priority areas for conservation, establishing protected areas, and implementing conservation measures for vulnerable ecosystems and species. It also assists in assessing the effectiveness of existing policies and identifying areas where policy interventions are needed.

Public Awareness and Education: Data and statistical information on the ecological impact of disasters are essential for raising public awareness and educating communities about the importance of environmental conservation. Effective communication of scientific findings and data-driven insights helps create awareness about the value of ecosystems, the risks they face, and the need for sustainable practices and disaster preparedness.

International Collaboration and Reporting: Data and statistical information are utilized in international collaboration and reporting efforts related to ecological impact and conservation. India participates in global initiatives such as the Convention on Biological Diversity (CBD) and the United Nations Framework Convention on Climate Change (UNFCCC). Accurate and comprehensive data is crucial for reporting on progress, sharing best practices, and participating in international forums to address ecological challenges.

Data Accessibility and Sharing: Efforts are made to improve the accessibility and sharing of ecological data and statistical information. Open data initiatives, online platforms, and databases are developed to facilitate data sharing among researchers, policymakers, and the general public. This accessibility promotes transparency, collaboration, and wider engagement in addressing ecological challenges and disaster management.

In conclusion, data and statistical information are essential for understanding and addressing the ecological impact of disasters in the Indian context. They contribute to evidence-based decision-making, policy formulation, and the development of conservation strategies. By utilizing data-driven approaches, India can better mitigate the ecological impact of disasters, promote sustainable development, and ensure the long-term conservation of its rich biodiversity and ecosystems.

5.7 Economical Impact of Disasters

The economic impact of disasters refers to the consequences and effects that disasters have on the economic systems, infrastructure, industries, and livelihoods of a region or country. It encompasses both the immediate and long-term economic losses, disruptions to economic activities, and the challenges faced in recovery and rebuilding efforts.

Direct Economic Losses: Disasters result in direct economic losses, including damage to physical infrastructure, buildings, agriculture, industries, and public utilities. This includes the destruction of roads, bridges, schools, hospitals, power plants, communication networks, and other critical infrastructure. Direct economic losses also encompass the loss of physical assets, inventory, and productive capacity.

Indirect Economic Losses: Disasters can also lead to indirect economic losses, which result from disruptions in economic activities and supply chains. These include business interruptions, production stoppages, reduced trade, job losses, and reduced consumer spending. Indirect economic losses can extend beyond the disaster-affected areas and impact regional and national economies.

Impact on Industries and Sectors: Disasters can have a significant impact on specific industries and sectors. For example, agricultural losses due to floods or droughts can result in crop failures, livestock deaths, and reduced agricultural productivity. Natural resource-based industries, such as fishing or forestry, can be severely affected by disasters, leading to loss of livelihoods and reduced economic output.

Loss of Employment and Livelihoods: Disasters can lead to a loss of employment and livelihoods, particularly in sectors heavily impacted by the disaster. Business closures, layoffs, and the destruction of small and medium-sized enterprises can result in job losses and income reduction. This affects individuals and communities, creating socio-economic challenges and exacerbating poverty and inequality.

Impacts on Trade and Tourism: Disasters can disrupt trade and tourism, leading to economic losses at national and regional levels. Disruptions in transportation infrastructure, port closures, and damage to tourism facilities and attractions can result in decreased tourist arrivals and reduced export and import activities. This affects foreign exchange earnings, tax revenues, and the overall economic performance.

Government Expenditures and Fiscal Impact: Disasters often require significant government expenditures for emergency response, relief operations, and post-disaster recovery and reconstruction. These expenditures can strain public finances, impact budget allocations for other sectors, and result in increased borrowing or deficits. The fiscal impact of disasters can have long-term consequences for economic stability and development priorities.

Impact on Small and Medium-sized Enterprises (SMEs): Small and medium-sized enterprises (SMEs) are particularly vulnerable to the economic impact of disasters. They often lack the resources, financial reserves, and insurance coverage to recover from losses. Disruptions to their operations can lead to closures, bankruptcies, and long-term economic hardships for SME owners and employees.

Infrastructure Rehabilitation and Reconstruction: The economic impact of disasters includes the cost of infrastructure rehabilitation and reconstruction. Rebuilding damaged or destroyed infrastructure, such as roads, bridges, schools, hospitals, and utilities, requires significant investment and resources. The cost of reconstruction can strain public finances and delay economic recovery.

Insurance and Risk Transfer: Disasters highlight the importance of insurance and risk transfer mechanisms to mitigate economic losses. Insurance coverage for properties, assets, and businesses can help individuals and businesses recover more quickly from the financial impact of disasters. Risk transfer mechanisms, such as catastrophe bonds or reinsurance, can help governments and businesses share the financial burden of large-scale disasters.

Economic Recovery and Resilience: Efforts to enhance economic recovery and resilience involve implementing strategies to restore economic activities, rebuild infrastructure, and revitalize affected industries. This includes targeted investments, business support programs, job creation initiatives, and promoting economic diversification. Building economic resilience involves adopting risk-informed development practices, strengthening disaster risk management capacities, and integrating disaster risk reduction into development planning.

Cost-Benefit Analysis and Decision-making: Data and statistical information on the economic impact of disasters are used in cost-benefit analysis to evaluate the feasibility and effectiveness of risk reduction measures, preparedness initiatives, and investment decisions. This analysis helps policymakers and stakeholders make informed decisions about resource allocation, prioritize investments, and select strategies that maximize benefits and reduce future economic losses.

International Aid and Support: The economic impact of disasters often necessitates international aid and support. International organizations, donor countries, and development partners provide financial assistance, technical expertise, and capacity-building support to help affected countries recover and rebuild their economies. Collaboration and partnerships with the international community are vital for addressing the economic impact of disasters.

Macroeconomic Effects: Disasters can have macroeconomic effects on a country's overall economy. These effects include reduced GDP growth, increased inflation, decreased investment and savings, and reduced tax revenues. The macroeconomic impacts can affect multiple sectors of the economy, leading to a slowdown in economic development and affecting the overall quality of life for the population.

Financial Sector Implications: Disasters can have implications for the financial sector, including banks, insurance companies, and capital markets. The financial sector may face increased loan defaults, insurance claims, and reduced liquidity. It may also experience a decline in investor confidence and increased uncertainty, impacting financial markets and investment decisions.

Long-term Economic Development: Disasters can have long-term implications for a country's economic development. The diversion of resources towards emergency response and recovery can delay or redirect investments in long-term development projects and infrastructure. This delay can have lasting effects on economic growth, employment opportunities, and poverty reduction efforts.

Income Inequality and Vulnerable Groups: Disasters can exacerbate income inequality and disproportionately impact vulnerable groups in society. Low-income households, informal workers, and marginalized communities often lack the resources and social protection systems to cope with the economic shocks caused by disasters. The economic impact can widen existing inequalities and hinder efforts to achieve sustainable and inclusive development.

Agriculture and Food Security: Disasters can significantly affect agriculture and food security, particularly in countries where agriculture plays a vital role in the economy and livelihoods. Crop failures, livestock losses, and damage to agricultural infrastructure can lead to decreased food production, increased food prices, and reduced food availability. This can have far-reaching consequences for food security and nutrition.

Infrastructure Investment and Resilience: The economic impact of disasters highlights the importance of investing in resilient infrastructure. Infrastructure resilience involves designing and constructing infrastructure that can withstand and recover from the impact of disasters. Investing in resilient infrastructure can help minimize economic losses, reduce the need for costly post-disaster reconstruction, and ensure the continuity of essential services.

Insurance Penetration and Disaster Risk Financing: The economic impact of disasters underscores the importance of insurance penetration and disaster risk financing mechanisms. Increasing insurance coverage, both at the individual and national level, can help transfer the financial burden of disasters and facilitate quicker recovery. Governments can also explore disaster risk financing mechanisms such as contingency funds and catastrophe bonds to supplement their financial resources during post-disaster recovery.

Business Continuity Planning and Risk Management: Business continuity planning and risk management are essential for minimizing the economic impact of disasters on businesses. Developing robust risk management strategies, including disaster preparedness, supply chain resilience, and business interruption insurance, can help businesses recover more quickly and reduce the economic losses associated with disruptions.

Economic Diversification: Disasters often reveal vulnerabilities in economies that are heavily reliant on a single sector or industry. Economic diversification, through the development of multiple sectors and industries, can help reduce the economic vulnerability to disasters. Diversification provides alternative sources of income and employment, allowing for more resilient economic growth.

5.7.1 Economic Impact Assessment:

Conducting comprehensive economic impact assessments following a disaster is crucial for understanding the magnitude of the economic losses and formulating effective recovery strategies. Economic impact assessments involve analysing the direct and indirect economic losses, estimating the costs of recovery and reconstruction, and identifying potential opportunities for economic growth and development.

Public-Private Partnerships: Engaging the private sector through public-private partnerships can enhance the resilience of economies and businesses. Collaborations between governments, businesses, and non-governmental organizations can support disaster risk reduction initiatives, enhance preparedness, and facilitate faster recovery. Public-private partnerships can leverage resources, expertise, and innovative solutions to address the economic impact of disasters.

Loss and Damage Assessment: Data and statistical information are used to assess the magnitude of economic losses and damages caused by disasters. This includes estimating the cost of infrastructure damage, the value of assets and properties affected, and the economic losses incurred by various sectors. These assessments provide a quantitative understanding of the economic impact, helping in resource allocation and planning for recovery and reconstruction efforts.

Sector-specific Analysis: Data and statistics are employed to analyse the economic impact on specific sectors and industries. This includes assessing the losses incurred by agriculture, manufacturing, services, tourism, and other sectors affected by the disaster. Sector-specific analysis helps in identifying the extent of disruption, estimating the financial losses, and formulating targeted interventions and support for affected industries.

Employment and Income Impact: Data and statistics play a crucial role in evaluating the impact of disasters on employment and income levels. Surveys and statistical data are used to assess the number of jobs lost, the income reduction faced by affected individuals and households, and the overall impact on livelihoods. This information helps in designing and implementing measures to support affected populations and promote economic recovery.

Small and Medium-sized Enterprises (SMEs) Assessment: SMEs form a significant part of the Indian economy, and data and statistical information are utilized to assess the impact of disasters on these enterprises. Surveys and statistical data help in evaluating the financial losses faced by SMEs, their ability to cope with the impacts, and their recovery prospects. This information guides policy interventions and support measures to facilitate the revival of SMEs and promote their resilience.

Trade and Supply Chain Disruptions: Data and statistics are employed to analyse the disruptions in trade and supply chains caused by disasters. This includes assessing the impact on import and export activities, identifying bottlenecks in supply chains, and quantifying the financial losses incurred by businesses. Understanding the trade and supply chain disruptions helps in formulating strategies to mitigate the economic impact and restore business operations.

Household Income and Expenditure Surveys: Household income and expenditure surveys provide valuable data for assessing the economic impact of disasters at the household level. These surveys collect information on income sources, expenditure patterns, and socio-economic characteristics of households. Analysing this data helps in understanding the financial vulnerabilities of households, identifying the most affected groups, and designing targeted assistance programs.

Financial and Insurance Data: Financial and insurance data are important sources of information for understanding the economic impact of disasters. This includes data on insurance claims, insurance penetration rates, and the financial health of insurance companies. Analysing this data helps in evaluating the effectiveness of insurance coverage in mitigating the economic losses and identifying gaps in insurance coverage.

Government Budgetary Data: Government budgetary data provides insights into the financial resources allocated for disaster response, recovery, and reconstruction. It helps in understanding the fiscal impact of disasters and the government's ability to finance recovery efforts. Analysing budgetary data aids in identifying the allocation of funds for various sectors and assessing the adequacy of resources for post-disaster recovery.

Long-term Economic Indicators: Long-term economic indicators, such as GDP growth rates, investment levels, and employment statistics, are monitored to assess the overall economic performance and resilience of the country. These indicators help in understanding the long-term economic consequences of disasters and tracking the progress of recovery and reconstruction efforts over time.

International Reporting and Comparisons: Data and statistical information are used for international reporting and comparisons. India participates in global initiatives, such as the Sendai Framework for Disaster Risk Reduction, and provides data on economic losses and recovery efforts. Comparative analysis with other countries helps in identifying best practices, learning from experiences, and benchmarking progress in disaster management and economic resilience.

Data Sharing and Accessibility: Efforts are made to improve data sharing and accessibility in India. Open data initiatives, online platforms, and databases are developed to facilitate access to data and statistics related to disaster impacts. This enables researchers, policymakers, and the general public to utilize the information for analysis, planning, and decision-making processes.

Thus, data and statistical information are crucial for assessing and understanding the economic impact of disasters in the Indian context. They provide quantitative insights into the magnitude of losses, sector-specific impacts, employment and income effects, and trade disruptions. By utilizing data-driven approaches, policymakers can make informed decisions, allocate resources effectively, and implement targeted interventions to mitigate the economic impact of disasters and foster sustainable economic recovery.

5.8 Political Impact of Disasters

The political impact of disasters refers to the effects that disasters have on political systems, governance structures, and decision-making processes. Disasters can significantly influence political dynamics and have implications for governance, policy-making, public trust, and social cohesion. Here are the key aspects of the political impact of disasters:

Crisis Management and Leadership: Disasters often require immediate crisis management and effective leadership from political leaders. The response and recovery efforts following a disaster can shape public perception of leaders and governments. The effectiveness of crisis management, coordination, and decision-making during a disaster can impact the reputation and legitimacy of political leaders and institutions.

Policy Priorities and Agenda Setting: Disasters can shift policy priorities and redirect government resources. The immediate response to a disaster may necessitate diverting funds, personnel, and attention from other areas of governance. Disasters can influence the policy agenda, leading to increased emphasis on disaster risk reduction, climate change adaptation, and emergency management in policy frameworks.

Governance and Institutional Performance: Disasters can expose weaknesses in governance and institutional systems. They reveal the effectiveness of institutions in disaster preparedness, response, and recovery. The performance of government agencies, disaster management authorities, and local administrations during and after a disaster can impact public perception of governance and the credibility of institutions.

Political Accountability and Transparency: Disasters can create opportunities for political accountability and transparency. The public scrutiny following a disaster can led to increased demands for transparency, accountability, and good governance. Citizens and civil society organizations may hold political leaders and institutions responsible for any shortcomings in disaster management, recovery efforts, or corruption-related issues.

Social Cohesion and Political Stability: Disasters can have both positive and negative effects on social cohesion and political stability. In some cases, disasters can foster solidarity and cooperation among citizens, leading to a sense of community resilience. However, if the disaster response is perceived as inadequate or unequal, it can fuel social tensions, protests, and political instability.

Disaster Risk Governance: Disasters can prompt changes in disaster risk governance and policy frameworks. They can lead to the revision or development of laws, regulations, and policies related to disaster management, land-use planning, building codes, and risk reduction. Disasters provide opportunities to strengthen disaster risk governance structures and enhance coordination between different levels of government.

Political Economy: Disasters can impact the political economy of a region or country. Economic activities may be disrupted, leading to changes in employment patterns, income distribution, and wealth disparities. Political actors and interest groups may attempt to influence the allocation of resources and aid distribution for their own political gain. The political economy considerations in post-disaster recovery and reconstruction can influence power dynamics and political decision-making.

International Relations and Cooperation: Disasters can have implications for international relations and cooperation. They can prompt international assistance and cooperation, leading to collaboration between governments, donor countries, and international organizations. Disasters can also impact regional dynamics and cooperation frameworks, such as cross-border collaboration on disaster response and sharing of best practices.

Public Trust and Perception of Government: The way in which a government responds to and manages a disaster can significantly affect public trust and perception of the government's effectiveness. Transparency, timely communication, and efficient allocation of resources can enhance public trust in government institutions. Conversely, a perceived lack of preparedness or ineffective response can erode public trust and confidence in political leadership.

Policy Learning and Institutional Change: Disasters can be catalysts for policy learning and institutional change. Post-disaster assessments and evaluations can provide insights into strengths, weaknesses, and areas for improvement in disaster management systems. They can lead to the adoption of new policies, institutional reforms, and capacity-building measures to enhance disaster resilience and governance.

It is important to note that the political impact of disasters is complex and can vary depending on the context, the nature of the disaster, and the effectiveness of the political response. The extent to which disasters influence political dynamics and decision-making processes is influenced by factors such as governance structures, political culture, societal resilience, and the capacity of institutions to respond and recover.

Public Perception and Political Legitimacy: Disasters can shape public perception of political leaders and affect their legitimacy. How leaders respond to a disaster, communicate with the public, and coordinate relief efforts can influence public opinion and support. Effective leadership during a crisis can enhance the credibility and legitimacy of political leaders, while a perceived failure in crisis management can erode public trust and support.

Political Mobilization and Social Movements: Disasters can spark political mobilization and social movements. Civil society organizations, advocacy groups, and affected communities may organize to demand policy changes, accountability, and justice. Disasters can serve as catalysts for social and political movements focused on issues such as climate change, environmental justice, or disaster risk reduction.

Policy Shifts and Reforms: Disasters can lead to policy shifts and reforms in various areas. Governments may review and revise policies related to disaster management, climate change adaptation, urban planning, and infrastructure resilience. Lessons learned from disasters can prompt changes in governance structures, regulations, and the allocation of resources to prevent similar occurrences in the future.

Political Fragmentation and Power Struggles: Disasters can expose existing political fragmentation and power struggles. Political actors may exploit disasters to advance their own interests, engage in blame-shifting, or use relief efforts for political gain. Disasters can intensify existing political divisions and lead to conflicts over resource allocation, decision-making authority, and the distribution of aid.

Emergency Powers and Decision-making: Disasters often require the activation of emergency powers and decision-making mechanisms. Governments may introduce temporary measures, such as emergency declarations, to streamline decision-making, coordinate response efforts, and mobilize resources. The exercise of emergency powers can have implications for civil liberties, human rights, and the balance of power between different branches of government.

Public Policy Response: Disasters can influence the formulation and implementation of public policies. They may highlight the need for investment in disaster risk reduction, climate change mitigation, and infrastructure resilience. Disasters can also lead to the development of social protection programs, safety regulations, and building codes aimed at reducing vulnerability and enhancing public safety.

Political Will for Change: Disasters can generate political will for change and prompt action on long-standing issues. They can create an opportunity for governments to address underlying vulnerabilities, invest in resilience, and tackle systemic challenges. Disasters can mobilize public support and create a sense of urgency for policy reforms and investments in disaster risk reduction and preparedness.

International Reputation and Diplomacy: The response to disasters can influence a country's international reputation and diplomatic relations. How a government handles a disaster, cooperates with international partners, and accepts or mobilizes international assistance can impact its standing in the international community. Disasters can shape perceptions of a country's capacity to manage crises and affect diplomatic ties and cooperation.

Political Commitment to Risk Reduction: Disasters can shape the political commitment to disaster risk reduction and resilience-building. High-impact disasters can serve as wake-up calls, prompting governments to prioritize risk reduction measures, allocate resources, and establish long-term strategies for resilience. Political commitment and sustained efforts are crucial for implementing effective disaster risk reduction policies and practices.

Media and Public Opinion Influence: The media and public opinion play a significant role in shaping the political impact of disasters. Media coverage, public discourse, and social media conversations can influence public opinion, hold political leaders accountable, and shape policy debates. The media can highlight issues of concern, amplify voices of affected communities, and foster transparency in disaster management.

5.8.1 Political Impact Assessment of Disaster

The political impact of disasters encompasses a wide range of effects on governance, leadership, policy-making, public perception, and international relations. Disasters can influence political dynamics, shape policy agendas, and mobilize social and political movements. It is important for governments to be proactive in their disaster response, foster transparency, accountability, and public trust, and prioritize long-term resilience-building efforts to effectively address the political impact of disasters.

Election and Political Behaviour Analysis: Data and statistics are used to analyse the impact of disasters on elections and political behaviour. Researchers examine voting patterns, political preferences, and changes in voter behaviour following a disaster. They analyse electoral data to understand how disasters shape political dynamics and influence voting decisions.

Public Opinion Surveys: Public opinion surveys provide valuable data on the political impact of disasters. These surveys collect information on public perceptions, attitudes, and trust in political leaders and institutions during and after a disaster. Analysing survey data helps assess the effectiveness of political responses, the level of public satisfaction, and the overall impact on political support.

Policy and Legislative Changes: Data and statistics are employed to assess policy and legislative changes following a disaster. Researchers analyse government reports, policy documents, and legislative records to identify new laws, regulations, and policy reforms that were implemented as a result of the disaster. This data helps evaluate the political will for change and the effectiveness of policy responses.

Government Decision-making and Resource Allocation: Data and statistical information are utilized to analyse government decision-making and resource allocation in disaster management. Researchers examine budgetary data, expenditure reports, and government records to understand how resources are allocated for disaster response, recovery, and preparedness. This data provides insights into the political priorities and resource distribution processes.

Media Analysis: Data and statistics are used to analyse media coverage of disasters and their political impact. Researchers examine news articles, television broadcasts, and social media trends to assess how the media frames disaster events, reports on political responses, and shapes public opinion. Media analysis helps understand the role of the media in influencing the political narrative.

Political Party Response and Positioning: Data and statistics are employed to analyse the response and positioning of political parties during and after a disaster. Researchers examine party manifestos, statements, and public speeches to assess how political parties frame their response, propose policy solutions, and position themselves in relation to the disaster. This data helps understand party strategies and political messaging.

International Comparisons and Rankings: Data and statistical information are used to compare the political response to disasters across countries. Global rankings and indices, such as the World Risk Index or the Global Peace Index, utilize data and statistical indicators to assess the political preparedness, response, and resilience of countries. These comparisons help identify areas for improvement and best practices.

Data-driven Policy Formulation: Data and statistics support evidence-based policy formulation in disaster management. Government agencies and policymakers utilize data on disaster impacts, public opinion, and policy evaluations to design effective policies and programs. Data-driven policy formulation helps ensure that political decisions are grounded in empirical evidence and contribute to better disaster governance.

Monitoring and Evaluation: Data and statistical information are essential for monitoring and evaluating the effectiveness of political responses to disasters. Indicators are developed to track progress in disaster risk reduction, resilience-building, and policy implementation. Monitoring and evaluation data help assess the impact of political actions, identify gaps, and guide policy adjustments.

International Reporting and Accountability: Data and statistics play a crucial role in international reporting and accountability. Governments provide data on the political impact of disasters, policy responses, and progress in disaster risk reduction through international frameworks like the Sendai Framework for Disaster Risk Reduction. This data enables international comparisons, peer learning, and accountability mechanisms.

Historical Analysis: Data and statistics from past disasters are analysed to understand the long-term political impact. Researchers examine historical records, archival data, and official reports to identify patterns, trends, and lessons learned from previous disasters. Historical analysis helps inform future political decision-making and policy responses.

Thus, data and statistical information are essential for understanding the political impact of disasters in the Indian context. They help analyse election behaviour, public opinion, policy changes, resource allocation, media dynamics, and political party responses. By utilizing data-driven approaches, policymakers and researchers can better understand the political dimensions of disasters and enhance disaster governance and political resilience.

CHAPTER 6

Health and Psycho-Social Issues in Disasters

6.1 Health Impact of Disasters

The health impact of disasters refers to the effects that disasters have on the physical, mental, and social well-being of individuals and communities. Disasters can lead to a range of health consequences, including injuries, illness, psychological distress, and increased vulnerability to diseases. Here are the key aspects of the health impact of disasters:

Injuries and Trauma: Disasters can result in a significant number of injuries and trauma. These injuries can be caused by various factors, such as collapsing structures, debris, flooding, or fires. Injuries can range from minor cuts and bruises to severe trauma requiring medical intervention. Prompt and appropriate medical care is crucial in addressing injuries and preventing further complications.

Communicable Diseases: Disasters can increase the risk of communicable diseases due to factors such as overcrowding, displacement, lack of clean water, poor sanitation, and disrupted healthcare systems. Infectious diseases like diarrehea, respiratory infections, vector-borne diseases (e.g., malaria, dengue fever), and waterborne diseases (e.g., cholera) can spread more easily in post-disaster settings. Disease surveillance and timely public health interventions are essential to prevent disease outbreaks.

Mental Health and Psychosocial Support: Disasters can have a significant impact on mental health and well-being. The stress, trauma, and disruption caused by disasters can lead to psychological distress, anxiety, depression, post-traumatic stress disorder (PTSD), and other mental health conditions. Psychosocial support services, including counselling, community-based interventions, and mental health outreach, are crucial in addressing the psychological impact and promoting resilience.

Vulnerable Populations: Certain populations are more vulnerable to the health impacts of disasters. This includes children, older adults, pregnant women, individuals with chronic illnesses, persons with disabilities, and marginalized or disadvantaged groups. These vulnerable populations may face increased risks, limited access to healthcare, and specific health needs that require targeted interventions and support.

Healthcare Infrastructure and Services: Disasters can severely disrupt healthcare infrastructure and services, making it challenging to provide essential medical care. Hospitals, clinics, and healthcare facilities may be damaged or overwhelmed, limiting the capacity to treat injured individuals and manage health emergencies. Strengthening healthcare infrastructure, disaster preparedness, and emergency response systems are critical in addressing the health impact of disasters.

Access to Essential Services: Disasters can disrupt access to essential services such as clean water, food, shelter, and sanitation facilities. Lack of access to safe drinking water and sanitation can increase the risk of waterborne diseases, while inadequate nutrition can lead to malnutrition and weakened immune systems. Ensuring the availability of essential services during and after a disaster is crucial to mitigate the health impact.

Displacement and Migration: Disasters often result in population displacement and migration. Displaced populations face numerous health challenges, including increased risks of infectious diseases, inadequate access to healthcare, mental health issues, and loss of social support networks. Providing adequate shelter, healthcare, and social support to displaced populations is vital to address their specific health needs.

Environmental Health Risks: Disasters can introduce environmental health risks that impact the health of affected populations. This includes exposure to hazardous substances, air pollution, chemical spills, and contaminated water sources. These environmental health risks can have both immediate and long-term health consequences, necessitating monitoring, remediation, and public health interventions.

Resilience and Health Systems Strengthening: Disasters highlight the importance of building resilient health systems. Strengthening healthcare infrastructure, training healthcare professionals in disaster management, improving disease surveillance, and enhancing emergency response capacities are key components of health system resilience. Building resilient health systems helps in mitigating the health impacts of disasters and improving overall healthcare delivery.

Risk Communication and Public Health Messaging: Effective risk communication and public health messaging are critical in addressing the health impact of disasters. Clear and timely information helps individuals and communities understand health risks, preventive measures, and available healthcare services. Public health campaigns, community engagement, and collaboration with local leaders and organizations play a vital role in disseminating accurate information and promoting healthy behaviours.

Data and Surveillance Systems: Data and surveillance systems are essential for monitoring and responding to the health impact of disasters. Robust data collection, disease surveillance, and health assessments provide valuable information on the prevalence of diseases, health needs, and emerging health trends. This data helps inform public health interventions, resource allocation, and policy decisions.

International Collaboration and Support: International collaboration and support are crucial in addressing the health impact of disasters. This includes cooperation between countries, sharing best practices, and providing technical assistance and resources. International organizations, such as the World Health Organization (WHO) and humanitarian agencies, play a vital role in coordinating and providing support for health-related interventions in disaster-affected areas.

Long-Term Health Effects: Disasters can have long-term health effects that extend beyond the immediate aftermath. For example, exposure to environmental hazards or hazardous substances during a disaster can led to chronic health conditions and increased risks of diseases in the future. It is essential to consider the long-term health implications and provide ongoing healthcare and support to affected populations.

Access to Healthcare: Disasters can disrupt access to healthcare services, particularly in remote or affected areas. Damage to healthcare facilities, infrastructure, and transportation systems can limit the availability of medical care. Ensuring access to healthcare services, including emergency medical care, primary healthcare, and specialized services, is crucial to meet the health needs of disaster-affected populations.

Health Inequities: Disasters often exacerbate existing health inequities and inequalities. Vulnerable populations, such as those living in poverty, marginalized communities, or remote areas, may experience greater health impacts due to pre-existing health conditions, limited access to healthcare, and reduced resources.

Addressing health inequities requires targeted interventions and a focus on inclusive and equitable healthcare delivery.

Health Surveillance and Early Warning Systems: Health surveillance and early warning systems are essential for detecting and responding to health risks during and after disasters. Monitoring and tracking disease outbreaks, injuries, and other health indicators help identify emerging health concerns, guide resource allocation, and support timely public health interventions. Strengthening health surveillance systems is crucial for effective disaster response.

Community Engagement and Participation: Community engagement and participation are key to addressing the health impact of disasters. Engaging affected communities in decision-making, risk communication, and health promotion activities can enhance the effectiveness of health interventions. Empowering communities to actively participate in their own recovery and rebuilding efforts promotes resilience and fosters community ownership of health initiatives.

Capacity Building and Training: Building the capacity of healthcare workers, first responders, and community members is vital for effective disaster response and addressing the health impact. Training programs on disaster management, emergency medical care, mental health support, and public health interventions equip individuals and organizations with the skills and knowledge to respond to health emergencies.

Health System Preparedness: Health system preparedness is crucial for mitigating the health impact of disasters. This includes developing disaster response plans, establishing coordination mechanisms, pre-positioning essential medical supplies, and conducting simulation exercises and drills. Preparedness efforts ensure a swift and coordinated response, reducing the health risks and minimizing the burden on healthcare systems.

Lessons Learned and Knowledge Sharing: Disasters provide opportunities for learning and knowledge sharing. Evaluating past disaster responses, identifying gaps, and sharing best practices contribute to continuous improvement in disaster management and health response. Collaboration between local, national, and international stakeholders facilitates the exchange of experiences, lessons learned, and innovative approaches to address the health impact of disasters.

Research and Innovation: Research and innovation play a crucial role in understanding the health impact of disasters and developing effective interventions. Studies on disaster epidemiology, public health interventions, mental health support, and healthcare delivery provide evidence-based insights that inform policy and practice. Encouraging research collaboration and fostering innovation in disaster health management contribute to improved health outcomes.

Financing and Resource Mobilization: Adequate financing and resource mobilization are essential for addressing the health impact of disasters. Governments, international organizations, and humanitarian agencies need to allocate sufficient resources to support health interventions, strengthen healthcare systems, and promote resilience. Securing sustainable funding streams and exploring innovative financing mechanisms are critical for long-term health impact mitigation.

Thus, the health impact of disasters encompasses a broad range of physical, mental, and social consequences. Addressing the health impact requires a multi-sectoral and holistic approach that includes healthcare delivery, public health interventions, community engagement, capacity building, and research. By prioritizing the health and well-being of affected populations, governments, healthcare systems, and communities can effectively mitigate the health risks and promote resilience in the face of disasters.

6.1.1 Assessment of Health Impact of Disaster

Disease Surveillance: Data and statistics are collected through disease surveillance systems to monitor the occurrence and spread of diseases in disaster-affected areas. This includes tracking communicable diseases, vector-borne diseases, waterborne diseases, and other health indicators. Disease surveillance data helps identify disease hotspots, trends, and patterns, enabling public health authorities to respond effectively.

Epidemiological Studies: Epidemiological studies are conducted to analyse the health impact of disasters and assess the prevalence of specific health conditions. These studies collect data on the incidence of injuries, diseases, mental health disorders, and other health outcomes among affected populations. By analysing epidemiological data, researchers can identify risk factors, assess the burden of disease, and inform targeted interventions.

Mortality and Morbidity Data: Data on mortality and morbidity provide insights into the health consequences of disasters. Mortality data record the number of deaths caused directly or indirectly by the disaster, while morbidity data capture the incidence and severity of injuries and illnesses. Analysing mortality and morbidity data helps identify vulnerable populations, assess the effectiveness of interventions, and inform future disaster planning.

Health Facility Data: Health facility data provides information on the utilization of healthcare services during and after disasters. This includes data on emergency room visits, hospital admissions, outpatient visits, and the types of health services provided. Analysing health facility data helps assess the capacity of healthcare systems, identify areas of need, and allocate resources accordingly.

Health Surveys: Health surveys are conducted to gather information on the health status, healthcare access, and health-related behaviours of affected populations. Surveys capture data on injuries, diseases, mental health, access to healthcare services, and health-seeking behaviours. Survey data enables a comprehensive assessment of the health impact and helps tailor interventions to meet the specific needs of affected communities.

Health Infrastructure Mapping: Data on health infrastructure, such as hospitals, clinics, and healthcare facilities, are mapped to assess their spatial distribution and accessibility in disaster-prone areas. Geographic Information Systems (GIS) technology is often used to map health infrastructure data and overlay it with disaster risk maps. This helps identify gaps in healthcare coverage and informs resource allocation and planning.

Health Expenditure and Financing: Data on health expenditure and financing are crucial for understanding the financial aspects of addressing the health impact of disasters. This includes tracking government spending on healthcare services, disaster response, and healthcare infrastructure. Analysing health financing data helps evaluate the adequacy of funding, identify areas of improvement, and advocate for increased investment in disaster healthcare.

Health Behaviour Surveys: Health behaviour surveys collect data on health-related knowledge, attitudes, and practices among disaster-affected populations. This includes information on hygiene practices, preventive measures, healthcare-seeking behaviours, and adherence to health recommendations. Understanding health behaviour data helps design targeted health promotion campaigns and improve health education initiatives.

Demographic and Socioeconomic Data: Demographic and socioeconomic data are essential for understanding the social determinants of health in disaster-affected populations. This includes data on age, gender, income, education, and other demographic factors. Analysing demographic and socioeconomic data helps identify vulnerable groups, assess health disparities, and design inclusive and equitable health interventions.

Integration of Data Sources: Integrating data from various sources, including health records, population census data, and disaster databases, helps create a comprehensive picture of the health impact of disasters. Linking data sources enables researchers and policymakers to analyse relationships between disaster events, health outcomes, and socioeconomic factors. Integrated data analysis provides a more robust understanding of the health impact and supports evidence-based decision-making.

Data Visualization and Geographic Analysis: Data visualization and geographic analysis techniques, such as maps, charts, and spatial analysis, are used to present health data in a visually informative manner. This helps identify geographic disparities, hotspot areas, and health trends. Data visualization aids in communicating complex health information to policymakers, stakeholders, and the public.

Research and Evidence Generation: Data and statistical information support research and evidence generation on the health impact of disasters. Researchers use quantitative and qualitative data to conduct studies, evaluate interventions, and identify best practices. Robust research and evidence contribute to the development of policies, guidelines, and interventions that effectively address the health impact of disasters.

Monitoring and Evaluation: Data and statistics are used for monitoring and evaluating health interventions in disaster-affected areas. Indicators are developed to assess the effectiveness and impact of health programs, measure progress towards health goals, and identify areas for improvement. Monitoring and evaluation data guide decision-making, inform resource allocation, and support evidence-based practice.

International Reporting and Benchmarking: Data and statistical information are crucial for international reporting and benchmarking of health outcomes in disaster-affected regions. Countries report health-related data to international organizations such as the World Health Organization (WHO), contributing to global databases and assessments. Benchmarking enables countries to compare their health indicators, identify gaps, and learn from international best practices.

Thus, data and statistical information are essential for understanding and addressing the health impact of disasters in the Indian context. Data collection, analysis, and integration facilitate evidence-based decision-making, resource allocation, and policy development. By utilizing data-driven approaches, policymakers, researchers, and healthcare professionals can effectively respond to the health needs of disaster-affected populations and enhance overall disaster healthcare.

6.2 Psycho-Social Issues Related to Various Disaster Impact

Psycho-social issues refer to the psychological and social challenges that individuals and communities face in the aftermath of a disaster. These issues arise from the combination of psychological distress and the disruption of social support systems caused by the disaster. Here are various psycho-social issues related to different disaster impacts:

Psychological Distress: Disasters can lead to significant psychological distress among affected individuals. This includes symptoms of anxiety, depression, post-traumatic stress disorder (PTSD), grief, and loss. The experience of witnessing or experiencing traumatic events, loss of loved ones, displacement, and the uncertainty of the future contribute to psychological distress.

Trauma and Emotional Reactions: Disasters can cause trauma, triggering emotional reactions such as fear, anger, guilt, and helplessness. Trauma may result from direct exposure to the disaster event, experiencing injuries or loss, or witnessing traumatic events. Emotional reactions can vary widely among individuals, and some may struggle with emotional regulation and coping with overwhelming emotions.

Bereavement and Loss: Disasters often result in loss of lives, homes, possessions, and communities. The grieving process following such losses can be complex and prolonged. Bereaved individuals may experience intense grief, feelings of emptiness, and a sense of disconnection from others. Support and interventions that address the specific needs of the bereaved are crucial for their healing process.

Social Disruption and Displacement: Disasters disrupt social networks, community structures, and support systems. Displaced individuals may experience a sense of dislocation, loss of social connections, and feelings of isolation. Displacement can lead to challenges in accessing basic needs, healthcare, and social support. The loss of familiar surroundings and social support networks can contribute to psychological distress.

Family and Relationship Strain: Disasters can strain family and interpersonal relationships. The stress and challenges associated with the disaster can lead to increased conflict, domestic violence, and breakdown of relationships. Changes in living conditions, financial stress, and displacement can further exacerbate these issues. Strengthening family and social support systems is crucial in promoting resilience and recovery.

Stigma and Discrimination: Some individuals and communities may experience stigma and discrimination following a disaster. This can be due to factors such as loss of homes, changes in socioeconomic status, or belonging to marginalized groups. Stigma and discrimination can have negative impacts on mental health, social integration, and community cohesion.

Disruption of Daily Routines and Identity: Disasters disrupt daily routines and roles, leading to a loss of structure and identity. Disrupted routines and roles can impact individuals' sense of normalcy, purpose, and self-identity. Adjusting to new circumstances, such as temporary housing, changes in employment, or altered social roles, can be challenging and contribute to psychological distress.

Coping and Resilience: Disasters require individuals and communities to adapt and cope with challenging circumstances. The ability to cope effectively varies among individuals and can be influenced by factors such as personal resilience, social support, and access to resources. Building coping skills and fostering resilience are crucial in mitigating the psycho-social impact of disasters.

Community Rebuilding and Social Cohesion: Communities affected by disasters often face the task of rebuilding their social fabric and fostering social cohesion. Rebuilding communities require collaborative efforts, participation, and engagement from community members. The process of community rebuilding can promote a sense of purpose, connectedness, and collective resilience.

Access to Mental Health Support: Providing access to mental health support services is crucial for addressing psycho-social issues in disaster-affected populations. This includes ensuring access to trained mental health professionals, counselling services, and psychosocial support programs. Community-based and culturally appropriate interventions are important in meeting the diverse needs of individuals and communities.

Empowerment and Participation: Empowering individuals and communities to actively participate in the recovery and decision-making process promotes a sense of control, resilience, and well-being. Encouraging participation in community initiatives, decision-making forums, and recovery planning helps individuals regain a sense of agency and rebuild their lives.

Training and Capacity Building: Building the capacity of healthcare providers, community leaders, and first responders in recognizing and addressing psycho-social issues is essential. Training programs on psychological first aid, trauma-informed care, and psychosocial support equip individuals with the skills and knowledge to provide effective support to affected populations.

Children and Vulnerable Populations: Children and vulnerable populations, such as older adults, individuals with disabilities, and marginalized groups, may experience unique psycho-social issues following a disaster. Children may exhibit behavioural changes, fear, anxiety, and difficulty coping with the disruption. Vulnerable populations may face additional challenges due to limited resources, access barriers, and pre-existing health conditions. Tailored interventions and support are necessary to address their specific psycho-social needs.

Secondary Traumatic Stress: Professionals and volunteers involved in disaster response and recovery efforts may experience secondary traumatic stress. This is a result of exposure to the trauma and suffering of others. Caregivers, healthcare providers, and emergency responders are particularly susceptible to secondary traumatic stress. Providing support and resources for self-care, debriefing, and mental health services for these individuals is essential.

Cultural and Language Considerations: Cultural and language factors play a significant role in psycho-social issues following a disaster. Cultural beliefs, practices, and norms influence how individuals and communities perceive and respond to traumatic events. Language barriers can limit access to information and support services. It is important to consider cultural and language diversity when designing interventions and ensuring the availability of culturally sensitive mental health services.

Community Resilience and Social Support: Community resilience and social support networks are vital in addressing psycho-social issues. Strong social networks, cohesive communities, and supportive relationships contribute to individuals' ability to cope with the stress and challenges of disasters. Promoting community resilience through community engagement, mutual support, and strengthening social capital can mitigate the psycho-social impact.

Gender-specific Psycho-social Issues: Gender-specific psycho-social issues may arise following a disaster. Women, men, and gender minorities may have different experiences and needs. For example, women may face gender-based violence, reproductive health challenges, or caregiving burdens. Understanding and addressing gender-specific psycho-social issues through gender-sensitive interventions is important for promoting gender equality and well-being.

Resettlement and Rehabilitation Challenges: In cases where displacement or relocation is necessary, psycho-social issues can arise during resettlement and rehabilitation processes. Displaced individuals may experience a sense of loss, disorientation, and difficulty adjusting to new environments. Providing support and assistance in terms of housing, livelihoods, and community integration can help mitigate the psycho-social challenges associated with resettlement.

Information and Communication: Effective communication and accurate information sharing are crucial in addressing psycho-social issues. Accessible, reliable, and timely information helps reduce uncertainty, alleviate anxiety, and promote trust among affected populations. Utilizing multiple communication channels, employing culturally appropriate messaging, and ensuring language accessibility are key considerations in effective communication.

Long-Term Psycho-social Support: Recovery from psycho-social issues may extend beyond the immediate aftermath of a disaster. Long-term psycho-social support is often necessary to address the lasting effects of trauma, loss, and disruption. This can include continued access to mental health services, community-based support groups, and programs that promote resilience and well-being.

Research and Evidence: Research and evidence-generation efforts are vital in advancing the understanding of psycho-social issues and informing effective interventions. Conducting studies on the psycho-social impact of disasters, evaluating the effectiveness of interventions, and identifying best practices contribute to evidence-based approaches in addressing psycho-social needs.

Integration of Mental Health in Disaster Planning: Integrating mental health considerations into disaster planning and preparedness efforts is essential. This includes developing mental health components in disaster response plans, training emergency responders in psychological first aid, and incorporating mental health assessments and support services into emergency response systems.

It is important to note that psycho-social issues can vary based on the nature and severity of the disaster, cultural context, and individual experiences. Tailoring interventions to address specific psycho-social needs and promoting community resilience are key in supporting the psychological and social well-being of disaster-affected populations.

Addressing psycho-social issues requires a comprehensive and multi-dimensional approach that encompasses mental health support, community engagement, social support systems, and cultural sensitivity. By recognizing and responding to the psycho-social needs of affected individuals and communities, disaster management efforts can promote resilience, recovery, and well-being in the aftermath of a disaster.

6.3 Public Health Challenges During Disasters

Public health challenges during disasters in India are complex and significant, as the country is prone to a variety of natural and man-made disasters due to its geographical location, climate, and population density. Disasters can include earthquakes, floods, cyclones, droughts, industrial accidents, disease outbreaks, and more. During such events, public health becomes a critical concern as the impact on the health and well-being of individuals and communities can be devastating. Here are some key aspects of the public health challenges faced during disasters in India:

Infrastructure Damage and Healthcare Access: Disasters often result in the destruction of critical infrastructure, including healthcare facilities such as hospitals, clinics, and primary health centers. This hampers access to medical services for both disaster-related injuries and pre-existing health conditions. Roads, bridges, and communication networks may also be damaged, making it difficult for medical teams and relief workers to reach affected areas promptly.

Injuries and Casualties: Disasters can cause a large number of injuries and fatalities, overwhelming the existing healthcare facilities. Trauma care, emergency services, and medical supplies may be insufficient to handle the sudden surge in patients, leading to delayed or inadequate treatment.

Waterborne Diseases: Flooding, a common occurrence during disasters like monsoons and cyclones, can contaminate water sources, leading to outbreaks of waterborne diseases such as cholera, typhoid, and diarrhea. Lack of access to clean drinking water and proper sanitation facilities exacerbates the risk of these diseases spreading rapidly.

Vector-Borne Diseases: Stagnant water after flooding provides breeding grounds for mosquitoes, leading to an increased risk of vector-borne diseases like malaria and dengue. Displaced populations, living in temporary shelters, may be more vulnerable to these diseases due to inadequate protection from mosquito bites.

Malnutrition and Food Insecurity: Disasters can disrupt agricultural activities, damage crops, and compromise food supplies, leading to food scarcity and price hikes. People in disaster-hit areas may face malnutrition and nutritional deficiencies, especially vulnerable groups such as children, pregnant women, and the elderly.

Mental Health Concerns: Disasters have a profound psychological impact on individuals and communities, leading to increased stress, anxiety, depression, and trauma. The loss of loved ones, livelihoods, and property can lead to long-term mental health challenges that require appropriate support and counselling services.

Infectious Disease Outbreaks: In crowded and unsanitary conditions, infectious diseases can spread rapidly, particularly respiratory infections like influenza. Displacement and the gathering of people in relief camps or shelters can facilitate the transmission of diseases.

Vulnerable Populations: Disasters disproportionately affect vulnerable populations, including the poor, elderly, disabled, and marginalized communities, who may face additional challenges in accessing healthcare and relief services.

Healthcare Workforce Strain: The healthcare system may already be strained before a disaster, and the event can further burden the healthcare workforce with additional responsibilities and long working hours.

Communicable Diseases and Epidemics: Disasters often lead to overcrowded and unsanitary conditions in evacuation centers or relief camps. These settings can facilitate the rapid spread of communicable diseases, such as respiratory infections (e.g., flu, COVID-19), measles, and tuberculosis. Lack of access to proper hygiene facilities, clean water, and sanitation increases the risk of disease transmission among the displaced population.

Medical Supply Chain Disruptions: Disasters can disrupt the supply chain for medicines, vaccines, medical equipment, and other essential healthcare supplies. Roads may be blocked, warehouses damaged, or transportation networks disrupted, hindering the timely delivery of critical medical resources. This can create shortages and difficulties in providing adequate medical care to disaster-affected communities.

Mass Displacement and Healthcare Continuity: Disasters often result in the mass displacement of people from their homes and communities. Ensuring healthcare continuity for those displaced can be a major challenge. Establishing temporary medical facilities, providing medical records, and ensuring the availability of essential medications become crucial tasks.

Nutritional Needs and Food Safety: Disruptions to food production and distribution systems can lead to food shortages and unsafe food practices. Proper food safety measures must be implemented in relief camps to prevent foodborne illnesses, and nutritional requirements should be met, especially for vulnerable groups.

Limited Access to Specialized Care: Some disasters may cause severe injuries and health conditions requiring specialized medical care, such as surgeries or treatments for chronic illnesses. Access to such specialized care might be limited in disaster-affected areas, necessitating timely evacuation or transfers to hospitals in relatively safer regions.

Emergency Medical Evacuations: In areas with challenging terrain or remote locations, conducting emergency medical evacuations can be difficult during disasters. Adequate transportation and communication systems need to be in place to ensure timely evacuations of critically ill or injured individuals.

Psychosocial Support: Psychological first aid and mental health support are essential components of disaster response. Survivors may experience trauma, grief, and emotional distress, which can impact their overall well-being and recovery. Trained mental health professionals and counsellors should be available to provide psychosocial support to affected individuals and communities.

Disease Surveillance and Early Warning Systems: Robust disease surveillance systems are critical during disasters to detect and respond promptly to disease outbreaks. Early warning systems, especially for weather-related disasters, can help in initiating preventive measures and evacuations to minimize the impact on public health.

Community Engagement and Education: Engaging with local communities and raising awareness about disaster preparedness, hygiene practices, and disease prevention can empower individuals to take appropriate actions during emergencies. Education programs can also help reduce misinformation and promote healthier behaviours.

Coordination and Collaboration: Effective disaster response requires seamless coordination and collaboration among various stakeholders, including government agencies, healthcare providers, NGOs, international organizations, and volunteers. Well-coordinated efforts can optimize the allocation of resources and maximize the impact of relief and healthcare services.

Long-Term Health Impacts: Disasters can have long-term health effects on affected populations, including chronic health conditions, disabilities, and increased vulnerability to future disasters. Post-disaster healthcare systems should be equipped to handle the long-term health needs of the affected communities.

To address these public health challenges, effective disaster preparedness, response, and recovery strategies are essential. Improved coordination between various government agencies, healthcare institutions, NGOs, and international organizations can help in providing timely and adequate medical assistance and relief to affected communities. Investing in disaster-resistant infrastructure, early warning systems, and community education can also play a crucial role in reducing the impact of disasters on public health in India.

Addressing public health challenges during disasters in India requires a comprehensive and multi-faceted approach. This involves not only responding to immediate medical needs but also implementing measures for disaster preparedness, strengthening healthcare infrastructure, promoting community resilience, and ensuring the availability of essential medical supplies. The integration of public health considerations into disaster management plans can significantly reduce the health impact of disasters and contribute to the well-being and recovery of affected populations.

6.4 Public Health Challenges Addressed by Government

The Government of India addresses public health challenges posed by various disasters through a multi-tiered approach, involving preparedness, response, and recovery measures. The responsibility for disaster management and public health primarily lies with the National Disaster Management Authority (NDMA), State Disaster Management Authorities (SDMAs), and District Disaster Management Authorities (DDMAs), with support from various ministries, departments, and agencies.

Disaster Management Plans:

The government develops comprehensive disaster management plans that encompass various aspects, including public health. These plans outline the roles and responsibilities of different agencies and specify actions to be taken during each phase of the disaster management cycle (mitigation, preparedness, response, and recovery).

Capacity Building and Training: The government conducts training programs for various stakeholders, including healthcare professionals, emergency responders, and community volunteers, to enhance their capacity to respond effectively during disasters. Specialized training on disaster-specific health issues, like managing disease outbreaks, trauma care, and psychosocial support, is also provided.

Early Warning Systems: The government invests in early warning systems to provide timely alerts for impending disasters, especially weather-related events like cyclones, floods, and heatwaves. Early warnings help in proactive evacuation and preparedness, minimizing the impact on public health.

Emergency Medical Services: The government ensures the availability of emergency medical services, including ambulances and medical teams, to respond promptly to medical emergencies during disasters. Mobile medical units may be deployed to provide healthcare in remote and inaccessible areas.

Healthcare Infrastructure and Resources: Strengthening healthcare infrastructure in disaster-prone areas is a priority. This includes establishing and upgrading hospitals, primary health centers, and medical facilities to handle increased patient load during disasters. Ensuring an adequate stock of medicines, vaccines, medical equipment, and supplies is critical to meet the surge in healthcare demands.

Disease Surveillance and Control: The government maintains disease surveillance systems to detect and respond to disease outbreaks promptly. Rapid response teams are activated to investigate and contain outbreaks, and preventive measures such as vaccination drives may be implemented.

Public Health Campaigns and Awareness: Public health campaigns are conducted to raise awareness about disaster preparedness, safe drinking water practices, hygiene, and disease prevention. The government disseminates health-related information through various media channels to educate the public.

Relief and Rehabilitation: During disasters, the government provides relief measures, including food, water, and shelter, to affected communities. Ensuring the safety and hygiene of relief camps is a priority to prevent the spread of diseases. Post-disaster rehabilitation efforts focus on restoring healthcare services, infrastructure, and support systems.

Mental Health Support: The government acknowledges the importance of psychosocial support for disaster survivors and provides counselling services to address mental health challenges. Specialized mental health teams are deployed to offer support and interventions.

Community Participation: The government encourages community participation in disaster management and public health initiatives. Local communities are involved in planning, response, and recovery efforts, as they have valuable knowledge of their areas and can play a significant role in disaster resilience.

Research and Development: The government promotes research and development in disaster management and public health to continuously improve preparedness and response strategies. Lessons learned from previous disasters are incorporated into future planning.

International Collaboration: The government collaborates with international organizations and other countries to access additional resources, expertise, and support during large-scale disasters.

It is important to note that while the government takes significant steps to address public health challenges during disasters, there are always opportunities for improvement. Investing in long-term disaster risk reduction, ensuring effective implementation of disaster management plans, and enhancing community resilience are ongoing efforts to enhance public health preparedness in India. Additionally, lessons learned from each disaster can guide the refinement of strategies and policies to better protect public health in the future.

6.5 Role of MoHFW in Disaster Management

The Ministry of Health and Family Welfare (MoHFW) in India plays a crucial role in disaster management, particularly in addressing public health challenges during various disasters. The ministry's responsibilities encompass disaster preparedness, response, and recovery measures to safeguard the health and well-being of affected communities.

Policy Formulation and Guidelines: The MoHFW is responsible for formulating national policies and guidelines related to public health aspects of disaster management. These policies provide a framework for disaster preparedness, response, and recovery, focusing on healthcare services, disease control, mental health support, and community engagement.

Coordination with Other Ministries and Agencies: The MoHFW collaborates with other ministries, including the National Disaster Management Authority (NDMA), Ministry of Home Affairs, Ministry of Defense, and State Governments, to ensure a coordinated and efficient response to disasters. This coordination helps in the timely mobilization of resources and enhances the effectiveness of disaster management efforts.

Healthcare Infrastructure and Resource Planning: The ministry is responsible for assessing and planning the healthcare infrastructure needed to manage potential health crises during disasters. This includes ensuring the availability of hospitals, medical facilities, and supplies in disaster-prone areas. Emergency medical response plans and medical stockpiles are developed to meet the increased demand for healthcare services during disasters.

Disease Surveillance and Control: The MoHFW maintains disease surveillance systems to detect and respond promptly to disease outbreaks during disasters. This includes monitoring infectious diseases, providing rapid diagnostic capabilities, and coordinating with state health departments to control the spread of diseases.

Public Health Communication and Awareness: The ministry engages in public health communication and awareness campaigns to educate the public about disaster preparedness, hygiene practices, and disease prevention. Information is disseminated through various media channels to reach a wide audience and ensure a well-informed public.

Emergency Medical Services: The MoHFW ensures the availability of emergency medical services, including ambulances, medical teams, and trained personnel, to respond promptly to medical emergencies during disasters. Mobile medical units and medical camps may be deployed to provide healthcare in remote and affected areas.

Mental Health Support: The ministry recognizes the importance of psychosocial support for disaster survivors and provides counselling services to address mental health challenges. Specialized mental health teams are deployed to offer support and interventions.

Capacity Building and Training: The MoHFW conducts training programs for healthcare professionals, emergency responders, and community volunteers to enhance their capacity to respond effectively during disasters. Specialized training on disaster-specific health issues, such as trauma care and disease outbreak management, is also provided.

Rehabilitation and Recovery: Post-disaster, the MoHFW contributes to the rehabilitation and recovery efforts, focusing on restoring healthcare services, infrastructure, and support systems in affected areas.

Research and Development: The ministry promotes research and development in disaster management and public health to continuously improve preparedness and response strategies. Lessons learned from previous disasters are incorporated into future planning.

Epidemic and Outbreak Management: The MoHFW takes a proactive approach to prevent and control disease outbreaks during disasters. This includes pre-positioning essential medicines, vaccines, and medical supplies to quickly respond to potential epidemics. Rapid response teams are activated to investigate and contain outbreaks, and preventive measures such as vaccination drives may be implemented.

Logistical Support and Resource Mobilization: During a disaster, the MoHFW plays a critical role in coordinating the logistics of healthcare resource deployment. This involves mobilizing medical personnel, equipment, and supplies to the affected areas. The ministry collaborates with the private sector, NGOs, and international organizations to leverage additional resources and support.

Assessment and Needs Analysis: The MoHFW conducts rapid health assessments to understand the immediate health needs of affected populations. This information guides the allocation of resources and helps in formulating targeted response strategies.

Technical Support to States and Union Territories: The MoHFW provides technical support and guidance to state governments and Union Territories in disaster-prone areas. This support ensures that local health authorities are well-prepared to handle disaster-related health challenges. The ministry may also deploy public health experts and emergency response teams to assist states in managing health crises.

Capacity Building at the Community Level: Recognizing the importance of community involvement, the MoHFW conducts capacity-building programs at the grassroots level. Local communities are trained to respond effectively during disasters, identify health risks, and implement preventive measures.

Coordinating Medical Relief and Aid: In collaboration with other ministries, the MoHFW facilitates the coordination of medical relief and aid from various sources, including international organizations and foreign governments. This coordination ensures that medical assistance reaches the affected areas in a timely and organized manner.

National Disaster Response Force (NDRF) Cooperation: The MoHFW collaborates with the National Disaster Response Force (NDRF) to integrate medical response capabilities into disaster operations. Medical teams from the NDRF, which include doctors, paramedics, and medical equipment, provide vital support during emergencies.

Research and Innovation for Resilience: The ministry encourages research and innovation in disaster management and public health to develop new solutions for enhancing disaster resilience. Studies on disaster impact, health risks, and best practices contribute to evidence-based policies and strategies.

Post-Disaster Public Health Surveys: After a disaster, the MoHFW conducts public health surveys to assess the health status of affected communities and identify any emerging health needs. The findings from these surveys inform ongoing recovery efforts and healthcare planning.

Cooperation with International Partners: The MoHFW collaborates with international organizations, such as the World Health Organization (WHO) and other countries, to share experiences, expertise, and best practices in disaster management and public health. International cooperation enhances India's ability to respond to large-scale disasters and public health emergencies.

The Ministry of Health and Family Welfare plays a vital role in integrating public health considerations into the overall disaster management framework. Its efforts are aimed at minimizing the impact of disasters on public health and ensuring the well-being of affected communities through timely and effective healthcare services.

Overall, the Ministry of Health and Family Welfare plays a central role in safeguarding public health during disasters. Its initiatives encompass disaster preparedness, response, and recovery efforts, with a focus on ensuring access to healthcare services, controlling disease outbreaks, and providing psychosocial support to affected communities. The ministry's proactive approach and collaborative efforts with various stakeholders contribute to building resilience and minimizing the impact of disasters on public health in India.

6.6 Role of NDMA in Disaster Management

The National Disaster Management Authority (NDMA) is the apex body responsible for disaster management in India. It plays a pivotal role in formulating policies, planning, coordinating, and implementing disaster management efforts across the country. The NDMA operates under the Ministry of Home Affairs and functions as the primary agency for disaster risk reduction and response.

Policy Formulation and Guidelines: The NDMA is responsible for formulating national policies, plans, and guidelines related to disaster management. It sets the overall direction and framework for disaster preparedness, mitigation, response, and recovery at the national level. These policies aim to integrate disaster risk reduction into development planning and ensure a well-coordinated and effective response to disasters.

Disaster Risk Assessment and Mapping: The NDMA conducts risk assessments to identify areas prone to various types of disasters, such as earthquakes, floods, cyclones, droughts, and industrial accidents. Vulnerability and hazard mapping are undertaken to understand the potential impact of disasters on different regions and communities.

Early Warning Systems: The NDMA is involved in establishing and strengthening early warning systems for various types of disasters. This includes weather-related events like cyclones, floods, and heatwaves, as well as geological events like earthquakes. Timely dissemination of warnings to the public and relevant authorities helps in saving lives and minimizing damage.

Capacity Building and Training: The NDMA conducts training programs and capacity-building initiatives for various stakeholders involved in disaster management, including government officials, emergency responders, community volunteers, and NGOs. Training covers aspects such as disaster response protocols, first aid, search and rescue techniques, and incident command systems.

Coordination and Collaboration: The NDMA facilitates coordination among various ministries, departments, and agencies involved in disaster management at the national, state, and district levels. It collaborates with state governments, Union Territories, and other stakeholders to ensure a well-coordinated and integrated response to disasters.

Response Planning and Preparedness: The NDMA assists in formulating national and state-level disaster response plans. These plans outline the roles and responsibilities of different agencies, resource requirements, and the coordination mechanism during disasters. Regular mock drills and exercises are conducted to test the preparedness of various stakeholders and improve the effectiveness of response efforts.

Post-Disaster Assessment and Recovery: The NDMA is involved in post-disaster assessment to evaluate the impact of a disaster and the effectiveness of the response. based on the assessment, it helps in formulating strategies for recovery and rehabilitation, including measures to restore essential services and infrastructure.

Technology and Innovation: The NDMA leverages technology and innovation for disaster risk reduction and response. This includes the use of geospatial technology, remote sensing, and data analytics for better disaster planning and decision-making.

Public Awareness and Education: The NDMA conducts public awareness campaigns to educate citizens about disaster preparedness, safe practices, and evacuation procedures. The authority emphasizes community participation and involvement in disaster risk reduction efforts.

International Cooperation: The NDMA collaborates with international organizations and other countries to access additional resources, expertise, and support during large-scale disasters. It shares experiences, best practices, and lessons learned with other nations to strengthen global disaster management efforts.

Research and Development: The NDMA promotes research and development in disaster management to continuously improve preparedness and response strategies. It supports studies on disaster impact, risk assessment, early warning systems, and resilience-building measures.

The NDMA's role in disaster management is comprehensive, covering all phases of the disaster management cycle. By providing strategic direction, coordination, and technical support, the NDMA aims to enhance India's disaster resilience and reduce the impact of disasters on communities and infrastructure. The authority's efforts are crucial in safeguarding lives, protecting livelihoods, and promoting sustainable development in the face of natural and man-made disasters.

6.6.1 Awareness Programs and Strategies by NDMA

The National Disaster Management Authority (NDMA) of India runs various programs and strategies to raise awareness and promote disaster management preparedness among different segments of society. These initiatives aim to educate and empower people to understand the risks associated with disasters, adopt preventive measures, and respond effectively in times of crisis. Here are some of the key programs and strategies undertaken by NDMA for disaster management awareness:

School Safety Program: The School Safety Program focuses on creating a safe and resilient school environment by integrating disaster management concepts into the school curriculum. It involves training teachers, students, and school staff on disaster preparedness, conducting mock drills, and establishing School Disaster Response Teams (SDRTs) to handle emergencies.

Community-Based Disaster Risk Reduction (CBDRR): NDMA promotes community participation and engagement in disaster risk reduction efforts through the Community-Based Disaster Risk Reduction program. The program encourages local communities to identify and address their unique vulnerabilities, conduct risk assessments, and develop localized response plans.

Mass Awareness Campaigns: NDMA conducts mass awareness campaigns through various media channels, including television, radio, print, and social media, to disseminate information about disaster preparedness and safety measures. These campaigns often focus on specific types of disasters, such as earthquakes, floods, cyclones, and fire safety.

National Disaster Response Force (NDRF) Awareness Program: The NDRF Awareness Program aims to educate citizens about the role and capabilities of the National Disaster Response Force (NDRF) in disaster response and rescue operations. It helps people understand how to seek help and support from NDRF during emergencies.

Information, Education, and Communication (IEC) Materials: NDMA develops and distributes Information, Education, and Communication (IEC) materials, including brochures, posters, leaflets, and booklets, in various regional languages to reach a wider audience. These materials provide practical tips and guidelines for disaster preparedness and response.

Mock Drills and Tabletop Exercises: To enhance disaster preparedness and response capacities, NDMA organizes mock drills and tabletop exercises at various levels, involving government officials, emergency responders, and the public. These exercises simulate disaster scenarios and test the effectiveness of response plans and coordination mechanisms.

School and College Competitions: NDMA conducts various competitions and contests in schools and colleges to encourage young minds to actively participate in disaster management awareness initiatives. Competitions may include poster-making, essay writing, and quiz competitions on disaster-related topics.

International Day for Disaster Reduction (IDDR) Celebrations: NDMA observes the International Day for Disaster Reduction (IDDR) on October 13th each year to promote global awareness about disaster risk reduction. Special events, workshops, and seminars are organized to discuss disaster-related issues and share best practices.

Capacity Building Workshops and Training: NDMA conducts capacity-building workshops and training programs for stakeholders, including government officials, NGOs, community leaders, and volunteers. These programs aim to build technical skills and knowledge related to disaster management.

National Disaster Management Guidelines and Manuals: NDMA publishes comprehensive guidelines and manuals on various aspects of disaster management, including community-based disaster preparedness, hospital safety, and school safety. These documents serve as reference materials for various stakeholders involved in disaster management.

Media Sensitization Workshops: NDMA organizes media sensitization workshops to build the capacity of journalists and media professionals in reporting on disasters accurately and responsibly. The workshops emphasize the role of media in disseminating accurate information during emergencies.

By implementing these programs and strategies, NDMA aims to foster a culture of disaster resilience, where individuals, communities, and institutions are better prepared to mitigate the impact of disasters and respond effectively to protect lives and property. Public awareness and participation are considered key elements in building a safer and more disaster-resilient India.

6.7 Role of WHO in Disaster Management

The World Health Organization (WHO) plays a crucial role in disaster management by providing leadership, technical expertise, and coordination in public health response during emergencies and disasters. As the leading international public health agency, the WHO collaborates with countries and other partners to strengthen disaster preparedness, response, and recovery efforts.

Emergency Response Coordination: The WHO coordinates and supports the health response during emergencies and disasters, including outbreaks, natural disasters, conflicts, and complex emergencies. It works with national health authorities, other United Nations agencies, and humanitarian partners to ensure a well-coordinated and effective response.

Health Needs Assessment: During a disaster, the WHO conducts rapid health needs assessments to identify the immediate health needs of affected populations. The assessments help determine the priority areas for health intervention and resource allocation.

Public Health Emergency Declarations: The WHO has the authority to declare a Public Health Emergency of International Concern (PHEIC) when a health event poses a significant risk to multiple countries and requires international cooperation. This declaration mobilizes global response efforts and resources to address the emergency.

Health Information and Guidance: The WHO provides evidence-based health information, guidelines, and technical advice to affected countries on various aspects of disaster management, including disease control, trauma care, mental health support, and healthcare delivery in emergencies.

Logistical Support and Medical Supplies: The organization facilitates the deployment of medical personnel, supplies, and equipment to support affected countries' healthcare systems. It also maintains a Strategic Health Operations Center to manage health emergency response logistics.

Disease Surveillance and Control: The WHO supports disease surveillance systems to detect and respond to disease outbreaks during disasters. It helps countries implement measures for disease control and prevention, such as vaccination campaigns and disease containment strategies.

Health Cluster Coordination: In humanitarian crises, the WHO leads the Health Cluster, which is a group of organizations working together to provide health services in emergencies. The Health Cluster coordinates health activities, resource mobilization, and service delivery to ensure a coherent and effective health response.

Training and Capacity Building: The WHO conducts training programs and capacity-building initiatives for healthcare professionals and emergency responders to enhance their preparedness and response skills. These programs include training on specific health interventions required during disasters.

Public Health Risk Communication: The WHO engages in risk communication to inform the public, health workers, and decision-makers about health risks, protective measures, and response actions during disasters. Timely and accurate communication helps dispel misinformation and supports informed decision-making.

Mental Health and Psychosocial Support: The WHO emphasizes the importance of mental health and psychosocial support during and after disasters. It provides guidance and resources to address the psychosocial needs of affected individuals and communities.

Research and Innovation: The WHO promotes research and innovation in disaster management and public health to develop new solutions for enhancing preparedness and response. It supports studies on disaster impact, health risks, and best practices for health interventions.

Advocacy and Policy Development: The WHO advocates for disaster risk reduction and health resilience at the global, regional, and national levels. It helps countries develop policies and strategies to integrate disaster risk reduction into their health systems and development plans.

Coordination of International Assistance: The WHO plays a central role in coordinating international assistance and support during large-scale disasters and emergencies. It mobilizes resources from member states, partner organizations, and donors to provide essential medical supplies, equipment, and funding for health interventions in affected countries.

Health System Strengthening: Disaster management efforts by the WHO often emphasize health system strengthening in vulnerable regions. This includes enhancing healthcare infrastructure, training healthcare workers, improving supply chain management, and ensuring access to essential health services.

Health and Disaster Risk Reduction Integration: The WHO advocates for integrating health concerns into disaster risk reduction strategies. This involves promoting risk-informed health policies, investing in healthcare infrastructure that can withstand disasters, and ensuring access to healthcare services during emergencies.

Capacity Building for National Health Authorities: The WHO works closely with national health authorities to build their capacity in disaster management and emergency response. Training programs, workshops, and exercises are conducted to enhance the skills and knowledge of local health professionals and emergency responders.

Monitoring and Evaluation: The WHO conducts ongoing monitoring and evaluation of health interventions during and after disasters to assess their effectiveness. This feedback loop allows for continuous improvement of disaster response strategies and programs.

One Health Approach: The WHO promotes a One Health approach, recognizing that the health of humans, animals, and the environment are interconnected. This approach considers the health impacts of disasters on both human and animal populations and emphasizes zoonotic disease surveillance and control.

Building Partnerships and Alliances: The WHO builds partnerships and alliances with various stakeholders, including other UN agencies, international organizations, NGOs, and academia, to strengthen global disaster management efforts. Collaboration with these partners allows for coordinated action and resource pooling.

Preparedness for Potential Global Health Threats: The WHO closely monitors potential global health threats, such as emerging infectious diseases and pandemics, and supports countries in their preparedness efforts. It establishes contingency plans, stockpiles essential medical supplies, and provides technical guidance to countries for effective response in case of a global health emergency.

Humanitarian Health Action: The WHO leads the health component of humanitarian response efforts in complex emergencies and protracted crises. It focuses on providing healthcare services, water, sanitation, nutrition, and disease control measures in displaced populations and vulnerable communities.

Disaster Risk Communication: The WHO supports countries in developing risk communication strategies to disseminate timely and accurate health information to the public before, during, and after disasters. Effective risk communication helps build public trust and encourages adherence to preventive measures.

Overall, the World Health Organization plays a critical role in strengthening health systems' resilience and response capacities to address public health challenges during disasters and emergencies worldwide. Its technical expertise, global reach, and coordination mechanisms contribute to effective disaster management and protect the health and well-being of affected populations. The WHO's multifaceted role in disaster management reflects its commitment to ensuring the health and well-being of populations affected by emergencies and disasters. By providing technical expertise, capacity building, and coordination, the WHO strengthens the global response to health-related crises, reduces the impact of disasters on communities, and contributes to building resilient health systems worldwide.

6.7.1 Awareness Strategies and Programs by WHO

The World Health Organization (WHO) implements various strategies and programs to raise awareness about disaster management and promote preparedness among communities, governments, and healthcare professionals worldwide. These initiatives aim to empower individuals and institutions with the knowledge and tools to effectively respond to disasters and protect public health. Here are some of the key strategies and programs run by WHO for awareness about disaster management:

Sendai Framework for Disaster Risk Reduction: The Sendai Framework is a global strategy adopted in 2015 to guide disaster risk reduction efforts worldwide. The WHO actively promotes the implementation of this framework, which emphasizes the importance of integrating health concerns into disaster risk reduction strategies.

Emergency and Disaster Risk Management (EDRM): EDRM is a comprehensive approach advocated by the WHO to enhance resilience and responsiveness to emergencies and disasters. The program emphasizes strengthening health systems, building capacity at all levels, and fostering partnerships for effective disaster management.

Health Emergency and Disaster Risk Management (Health EDRM) Training: The Health EDRM training program provides specialized courses and workshops to healthcare professionals and emergency responders. The training covers various aspects of disaster management, including preparedness, risk assessment, early warning systems, response planning, and recovery.

Emergency Medical Teams (EMTs) Initiative: The EMTs Initiative, led by the WHO, focuses on developing and coordinating the deployment of medical teams during emergencies and disasters. The program ensures that these teams are well-trained, qualified, and follow established standards to provide effective medical care in disaster-affected areas.

Public Health Emergency Operations Center (PHEOC): WHO supports countries in establishing and strengthening PHEOCs, which serve as central coordination hubs during health emergencies. PHEOCs facilitate real-time information sharing, decision-making, and resource allocation during disaster response.

Emergency Medical Teams (EMTs) Classification and Verification: The WHO classifies and verifies emergency medical teams to ensure their quality and capacity to respond effectively during disasters. Verified teams are listed in the WHO Global EMTs Registry, facilitating coordination and deployment during emergencies.

Health Cluster Coordination Training: The Health Cluster Coordination Training equips health professionals with the skills to coordinate and manage health clusters during humanitarian crises. The training emphasizes inter-agency collaboration and the integration of health services in humanitarian response.

Disaster and Emergency Events Preparedness (DEEP) Program: DEEP is a capacity-building program that enhances the preparedness of healthcare facilities and professionals to respond to emergencies and disasters. It includes scenario-based exercises and drills to test response plans and improve readiness.

Disaster Preparedness for Hospitals (DPH) Program: The DPH program focuses on strengthening the capacity of hospitals to withstand and respond to disasters. It includes risk assessment, safety audits, and planning for surge capacity during emergencies.

Mental Health and Psychosocial Support (MHPSS) in Emergencies: WHO runs programs to raise awareness about the importance of mental health and psychosocial support during and after disasters. The initiative aims to address the mental health needs of affected populations and reduce the long-term impact of traumatic events.

Global Health Security Agenda (GHSA): The GHSA, supported by WHO, focuses on strengthening global capacity to prevent, detect, and respond to infectious disease outbreaks and other health emergencies. It promotes collaboration among countries to build resilience against health threats.

Health and Climate Change: WHO's work on health and climate change emphasizes the link between climate-related disasters and public health impacts. Awareness campaigns highlight the importance of climate adaptation and mitigation measures for health protection.

These programs and strategies by WHO are part of a comprehensive approach to raise awareness and build capacity for disaster management at various levels. By disseminating knowledge, providing training, and fostering international collaboration, WHO contributes to global efforts in reducing disaster risks and protecting the health and well-being of communities around the world.

6.8 Psychosocial Support for Disaster Affected Populations

Providing mental health and psychosocial support (MHPSS) for disaster-affected populations is essential to help individuals cope with the emotional and psychological impacts of the traumatic event. Disasters can lead to increased stress, anxiety, depression, and other mental health challenges. Here are various ways to offer MHPSS to disaster-affected populations:

Crisis Counselling and Psychological First Aid (PFA): Trained mental health professionals and volunteers can provide crisis counselling and PFA immediately after the disaster. PFA involves active listening, empathy, and reassurance to help individuals feel supported and understood.

Community-based Support Groups: Establishing support groups within affected communities can create safe spaces for individuals to share their experiences, emotions, and coping strategies with others who have gone through similar situations.

Training Local Community Volunteers: Training local community members in basic counselling skills and techniques can extend the reach of MHPSS services and help identify individuals in need of more specialized support.

Psychological Debriefing: Psychological debriefing sessions, conducted by trained professionals, allow individuals to process their experiences and emotions in a structured and supportive environment.

Mental Health Hotlines and Helplines: Hotlines and helplines staffed by mental health professionals can provide immediate support, advice, and information to individuals seeking help for emotional distress.

Mobile Mental Health Clinics: Deploying mobile mental health clinics to disaster-affected areas allows for on-site psychological assessments and counselling services, particularly in remote or hard-to-reach locations.

Training Healthcare Workers in MHPSS: Training healthcare workers, including doctors, nurses, and emergency responders, in MHPSS enables them to identify and address mental health needs in the immediate aftermath of the disaster.

Child-Focused MHPSS Programs: Tailoring MHPSS interventions to the specific needs of children is crucial.

Child-friendly spaces and activities, as well as specialized counselling for children, can support their emotional recovery.

Promoting Resilience and Coping Skills: Providing information on coping strategies and resilience-building techniques can empower individuals to develop healthy ways of dealing with stress and trauma.

Incorporating Cultural and Spiritual Approaches: Recognizing and respecting cultural and spiritual practices can be important in MHPSS interventions, as these can serve as significant sources of support and coping for affected populations.

Referral Services: Establishing a referral network with mental health facilities and services ensures that individuals with more severe mental health needs can access appropriate and specialized care.

Training Educators and School Personnel: Supporting educators and school personnel in understanding the psychological needs of students after a disaster can create a safe and supportive learning environment.

Long-Term Support and Follow-up: Mental health support should extend beyond the immediate aftermath of the disaster. Providing long-term follow-up and care is crucial for sustained recovery.

Reducing Stigma and Raising Awareness: Public awareness campaigns can help reduce the stigma surrounding mental health issues and encourage affected individuals to seek support without fear of judgment.

Integration with Healthcare Services: Integrating mental health services with primary healthcare facilities ensures that MHPSS is accessible and part of routine healthcare.

By combining various MHPSS approaches and involving multiple stakeholders, including local communities, healthcare professionals, and organizations, disaster-affected populations can receive comprehensive and tailored support to cope with the emotional toll of the disaster and foster resilience in the face of adversity.

6.8.1 Importance of Psychosocial Support for Disaster Affected Populations

Providing mental health and psychosocial support (MHPSS) for disaster-affected populations is of paramount importance due to the significant impact disasters can have on individuals' emotional and psychological well-being. Disasters are traumatic events that can lead to a range of mental health challenges, including stress, anxiety, depression, post-traumatic stress disorder (PTSD), and other psychosocial difficulties. Here are the key reasons why offering MHPSS is crucial for disaster-affected populations:

Reducing Emotional Distress: Disasters can leave individuals feeling overwhelmed, scared, and emotionally distressed. MHPSS interventions help people process their emotions and cope with the trauma they have experienced, reducing emotional suffering.

Promoting Resilience and Coping: MHPSS empowers individuals with coping strategies and resilience-building techniques to better adapt to adverse circumstances. These skills enhance their ability to navigate the challenges posed by the disaster and rebuild their lives.

Supporting Recovery and Healing: Addressing mental health needs is an integral part of the overall recovery process after a disaster. MHPSS services facilitate healing and support individuals in regaining a sense of normalcy.

Enhancing Physical Health Outcomes: Mental and physical health are interconnected. Addressing mental health issues through MHPSS can positively impact physical health outcomes and promote overall well-being.

Strengthening Social Support Networks: MHPSS interventions, such as support groups, encourage social cohesion and bonding within affected communities. This sense of connection can be vital in the recovery process.

Mitigating Long-Term Psychological Impact: Untreated mental health issues resulting from the disaster can have long-term consequences on individuals and communities. Early intervention and support can prevent chronic mental health problems.

Supporting Vulnerable Populations: Certain groups, such as children, the elderly, and individuals with pre-existing mental health conditions, may be particularly vulnerable to the psychological impact of disasters. Targeted MHPSS interventions cater to the specific needs of these groups.

Facilitating Post-Trauma Adjustment: MHPSS helps individuals adjust to life after the traumatic event. It provides them with tools to manage triggers, anxiety, and distress associated with memories of the disaster.

Strengthening Community Resilience: By addressing mental health needs within the community, MHPSS contributes to building community resilience. Resilient communities are better equipped to cope with future challenges and disasters.

Improving Overall Quality of Life: Access to MHPSS can improve the overall quality of life for disaster-affected populations by supporting emotional well-being, interpersonal relationships, and social functioning.

Promoting Effective Disaster Response: Providing MHPSS during and after disasters helps stabilize affected individuals, enabling them to participate more effectively in response and recovery efforts.

Reducing Stigma around Mental Health: Offering MHPSS normalizes discussions about mental health and reduces stigma, making it more likely for individuals to seek help without hesitation.

Supporting Humanitarian Aid and Recovery Efforts: MHPSS is an essential component of humanitarian aid, ensuring the holistic well-being of disaster-affected populations alongside other life-saving interventions.

Enhancing Community Reintegration: MHPSS facilitates the reintegration of disaster survivors into their communities, workplaces, and social environments, promoting a sense of belonging and acceptance.

Contributing to Sustainable Development: By addressing mental health needs and fostering psychosocial well-being, MHPSS interventions contribute to the sustainable development of affected communities.

Thus, providing mental health and psychosocial support for disaster-affected populations is crucial for their emotional recovery, resilience, and overall well-being. It helps individuals and communities navigate the aftermath of the disaster, heal from the trauma, and rebuild their lives with greater strength and adaptability. Moreover, MHPSS interventions contribute to more effective disaster response and recovery efforts, ultimately leading to more resilient and thriving communities in the long term.

6.8.2 Aspects of Disease Outbreaks

Disease outbreaks are a significant public health concern during and after various natural disasters. Disasters can create conditions conducive to the spread of infectious diseases, posing additional challenges to disaster response and recovery efforts. Several aspects contribute to disease outbreaks during different types of natural disasters:

Contaminated Water Sources: Disasters such as floods and hurricanes can damage water supply systems and contaminate water sources with sewage, debris, and pollutants. Contaminated water can lead to waterborne diseases like cholera, dysentery, and hepatitis A.

Lack of Sanitation Facilities: Disasters may disrupt sanitation facilities and waste disposal systems, leading to poor hygiene conditions. The lack of proper sanitation can result in the spread of diseases like diarrheal illnesses, typhoid, and other enteric infections.

Displacement and Crowded Shelters: Disasters can force people to evacuate their homes and seek refuge in temporary shelters, evacuation centers, or crowded areas. Such conditions can promote the transmission of respiratory infections and communicable diseases.

Vector-Borne Diseases: Natural disasters can create breeding grounds for disease-carrying vectors like mosquitoes, flies, and rodents. Stagnant water after floods and disrupted waste management attracts vectors that can transmit diseases such as malaria, dengue fever, and leptospirosis.

Inadequate Health Services: Disasters can overwhelm healthcare facilities, disrupt supply chains, and hinder access to medical services. This can lead to delays in diagnosing and treating diseases, exacerbating their impact.

Mental Health Challenges: Natural disasters can lead to emotional distress, anxiety, and trauma, affecting mental health. Psychological factors can weaken the immune system and increase susceptibility to diseases.

Inadequate Nutrition: Disasters may disrupt food supply chains, leading to food shortages and malnutrition. Malnourished individuals are more vulnerable to infectious diseases and have reduced immunity.

Vector Control Challenges: After disasters, vector control measures may be challenging to implement due to resource constraints and disrupted infrastructure. This can result in increased vector populations and disease transmission.

Post-Disaster Health Risks: In the aftermath of disasters, individuals engaged in cleanup and reconstruction activities may be exposed to hazardous materials, leading to respiratory problems and other health issues.

Disease Importation: Disasters can cause population movements, including displaced individuals crossing borders. This movement can facilitate the spread of diseases across regions or countries.

Disruption of Disease Surveillance: Disasters can disrupt disease surveillance systems, making it challenging to track and respond to disease outbreaks effectively.

Reduced Access to Medications: Disasters may disrupt the supply of essential medications and vaccines, leading to reduced access to preventive and curative healthcare. Addressing Disease Outbreaks during Natural Disasters:

Preparedness and Response Planning: Governments and health authorities need to have disaster-specific preparedness and response plans in place, including measures to prevent and control disease outbreaks.

Rapid Assessment and Early Warning: Conducting rapid health assessments during and after disasters helps identify potential disease outbreaks early and triggers timely response measures.

Health Education and Communication: Public health authorities should conduct health education campaigns to raise awareness about disease risks, prevention, and hygiene practices.

Water, Sanitation, and Hygiene (WASH) Interventions: Providing access to safe drinking water, sanitation facilities, and promoting good hygiene practices are crucial in preventing waterborne diseases.

Vector Control Measures: Implementing vector control strategies, such as insecticide-treated bed nets and environmental management, can reduce the risk of vector-borne diseases.

Healthcare Infrastructure Strengthening: Strengthening healthcare infrastructure and capacity ensures that health services can effectively respond to disease outbreaks during and after disasters.

Mental Health and Psychosocial Support (MHPSS): Including MHPSS in disaster response efforts helps address emotional distress and promotes overall well-being.

Surveillance and Reporting Systems: Maintaining disease surveillance and reporting systems during and after disasters facilitates early detection and response to outbreaks.

Vaccination Campaigns: Implementing vaccination campaigns in disaster-affected areas can protect populations from vaccine-preventable diseases.

Coordination and Partnerships: Collaboration among local, national, and international organizations is essential in coordinating resources and expertise to address disease outbreaks during disasters. By addressing these various aspects and implementing appropriate measures, health authorities and disaster response teams can mitigate the risk of disease outbreaks, protect the health of affected populations, and support post-disaster recovery efforts.

Coordination of Health and Disaster Response Agencies: Effective coordination between health agencies and disaster response teams is crucial to ensure a swift and well-coordinated response to disease outbreaks. Clear communication channels and established protocols facilitate the integration of health considerations into disaster response plans.

Surge Capacity Planning: Health facilities must have surge capacity plans to accommodate an increased number of patients during disasters and disease outbreaks. Planning for additional healthcare staff, beds, medical supplies, and equipment is essential to manage the surge in healthcare needs.

Isolation and Quarantine Measures: Implementing isolation and quarantine measures can help prevent the spread of infectious diseases among disaster-affected populations. Identifying and isolating infected individuals and providing appropriate medical care are vital components of outbreak control.

Rapid Diagnostic Testing: Rapid and accurate diagnostic testing is essential for early detection of infectious diseases during disasters. Deploying mobile diagnostic units to affected areas can expedite testing and facilitate prompt intervention.

Prepositioning Medical Supplies: Prepositioning medical supplies, including medicines, vaccines, personal protective equipment (PPE), and diagnostic kits, in disaster-prone areas can ensure timely access during emergencies.

Community Engagement and Participation: Engaging affected communities in disease outbreak response efforts enhances the effectiveness and acceptance of public health interventions. Community participation in surveillance, contact tracing, and health education fosters a sense of ownership and responsibility.

Epidemic Risk Mapping: Conducting epidemic risk mapping can identify vulnerable areas and populations at higher risk of disease outbreaks during disasters. This information aids in targeted interventions and resource allocation.

Intersectoral Collaboration: Collaboration between health and other sectors, such as water and sanitation, housing, and education, is essential for addressing the root causes of disease outbreaks and implementing holistic interventions.

One Health Approach: Adopting a One Health approach, which recognizes the interconnectedness of human, animal, and environmental health, is critical in addressing zoonotic diseases during disasters.

Post-Disaster Surveillance and Monitoring: Continued surveillance and monitoring after disasters are essential to identify any delayed disease outbreaks or emerging health issues. Post-disaster health assessments can inform long-term recovery plans.

Capacity Building and Training: Regular training of healthcare personnel, first responders, and community health workers in disease outbreak management equips them with the skills and knowledge needed to respond effectively.

Research and Innovation: Investing in research and innovation in disaster health management can lead to the development of new technologies, diagnostic tools, and strategies for outbreak prevention and control.

Cross-Border Collaboration: For transboundary disasters, cross-border collaboration between neighbouring countries is crucial to address shared health risks and facilitate coordinated responses.

By addressing these various aspects of disease outbreaks during natural disasters, health authorities can better anticipate and respond to potential health threats, safeguarding the well-being of disaster-affected populations. Timely and effective intervention not only saves lives but also contributes to the long-term recovery and resilience of communities affected by disasters.

CHAPTER 7

Demographic Aspects in Disaster Management

7.1 Demographic Aspects of Disaster Impact

Demographic aspects play a significant role in understanding the impact of disasters on different population groups. Here are some key points regarding the demographic aspects of disaster impact, specifically focusing on gender, age, and special needs:

Gender: Disasters can affect genders differently due to social, cultural, and economic factors. Understanding gender dynamics is crucial for addressing the specific needs and vulnerabilities of men, women, girls, and boys during and after disasters. Here are some considerations related to gender:

a. Gender-Based Violence: Women and girls may face an increased risk of gender-based violence during and after disasters. Disruption of social structures, displacement, and increased stress contribute to this vulnerability. It is important to implement measures to prevent and respond to gender-based violence, including safe spaces, psychosocial support, and gender-sensitive services.

b. Caregiving Roles: Women often bear additional caregiving responsibilities during and after disasters. They may be responsible for the care and safety of children, elderly family members, and other vulnerable individuals. Supporting women's caregiving roles through accessible services and resources is essential.

c. Decision-Making and Participation: Ensuring women's meaningful participation in decision-making processes and leadership roles during disaster response and recovery efforts is crucial. Including women's perspectives and expertise promotes more inclusive and effective interventions.

Age: Different age groups have distinct vulnerabilities and needs during and after disasters. Here are some age-specific considerations:

a. Children: Children are particularly vulnerable during disasters due to their physiological, psychological, and developmental characteristics. They may experience fear, trauma, separation anxiety, and disruption of routines. Special attention should be given to providing safe spaces, psychosocial support, and education services tailored to their needs.

b. Elderly: Older adults may face challenges related to physical health, mobility, and chronic conditions during and after disasters. They may require assistance with evacuation, access to medication, and support in coping with the emotional impact of the disaster. Strategies should be in place to ensure their safety and well-being.

c. Youth: Adolescents and young adults may have unique psychosocial needs and may face challenges related to education, employment, and social integration. Engaging youth in disaster risk reduction activities and providing platforms for their participation can contribute to their resilience and empowerment.

Special Needs: Individuals with special needs require specific considerations and support to ensure their safety and well-being during disasters. Here are some aspects to consider:

a. Disabilities: Individuals with disabilities may face barriers in accessing information, evacuation, and receiving appropriate assistance. Providing accessible communication, transportation, shelters, and healthcare services is vital. Disability-inclusive emergency planning and coordination are necessary to address their specific needs.

b. Chronic Illnesses and Medical Conditions: Individuals with chronic illnesses, medical conditions, or specific healthcare needs may require ongoing medical care and access to medication during and after disasters. Ensuring continuity of care, medication availability, and access to specialized medical services is crucial.

c. Language and Cultural Considerations: Individuals with limited English proficiency and diverse cultural backgrounds may require language support and culturally sensitive services. Providing interpretation services, translated materials, and culturally appropriate support are essential for effective communication and understanding.

Understanding the demographic aspects of disaster impact helps in developing targeted interventions, allocating resources, and promoting inclusivity in disaster management. It is important to engage with diverse communities, involve relevant stakeholders, and adopt a holistic approach that addresses the specific needs and vulnerabilities of different demographic groups. By considering gender, age, and special needs, disaster management efforts can become more equitable, effective, and responsive to the diverse populations affected by disasters.

Gender and Vulnerability: Gender plays a significant role in determining vulnerability to disasters. Socio-cultural norms, economic disparities, and power dynamics can exacerbate the impact of disasters on certain gender groups. For example:

a. Women and girls may face greater challenges in accessing resources, healthcare, and decision-making processes. Their limited mobility, caregiving responsibilities, and social roles can increase their vulnerability during and after disasters.

b. Men may face specific challenges related to traditional gender roles, such as providing for their families and maintaining livelihoods. These roles can put them at increased risk during disaster situations.

c. LGBTQ+ individuals may experience unique challenges and discrimination, including limited access to services and support networks. Recognizing and addressing their specific needs is important for promoting inclusivity and equality in disaster management.

Age and Vulnerability: Different age groups have varying levels of vulnerability to disasters. Understanding age-specific needs and vulnerabilities is crucial for effective disaster response and recovery efforts. Here are some considerations:

a. Infants and young children: They depend on caregivers for their well-being and are particularly vulnerable during disasters. They may require special nutrition, hygiene, and protection measures.

b. older adults: They may have limited mobility, chronic health conditions, and reduced resilience, making them more susceptible to the physical and psychological impact of disasters. Supportive measures such as accessible evacuation plans, medical assistance, and social support are essential.

c. Adolescents and youth: They may experience unique psycho-social challenges related to identity formation, education, and social integration. Engaging youth in disaster risk reduction efforts and providing psychosocial support can promote their resilience and empowerment.

Special Needs and Vulnerability: Individuals with special needs have specific vulnerabilities that require tailored support and accommodations during disasters. Here are some considerations:

a. Physical disabilities: Individuals with physical disabilities may face challenges related to mobility, evacuation, and accessing essential services. Providing accessible infrastructure, transportation, and communication options is crucial.

b. Sensory disabilities: Individuals with hearing or vision impairments may require specific accommodations, such as sign language interpretation or visual aids, to ensure effective communication and access to information.

c. Cognitive disabilities: Individuals with cognitive disabilities may have difficulties understanding and following emergency procedures. Providing clear instructions, visual aids, and support from trained personnel can help address their needs.

Data and Monitoring: Collecting demographic data during and after disasters is important for identifying vulnerable groups, assessing the impact, and targeting interventions. Disaggregating data by gender, age, and special needs allows for a more nuanced understanding of the diverse populations affected by disasters. Regular monitoring of demographic trends helps identify emerging vulnerabilities and track progress in addressing the specific needs of different groups.

Community Engagement and Participation: Engaging with affected communities and involving them in decision-making processes is crucial for effective disaster management. Including diverse demographic groups in planning, response, and recovery efforts ensures their unique perspectives, needs, and capacities are considered. Community engagement promotes ownership, resilience, and sustainable solutions.

Capacity Building and Training: Building the capacity of responders, healthcare providers, and community members in understanding and addressing the demographic aspects of disaster impact is essential. Training programs can help enhance awareness, cultural competence, and sensitivity towards the needs of different demographic groups. Capacity building efforts should focus on inclusive practices, communication strategies, and equitable service provision.

By considering the demographic aspects of disaster impact, disaster management efforts can address the specific needs, vulnerabilities, and strengths of diverse population groups.

Recognizing the intersecting factors of gender, age, and special needs ensures that interventions are tailored, inclusive, and equitable, leading to more effective and resilient communities in the face of disasters.

7.2 Effect of Hazard Location on Disaster Impact

The location of hazards plays a crucial role in determining the impact of disasters. Different geographic areas have varying degrees of susceptibility to specific hazards based on their environmental, geographical, and geological characteristics. Here are key points explaining the effects of hazard location on disaster impact:

Environmental Factors: The natural environment, including topography, climate, and ecosystems, influences the severity and frequency of hazards. Here are some considerations:

a. Topography: Areas with steep slopes, unstable soils, or proximity to water bodies are more prone to landslides, erosion, and flooding. Steep terrain can amplify the speed and magnitude of cascading events, increasing the destructive potential.

b. Climate: Climate patterns, such as heavy rainfall, high temperatures, or drought conditions, can contribute to the occurrence and intensity of certain hazards. For example, areas with high rainfall are more susceptible to flooding, while regions experiencing prolonged drought are at risk of drought-related impacts.

c. Ecosystems: Healthy ecosystems, such as forests, wetlands, and coastal mangroves, can act as natural buffers and mitigate the impacts of hazards. Destruction or degradation of these ecosystems reduces their protective functions, making the surrounding areas more vulnerable to disasters.

Geological Factors: The geological characteristics of an area significantly influence the types and intensities of hazards. Here are some considerations:

a. Tectonic Activity: Areas located near tectonic plate boundaries, fault lines, or active volcanic zones are more prone to earthquakes, volcanic eruptions, and associated hazards like tsunamis.

b. b. Soil Composition: The composition and stability of soils affect the susceptibility to landslides and soil erosion. Loose, unstable soils are more prone to erosion, while saturated soils on slopes increase the likelihood of landslides.

c. c. Geographical Features: Certain geographical features, such as proximity to coastlines or river systems, influence the susceptibility to coastal erosion, river flooding, and associated hazards. Coastal areas are at risk of storm surges, while regions near major rivers are prone to riverine flooding.

Human Settlement Patterns: The distribution and density of human settlements in hazard-prone areas can greatly impact disaster impacts. Here are some considerations:

a. a. Urbanization and Infrastructure: Rapid urbanization and inadequate infrastructure planning can lead to settlements in high-risk areas, such as floodplains or landslide-prone slopes. Population density and the presence of critical infrastructure in hazard-prone zones increase the potential for severe impacts during disasters.

b. b. Informal Settlements: Informal settlements or slums often develop in hazard-prone areas due to social, economic, and spatial factors. These settlements typically lack proper infrastructure, emergency preparedness, and access to essential services, making their residents more vulnerable to disasters.

c. c. Population Growth: Rapid population growth in hazard-prone areas exacerbates the risk and impact of disasters. Increased population density puts a higher number of people at risk and intensifies the demand for resources and services during and after disasters.

Socio-economic Factors: Socio-economic conditions can influence the vulnerability and resilience of communities to hazards. Here are some considerations:

a. Poverty and Inequality: Areas with high poverty rates and income inequality tend to have limited resources, inadequate infrastructure, and reduced access to healthcare and education. These factors amplify vulnerability and hinder effective disaster preparedness and response.

b. Education and Awareness: The level of education and awareness within a community impacts preparedness and response capacities. Well-informed and educated communities are more likely to adopt preventive measures, engage in early warning systems, and respond effectively to disaster events.

c. Livelihoods and Economic Dependence: The reliance on specific industries or economic activities, such as agriculture, fishing, or tourism, can make communities more susceptible to the impacts of hazards. Disruptions to these livelihoods can have long-lasting socio-economic consequences.

Vulnerable Populations: The location of hazards can have differential impacts on vulnerable populations. These groups may include low-income communities, marginalized populations, people with disabilities, and elderly individuals. Hazard-prone areas with a concentration of vulnerable populations may experience heightened risk and increased challenges in disaster preparedness, response, and recovery.

Connectivity and Accessibility: The location of hazards can affect the connectivity and accessibility of affected areas. Disasters such as floods, landslides, or earthquakes can damage critical infrastructure, including roads, bridges, and communication networks. This can hinder rescue and relief operations, delay access to affected communities, and impede the delivery of essential services.

Cascading Effects: The location of hazards can trigger cascading effects that propagate beyond the immediate impact zone. For example, a major earthquake in a densely populated urban area can result in infrastructure damage, disruptions in water and power supply, and secondary hazards such as fires or gas leaks. These cascading effects can exacerbate the overall impact of the disaster and challenge response efforts.

Environmental and Biodiversity Loss: Hazard-prone areas may be rich in biodiversity and ecosystems that provide important ecological services. Disasters can lead to significant environmental degradation, habitat loss, and damage to ecosystems. This loss of environmental resources can have long-term consequences for biodiversity, ecosystem services, and the overall resilience of the affected region.

Climate Change Interactions: The location of hazards can interact with climate change dynamics, influencing the frequency and intensity of certain disasters. Climate change-related factors such as rising sea levels, changing precipitation patterns, and increased temperatures can amplify the impact of hazards in vulnerable areas. Understanding these interactions is crucial for developing climate-resilient strategies and adaptation measures.

Historical and Cultural Significance: Some hazard-prone areas may have historical or cultural significance. Disasters can result in the destruction or damage of culturally important sites, monuments, and heritage buildings. The loss of cultural heritage can have profound impacts on the identity, traditions, and sense of place for affected communities.

Tourism and Economic Impact: Hazard-prone areas that rely on tourism as a significant source of income may experience severe economic impacts. Disasters can disrupt tourism activities, damage infrastructure, and negatively affect local businesses. The recovery and rebuilding of tourism-dependent areas require targeted efforts to restore confidence and attract visitors.

Cross-Border Impact: Certain hazards, particularly those related to climate change or transboundary rivers, can have cross-border implications. Disasters in one country can affect neighbouring regions, resulting in shared challenges and the need for international cooperation in response and recovery efforts.

Coastal Hazards: Coastal areas are prone to hazards such as hurricanes, storm surges, and sea-level rise. Low-lying regions along coastlines, such as the Sundarbans in India, are highly vulnerable to the impacts of cyclones and coastal flooding. These areas experience significant damage to infrastructure, agricultural land, and natural ecosystems. The frequency and intensity of coastal hazards are influenced by factors such as proximity to the ocean, coastal geomorphology, and climate change dynamics.

Himalayan Region Hazards: The Himalayan region in India is prone to hazards such as earthquakes, landslides, and glacial lake outburst floods (GLOFs). The rugged topography and tectonic activity make this region susceptible to devastating earthquakes, such as the 2015 earthquake in Nepal. Landslides are common in hilly areas, impacting transportation routes, settlements, and agricultural land. Glacier retreat and the formation of unstable glacial lakes increase the risk of GLOFs, posing a significant threat to downstream communities.

Floodplains: Areas situated in floodplains, such as the Gangetic plains in India, are susceptible to riverine flooding. Heavy monsoon rainfall and overflowing rivers result in extensive flooding, leading to displacement, loss of livelihoods, damage to infrastructure, and disruption of essential services. Floodplains are highly populated regions, and the impact is intensified due to the concentration of people and infrastructure in these areas.

Urban Centers: Urban areas are vulnerable to multiple hazards due to high population density, inadequate infrastructure, and rapid urbanization. Cities like Mumbai, Kolkata, and Chennai are exposed to cyclones, flooding, and heatwaves. The urban heat island effect, combined with climate change, exacerbates the impacts of heatwaves, leading to heat-related illnesses and increased mortality rates. Urban areas also face the risks of building collapses during earthquakes or structural failures during floods.

Industrial Zones: Hazardous industrial installations, such as chemical plants or nuclear power plants, are located in specific zones. Accidents or incidents in these facilities can have severe consequences, including toxic chemical spills, fires, or radiation leaks. Bhopal, India, witnessed one of the worst industrial disasters in history when a gas leak occurred at a pesticide plant in 1984, resulting in thousands of deaths and long-term health impacts on the affected population.

Hill Stations and Tourist Destinations: Hill stations and tourist destinations are often located in hazard-prone areas. For example, hill stations in the Western Ghats region of India are exposed to landslides and flash floods during the monsoon season. These disasters pose risks to the safety of residents and tourists, as well as the infrastructure and economy of these popular tourist destinations.

Understanding the effects of hazard location on disaster impact helps inform risk assessments, land-use planning, and disaster management strategies. It enables policymakers, planners, and communities to make informed decisions regarding infrastructure development, early warning systems, evacuation plans, and resilience-building measures. By considering the unique characteristics and vulnerabilities associated with hazard-prone locations, effective measures can be implemented to reduce the impact of disasters and enhance the resilience of communities. It allows for the prioritization of resources, risk reduction measures, and targeted investments in infrastructure and community resilience. By considering the unique characteristics and interactions of hazards within specific locations, disaster management efforts can be better tailored to address the specific needs and challenges of the affected areas. By considering the vulnerabilities and characteristics of different locations, policymakers, planners, and communities can implement appropriate land-use planning, early warning systems, evacuation plans, and infrastructure improvements. This ensures a more resilient and prepared response to disasters in hazard-prone areas.

7.3 Gender Considerations in Disaster Management

Gender considerations in disaster management refer to the recognition of gender-specific vulnerabilities, needs, and capacities of individuals during all phases of disaster management, including preparedness, response, recovery, and reconstruction. It acknowledges that disasters can affect men, women, boys, and girls differently due to pre-existing social norms, roles, and inequalities. Integrating gender considerations into disaster management ensures that the needs and perspectives of all genders are considered, promoting more inclusive and effective responses. Here are some key aspects of gender considerations in disaster management:

Gender Roles and Responsibilities: Disasters can disrupt traditional gender roles and responsibilities. For example, women may take on additional caregiving responsibilities, and men may be involved in disaster response and recovery activities. Understanding these shifts is vital for providing appropriate support to affected populations.

Gender-Specific Vulnerabilities: Disasters can exacerbate existing gender disparities, making certain groups more vulnerable to the impacts. For instance, pregnant women, lactating mothers, and elderly women may have specific health and safety needs that require targeted attention.

Violence and Exploitation: Disasters can increase the risk of gender-based violence, including domestic violence and sexual exploitation. Safe spaces and protection mechanisms must be established to ensure the safety and security of all individuals, especially women and girls.

Access to Resources and Services: Gender inequalities can affect access to resources and services during disasters. Women may face barriers in accessing relief materials or health services. Ensuring equitable distribution and accessibility is essential.

Women's Participation and Decision-Making: Women's active participation in disaster management is crucial. Engaging women in decision-making processes enhances the effectiveness and inclusivity of response efforts.

Data Collection and Analysis: Gender-disaggregated data collection and analysis are essential to understand the distinct needs and impacts experienced by different genders. This data informs targeted interventions and policy-making.

Gender-Responsive Communication: Communication strategies during disasters should consider the diverse information needs of all genders, including language, literacy levels, and cultural considerations.

Women as First Responders: Recognizing and supporting women as first responders is essential. Women are often the first to provide care and support within their families and communities during and after disasters.

Gender-Responsive Shelters and Facilities: Shelters and facilities should be designed with gender-specific needs in mind, providing separate and safe spaces for women and men.

Livelihoods and Economic Recovery: Disasters can disproportionately impact women's livelihoods. Gender-responsive economic recovery measures should be implemented to support women's income-generating activities.

Training and Capacity Building: Building the capacity of disaster management personnel in gender-sensitive approaches ensures a more effective response to the diverse needs of affected populations.

Engaging Men and Boys: Engaging men and boys in gender-transformative approaches helps challenge harmful gender norms and fosters a more equal and supportive environment during and after disasters.

Reproductive Health and Hygiene Needs: During disasters, women and girls may face challenges related to reproductive health, menstrual hygiene, and access to essential healthcare services. Adequate provision of hygiene kits, maternal care, and reproductive health services are crucial to address these specific needs.

Gender-Responsive Evacuation and Mobility: Evacuation plans and transportation arrangements should be designed with consideration of gender-specific needs. For instance, ensuring safe and accessible transportation for pregnant women, elderly women, and women with disabilities.

Women's Leadership and Expertise: Women's leadership and expertise are valuable assets in disaster management. Acknowledging and promoting women's leadership in decision-making processes enhances the effectiveness of disaster response and ensures diverse perspectives are considered.

Intersectionality and Marginalized Groups: Gender considerations should also consider intersectionality, recognizing that individuals may face multiple forms of discrimination based on factors such as race, ethnicity, class, and disability. Disaster responses should be inclusive and address the specific needs of marginalized groups.

Women's Economic Empowerment: Post-disaster recovery efforts present opportunities for women's economic empowerment. Integrating gender-responsive livelihood programs and access to credit and resources can support women in rebuilding their lives and communities.

Promoting Gender Equality as a Resilience Strategy: Gender equality is not only a human rights imperative but also a resilience strategy. Empowering women and girls with education, skills, and decision-making power strengthens the overall capacity of communities to respond to and recover from disasters.

Cultural Sensitivity: Disaster management efforts should be culturally sensitive and respectful of diverse gender norms and practices. Engaging with local communities and understanding their unique gender dynamics is essential for effective and sustainable interventions.

Gender-Responsive Budgeting: Allocating resources with a gender-responsive approach ensures that funds are used effectively to address the specific needs and priorities of different genders in disaster management.

Inclusive Training and Capacity Building: Training programs for disaster management personnel should include modules on gender sensitivity and the integration of gender considerations. This helps enhance the capacity of responders to meet the diverse needs of affected populations.

Gender-Responsive Recovery Policies: Post-disaster recovery policies should consider the differentiated impact on women and men and address gender inequalities to build back better and more resilient communities.

Data Disaggregation for Informed Decision-Making: Collecting disaggregated data based on gender allows for evidence-based decision-making, ensuring that interventions are targeted and responsive to the needs of all genders.

Gender considerations in disaster management promote social justice, reduce vulnerability, and contribute to more sustainable and resilient communities. Integrating a gender perspective into policies, plans, and programs ensures that no one is left behind in disaster response and recovery efforts. By integrating gender considerations into disaster management, policymakers, governments, and organizations can create more equitable and effective responses that prioritize the well-being and empowerment of all individuals affected by disasters. These efforts contribute to building a more inclusive and resilient society, where everyone has the opportunity to thrive, regardless of their gender.

7.4 Age-Specific Vulnerabilities and Needs

Age-specific vulnerabilities and needs in disaster management refer to the recognition of different age groups' distinct vulnerabilities and requirements during all phases of disaster management, including preparedness, response, recovery, and reconstruction. Each age group, from infants to the elderly, experiences disasters differently and has specific needs that must be addressed to ensure their safety, well-being, and resilience. Here are some key age-specific vulnerabilities and needs in disaster management:

Infants and Young Children (0-5 years): Infants and young children are entirely dependent on caregivers for their safety and well-being. They may require specialized care, including safe shelter, adequate nutrition, and access to clean water and sanitation facilities. Ensuring access to infant formula, baby food, diapers, and hygiene items is essential during disasters. Child-friendly spaces and psychosocial support can help alleviate stress and trauma for young children.

Children (6-12 years): Children may experience fear and anxiety during disasters, and their coping mechanisms may vary based on age and personality. Education continuity is crucial for their emotional well-being and development. Temporary learning spaces and educational materials should be provided. Providing age-appropriate information about the disaster and its impacts can help children better understand and cope with the situation.

Adolescents and Youth (13-17 years): Adolescents may experience increased stress and emotional challenges during disasters. Access to mental health and psychosocial support services is critical to address their unique emotional needs. Engaging youth in disaster preparedness and response activities can empower them to take an active role in their communities.

Adults (18-64 years): Adults are often the primary caregivers and breadwinners for their families, making their well-being essential for overall family resilience. Economic livelihoods and access to employment opportunities should be considered during the recovery phase. Ensuring access to healthcare services, including reproductive health, is crucial for adult populations.

Elderly (65 years and older): The elderly may face mobility challenges and chronic health conditions that can be exacerbated during disasters. They may require assistance with evacuation and accessing relief services. Special attention should be given to providing appropriate medical care, medication, and assistive devices.

Persons with Disabilities: Persons with disabilities face unique challenges during disasters, including access to transportation and evacuation shelters. Disaster management plans should include accessible communication, evacuation procedures, and specialized support services.

Pregnant and Lactating Women: Pregnant and lactating women have specific health and nutrition needs that must be addressed during disasters. Access to maternal healthcare services and safe spaces for breastfeeding are crucial.

Single-Parent Households: Single-parent households may have additional challenges during disasters, as the primary caregiver may face increased responsibilities. Supporting single-parent households with resources and psychosocial support can be beneficial.

Migrants, Refugees, and Displaced Populations: Migrants, refugees, and displaced populations are often more vulnerable during disasters due to their marginalized status and limited access to resources. Culturally sensitive support and access to information in their languages are essential for their well-being.

Homeless Populations: Homeless populations are particularly vulnerable during disasters, as they lack permanent shelter and may have limited access to relief services. Special measures should be taken to provide them with safe shelter and essential supplies.

Child Protection and Family Reunification: During disasters, there is an increased risk of child separation from their families. Establishing child protection mechanisms and family reunification systems are crucial to ensure the safety and well-being of separated children.

Geriatric Care and Dignity: Elderly individuals may require specialized geriatric care and assistance with daily activities, particularly during evacuations and sheltering. Providing a sense of dignity and respect to elderly populations is essential to maintain their mental and emotional well-being.

Language and Communication Barriers: People from diverse linguistic backgrounds may face communication challenges during disasters. Providing information in multiple languages and using culturally sensitive communication methods can improve access to critical information.

Education and Continuity of Learning: Disasters disrupt educational activities, affecting the learning and developmental needs of children and youth. Establishing temporary learning centers, distributing educational materials, and ensuring continuity of education are crucial.

Gender-Sensitive Support: Gender-specific vulnerabilities, as discussed earlier, are vital considerations during disaster management. Ensuring access to menstrual hygiene products for women and girls and considering the privacy and safety needs of women in shelters are examples of gender-sensitive support.

Psychosocial Support and Trauma Healing: All age groups may experience emotional trauma during disasters. Providing psychosocial support, counselling, and trauma healing services can help individuals cope with their experiences and build resilience.

Addressing Specific Health Needs: Individuals with chronic illnesses, such as diabetes or respiratory conditions, require continuous access to medications and medical care during disasters. Pregnant women may need specialized care to ensure safe deliveries and postnatal support.

Inclusive Evacuation and Sheltering: Evacuation plans and shelters should be inclusive and accessible to all, including persons with disabilities, the elderly, pregnant women, and families with young children. Providing separate spaces for families and ensuring child-friendly spaces are essential for the well-being of families with children.

Protection from Exploitation and Abuse: Disasters can increase the risk of human trafficking, child labour, and other forms of exploitation. Implementing protective measures and monitoring systems are essential to prevent such incidents.

Cultural and Religious Sensitivity: Understanding and respecting the cultural and religious practices of different age groups is crucial during disaster management. Providing culturally appropriate food, prayer spaces, and rituals can help maintain a sense of normalcy and comfort during difficult times.

Long-Term Rehabilitation and Support: Post-disaster recovery efforts should include long-term rehabilitation and support programs, particularly for vulnerable age groups, to ensure their sustained well-being and resilience.

Social and Community Support Networks: Utilizing existing social and community support networks can strengthen the disaster response and recovery efforts, particularly for vulnerable individuals and households.

Addressing age-specific vulnerabilities and needs requires a holistic and coordinated approach involving various stakeholders, including government agencies, civil society organizations, communities, and families. By integrating age-specific considerations into disaster management planning and practices, societies can build more inclusive, resilient, and compassionate systems that prioritize the well-being of all age groups during and after disasters.

7.5 Considerations for Special needs Populations

Considerations for special needs populations in disaster management involve recognizing the unique vulnerabilities and requirements of individuals with disabilities and other special needs during all phases of disaster management, including preparedness, response, recovery, and reconstruction. These considerations aim to ensure that disaster management efforts are inclusive, equitable, and responsive to the diverse needs of all individuals, regardless of their abilities or special requirements. Here are some key considerations for special needs populations in disaster management:

Inclusive Preparedness Planning: Integrating individuals with disabilities and special needs into disaster preparedness planning ensures that their specific requirements are addressed. This includes understanding mobility challenges, communication needs, and medical considerations. Inclusive planning involves consulting with special needs advocacy groups and organizations to gather insights and perspectives.

Accessible Evacuation and Sheltering: Evacuation plans and shelter facilities should be designed to accommodate individuals with disabilities. This includes providing accessible transportation, ramps, and elevators for mobility aids. Special needs populations may require separate spaces in shelters for privacy, medical care, or assistance.

Communication Accessibility: Disaster alerts and information should be disseminated through multiple communication channels to ensure accessibility for individuals with various disabilities. Providing information in Braille, sign language interpretation, or easy-to-read formats enhances communication for people with visual, hearing, or cognitive impairments.

Medical Support and Supplies: Special needs populations may rely on medical equipment, assistive devices, or medication that must be accounted for during disaster planning. Ensuring access to medical supplies and necessary equipment in shelters and relief centers is critical.

Psychosocial Support and Sensory Considerations: Disasters can be stressful for everyone, including special needs populations. Providing psychosocial support, counselling, and sensory considerations can help individuals cope with the emotional impact of the disaster.

Personal Support Networks: Recognizing the importance of personal support networks, including family members, caregivers, and service animals, is essential in disaster response efforts. Preserving the unity of support networks during evacuation and sheltering is crucial for the well-being of individuals with special needs.

Training and Sensitization: Disaster management personnel, first responders, and volunteers should receive training on disability-inclusive practices and sensitization to the diverse needs of special populations. Disability-inclusive training ensures that responders can provide appropriate assistance and support.

Engagement and Participation: Involving individuals with disabilities and special needs in disaster management planning and decision-making processes empowers them to contribute their insights and experiences. Engaging with special needs advocacy groups fosters collaboration and ensures that planning is representative of the community's needs.

Accessibility in Relief Distribution: Relief distribution centers should be designed to ensure accessibility for individuals with disabilities. This includes helping in navigating queues and accessing relief materials.

Post-Disaster Recovery and Rehabilitation: Post-disaster recovery efforts should address the specific needs of special needs populations in rebuilding infrastructure and providing support services.

By incorporating these considerations into disaster management strategies, communities can foster a more inclusive and supportive environment for individuals with disabilities and special needs. An inclusive approach not only ensures the safety and well-being of special needs populations during disasters but also promotes social cohesion and resilience within the community as a whole.

7.6 Inclusive Approach in Disaster Management

A general inclusive approach in disaster management involves recognizing and addressing the diverse needs, vulnerabilities, and capacities of all individuals, including those from marginalized or vulnerable groups. It aims to ensure that no one is left behind and that disaster management efforts are equitable, accessible, and responsive to the needs of the entire community. Here are some key considerations for adopting an inclusive approach in disaster management:

Engaging Diverse Stakeholders: Inclusive disaster management involves engaging diverse stakeholders, including government agencies, civil society organizations, community leaders, local residents, and representatives from marginalized groups. Including representatives from marginalized communities in decision-making processes ensures that their perspectives and needs are considered in disaster planning and response efforts.

Disaggregated Data Collection: Collecting disaggregated data based on characteristics such as age, gender, disability, ethnicity, and socio-economic status provides insights into the diverse needs of the community. Data helps identify vulnerable groups, assess their specific risks, and design targeted interventions.

Community-Based Approaches: Engaging local communities in disaster management fosters ownership, empowerment, and resilience. Local knowledge and community-based strategies can complement formal disaster management efforts.

Accessibility and Communication: Ensuring accessibility in disaster management includes providing information and communication in multiple formats, languages, and modalities to reach diverse populations, including those with disabilities. Information should be disseminated through various channels to cater to different preferences and needs.

Addressing Language Barriers: Language diversity in multicultural communities requires effective translation and interpretation services during disaster communications and interactions. Language considerations help ensure everyone can understand and respond appropriately to disaster messages.

Inclusive Training and Capacity Building: Training programs for disaster management personnel, responders, and volunteers should include modules on diversity and inclusion. Building capacity in disability-inclusive practices, cultural sensitivity, and gender considerations enhances the effectiveness of disaster response.

Universal Design and Accessibility: Incorporating universal design principles in the construction of infrastructure, evacuation routes, and shelters ensures accessibility for people with disabilities and other special needs. Barrier-free facilities benefit everyone and promote social inclusion.

Cultural Sensitivity and Respect: Cultural sensitivity ensures that disaster management efforts respect and integrate the cultural practices, beliefs, and values of diverse communities. Understanding cultural norms and practices helps build trust and acceptance during disaster response.

Psychosocial Support and Mental Health: Disaster management should prioritize psychosocial support and mental health services for individuals and communities affected by disasters. Trauma healing and emotional support are critical components of the recovery process.

Gender Considerations: Gender-sensitive disaster management recognizes the different experiences and vulnerabilities of men, women, boys, and girls. Promoting gender equality and empowering women contribute to more effective and resilient disaster management.

Disability-Inclusive Approaches: Disability-inclusive disaster management ensures that the needs and rights of people with disabilities are fully integrated into all phases of disaster management. Accessible evacuation, communication, and facilities are essential components of disability-inclusive approaches.

Accountability and Feedback Mechanisms: Establishing mechanisms for feedback and accountability helps evaluate the effectiveness of disaster management efforts and address any gaps or concerns raised by the community.

By adopting an inclusive approach in disaster management, communities can build stronger social cohesion, enhance resilience, and ensure that disaster responses are better tailored to the specific needs and contexts of the people they serve. A focus on equity, accessibility, and respect for diversity fosters a more compassionate and responsive disaster management system that promotes the well-being and safety of all individuals, regardless of their backgrounds or circumstances.

7.6.1 Importance of an Inclusive Approach

The importance of an inclusive approach in disaster management cannot be overstated. Adopting an inclusive approach ensures that all individuals, regardless of their age, gender, disability, ethnicity, socio-economic status, or other characteristics, are considered and accounted for throughout all phases of disaster management. Here are some key reasons why an inclusive approach is crucial:

Equity and Social Justice: An inclusive approach promotes equity and social justice by addressing the needs and vulnerabilities of marginalized and vulnerable groups. It helps reduce disparities and ensures that resources and assistance are distributed more fairly among affected populations.

Effective Risk Reduction: Identifying and addressing the unique vulnerabilities of different groups improves the effectiveness of disaster risk reduction strategies. Tailoring interventions to specific needs enhance the overall resilience of communities.

Better Preparedness and Response: Inclusive disaster management planning considers the diverse needs of the community, enabling more effective preparedness and response efforts. By involving all stakeholders, including representatives from marginalized groups, plans can be more comprehensive and responsive.

Enhanced Community Resilience: An inclusive approach fosters a sense of ownership and empowerment within communities. Engaging diverse stakeholders and considering their perspectives promotes community cohesion and resilience.

Ensuring No One is Left Behind: An inclusive approach ensures that no individual or group is overlooked or excluded from disaster management efforts. It prioritizes the most vulnerable populations and provides targeted support to those who may face greater challenges during disasters.

Psychosocial Support and Mental Health: Disasters can take a toll on mental health and psychosocial well-being. An inclusive approach addresses the emotional and psychological needs of diverse populations, promoting healing and resilience.

Cultural Sensitivity and Respect: An inclusive approach fosters cultural sensitivity and respect for diverse cultural practices, beliefs, and languages. It helps build trust and acceptance, improving community engagement during disaster management.

Building Trust and Collaboration: Inclusive disaster management builds trust between communities and authorities, encouraging collaboration and cooperation during emergencies. Engaging marginalized groups and involving them in decision-making strengthens community-government partnerships.

Disability-Inclusive Disaster Management: Incorporating disability-inclusive practices ensures that individuals with disabilities are not overlooked or excluded. Accessible infrastructure, communication, and support services benefit everyone and promote social inclusion.

Gender-Responsive Approach: Gender-responsive disaster management recognizes and addresses the different needs and vulnerabilities of men, women, boys, and girls. Empowering women and involving them in decision-making enhances the effectiveness of disaster responses.

Accountability and Transparency: An inclusive approach promotes accountability and transparency in disaster management efforts. Mechanisms for feedback and evaluation ensure that the community's needs and concerns are addressed.

In conclusion, an inclusive approach in disaster management is essential for building more resilient and compassionate communities. It ensures that disaster responses are tailored to meet the diverse needs of all individuals and that the most vulnerable are prioritized. By involving all stakeholders, respecting cultural diversity, and promoting equity and social justice, an inclusive approach fosters a stronger, more cohesive society that is better prepared to face and recover from disasters.

CHAPTER 8

Global and National Disaster Trends

8.1 Global Disasters Trends

Global disaster trends refer to the patterns and changes observed in the occurrence, impact, and characteristics of disasters on a global scale. Understanding these trends is essential for effective disaster risk reduction, preparedness, and response efforts. Here are some key points to explain global disaster trends:

Increasing Frequency: Over the past few decades, there has been an increase in the frequency of natural disasters worldwide. This can be attributed to various factors, including climate change, population growth, urbanization, and environmental degradation.

The frequency of extreme weather events such as hurricanes, heatwaves, floods, and wildfires has been particularly notable.

Rising Economic Losses: Global disasters have led to significant economic losses, which have been on the rise. The increasing exposure of populations and assets in hazard-prone areas has contributed to higher economic impacts. Climate-related disasters, in particular, have caused substantial financial losses due to damage to infrastructure, agriculture, and businesses.

Shifting Patterns: While natural disasters have been a recurring phenomenon, there have been noticeable shifts in the patterns and types of disasters. Climate change has influenced the intensity and distribution of hazards, resulting in altered patterns of extreme weather events. For example, some regions experience more intense rainfall and flooding, while others face prolonged droughts and heatwaves.

Impact on Vulnerable Populations: Disasters disproportionately affect vulnerable populations, including the poor, marginalized communities, and those with limited resources. These groups often face higher risks due to inadequate infrastructure, limited access to essential services, and social and economic inequalities. Global disaster trends highlight the need for targeted interventions to address the specific vulnerabilities of these populations.

Technological Disasters: Alongside natural disasters, there has been an increase in technological disasters, including industrial accidents, chemical spills, and infrastructure failures. Technological disasters can have severe environmental, social, and economic consequences, often requiring specialized response and recovery efforts.

Regional Variations: Disaster trends vary across different regions of the world. Some regions are more prone to certain types of hazards, such as hurricanes in the Atlantic Basin, earthquakes in the Pacific Ring of Fire, or droughts in arid regions. Understanding regional variations helps in developing context-specific strategies and measures to mitigate risks.

Interconnectedness and Global Impacts: Disasters are increasingly interconnected and can have cascading effects beyond national borders. For example, climate-related events in one region can lead to food and water scarcity, displacement, and migration, affecting neighbouring countries and even global markets. The interconnectedness of disasters highlights the need for international cooperation, information sharing, and coordinated response efforts.

Data and Monitoring: Advances in technology and data collection have improved the monitoring and documentation of global disaster trends. Organizations such as the United Nations Office for Disaster Risk Reduction (UNDRR) and international databases like EM-DAT (Emergency Events Database) provide valuable data on disaster occurrences, impacts, and trends. This information helps in identifying areas of focus, setting priorities, and evaluating the effectiveness of disaster risk reduction measures.

Climate Change and Future Projections: Climate change is expected to have a significant impact on future disaster trends. As the planet continues to warm, the frequency and intensity of extreme weather events are projected to increase. This includes more intense storms, heatwaves, droughts, and rising sea levels. Understanding these projections informs the development of adaptive strategies and resilience-building measures.

Monitoring global disaster trends helps policymakers, governments, and organizations to identify emerging risks, allocate resources effectively, and develop proactive strategies to reduce disaster impacts. It underscores the importance of investing in disaster risk reduction, climate change adaptation, and building resilient communities worldwide.

Urbanization and Megacities: The rapid growth of urban areas, particularly in developing countries, has led to an increase in disaster risks. As more people settle in cities and megacities, the vulnerability to hazards such as earthquakes, floods, and heatwaves intensifies. The concentration of populations and assets in urban areas amplifies the potential impact of disasters and necessitates specific urban resilience strategies.

Multi-Hazard Scenarios: Global disaster trends indicate that many regions face the risks of multiple hazards. For example, coastal areas may experience the combined impacts of hurricanes, storm surges, and sea-level rise. These multi-hazard scenarios pose complex challenges for disaster management, requiring integrated approaches that consider the interactions and cumulative effects of different hazards.

Climate-related Disasters: Climate change has contributed to the intensification and alteration of certain types of disasters. Heatwaves, wildfires, intense rainfall, and tropical cyclones have demonstrated increasing trends in frequency, intensity, or both. Climate-related disasters pose significant challenges in terms of adaptation, as they require long-term planning, policy changes, and measures to reduce greenhouse gas emissions.

Displacement and Migration: Disasters, both natural and man-made, contribute to population displacement and migration. The impacts of climate change, including sea-level rise, droughts, and land degradation, are anticipated to lead to increased displacement in the future. Understanding the links between disasters, displacement, and migration is crucial for addressing the needs of affected populations, ensuring their protection, and managing social, economic, and environmental implications.

Data and Technology: Advances in technology, remote sensing, and data analytics have improved our ability to monitor and analyse global disaster trends. Real-time monitoring systems, satellite imagery, and machine learning algorithms help in early warning, rapid damage assessments, and informed decision-making. These technological advancements enhance our understanding of disaster trends, improve response efforts, and support evidence-based policies.

Sustainable Development Goals (SDGs): Global disaster trends are interconnected with the SDGs, a set of global goals adopted by the United Nations to address social, economic, and environmental challenges. Disasters can hinder progress towards achieving the SDGs, and conversely, achieving the SDGs contributes to disaster risk reduction and resilience-building. Understanding global disaster trends helps align disaster risk reduction efforts with the broader sustainable development agenda.

Global Cooperation and Partnerships: Addressing global disaster trends requires international cooperation, partnerships, and knowledge sharing. Countries and organizations collaborate to exchange best practices, share resources, and support capacity-building initiatives. Global frameworks, such as the Sendai Framework for Disaster Risk Reduction and the Paris Agreement on climate change, provide platforms for cooperation and coordination.

Monitoring global disaster trends allows for evidence-based decision-making, policy formulation, and the development of effective strategies to reduce disaster risks and enhance resilience at the global level. By understanding the evolving nature of disasters, policymakers, governments, and organizations can prioritize investments, build partnerships, and take proactive measures to protect lives, preserve ecosystems, and promote sustainable development.

Increasing Frequency: The United Nations Office for Disaster Risk Reduction (UNDRR) reported an average of 6,681 disasters worldwide between 2000 and 2019, representing a significant increase compared to previous decades. The Centre for Research on the Epidemiology of Disasters (CRED) recorded an average of 334 weather-related disasters per year between 2000 and 2019, which is almost double the average of the 1980s. According to the World Meteorological Organization (WMO), the number of climate-related disasters has tripled since the 1960s.

Rising Economic Losses: The United Nations International Strategy for Disaster Reduction (UNISDR) estimated that the global economic losses from disasters between 2000 and 2019 exceeded $2.97 trillion. The Munich Reinsurance Company reported that weather-related disasters caused economic losses of $1.63 trillion between 2000 and 2019.

Climate-related Disasters: The Intergovernmental Panel on Climate Change (IPCC) stated that climate change is increasing the frequency and intensity of heatwaves, droughts, floods, and storms worldwide. The World Bank estimated that climate change could push over 100 million people into poverty by 2030 due to the increased frequency of climate-related disasters.

Regional Variations: The Asia-Pacific region is the most disaster-prone, accounting for around 40% of all disasters and over 80% of the world's total affected population.

Small island developing states (SIDS) face significant vulnerability to climate change and are disproportionately affected by sea-level rise, storms, and coastal hazards. Africa is also highly susceptible to a range of hazards, including droughts, floods, and desertification.

Technological Disasters: The International Federation of Red Cross and Red Crescent Societies (IFRC) reported an increasing trend in technological disasters, including industrial accidents, chemical spills, and nuclear incidents. The Global Assessment Report on Disaster Risk Reduction highlighted the risks associated with emerging technologies such as cybersecurity threats and digital vulnerabilities.

Humanitarian Impact: The United Nations estimates that an average of 108 million people worldwide requires humanitarian assistance each year due to natural disasters and conflicts. The Internal Displacement Monitoring Centre (IDMC) reported that an average of 22.5 million people were displaced annually between 2008 and 2019 due to natural disasters.

Data and Reporting: The Emergency Events Database (EM-DAT), maintained by CRED, provides comprehensive data on global disasters, including information on their impact, human casualties, and economic losses. The UNISDR's Global Assessment Report on Disaster Risk Reduction provides detailed analysis and assessment of global disaster trends, risks, and progress in disaster risk reduction efforts. These statistics highlight the increasing frequency and impacts of disasters worldwide, particularly those related to climate change. They emphasize the urgent need for effective disaster risk reduction measures, climate adaptation strategies, and international cooperation to build resilience and reduce the human, economic, and environmental costs of disasters.

8.2 Disasters Trends in India

Disaster trends in India reflect the occurrence, impacts, and characteristics of disasters within the country. India is a diverse nation with varied geographical features, climate patterns, and socio-economic conditions, which contribute to a wide range of hazards. Here are key points to explain disaster trends in India:

Climate-related Disasters: India is highly susceptible to climate-related disasters such as floods, cyclones, heatwaves, droughts, and landslides. These disasters are influenced by the country's monsoon climate, geographical location, and topography. The frequency and intensity of climate-related disasters have shown notable trends in recent years, including an increase in extreme rainfall events and heatwaves.

Floods: Flooding is a recurring disaster in India, affecting both riverine and coastal areas. Heavy monsoon rains, coupled with inadequate drainage systems and deforestation, contribute to frequent floods. Northern and northeastern states, including Assam and Bihar, are particularly prone to riverine flooding, while coastal regions like Gujarat and Odisha face the risks of cyclone-induced storm surges and coastal flooding.

According to the National Crime Records Bureau (NCRB), floods accounted for 36.2% of the total natural disasters in India between 2001 and 2014. The Central Water Commission reported that, on average, around 7.5% of the total geographical area of India is affected by floods every year. The Indian Meteorological Department (IMD) recorded that the number of extreme rainfall events (over 204 mm per day) increased from 16 events in 1950 to 49 events in 2019.

Cyclones: India's coastal regions, especially the eastern and western coasts, are prone to cyclones. The Bay of Bengal witnesses cyclones that often make landfall in states like Odisha and West Bengal, while the Arabian Sea is known for cyclones affecting states like Gujarat and Maharashtra. Recent years have seen an increase in the frequency and intensity of cyclones, necessitating improved early warning systems, evacuation plans, and coastal infrastructure.

India's east coast, particularly the Bay of Bengal region, is prone to cyclones. The IMD reported that the average annual frequency of cyclones is around five to six. In recent years, severe cyclonic storms like Cyclone Fani in 2019 and Cyclone Amphan in 2020 have caused significant damage and displacement in coastal regions of Odisha and West Bengal, respectively.

Heatwaves: India experiences severe heatwaves, particularly in the summer months, with temperatures soaring above 40 degrees Celsius in many regions. Heatwaves pose significant risks to human health, especially for vulnerable populations. Urban areas with high population density, such as Delhi and Chennai, face additional challenges due to the urban heat island effect.

The IMD recorded that the number of heatwave days in India has been increasing in recent years. For example, in 2019, there were 262 heatwave days across the country, compared to 174 in 2018. The Indian Council of Medical Research (ICMR) estimated that heatwaves caused approximately 4,620 deaths in India between 2010 and 2019.

Landslides: Hilly regions, including the Himalayan states of Uttarakhand, Himachal Pradesh, and parts of Northeast India, are prone to landslides. Deforestation, unplanned construction, and heavy rainfall contribute to slope instability and landslides. The devastating landslide in Kedarnath in 2013 highlighted the vulnerability of hilly areas to this hazard.

The Geological Survey of India (GSI) has identified around 15 landslide-prone states in India, including Himachal Pradesh, Uttarakhand, and parts of Northeast India. According to the National Disaster Management Authority (NDMA), landslides have accounted for around 10% of the total deaths due to natural disasters in India.

Droughts: Certain regions of India, such as Rajasthan, Gujarat, and parts of Maharashtra, are prone to droughts due to low rainfall and arid climatic conditions. Droughts impact agriculture, water availability, and livelihoods, posing significant challenges for rural communities. Climate change and changing precipitation patterns have contributed to the increasing frequency and severity of droughts in some areas.

The Drought Early Warning System (DEWS) reported that around 26% of India's land area was affected by drought conditions in 2020. According to the NCRB, from 2001 to 2014, droughts accounted for approximately 8.5% of the total natural disasters in India.

Earthquakes: India is located in a seismically active region, with several earthquake-prone zones. The Himalayan region, particularly the states of Jammu and Kashmir, Himachal Pradesh, and Uttarakhand, is at high risk of earthquakes. Other regions like the northeastern states and Gujarat also face earthquake risks. Regular monitoring, seismic building codes, and public awareness are critical for mitigating earthquake impacts.

India falls under Zone II to Zone V in terms of seismic vulnerability. The northeastern states, Jammu and Kashmir, and parts of Himachal Pradesh and Uttarakhand are classified as high-risk seismic zones. The National Centre for Seismology (NCS) recorded around 1,000 earthquakes annually in India, with varying magnitudes.

Industrial Disasters: India has witnessed industrial disasters, including chemical accidents, gas leaks, and major fires. Incidents such as the Bhopal gas tragedy in 1984 and the Visakhapatnam gas leak in 2020 highlighted the need for stringent safety regulations and risk management in industrial facilities.

The National Crime Records Bureau reported that industrial accidents accounted for approximately 4% of the total accidental deaths in India in 2019. Major incidents like the Bhopal gas tragedy in 1984 resulted in thousands of deaths and long-term health impacts on the affected population.

Urban Disasters: Rapid urbanization and inadequate infrastructure in Indian cities contribute to urban disasters. Building collapses, fires, and accidents in densely populated urban areas pose risks to residents. Mumbai, Delhi, Kolkata, and other major cities face challenges related to urban disasters and the need for improved urban planning and disaster management strategies.

According to the NCRB, building collapses accounted for around 3% of the total accidental deaths in India in 2019. The Fire Services Department reported around 20,000 fire incidents in India's major cities in 2019.

Data and Preparedness: Enhancing data collection, monitoring, and early warning systems is crucial for disaster preparedness and response in India. The country has made efforts to improve disaster management capacities, including the establishment of the National Disaster Management Authority (NDMA) and the development of disaster management plans at various levels. However, there is still a need for continued investment in risk assessment, capacity building, and community preparedness.

Understanding disaster trends in India helps policymakers, government agencies, and communities to develop context-specific strategies, allocate resources effectively, and implement measures to reduce risks, enhance preparedness, and build resilience. It highlights the importance of integrating disaster risk reduction into development planning, strengthening early warning systems, improving infrastructure resilience, and promoting community engagement in disaster management processes.

8.3 Historical Disasters in India

India has a long history of experiencing various natural and human-made disasters that have had significant impacts on the nation's population, economy, and infrastructure. Here are some notable historical disasters in India:

Bhuj Earthquake (2001): On January 26, 2001, a devastating earthquake struck the city of Bhuj in Gujarat, measuring 7.7 on the Richter scale. The earthquake caused extensive damage to buildings, infrastructure, and resulted in the loss of thousands of lives. It was one of the most destructive earthquakes in Indian history, affecting millions of people across the region.

Bhopal Gas Tragedy (1984): On December 2-3, 1984, a gas leak from the Union Carbide pesticide plant in Bhopal, Madhya Pradesh, resulted in one of the world's worst industrial disasters. The release of methyl isocyanate gas and other toxic chemicals caused the death of thousands of people and left many others with severe health issues.

Great Bengal Famine (1943-1944): The Great Bengal Famine was a severe food crisis that occurred during World War II, affecting the Bengal province of British India (now West Bengal and Bangladesh). The famine resulted from a combination of factors, including crop failure, war-related disruptions, and economic policies that exacerbated the food shortage. Millions of people died due to starvation and malnutrition during this period.

Cyclone Nargis (2008): Cyclone Nargis, which struck Myanmar (Burma) on May 2, 2008, had a significant impact on the eastern coastal regions of India, particularly in West Bengal and Odisha. The cyclone caused widespread destruction, claiming thousands of lives and displacing millions of people.

Kedarnath Flash Floods (2013): In June 2013, heavy rainfall and cloudbursts triggered flash floods and landslides in the Uttarakhand region, particularly affecting the pilgrimage site of Kedarnath. The disaster led to the loss of thousands of lives, massive destruction of infrastructure, and the displacement of numerous people.

Indian Ocean Tsunami (2004): The Indian Ocean Tsunami, also known as the Boxing Day Tsunami, occurred on December 26, 2004. The undersea earthquake off the coast of Sumatra generated massive tsunamis that affected several countries, including India's eastern and southeastern coastal regions. The tsunami caused widespread devastation, claiming thousands of lives in India, particularly in the Andaman and Nicobar Islands, Tamil Nadu, and Kerala.

Assam Earthquake (1950): On August 15, 1950, an earthquake with a magnitude of 8.6 struck Assam, causing significant damage to infrastructure and resulting in thousands of fatalities. The earthquake was one of the most powerful and deadliest to hit the region.

Banaskantha Floods (2017): In July 2017, heavy monsoon rains and flooding severely affected the Banaskantha district of Gujarat. The floods caused extensive damage to property, agricultural lands, and resulted in loss of lives and displacement of people.

Daulatabad Earthquake (1327): The Daulatabad earthquake, also known as the "Devagiri earthquake," occurred in the present-day Maharashtra region in 1327. It is considered one of the deadliest earthquakes in Indian history, causing widespread destruction and loss of life.

These historical disasters illustrate the vulnerability of India to a range of natural and human-made catastrophes. They have had profound social, economic, and environmental consequences, leading to efforts in disaster preparedness, mitigation, and response to reduce the impact of future disasters on the nation and its people.

8.4 Case Study – Bhuj Earthquake

The Bhuj Earthquake, also known as the Gujarat Earthquake, occurred on January 26, 2001, in the western Indian state of Gujarat. It was a devastating earthquake, measuring 7.7 on the Richter scale, with its epicenter near the town of Bhuj. The earthquake caused widespread destruction, resulted in the loss of thousands of lives, and had a significant impact on the affected region. Here are various aspects of disaster management during the Bhuj Earthquake:

Emergency Response and Search and Rescue: The immediate priority after the earthquake was to conduct search and rescue operations to locate and save survivors trapped under collapsed buildings and debris. Indian and international teams of rescue personnel were deployed to the affected areas to assist in rescue efforts.

Medical Aid and Healthcare: Setting up medical camps and field hospitals was crucial to provide emergency medical aid to the injured. Medical teams, including doctors, nurses, and paramedics, were mobilized to treat the wounded and provide essential medical services.

Shelter and Relief Camps: Displaced individuals and families were provided with temporary shelter in relief camps set up in safe locations. Adequate provisions for food, water, clothing, and other essential supplies were made available to those staying in the camps.

Infrastructure Restoration: Restoring critical infrastructure such as roads, bridges, power supply, and communication networks was a significant priority to facilitate the movement of relief and rescue teams and coordinate the response efforts effectively.

Coordination and Logistics: Disaster management agencies and government authorities worked together to ensure effective coordination and logistics in the distribution of relief materials and resources to affected areas.

Public Awareness and Communication: Providing accurate and timely information to the public was crucial to prevent panic and aid in response efforts. Public awareness campaigns were launched to educate people about safety measures and procedures during and after the earthquake.

Assessment and Damage Estimation: Conducting rapid damage and needs assessments helped determine the scale of destruction and the requirements for relief and recovery efforts. The assessments aided in resource allocation and decision-making for the deployment of personnel and equipment.

Psychosocial Support: Providing psychosocial support to survivors and affected communities was essential to help them cope with the trauma and emotional impact of the disaster. Counselling services were made available to those who needed emotional support.

International Assistance: Given the scale of the disaster, international assistance and humanitarian aid were sought and received from various countries and organizations. This support played a significant role in enhancing the response and relief efforts.

Recovery and Rehabilitation: Once the immediate response phase was over, efforts were focused on long-term recovery and rehabilitation of the affected areas and communities. Reconstruction of damaged buildings, infrastructure, and livelihood support for those who lost their homes and livelihoods were prioritized.

Lessons Learned and Policy Changes:

The Bhuj Earthquake prompted a re-evaluation of disaster preparedness and response capabilities in India. It led to policy changes, updates in building codes, and improvements in disaster management practices to enhance the country's resilience to future earthquakes and disasters.

The Bhuj Earthquake was a tragic event that highlighted the importance of effective disaster management and the need for comprehensive preparedness, response, and recovery plans. It served as a learning experience for India's disaster management authorities, prompting improvements in disaster response systems and strategies to minimize the impact of future disasters on human lives and communities.

8.4.1 Lesson Learnt from Disaster Management during Bhuj Earthquake

The Bhuj Earthquake, which occurred on January 26, 2001, in Gujarat, India, provided several crucial lessons in disaster management. The earthquake had a magnitude of 7.7 on the Richter scale and caused extensive damage, resulting in the loss of thousands of lives and widespread destruction of buildings and infrastructure. Here are some of the key lessons learned from disaster management during the Bhuj Earthquake:

Importance of Early Warning Systems: The Bhuj Earthquake highlighted the critical need for early warning systems, especially for seismic events. Early warning systems can provide alerts before an earthquake strikes, giving people valuable seconds to minutes to take protective actions or evacuate, thereby reducing casualties and injuries.

Disaster Preparedness and Training: The earthquake underscored the importance of disaster preparedness and training for communities, government agencies, and emergency responders. Regular drills and training exercises can help people understand their roles during emergencies and respond more effectively when disasters occur.

Strengthening Building Codes and Infrastructure: The earthquake exposed vulnerabilities in building structures and infrastructure. Implementing and enforcing robust building codes can ensure that structures are more resistant to seismic forces, reducing the risk of building collapses during earthquakes.

Importance of Public Awareness and Education: Enhancing public awareness about earthquake risks and preparedness measures is crucial to ensure that individuals and communities know how to respond when an earthquake strikes.

Educational campaigns can promote safety practices, evacuation procedures, and the importance of staying informed during disasters.

Effective Coordination and Communication: The Bhuj Earthquake emphasized the need for effective coordination and communication among various agencies, including government departments, non-governmental organizations, and international aid organizations. Clear communication channels can facilitate the efficient deployment of resources and assistance to affected areas.

Community Engagement and Resilience: Involving local communities in disaster management planning and decision-making can enhance disaster resilience. Empowering communities to take proactive measures, such as retrofitting buildings and developing community-based emergency response plans, can improve their ability to cope with disasters.

Psychosocial Support and Mental Health Services: The earthquake highlighted the importance of providing psychosocial support and mental health services to survivors and affected communities. Trauma, grief, and emotional distress were prevalent after the disaster, and addressing mental health needs is essential for long-term recovery.

Capacity Building of Emergency Responders: Strengthening the capacity of emergency responders, including firefighters, search and rescue teams, and medical personnel, is critical to mounting an effective response to large-scale disasters.

Integration of Technology in Disaster Management: Leveraging technology, such as remote sensing, geographic information systems (GIS), and social media, can enhance disaster management efforts, including damage assessment, resource allocation, and public information dissemination.

International Cooperation and Aid: The Bhuj Earthquake highlighted the significance of international cooperation and aid during disasters. The disaster prompted a global humanitarian response, emphasizing the importance of solidarity and support from the international community.

Post-Disaster Recovery and Rehabilitation:

The earthquake emphasized the need for long-term recovery and rehabilitation efforts to rebuild infrastructure, restore livelihoods, and support affected communities in their journey towards recovery. Learning from the Bhuj Earthquake has contributed to the improvement of disaster management practices not only in India but also globally. The lessons learned from this tragic event have led to reforms and policy changes aimed at enhancing disaster preparedness, response, and recovery measures to minimize the impact of future disasters on human lives and communities.

8.5 Case Study – Indian Ocean Tsunami (2004)

The Indian Ocean Tsunami, also known as the Boxing Day Tsunami, occurred on December 26, 2004. It was triggered by a massive undersea earthquake off the west coast of northern Sumatra, Indonesia. The earthquake had a magnitude of 9.1-9.3 and generated tsunamis that affected several countries bordering the Indian Ocean, causing one of the deadliest natural disasters in recorded history. Here are various aspects of disaster management during the Indian Ocean Tsunami:

Early Warning Systems: At the time of the tsunami, there was no regional tsunami warning system in the Indian Ocean. After the disaster, there was a realization of the need for such a system to provide timely alerts for future tsunamis. The Indian Ocean Tsunami Warning and Mitigation System (IOTWMS) was subsequently established to enhance early warning capabilities and improve disaster preparedness.

Emergency Response and Search and Rescue: In the immediate aftermath of the tsunami, search and rescue operations were launched to locate and save survivors and retrieve bodies of victims. Local authorities and international teams worked together to clear debris and search for survivors trapped under collapsed buildings and rubble.

Medical Aid and Healthcare: Medical teams and relief organizations provided emergency medical aid to the injured, including treatment for injuries and infections resulting from the disaster. Field hospitals and medical camps were set up in affected areas to provide healthcare services.

Shelter and Relief Camps: Temporary shelters and relief camps were established to accommodate displaced individuals and families who lost their homes in the disaster. Relief camps provided food, water, and basic amenities to those seeking refuge.

Public Awareness and Education: The Indian Ocean Tsunami underscored the need for public awareness and education about tsunamis and other natural hazards. Awareness campaigns were conducted to educate coastal communities about tsunami warning signs, evacuation procedures, and safety measures.

Identification and Management of Dead Bodies: Proper management and identification of dead bodies were essential to respect the dignity of the deceased and provide closure to their families. Forensic experts and disaster management teams worked to identify bodies and conduct appropriate burials or cremations.

Coordination and Logistics: Effective coordination among national governments, international organizations, and humanitarian agencies was crucial for the efficient distribution of relief materials and resources. Logistics support was essential to ensure that aid reached the affected areas promptly.

Psychosocial Support: The tsunami caused immense trauma and grief among survivors, especially those who lost family members and witnessed the destruction. Psychosocial support services, including counselling and trauma healing, were offered to help survivors cope with the emotional impact of the disaster.

International Aid and Support: The scale of the disaster prompted an outpouring of international aid and support from governments, organizations, and individuals worldwide. This aid played a vital role in supplementing local relief efforts and supporting the affected communities in their recovery.

Reconstruction and Rehabilitation: The long-term recovery phase involved rebuilding infrastructure, homes, schools, and healthcare facilities in the affected regions. Livelihood support was provided to help affected communities regain economic stability.

Coastal Zone Management and Tsunami Preparedness: The Indian Ocean Tsunami highlighted the need for coastal zone management and land-use planning to reduce vulnerability to future tsunamis. Governments implemented measures such as the construction of tsunami-resistant buildings and the establishment of evacuation routes and assembly points.

Regional Cooperation and Capacity Building: The disaster emphasized the importance of regional cooperation in disaster management and early warning systems. Countries in the Indian Ocean region collaborated to enhance their disaster preparedness and response capacities through training, information sharing, and joint exercises.

The Indian Ocean Tsunami had a profound impact on disaster management practices not only in the affected countries but also globally. It led to improvements in early warning systems, disaster preparedness, and international cooperation to enhance resilience against tsunamis and other natural disasters.

8.5.1 Lesson Learnt from DM during Tsunami

The Indian Ocean Tsunami, also known as the Boxing Day Tsunami, was a devastating disaster that struck on December 26, 2004. Triggered by a massive undersea earthquake off the coast of Sumatra, Indonesia, the tsunami affected several countries bordering the Indian Ocean. The disaster had a profound impact on disaster management practices and led to several important lessons learned:

Importance of Early Warning Systems: One of the most significant lessons from the Indian Ocean Tsunami was the urgent need for early warning systems for tsunamis. The disaster exposed the lack of a comprehensive regional warning system in the Indian Ocean, which could have provided timely alerts to vulnerable communities.

Strengthening Communication Infrastructure: The tsunami highlighted the importance of robust communication infrastructure for disseminating timely warnings and critical information to at-risk populations. Improving communication channels with remote and isolated communities can enhance disaster preparedness and response.

Regional Cooperation and Information Sharing: The Indian Ocean Tsunami emphasized the necessity of regional cooperation and information sharing among countries to enhance early warning capabilities. The establishment of the Indian Ocean Tsunami Warning and Mitigation System (IOTWMS) aimed to foster collaboration among nations and improve regional tsunami monitoring and response.

Education and Public Awareness: The disaster underscored the importance of public awareness and education about tsunamis and other natural hazards. Educational programs and campaigns have since been developed to raise awareness about warning signs, evacuation procedures, and safety measures during tsunamis.

Integration of Indigenous Knowledge: Recognizing and incorporating local knowledge and traditional practices can contribute to more effective disaster preparedness and response. Indigenous communities often possess valuable knowledge of environmental cues and early warning signs that can complement scientific data.

Infrastructure Resilience: The Indian Ocean Tsunami exposed the vulnerability of coastal infrastructure and buildings to tsunamis. Implementing and enforcing building codes that account for tsunami risks can enhance the resilience of structures and reduce casualties during future events.

Effective Disaster Response and Coordination: The tsunami demonstrated the importance of timely and well-coordinated disaster response efforts. Efficient coordination among national authorities, international agencies, and humanitarian organizations is crucial to ensure the rapid and effective delivery of relief and aid.

Capacity Building and Training: Strengthening the capacity of emergency responders, local communities, and government agencies can lead to more efficient disaster management. Training programs for first responders and disaster management personnel improve their ability to handle crises effectively.

Use of Technology and Remote Sensing: The Indian Ocean Tsunami highlighted the utility of technology, such as remote sensing and geographic information systems (GIS), in disaster monitoring and response. Utilizing satellite data and real-time information can aid in rapid assessment and decision-making during emergencies.

Community-Based Disaster Preparedness: Empowering communities to develop their disaster preparedness plans and response strategies can enhance resilience and self-sufficiency during emergencies.

Psychosocial Support and Mental Health Services: The tsunami demonstrated the importance of providing psychosocial support and mental health services to survivors and affected communities to cope with trauma and emotional distress.

International Solidarity and Aid: The scale of the disaster prompted a global humanitarian response, highlighting the significance of international solidarity and support during large-scale disasters.

The lessons learned from the Indian Ocean Tsunami have influenced disaster management practices worldwide. They have led to reforms, policy changes, and increased efforts to enhance early warning systems, strengthen community resilience, and improve disaster preparedness, response, and recovery measures to minimize the impact of future tsunamis and natural disasters.

8.6 Case Study – Kedarnath Flash Floods (2013)

The Kedarnath Flash Floods occurred in June 2013 in the state of Uttarakhand, India. The disaster was triggered by heavy monsoon rains and cloudbursts, which caused flash floods and landslides in the region, particularly affecting the Kedarnath Valley and surrounding areas. The floods resulted in widespread devastation, loss of lives, and significant damage to infrastructure and property. Here are various aspects of disaster management during the Kedarnath Flash Floods:

Emergency Response and Search and Rescue: Immediate search and rescue operations were launched to locate and save survivors trapped in debris and flooded areas. The Indian Army, National Disaster Response Force (NDRF), and other agencies were involved in rescue efforts.

Medical Aid and Healthcare: Medical teams were deployed to provide emergency medical aid and treat injuries and illnesses among survivors and affected communities. Field hospitals and medical camps were set up to cater to the healthcare needs of those impacted by the floods.

Shelter and Relief Camps: Temporary shelters and relief camps were established to provide safe accommodations to displaced individuals and families. The camps offered food, water, and other essential supplies to those seeking refuge.

Evacuation and Transportation: Evacuation of stranded individuals from remote and inaccessible areas was a significant challenge due to damaged infrastructure and disrupted transportation. Helicopters and other means of aerial transport were utilized to rescue people in remote regions.

Coordination and Logistics: Coordinated efforts among various agencies, including the central government, state authorities, and non-governmental organizations, were crucial for efficient relief and rescue operations. Logistics support was essential to ensure the timely delivery of relief materials to affected areas.

Identification and Management of Dead Bodies: Proper identification and management of dead bodies were necessary to handle the aftermath of the disaster with sensitivity and respect. Forensic experts and disaster management teams worked to identify bodies and facilitate their proper handling and disposal.

Rehabilitation and Reconstruction: The long-term recovery phase focused on the rehabilitation and reconstruction of damaged infrastructure, buildings, and livelihoods. Support was provided to help affected communities rebuild their lives and regain economic stability.

Psychosocial Support: Survivors of the flash floods experienced trauma and emotional distress. Psychosocial support services, including counselling and mental health assistance, were offered to help individuals cope with the aftermath of the disaster.

Infrastructure Restoration and Risk Reduction Measures: Restoring critical infrastructure, including roads, bridges, and communication networks, was essential to facilitate recovery efforts and access to affected areas. Risk reduction measures, such as slope stabilization and disaster-resilient infrastructure, were implemented to mitigate the impact of future disasters.

Disaster Preparedness and Early Warning Systems: The Kedarnath Flash Floods underscored the need for disaster preparedness and early warning systems in mountainous regions prone to flash floods and landslides. Efforts were made to strengthen early warning capabilities and improve communication systems to alert communities about impending disasters.

Community Participation and Resilience Building: Involving local communities in disaster management efforts and decision-making processes was crucial to building resilience and promoting sustainable recovery. Training and capacity-building programs were conducted to equip communities with knowledge and skills to respond effectively to disasters.

The Kedarnath Flash Floods were a tragic event that exposed vulnerabilities in disaster preparedness and infrastructure resilience in the region. The disaster prompted the implementation of measures to enhance disaster management capabilities, improve early warning systems, and invest in sustainable development to reduce the impact of future floods and landslides in Uttarakhand.

8.6.1 Lesson Learnt from DM during Kedarnath Flash Floods

The Kedarnath Flash Floods occurred in June 2013 in the state of Uttarakhand, India. The disaster was triggered by heavy monsoon rains and cloudbursts, leading to flash floods and landslides in the region, particularly affecting the Kedarnath Valley and surrounding areas. The flash floods caused widespread devastation, loss of lives, and significant damage to infrastructure and property. From the disaster management perspective, the Kedarnath Flash Floods offered several critical lessons:

Improved Early Warning Systems: The disaster highlighted the need for enhanced early warning systems for extreme weather events, especially in regions prone to flash floods and landslides.

Timely warnings can help authorities and communities take necessary precautionary measures and evacuate vulnerable areas.

Integrated Disaster Management Planning: The floods underscored the importance of comprehensive and integrated disaster management planning, encompassing risk assessment, prevention, preparedness, response, and recovery. Such planning should consider the region's geographical vulnerabilities and incorporate multi-hazard approaches.

Ecosystem-based Disaster Risk Reduction: The Kedarnath Flash Floods showed the significance of maintaining healthy ecosystems, including forests and wetlands, as they can act as natural buffers and reduce the impact of floods and landslides. Implementing ecosystem-based disaster risk reduction measures can contribute to greater resilience.

Infrastructure Resilience and Building Codes: The floods exposed the vulnerability of infrastructure, particularly roads, bridges, and buildings, to extreme weather events. Strengthening building codes and ensuring the construction of resilient infrastructure can mitigate damage and loss of life during disasters.

Effective Land Use Planning: The disaster emphasized the need for better land use planning, particularly in hilly and ecologically sensitive areas. Prohibiting construction in high-risk zones and enforcing zoning regulations can prevent settlements in hazardous locations.

Investment in Communication Infrastructure: The floods revealed the importance of investing in robust communication infrastructure to maintain connectivity during disasters. Reliable communication networks are vital for coordinating response efforts and disseminating information to affected communities.

Capacity Building of Local Communities: Strengthening the capacity of local communities in disaster preparedness and response can significantly improve their ability to cope with emergencies. Training programs and awareness campaigns can empower communities to take proactive measures.

Air Rescue Operations: The floods highlighted the value of air rescue operations in inaccessible and remote areas, especially in the immediate aftermath of disasters. Helicopters and aerial support can be instrumental in evacuating stranded individuals and delivering essential relief supplies.

Psychosocial Support Services: The Kedarnath Flash Floods emphasized the importance of providing psychosocial support services to survivors and affected communities. Addressing trauma and mental health needs is crucial for facilitating long-term recovery.

Effective Coordination and Multi-agency Response: The disaster emphasized the need for coordinated response efforts involving various government agencies, non-governmental organizations, and international partners. Efficient coordination can optimize resource allocation and support affected communities more effectively.

Climate Change Adaptation: The Kedarnath Flash Floods served as a reminder of the increasing risks posed by climate change-induced extreme weather events. Disaster management plans should consider climate change adaptation measures to address evolving risks.

Learning from Past Disasters: The floods highlighted the importance of learning from past disasters to improve disaster management practices. Post-disaster assessments and evaluations can inform future preparedness and response strategies.

The lessons learned from the Kedarnath Flash Floods have contributed to enhancing disaster management practices in Uttarakhand and other vulnerable regions. They have emphasized the significance of preparedness, resilience-building, and community engagement in reducing the impact of disasters on human lives and communities.

8.7 Case Study – Cyclone Nargis (2008)

Cyclone Nargis was a powerful tropical cyclone that struck Myanmar (Burma) on May 2, 2008. It was one of the deadliest cyclones in recorded history, causing widespread devastation and loss of lives in the affected regions. The disaster management efforts during Cyclone Nargis faced numerous challenges due to the political context of Myanmar, but various aspects of disaster management were implemented to respond to the crisis:

Early Warning and Preparedness: Cyclone Nargis highlighted the importance of early warning systems and disaster preparedness in vulnerable coastal areas. However, Myanmar's government faced criticism for not issuing timely and adequate warnings before the cyclone struck.

Emergency Response and Search and Rescue: Immediate search and rescue operations were hindered by the lack of resources and access to affected areas. The military junta's response was criticized for being slow and insufficient in helping affected communities.

International Aid and Assistance: The scale of the disaster prompted an international humanitarian response from various countries and organizations. However, the Myanmar government initially restricted foreign aid and access to the affected regions, creating challenges for relief efforts.

Medical Aid and Healthcare: Medical teams and relief organizations provided emergency medical aid to treat injuries, infections, and illnesses resulting from the cyclone. Field hospitals and medical camps were set up to provide healthcare services to affected communities.

Shelter and Relief Camps: Temporary shelters and relief camps were established to accommodate displaced individuals who lost their homes in the cyclone. However, limited resources and logistical challenges affected the provision of adequate shelter and amenities in some camps.

Food and Water Supply: The cyclone caused widespread destruction of food supplies and water sources, leading to shortages of food and clean water for affected communities. Relief agencies and organizations focused on providing food aid and restoring access to safe drinking water.

Logistics and Access to Affected Areas: Damage to infrastructure, including roads and communication networks, made it challenging to reach remote and isolated communities in need of assistance. International aid agencies faced difficulties in accessing affected regions due to restrictions imposed by the Myanmar government.

Psychosocial Support: Survivors of Cyclone Nargis experienced trauma and emotional distress. Psychosocial support services, including counselling, were crucial to help individuals cope with the aftermath of the disaster.

Coordination and Information Sharing: Effective coordination among humanitarian organizations, national authorities, and international agencies was essential to streamline relief efforts. Information sharing and collaboration helped avoid duplication of efforts and targeted assistance where it was needed the most.

Recovery and Reconstruction: The long-term recovery phase involved rebuilding infrastructure, homes, schools, and healthcare facilities in the affected regions. Support was provided to help affected communities recover economically and socially.

Disaster Risk Reduction and Preparedness for the Future: Cyclone Nargis underscored the need for disaster risk reduction measures and preparedness planning for future cyclones and natural disasters. Advocacy for building cyclone-resistant structures and early warning systems gained importance in the post-cyclone recovery process.

Cyclone Nargis brought attention to the importance of effective disaster management and humanitarian response. The challenges faced during this disaster highlighted the significance of international cooperation, timely response, and disaster preparedness measures in saving lives and reducing the impact of natural disasters on vulnerable communities. It also emphasized the need for transparent and collaborative approaches to disaster management, even in complex political contexts.

8.7.1 Lesson Learnt from DM during Cyclone

Cyclone Nargis was a powerful tropical cyclone that struck Myanmar (Burma) on May 2, 2008. The cyclone caused widespread devastation, particularly in the Irrawaddy Delta region, resulting in the loss of thousands of lives and extensive damage to infrastructure and property. The disaster management efforts during Cyclone Nargis faced various challenges due to the political context of Myanmar, but several crucial lessons were learned:

Importance of Early Warning Systems: One of the most significant lessons from Cyclone Nargis was the critical need for early warning systems for tropical cyclones. Timely and accurate forecasts and warnings can provide communities with essential information to take precautionary measures and evacuate to safer areas.

Disaster Preparedness and Training: The cyclone highlighted the importance of disaster preparedness and training for communities, government agencies, and emergency responders. Regular drills and exercises can help people understand their roles during emergencies and respond more effectively when disasters occur.

Effective Communication and Information Sharing: The disaster exposed the importance of robust communication infrastructure for disseminating timely warnings and critical information to at-risk populations. Improving communication channels can enhance disaster preparedness and response.

Community-Based Disaster Response: Cyclone Nargis underscored the significance of involving local communities in disaster response efforts. Empowering communities to develop their response plans and strategies can improve their ability to cope with disasters and reduce their vulnerability.

Capacity Building of Emergency Responders: The cyclone highlighted the need to strengthen the capacity of emergency responders, including firefighters, search and rescue teams, and medical personnel. Training programs for first responders and disaster management personnel improve their ability to handle crises effectively.

Effective Coordination and Resource Allocation: The cyclone emphasized the importance of effective coordination among national authorities, international agencies, and humanitarian organizations. Efficient resource allocation and coordination can ensure the rapid and effective delivery of relief and aid to affected areas.

Accessibility of Disaster-Affected Areas: The cyclone revealed the challenges in accessing remote and isolated areas in the aftermath of a disaster. Pre-positioning resources and establishing reliable transportation routes can facilitate relief efforts to reach the affected communities more effectively.

Psychosocial Support and Mental Health Services: Cyclone Nargis demonstrated the importance of providing psychosocial support and mental health services to survivors and affected communities. Addressing trauma and emotional distress is crucial for facilitating long-term recovery.

Investment in Disaster-Resilient Infrastructure: The cyclone highlighted the need to invest in disaster-resilient infrastructure to withstand the impact of cyclonic winds and flooding. Building cyclone-resistant structures and strengthening critical infrastructure can mitigate damage and protect lives.

Cooperation and International Assistance: The scale of the disaster prompted international humanitarian response, underscoring the significance of international cooperation and support during large-scale disasters.

Post-Disaster Recovery and Rehabilitation: The cyclone emphasized the importance of long-term recovery and rehabilitation efforts to rebuild infrastructure, restore livelihoods, and support affected communities in their journey towards recovery.

Climate Change Adaptation: Cyclone Nargis served as a reminder of the increasing risks posed by climate change-induced extreme weather events. Disaster management plans should consider climate change adaptation measures to address evolving risks.

The lessons learned from Cyclone Nargis have influenced disaster management practices not only in Myanmar but also globally. They have led to reforms, policy changes, and increased efforts to enhance early warning systems, strengthen community resilience, and improve disaster preparedness, response, and recovery measures to minimize the impact of future cyclones and natural disasters.

8.8 Best Practices in Disaster Management

Global examples of best practices in disaster management showcase effective approaches and strategies implemented by various countries and organizations to mitigate the impact of disasters and improve resilience. These practices highlight successful disaster preparedness, response, and recovery efforts. Here are some notable examples:

Japan's Tsunami Early Warning System: Japan is renowned for its advanced tsunami early warning system. The Japan Meteorological Agency (JMA) operates the system, which combines seismic data and oceanic sensors to detect undersea earthquakes and issue timely tsunami warnings to coastal communities. The system's effectiveness was demonstrated during the 2011 Great East Japan Earthquake and Tsunami, where the early warnings saved numerous lives.

The Netherlands' Flood Risk Management: The Netherlands is a global leader in flood risk management. The country has implemented an intricate system of dikes, levees, and floodgates, known as the Delta Works, to protect its low-lying lands from the threat of flooding. The Delta Works is an impressive example of integrated water management and engineering solutions.

Australia's National Bushfire Warning System: Australia has developed a comprehensive national bushfire warning system to alert residents about impending bushfire threats. The system includes public awareness campaigns, real-time monitoring, and timely warnings through various communication channels to keep residents informed and safe during bushfire emergencies.

The United States' Disaster Preparedness and Response: The United States' Federal Emergency Management Agency (FEMA) plays a critical role in coordinating disaster preparedness and response efforts. FEMA's Incident Command System (ICS) is a standardized approach to command, control, and coordination of emergency response across different agencies and levels of government.

Community-Based Disaster Risk Reduction in the Philippines: The Philippines has implemented community-based disaster risk reduction (CBDRR) initiatives, empowering local communities to take proactive measures to reduce their vulnerability to disasters. The approach includes capacity building, risk assessment, and the creation of local contingency plans.

Germany's Flood Risk Management and Early Warning: Germany's early warning system for floods incorporates data from various sources, including rainfall forecasts, river levels, and soil moisture. This system allows authorities to issue timely warnings to communities at risk and helps prevent casualties and property damage during flood events.

Community Resilience in New Zealand: New Zealand focuses on building community resilience through various programs and initiatives. The "Get Ready, Get Thru" campaign encourages individuals and families to be prepared for emergencies, including earthquakes and tsunamis. The country also emphasizes local communities' involvement in disaster response and recovery efforts.

Chile's Earthquake-Resistant Building Codes: Chile is known for its stringent earthquake-resistant building codes, which are continuously updated based on scientific research and historical seismic events. These codes have played a crucial role in reducing casualties and damage during earthquakes.

Indonesia's Tsunami Preparedness and Education: Indonesia, being prone to tsunamis, has made significant efforts to improve tsunami preparedness and education. The country's Tsunami Early Warning System (InaTEWS) disseminates alerts to coastal communities through various channels, including sirens and mobile phones.

Global Partnerships for Disaster Response: International organizations, such as the International Federation of Red Cross and Red Crescent Societies (IFRC), the World Food Programme (WFP), and the United Nations Office for the Coordination of Humanitarian Affairs (OCHA), play critical roles in coordinating and supporting disaster response efforts worldwide. These partnerships facilitate the rapid mobilization of resources and expertise during emergencies.

These global examples of best practices in disaster management serve as models for other countries and organizations to learn from and adapt to their specific contexts. Implementing effective disaster management practices is crucial for enhancing resilience and minimizing the impact of natural and human-made disasters on communities and societies.

8.8.1 Best Practices of Disaster Management in India

India, being vulnerable to a wide range of natural and human-made disasters, has implemented several best practices in disaster management to enhance preparedness, response, and recovery efforts. These practices aim to minimize the impact of disasters on human lives, infrastructure, and the environment. Here are some notable best practices in disaster management in India:

National Disaster Management Plan (NDMP): India has developed the National Disaster Management Plan, a comprehensive document that outlines the country's approach to disaster management. It includes risk assessment, preparedness measures, response strategies, and recovery guidelines for various types of disasters.

Disaster Risk Reduction (DRR) Initiatives: India focuses on disaster risk reduction through various initiatives, including the implementation of the Sendai Framework for Disaster Risk Reduction. These efforts aim to strengthen disaster resilience by integrating risk reduction measures into development plans and policies.

Cyclone Early Warning Systems: India's Meteorological Department has established effective cyclone early warning systems, especially for coastal regions. These systems utilize weather monitoring, forecasting, and communication channels to issue timely warnings and evacuate vulnerable communities before cyclone landfalls.

Community-Based Disaster Preparedness: India emphasizes community-based disaster preparedness initiatives. These programs involve local communities in identifying risks, creating contingency plans, and conducting mock drills to enhance their capacity to respond to disasters effectively.

National Disaster Response Force (NDRF): India has set up the NDRF, a specialized force trained for disaster response and rescue operations. NDRF units are strategically stationed across the country to respond swiftly to emergencies.

Urban Disaster Management: Many Indian cities have developed urban disaster management plans to address the unique challenges of urban disasters, including fire safety, building collapses, and urban flooding.

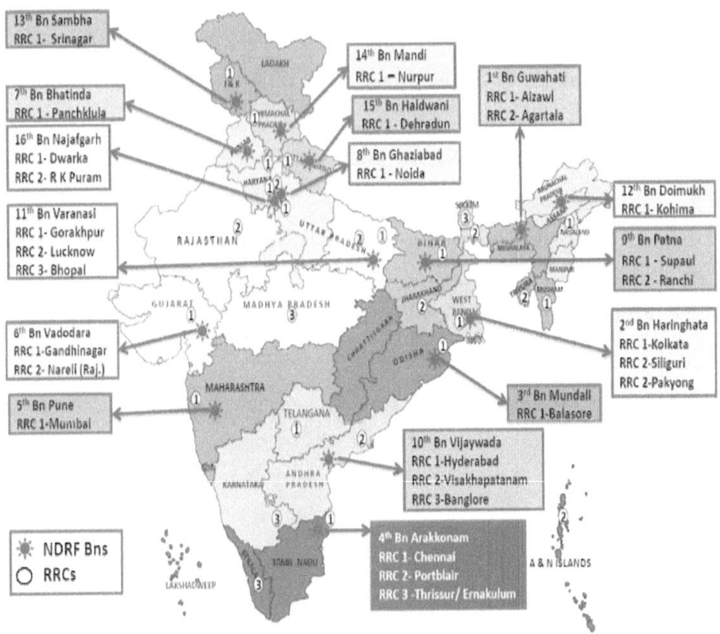

Figure 8.1 Map showing NDRF BNS locations

Earthquake-Resistant Building Codes: India has implemented earthquake-resistant building codes to ensure that new constructions, particularly in seismic-prone areas, are designed to withstand earthquakes and minimize casualties.

Satellite-Based Disaster Monitoring: India utilizes satellite technology for disaster monitoring and management. The Indian Space Research Organisation (ISRO) provides valuable data for monitoring floods, cyclones, and other natural disasters.

Education and Awareness Programs: India conducts public awareness and education programs to inform citizens about disaster risks, preparedness measures, and evacuation procedures. The "School Safety" program educates students on disaster management.

The National Institute of Disaster Management (NIDM): NIDM is a premier institute in India that conducts research, training, and capacity-building programs in disaster management. It plays a crucial role in building the capacity of stakeholders and disseminating knowledge.

Public-Private Partnerships: India encourages public-private partnerships in disaster management to harness expertise and resources from both sectors for a more effective response to disasters.

Flood Early Warning Systems: India has implemented flood early warning systems in vulnerable river basins to issue alerts before floods occur, allowing communities to take necessary precautions.

Climate Change Adaptation Measures: In recognition of the increasing impacts of climate change, India is integrating climate change adaptation measures into disaster management planning to address evolving risks.

Integrated Command and Control Centers (ICCCs): Some cities in India have established ICCCs to enable real-time monitoring of emergency situations and coordinate response efforts across various departments.

These best practices demonstrate India's commitment to disaster risk reduction, preparedness, and resilience-building. However, continuous evaluation, improvement, and implementation of lessons learned from past disasters are essential to further enhance India's disaster management capabilities.

8.8.2 Lesson Learnt from Global Disaster Trends

Global disaster trends offer valuable insights into the evolving nature of disasters and their impact on communities and societies worldwide. Analysing these trends helps identify lessons learned and informs disaster management strategies to build resilience and mitigate future risks. Here are some key lessons learned from global disaster trends:

Increasing Frequency and Intensity of Disasters: Global disaster trends show a rise in the frequency and intensity of natural disasters, such as hurricanes, floods, wildfires, and heatwaves. This emphasizes the urgency of proactive disaster risk reduction measures and climate change adaptation. According to the Centre for Research on the Epidemiology of Disasters (CRED) and the International Disaster Database (EM-DAT), the number of reported natural disasters has been increasing over the past few decades. For example, in the 1990s, there were an average of 322 reported natural disasters per year, while in the 2010s, the average increased to 354 reported disasters per year.

Urbanization and Disaster Vulnerability: The increasing concentration of populations in urban areas has led to higher vulnerability to disasters. Urban planning must integrate disaster risk reduction strategies, including resilient infrastructure and land use planning. The United Nations estimates that by 2050, around 68% of the world's population will live in urban areas, increasing the vulnerability of large populations to disasters in cities and urban centers.

Humanitarian and Development Nexus: Disaster trends underscore the interconnection between humanitarian response and long-term development. Addressing disaster risks and vulnerabilities must be integrated into development planning to achieve sustainable outcomes.

Importance of Early Warning Systems: Early warning systems are crucial for minimizing the impact of disasters. They provide timely alerts, enabling communities to take preventive actions, evacuate, and prepare for upcoming hazards. The Sendai Framework for Disaster Risk Reduction (2015-2030) emphasizes the need for countries to establish and strengthen early warning systems for various hazards. As of 2021, only about 50% of countries had multi-hazard early warning systems in place, leaving significant gaps in preparedness and response capabilities.

Disasters' Disproportionate Impact on Vulnerable Populations: Disaster trends reveal that vulnerable populations, such as the poor, children, elderly, and marginalized communities, suffer disproportionately during disasters. Ensuring their inclusion and protection in disaster management plans is critical. The United Nations Office for Disaster Risk Reduction (UNDRR) reports that between 1998 and 2017, around 1.3 million people were killed by disasters, and over four billion were affected. Vulnerable populations, such as women, children, elderly, and people with disabilities, are disproportionately affected during disasters.

Technology and Data for Disaster Management: Advancements in technology and data collection have revolutionized disaster management. Satellite imagery, remote sensing, and data analytics facilitate better risk assessment, preparedness, and response.

Community Resilience and Empowerment: Strengthening community resilience and empowering local communities to lead disaster preparedness and response efforts are crucial for more effective disaster management.

Importance of Disaster Risk Reduction (DRR): Disaster trends highlight the significance of investing in disaster risk reduction measures to reduce the human and economic costs of disasters in the long run.

Climate Change and Disaster Impacts: The correlation between climate change and the frequency of extreme weather events emphasizes the need for climate change mitigation and adaptation as part of disaster management strategies. The Intergovernmental Panel on Climate Change (IPCC) states that climate change is increasing the frequency and intensity of extreme weather events, including hurricanes, heatwaves, floods, and droughts. Between 2000 and 2019, climate-related disasters accounted for 83% of all recorded disasters, according to CRED's EM-DAT.

Cross-Border Cooperation and Solidarity: Disasters often transcend national boundaries, requiring international cooperation and solidarity in disaster response and recovery efforts.

Inclusive Disaster Communication: Accessible and inclusive communication channels are essential for disseminating information during disasters to reach all segments of society, including people with disabilities and language barriers.

Holistic Disaster Management Approach: Disaster trends underline the importance of a comprehensive, multi-hazard approach to disaster management that addresses various types of disasters and their potential cascading effects. The World Bank estimates that the cost of disasters and climate-related losses could reach $520 billion per year by 2050 if action is not taken to address disaster risks proactively. A comprehensive approach to disaster risk reduction could significantly reduce these costs.

Psychosocial Support and Mental Health: Disasters take a toll on mental health and psychosocial well-being. Providing psychosocial support and mental health services to survivors and affected communities is vital for long-term recovery. The World Health Organization (WHO) estimates that after a major disaster, up to 10% of the population affected may suffer from mental health issues, such as depression, anxiety, and post-traumatic stress disorder.

Preparedness for Slow-Onset Disasters: Slow-onset disasters, such as droughts and desertification, require preparedness and long-term resilience-building measures to mitigate their impact on agriculture, water resources, and livelihoods. The Food and Agriculture Organization (FAO) estimates that slow-onset disasters, such as droughts, result in annual economic losses of around $6-8 billion globally. It is essential to note that disaster data and trends are continuously changing, and new events can significantly impact these statistics. Up-to-date information from reputable sources such as the United Nations, World Bank, WHO, and CRED should be consulted for the most recent data on global disaster trends.

By learning from global disaster trends, policymakers, governments, and communities can take proactive measures to reduce disaster risks, enhance preparedness, and strengthen resilience. Collaboration between stakeholders at local, national, regional, and international levels is essential to build a more resilient world in the face of increasing disaster challenges.

8.8.3 Lessons Learnt from National Disaster Trends in India

Lessons learned from national disaster trends in India provide valuable insights into the country's disaster management efforts, challenges, and achievements. Analysing these trends helps identify areas for improvement and informs strategies to enhance preparedness, response, and recovery. Here are some key lessons learned from national disaster trends in India:

Multi-Hazard Approach: India is prone to a wide range of disasters, including earthquakes, cyclones, floods, droughts, landslides, and heatwaves. The multi-hazard nature of the country's risk landscape highlights the importance of adopting a comprehensive and integrated approach to disaster management.

Importance of Early Warning Systems: India has made significant progress in developing early warning systems for various hazards. The success of early warning systems during cyclones like Cyclone Phailin (2013) and Cyclone Fani (2019) demonstrated the importance of timely alerts in saving lives and enabling preparedness.

Community-Based Disaster Preparedness: The 1999 Odisha Super Cyclone was a turning point in disaster management in India. After the disaster, the country recognized the importance of involving local communities in disaster preparedness, response, and recovery efforts. Community-based disaster preparedness programs have since played a crucial role in enhancing resilience at the grassroots level.

Improving Cyclone Preparedness: India's experience with cyclones, such as the 1999 Odisha Super Cyclone and Cyclone Phailin, led to improvements in cyclone preparedness. Evacuation planning, cyclone shelters, and coordination among various agencies have been enhanced to minimize casualties during cyclones.

Flood Management and River Basin Planning: India faces annual flooding in various regions. Lessons from past floods, such as the 2013 Uttarakhand Floods, have highlighted the need for better flood management strategies, including river basin planning, early warning systems, and improved infrastructure.

Seismic Preparedness: India is situated in a seismically active region, and earthquakes pose a significant risk. The Bhuj Earthquake of 2001 demonstrated the importance of earthquake-resistant building codes and strengthened infrastructure to reduce casualties and damage during seismic events.

Landslide Risk Mitigation: Landslides are a recurring disaster in hilly regions of India. Landslide risk mitigation measures, such as slope stabilization and early warning systems, are crucial to protect vulnerable communities.

Climate Change Adaptation: India's vulnerability to climate change impacts, including extreme weather events and sea-level rise, necessitates the integration of climate change adaptation measures into disaster management planning.

Technology and Data Integration: India has been leveraging technology, such as satellite imagery, remote sensing, and Geographic Information System (GIS), to improve disaster monitoring, risk assessment, and response.

Strengthening Disaster Response Forces: The National Disaster Response Force (NDRF) and State Disaster Response Forces (SDRF) have played a vital role in disaster response. Continuous training and capacity building are essential to enhance their effectiveness.

Public Awareness and Education: Public awareness campaigns and education programs are essential to improve disaster literacy among citizens, enabling them to respond effectively during emergencies.

Collaboration and International Cooperation: India has collaborated with international organizations and neighbouring countries in disaster response and sharing best practices, demonstrating the significance of cross-border cooperation.

Post-Disaster Recovery and Rehabilitation: Timely and well-planned post-disaster recovery and rehabilitation efforts are critical for restoring livelihoods and rebuilding communities.

Integration of Disaster Risk Reduction in Development Planning: Integrating disaster risk reduction measures into development planning helps build resilience and reduce vulnerabilities.

India's experience with various disasters provides a wealth of knowledge for continuous improvement in disaster management. Regular evaluation, learning from past experiences, and adopting innovative solutions are crucial to strengthening India's disaster management capabilities and building a more resilient nation.

CHAPTER 9

Climate Change and Urban Disasters

9.1 Relation between Climate Change and Urban Disasters

Climate change and urban disasters are intricately linked, as the impacts of climate change exacerbate the risks and vulnerabilities of urban areas. Here is a detailed explanation of the relationship between climate change and urban disasters:

Urbanization and Climate Change: Urban areas are characterized by high population densities, extensive infrastructure, and concentrated economic activities. Rapid urbanization, particularly in developing countries, has led to the expansion of cities and increased vulnerability to climate change. Urban areas often experience the urban heat island effect, where temperatures are higher compared to surrounding rural areas due to the concentration of buildings, roads, and heat-absorbing materials.

Increased Frequency and Intensity of Extreme Weather Events: Climate change is causing an increase in the frequency and intensity of extreme weather events, such as heatwaves, heavy rainfall, hurricanes, and storms. Urban areas are particularly vulnerable to these events due to factors like inadequate drainage systems, impervious surfaces, and poor land use planning. Heatwaves in cities can lead to heat-related illnesses and deaths, particularly among vulnerable populations like the elderly and those with pre-existing health conditions. Heavy rainfall events can overwhelm urban drainage systems, leading to urban flooding and property damage.

Urban Flooding: Climate change intensifies the risks of urban flooding due to increased precipitation, sea-level rise, and changes in rainfall patterns. Urban areas, with their high percentage of impermeable surfaces like concrete and asphalt, have reduced natural water absorption capacity, resulting in surface runoff and increased flood risk. Urban infrastructure, including stormwater drainage systems, may be inadequate to handle the increased volume of water during intense rainfall events. Urban floods can disrupt transportation networks, damage buildings and infrastructure, contaminate water sources, and pose health risks due to waterborne diseases.

Coastal Hazards and Sea-Level Rise: Urban areas located along coastlines are at heightened risk due to rising sea levels and the increased intensity of coastal storms. Sea-level rise threatens low-lying coastal cities with inundation, saltwater intrusion into freshwater sources, and increased vulnerability to storm surges during hurricanes and cyclones.

Coastal erosion and land subsidence further exacerbate the risks faced by urban coastal areas.

Urban Infrastructure Resilience: Climate change requires urban areas to enhance their infrastructure resilience to withstand and adapt to changing climate conditions. This includes upgrading drainage systems, improving water management, enhancing building design standards, and implementing nature-based solutions like green infrastructure. Retrofitting existing buildings and infrastructure to be more resilient can help mitigate the impacts of urban disasters.

Integrated Urban Planning and Governance: Addressing the challenges of climate change and urban disasters requires integrated urban planning and governance approaches.

This involves coordination among various stakeholders, including city governments, urban planners, engineers, and community members. Climate-resilient urban planning should consider factors such as land use zoning, building codes, transportation systems, and the preservation of green spaces.

Community Engagement and Awareness: Building resilience in urban areas necessitates active community engagement and awareness. Communities should be involved in decision-making processes, disaster preparedness, and early warning systems. Public education and awareness campaigns can contribute to enhancing community resilience and promoting sustainable practices in urban areas.

Urban Heat Island Effect: The urban heat island effect refers to the phenomenon where urban areas experience higher temperatures compared to surrounding rural areas due to human activities and the built environment. Climate change exacerbates the urban heat island effect by increasing ambient temperatures and heatwaves. Higher temperatures in urban areas can have adverse effects on human health, particularly for vulnerable populations, and can increase energy demands for cooling.

Water Scarcity and Drought: Climate change can lead to water scarcity and drought conditions in urban areas. Rising temperatures and changes in precipitation patterns can reduce water availability, strain water resources, and increase the risk of water shortages in cities. Urban areas need to implement sustainable water management strategies, including water conservation measures, rainwater harvesting, and efficient water use practices.

Impacts on Vulnerable Communities: Urban disasters resulting from climate change disproportionately affect vulnerable communities, including low-income neighbourhoods and informal settlements. These communities often lack access to basic infrastructure and services, making them more susceptible to the impacts of urban disasters. Social inequities and limited resources can hinder their ability to adapt and recover from climate-related disasters.

Urban Biodiversity and Ecosystem Services: Climate change affects urban biodiversity and ecosystem services, such as green spaces, urban forests, and natural habitats. Loss of urban green spaces and vegetation can worsen the urban heat island effect and reduce the capacity for natural stormwater management. Protecting and enhancing urban biodiversity can contribute to climate resilience by providing ecosystem services and mitigating the impacts of climate change.

Sustainable Urban Development: Climate change and urban disasters necessitate a shift towards sustainable urban development practices. This includes promoting energy-efficient buildings, renewable energy, sustainable transportation, and green infrastructure. Sustainable urban development can help reduce greenhouse gas emissions, improve resilience to climate-related hazards, and enhance the quality of urban life.

It is crucial for urban areas to incorporate climate change adaptation and disaster risk reduction into their planning and development processes. This involves integrating climate considerations into urban policies, investing in resilient infrastructure, promoting sustainable practices, and fostering community participation. Addressing the impacts of climate change on urban disasters requires a multi-faceted approach that combines climate mitigation efforts, adaptation strategies, and urban planning measures. By integrating climate resilience into urban development, cities can become more sustainable, liveable, and resilient to the growing challenges posed by climate change. By taking proactive measures to address the challenges posed by climate change, urban areas can become more resilient, liveable, and sustainable in the face of urban disasters.

9.2 Preventive Measures to Reduce Impact of Climate Change

Preventive measures to reduce the impact of climate change on urban disasters involve a combination of mitigation and adaptation strategies. Here are some key preventive measures:

Climate Change Mitigation: Reduce greenhouse gas emissions: Implement measures to reduce carbon emissions from various sources, including industries, transportation, and energy production. This can involve transitioning to renewable energy sources, promoting energy efficiency, and adopting sustainable practices. Urban planning and design: Incorporate climate considerations into urban planning by promoting compact, mixed-use developments, efficient transportation systems, and green infrastructure. This can help reduce energy consumption, minimize carbon emissions, and create more sustainable and resilient cities.

Climate Change Adaptation: Enhance urban infrastructure resilience: Upgrade existing infrastructure and design new infrastructure to withstand climate-related hazards such as floods, heatwaves, and storms. This includes improving drainage systems, constructing flood-resistant buildings, and implementing nature-based solutions like green roofs and permeable pavements. Strengthen early warning systems: Develop robust early warning systems to provide timely alerts for approaching disasters. This can include weather monitoring, flood forecasting, and dissemination of warnings through various channels to reach vulnerable communities.

a) **Water management:** Implement sustainable water management practices, such as rainwater harvesting, water recycling, and efficient irrigation systems, to cope with water scarcity and drought conditions.

b) **Heatwave management:** Develop heat action plans to mitigate the impacts of heatwaves, including setting up cooling centers, implementing heat-resistant urban design, and providing public awareness campaigns on heat safety measures.

c) **Ecosystem preservation:** Protect and restore urban green spaces, natural habitats, and biodiversity. These natural elements provide multiple benefits, including temperature regulation, stormwater management, and carbon sequestration, which can help mitigate the impacts of climate change.

d) **Community engagement and capacity building**: Involve communities in climate change adaptation efforts through awareness campaigns, education, and training. Empowering communities with knowledge and skills can enhance their resilience and enable them to actively participate in disaster preparedness and response.

Integrated Governance and Collaboration:

a) **Develop comprehensive policies and regulations**: Formulate and enforce policies that integrate climate change adaptation and disaster risk reduction into urban planning, infrastructure development, and land-use management. This requires collaboration among government agencies, urban planners, policymakers, and community representatives.

b) **Multisectoral collaboration**: Foster partnerships and collaboration among different sectors, including government, academia, non-governmental organizations, and private sectors. This collective effort can enhance knowledge sharing, resource mobilization, and the implementation of climate change adaptation strategies.

c) **international cooperation**: Engage in international cooperation and knowledge exchange to learn from best practices and experiences in other cities and regions. Participate in global initiatives and networks that address climate change and urban resilience.

By implementing these preventive measures, urban areas can reduce their vulnerability to climate change, enhance their resilience to urban disasters, and promote sustainable development. It requires a holistic approach, long-term planning, and collaboration among stakeholders to build climate-resilient cities that can thrive in the face of climate change challenges.

Green Infrastructure: Implement green infrastructure strategies such as urban forests, parks, green roofs, and permeable surfaces. These features can help absorb rainwater, reduce urban heat island effects, improve air quality, and provide spaces for recreation and biodiversity. Promote urban agriculture and community gardens, which can contribute to food security, improve local resilience, and mitigate the heat island effect.

Risk-Informed Land Use Planning: Incorporate climate change projections and disaster risk assessments into land use planning processes. This includes avoiding high-risk areas prone to flooding, landslides, or other hazards when siting critical infrastructure and residential developments. Develop land use regulations and building codes that consider climate resilience and incorporate measures to protect against climate-related hazards.

Community-Based Disaster Risk Reduction: Foster community participation in disaster risk reduction and climate change adaptation through community-based organizations, local governance structures, and grassroots initiatives. Encourage the development of neighbourhood emergency response plans, community-based early warning systems, and capacity-building programs to enhance the resilience of vulnerable communities.

Knowledge Sharing and Capacity Building: Strengthen research and data collection on climate change impacts and urban disasters to inform evidence-based decision-making and planning. Enhance the capacity of local governments, urban planners, and professionals through training programs, workshops, and knowledge-sharing platforms. Promote information dissemination and public awareness campaigns to educate residents about climate change impacts, disaster risks, and preventive measures.

Financial Mechanisms and Insurance: Establish financial mechanisms to support climate change adaptation and disaster risk reduction efforts in urban areas, including dedicated funding sources, public-private partnerships, and insurance schemes. Encourage investments in resilient infrastructure, incentivize private sector engagement, and provide financial support to vulnerable communities for risk reduction measures.

International Support and Funding: Seek international support, funding, and technical assistance to enhance climate resilience in urban areas. This can be done through partnerships with international organizations, development agencies, and global climate initiatives.

Monitoring and Evaluation: Develop monitoring and evaluation frameworks to assess the effectiveness of climate change adaptation and disaster risk reduction measures in urban areas. Regularly review and update strategies based on lessons learned, changing climate patterns, and emerging risks.

By implementing these preventive measures, urban areas can reduce their vulnerability to climate change impacts and build resilience to urban disasters. It requires a comprehensive and integrated approach involving all levels of government, stakeholders, and communities to create sustainable, safe, and liveable cities in the face of climate change challenges.

9.3 Impact of Climate Change on Urban Areas

Climate change has significant impacts on urban areas due to their high population densities, infrastructure concentration, and economic activities. As global temperatures rise and extreme weather events become more frequent and intense, urban areas are particularly vulnerable to various environmental, social, and economic consequences. Here are some key impacts of climate change on urban areas:

Heat Island Effect: Urban areas often experience higher temperatures than surrounding rural areas, known as the heat island effect. Concrete, asphalt, and tall buildings absorb and retain heat, exacerbating heatwaves and posing health risks to residents, especially vulnerable populations like the elderly and children. According to a study conducted by the Indian Institute of Technology (IIT) Gandhinagar, urban areas in India can experience temperatures up to 5°C higher than nearby rural areas during heatwaves due to the heat island effect.

Extreme Heat and Heatwaves: Climate change leads to more frequent and intense heatwaves, putting urban residents at risk of heat-related illnesses and heat stress. Demand for cooling increases, leading to higher energy consumption and strain on the power grid. India has witnessed an increase in the frequency and intensity of heatwaves. In 2019, India experienced one of its longest and most intense heatwaves, with temperatures exceeding 50°C in some regions.

Urban Flooding: Intense rainfall events, coupled with impermeable surfaces in urban areas, can cause rapid runoff and flooding. Inadequate drainage systems exacerbate the risk of urban flooding, disrupting transportation, damaging property, and posing health hazards. According to the National Disaster Management Authority (NDMA), urban flooding is a recurrent problem in many Indian cities. In 2020, heavy monsoon rains caused severe flooding in cities like Mumbai, Hyderabad, and Bengaluru.

Sea Level Rise and Coastal Erosion: Urban areas located along coastlines face the risk of sea-level rise and coastal erosion due to melting ice caps and glaciers. Sea-level rise threatens low-lying coastal cities, leading to saltwater intrusion, property damage, and displacement of residents. A study by the Climate Central organization estimates that by 2050, more than 20 million people in India may be at risk of coastal flooding due to sea-level rise caused by climate change.

Water Scarcity and Drought: Climate change can alter precipitation patterns, leading to water scarcity and drought in some urban areas. Reduced water availability affects agriculture, industries, and households, impacting food security and economic activities. The Intergovernmental Panel on Climate Change (IPCC) projects that India may experience more frequent and prolonged droughts due to climate change, affecting water availability in urban areas.

Increased Storm Intensity: Urban areas are susceptible to intense storms, hurricanes, and cyclones due to climate change. These extreme weather events can cause significant damage to infrastructure, disrupt essential services, and displace residents. India's coastal cities are vulnerable to the increasing intensity of cyclones and storms. For instance, Cyclone Amphan, which hit West Bengal and Odisha in 2020, caused extensive damage to infrastructure and displaced thousands of people.

Health Impacts: Climate change in urban areas can lead to increased incidences of heat-related illnesses, respiratory issues due to air pollution, and vector-borne diseases. Poor air quality and heat stress affect public health, putting a strain on healthcare facilities and resources. According to a report by Lancet Countdown, India witnessed a significant increase in heat-related deaths, reaching 3,218 deaths in 2019, compared to 424 deaths in 2000.

Infrastructure Damage: More frequent extreme weather events can damage critical infrastructure, such as roads, bridges, buildings, and utilities. The cost of repairing and maintaining infrastructure increases, affecting municipal budgets. The Economic Survey of India 2019-2020 noted that climate-induced extreme weather events have caused damage to critical infrastructure, resulting in economic losses.

Economic Disruptions: Climate change impacts can disrupt economic activities, affecting businesses, trade, and productivity in urban centers. Increased costs due to damage repair, insurance claims, and energy demand add economic burdens. The Global Climate Risk Index 2021 ranked India among the top ten countries most affected by climate-related events from 2000 to 2019, with significant economic losses.

Social Inequity: Vulnerable populations, including low-income communities and marginalized groups, bear a disproportionate burden of climate change impacts in urban areas. Limited access to resources, information, and support systems exacerbates social inequities. A study by ActionAid India highlights that vulnerable urban communities, such as slum dwellers, are disproportionately impacted by climate change due to inadequate access to basic services and resources.

Population Displacement and Migration: Climate-induced impacts such as flooding and sea-level rise can lead to population displacement and migration from vulnerable urban areas to safer regions. Climate-induced impacts, such as floods and sea-level rise, have led to internal migration from climate-vulnerable regions to urban areas, increasing the strain on urban infrastructure and resources.

Urban Resilience Challenges:

Climate change presents significant challenges to urban resilience, requiring cities to invest in climate adaptation strategies, infrastructure upgrades, and disaster preparedness. A report by the World Bank states that rapid urbanization, combined with climate change impacts, presents significant challenges to urban resilience in India, requiring concerted efforts in building climate resilience.

To address the impacts of climate change on urban areas, comprehensive and proactive strategies are necessary. These may include climate-resilient urban planning, green infrastructure, sustainable transport, energy efficiency measures, and community engagement. By adopting measures to mitigate and adapt to climate change, cities can build greater resilience and protect the well-being of their residents and ecosystems.

These data and statistics underscore the urgent need for comprehensive climate adaptation and mitigation strategies in India's urban areas. Initiatives focused on sustainable urban planning, resilient infrastructure, improved disaster preparedness, and community engagement are critical to address the impacts of climate change and build more resilient and climate-resilient cities in India.

9.4 Urban Planning for Disaster Resilience

Urban planning for disaster resilience is a comprehensive approach that aims to design cities and urban areas to withstand and recover from natural and human-induced disasters. It involves integrating disaster risk reduction principles into the planning and development process to create safer, more sustainable, and resilient communities. Here are key aspects and strategies involved in urban planning for disaster resilience:

Risk Assessment and Vulnerability Mapping: Conducting a thorough risk assessment helps identify potential hazards and vulnerabilities in the urban area. Vulnerability mapping allows planners to pinpoint high-risk zones and tailor mitigation measures accordingly.

Land Use Planning and Zoning: Zoning regulations can help prevent or limit construction in high-risk areas, such as floodplains, seismic zones, or coastal regions prone to storm surges. Promoting mixed land-use can reduce the impact of disasters by decentralizing critical infrastructure and services.

Building Codes and Construction Standards: Implementing and enforcing stringent building codes and construction standards ensures that buildings can withstand natural hazards like earthquakes, hurricanes, and floods. Retrofitting existing structures can improve their resilience.

Green Infrastructure and Ecosystem-based Approaches: Incorporating green infrastructure, such as urban parks, wetlands, and green roofs, can help manage stormwater, reduce urban heat island effects, and improve air quality. Ecosystem-based approaches contribute to disaster risk reduction by enhancing natural buffers against hazards.

Safe and Resilient Infrastructure: Planning and designing infrastructure with resilience in mind, including roads, bridges, utilities, and transportation systems, can minimize disruptions during disasters. Ensuring redundancy and backup systems increases the capacity to withstand shocks.

Early Warning Systems and Communication: Integrating early warning systems into urban planning helps disseminate timely information to residents and authorities during emergencies. Communication networks that function during disasters are vital for coordination and response efforts.

Community Engagement and Participation: Involving local communities in the planning process empowers them and fosters a sense of ownership and responsibility for disaster resilience. Understanding local knowledge and traditional practices can inform more effective strategies.

Social Inclusion and Equity: Addressing the needs of vulnerable populations, such as low-income communities, the elderly, and persons with disabilities, is crucial in urban planning for disaster resilience. Ensuring that resilience measures benefit all segments of society promotes social equity.

Multi-stakeholder Collaboration: Disaster resilience requires collaboration among various stakeholders, including government agencies, private sector, academia, and civil society organizations. Coordinated efforts strengthen resilience strategies and resource allocation.

Climate Adaptation and Mitigation: Incorporating climate change projections and adaptation measures into urban planning ensures long-term resilience against changing climate patterns. Mitigation strategies to reduce greenhouse gas emissions contribute to overall disaster risk reduction.

Post-Disaster Recovery and Reconstruction Planning: Having post-disaster recovery and reconstruction plans in place enables a quicker and more effective response to rebuilding efforts. Designing resilient infrastructure and incorporating lessons learned from disasters improve future resilience.

Urban planning for disaster resilience requires a holistic and integrated approach that considers multiple hazards, climate change, socio-economic factors, and community dynamics. By adopting these strategies, cities and urban areas can enhance their ability to withstand, adapt to, and recover from disasters, thereby safeguarding the well-being and prosperity of their residents.

9.5 Urban Disasters in India

Urban Flooding in Mumbai: Mumbai, India's financial capital, is susceptible to heavy monsoon rains, leading to frequent urban flooding. In 2005, Mumbai experienced one of the worst floods in its history, resulting in over 1,000 deaths and extensive damage to infrastructure and property.

Chennai Floods: In 2015, Chennai, the capital city of Tamil Nadu, witnessed devastating floods that submerged entire neighbourhoods. The floods resulted in hundreds of deaths and caused significant economic losses.

Cyclone Fani in Odisha: In 2019, Cyclone Fani made landfall in Odisha, causing extensive damage to infrastructure and agriculture. However, effective disaster preparedness and evacuation measures saved countless lives.

Heatwaves in Urban Areas: Indian cities, especially in the northern and central regions, frequently experience severe heatwaves during the summer months. In 2019, India recorded its highest-ever temperature of 51°C in the city of Churu, Rajasthan.

Coastal Vulnerability: India's long coastline is highly vulnerable to sea-level rise and coastal erosion due to climate change. Coastal cities like Mumbai, Chennai, and Kolkata face increasing risks from storm surges and sea-level rise.

Data on disaster events in India underscores the need for effective urban planning for disaster resilience:

According to the Global Climate Risk Index 2021, India ranks among the top ten countries most affected by climate-related events from 2000 to 2019, experiencing significant economic losses and human impacts.

The National Disaster Management Authority (NDMA) reported that between 2005 and 2017, India witnessed over 250 disaster events, affecting millions of people and causing substantial damage to infrastructure and livelihoods.

The World Bank estimates that climate change could cause losses equivalent to 2.8% of India's GDP annually by 2050, affecting urban areas significantly.

In response to these challenges, India has taken various steps to enhance urban planning for disaster resilience:

The National Disaster Management Plan (NDMP) was launched in 2016 to guide disaster management efforts, including urban planning, across the country.

Initiatives like the Smart Cities Mission focus on promoting sustainable urban development and integrating disaster resilience into city planning.

City-specific disaster management plans are being developed to address the unique risks faced by different urban centers.

Climate change adaptation measures, such as constructing elevated roads and improving drainage systems, are being implemented in vulnerable cities.

Community-based disaster preparedness programs aim to enhance public awareness and participation in disaster resilience efforts.

Despite these efforts, there is still a need for continued investment in disaster-resilient urban planning, particularly as India continues to urbanize rapidly. Sustainable urban development, climate-responsive infrastructure, and inclusive planning are essential to ensure that India's urban areas can withstand and recover from the increasing challenges posed by climate change and natural disasters.

9.5.1 Role of Smart Cities for Disaster Resilience

Smart Cities play a crucial role in effective urban planning for disaster resilience by leveraging technology and data-driven approaches to enhance preparedness, response, and recovery efforts. The concept of Smart Cities emphasizes the integration of digital technologies, data analytics, and citizen engagement to create more sustainable, efficient, and resilient urban environments. Here are some key aspects of the role of Smart Cities in disaster resilience:

Early Warning Systems: Smart Cities utilize advanced sensor networks, weather forecasting, and data analytics to develop early warning systems for various hazards, such as floods, cyclones, and heatwaves. These systems enable timely dissemination of alerts to residents, allowing them to take preventive actions and evacuate if necessary.

Real-time Monitoring and Surveillance: Smart Cities employ real-time monitoring of critical infrastructure, such as bridges, roads, and utilities, to detect potential vulnerabilities or damage during disasters. Surveillance technologies help authorities assess the situation quickly and prioritize response efforts.

Data Analytics and Decision Support Systems: Smart Cities use data analytics to identify disaster risks, vulnerability hotspots, and patterns of exposure. Decision support systems aid urban planners and authorities in making informed decisions for disaster risk reduction and response strategies.

Climate-Responsive Infrastructure: Smart Cities incorporate climate-resilient infrastructure design, such as flood-resistant buildings, green spaces, and water management systems, into urban planning. These adaptive measures reduce the impact of disasters and enhance long-term resilience.

Citizen Engagement and Public Awareness: Smart Cities promote citizen engagement through mobile applications and social media platforms, encouraging residents to actively participate in disaster preparedness and response initiatives. Public awareness campaigns disseminate information on disaster risks, evacuation procedures, and safety measures.

Resilient Transportation Systems: Smart Cities implement intelligent transportation systems that facilitate smooth movement of people and goods during emergencies. Integrated transportation systems enable efficient evacuation and emergency response.

Energy Management and Backup Systems: Smart Cities employ energy management solutions and backup systems to ensure continuous power supply during disasters. Distributed energy sources, such as solar panels, reduce dependency on centralized power grids and enhance resilience.

Open Data Platforms: Smart Cities develop open data platforms that provide real-time information to the public, businesses, and government agencies during disasters. Open data facilitates collaboration and coordination among various stakeholders.

Community Resilience and Social Networks: Smart Cities support community-based disaster resilience initiatives that promote social networks and mutual aid among residents. Community resilience strengthens the capacity to cope with disasters and fosters self-help efforts.

Post-Disaster Recovery Planning: Smart Cities utilize post-disaster data and analytics to inform recovery and reconstruction efforts. Planning for resilient rebuilding helps cities bounce back more effectively after disasters.

Collaboration with Stakeholders: Smart Cities foster collaboration with various stakeholders, including government agencies, academia, private sector, and civil society organizations, to pool resources and expertise for disaster resilience initiatives.

By leveraging technology, data, and citizen engagement, Smart Cities enhance their ability to predict, prevent, and respond to disasters, reducing the human and economic toll of these events. Effective urban planning in Smart Cities embraces resilience as a core principle, ensuring that cities can adapt to changing environmental conditions, cope with shocks and stresses, and maintain a high quality of life for their residents in the face of adversity.

9.5.2 Indian Cities for Disaster Resilience

In the context of India, Smart Cities play a vital role in disaster resilience, especially as the country faces increasing urbanization and the challenges posed by climate change. Data and statistics from various sources highlight the need for disaster resilience in India's urban areas. According to the Global Climate Risk Index 2021, India ranked 7th in terms of climate-related events and 4th in terms of fatalities from 2000 to 2019. The Asian Development Bank estimates that India will need approximately USD 1 trillion for climate-resilient infrastructure development in its cities over the next decade. Here are specific examples and data highlighting the role of Smart Cities in effective urban planning for disaster resilience in India:

Early Warning Systems – Kolkata Floods: Kolkata, a city prone to urban flooding during heavy rains and cyclones, implemented a state-of-the-art early warning system. The system uses real-time data from weather stations, river gauges, and flood sensors to provide timely alerts to residents and authorities. During Cyclone Amphan in 2020, the early warning system helped in evacuating vulnerable communities, minimizing loss of life.

Real-time Monitoring and Surveillance – Gujarat Earthquake: In Gujarat, a Smart City initiative included installing seismic sensors and accelerometers in critical infrastructure and buildings. These sensors provide real-time data on ground movements during earthquakes, enabling rapid assessment of damage and response efforts.

Data Analytics and Decision Support Systems – Chennai Resilience Roadmap: Chennai, after facing severe floods in 2015, developed a Resilience Roadmap under the Smart City initiative. The roadmap utilizes data analytics to identify high-risk areas, vulnerable communities, and critical infrastructure. It helps in designing targeted disaster resilience measures, including stormwater management systems and climate-responsive infrastructure.

Climate-Responsive Infrastructure – Smart Cities Green Buildings: Several Smart Cities in India have adopted green building concepts in their infrastructure development. Green buildings are designed to reduce energy consumption, mitigate urban heat island effects, and withstand extreme weather events.

Citizen Engagement and Public Awareness – Pune Smart City App: Pune Smart City developed a mobile application that enables citizens to report infrastructure damage or emergencies during disasters. The app promotes citizen engagement and real-time information sharing with authorities, enhancing disaster response efficiency.

Resilient Transportation Systems – Delhi Integrated Command and Control Center (ICCC): Delhi's ICCC integrates traffic management and transportation systems to improve emergency response during disasters. Integrated transportation systems allow for dynamic rerouting of traffic during emergencies, facilitating evacuation and rescue operations.

Energy Management and Backup Systems – Nagpur Solar City: Nagpur, a designated Solar City, has increased its adoption of solar power to enhance energy resilience during disasters. Solar panels and renewable energy solutions ensure continuous power supply, reducing dependence on conventional grids.

Open Data Platforms – DataSmart Goa: Goa implemented the DataSmart initiative, providing open data on various aspects of urban living, including disaster risks. Open data platforms facilitate data-driven decision-making and public access to disaster-related information.

Community Resilience and Social Networks – Kochi Resilience Network: Kochi Smart City initiated a Resilience Network to engage local communities in disaster preparedness and response. Community-led initiatives and social networks enhance resilience and foster mutual support during disasters.

Post-Disaster Recovery Planning – Kerala Floods Recovery: After the devastating floods in Kerala in 2018, the state focused on data-driven recovery planning. The Kerala government utilized post-disaster data and analytics to prioritize rebuilding efforts and allocate resources efficiently.

By embracing Smart City initiatives, India can build more resilient urban areas that are better prepared to face the increasing challenges of natural disasters and climate change. Utilizing technology, data, and citizen engagement, Smart Cities can strengthen disaster response capacities, reduce vulnerability, and enhance the overall well-being of urban populations in the face of future challenges.

9.6 Inter Relation between ND, CC, SDG

The interrelation between natural disasters, climate change, and Sustainable Development Goals (SDGs) is complex and interconnected. Understanding these relationships is crucial for building a more resilient and sustainable future.

Natural Disasters and Climate Change: Natural disasters, such as hurricanes, floods, droughts, wildfires, and earthquakes, are events with significant adverse impacts on human populations and ecosystems. Climate change exacerbates the frequency and intensity of many natural disasters. For instance, rising global temperatures lead to more frequent and severe heatwaves, while warmer oceans fuel stronger hurricanes and cyclones. Climate change also contributes to sea-level rise, which intensifies the impacts of coastal flooding during storm surges and tsunamis.

Climate Change and Sustainable Development Goals (SDGs): Climate change poses a fundamental threat to achieving the SDGs, a set of 17 global goals adopted by all United Nations Member States in 2015 to address global challenges and ensure sustainable development by 2030. Climate change affects several SDGs directly and indirectly, including those related to poverty, hunger, health, clean water and sanitation, gender equality, affordable and clean energy, climate action, life below water, life on land, and partnerships for the goals. For example, climate change can exacerbate food insecurity (SDG 2) by impacting crop yields, lead to water scarcity (SDG 6), and cause health issues (SDG 3) due to extreme heat events and the spread of vector-borne diseases.

Natural Disasters and Sustainable Development Goals (SDGs): Natural disasters can have severe negative impacts on progress toward achieving the SDGs. Disasters can cause loss of life, displacement, destruction of infrastructure, disruption of economic activities, and increased vulnerability of marginalized communities, affecting numerous SDGs. For instance, disasters can hamper progress on poverty eradication (SDG 1) by pushing affected communities further into poverty and hinder progress on quality education (SDG 4) by damaging schools and disrupting education.

Climate Change Mitigation and Adaptation for Sustainable Development: Addressing climate change through mitigation and adaptation measures is vital for achieving sustainable development. Mitigation involves reducing greenhouse gas emissions to limit global warming and its impacts. Transitioning to renewable energy sources, improving energy efficiency, and promoting sustainable land-use practices are examples of climate change mitigation actions. Adaptation involves building resilience to the impacts of climate change. It includes measures such as strengthening infrastructure, implementing early warning systems, and developing climate-resilient agricultural practices.

Integrated Approach for Resilience and Sustainable Development: An integrated approach that addresses both climate change and natural disaster risks is essential for achieving sustainable development goals. This approach involves mainstreaming disaster risk reduction and climate adaptation into development planning and policy-making. Implementing resilient infrastructure, promoting sustainable land management, enhancing disaster preparedness, and empowering vulnerable communities are some strategies that align with both climate change and SDG objectives.

Thus, natural disasters and climate change are interconnected phenomena that have significant implications for achieving the SDGs. To address these challenges effectively, an integrated approach that combines climate change mitigation, adaptation, and disaster risk reduction is essential. By aligning efforts toward building resilience and sustainability, countries can work toward achieving the SDGs while simultaneously tackling the impacts of climate change and reducing the risks posed by natural disasters.

CHAPTER 10

Disaster Risk Reduction (DRR)

10.1 Disaster Risk Reduction (DRR)

Disaster Risk Reduction (DRR) is a systematic and strategic approach to minimize the vulnerabilities and enhance the resilience of communities, individuals, and infrastructure against the adverse impacts of natural and human-induced disasters. The primary goal of DRR is to prevent or reduce the loss of lives, livelihoods, assets, and overall societal well-being during disasters. It involves a range of policies, practices, and interventions aimed at understanding and addressing disaster risks to build more resilient societies. Here are the key aspects of Disaster Risk Reduction:

Risk Assessment and Understanding: DRR begins with a comprehensive risk assessment, which involves identifying and analysing potential hazards, vulnerabilities, and exposure of communities to those hazards. Understanding the risks enables stakeholders to prioritize efforts and allocate resources effectively.

Early Warning Systems and Preparedness: DRR emphasizes the importance of early warning systems to detect and communicate potential disaster events promptly. Early warning systems help in evacuating at-risk populations, implementing response plans, and minimizing loss of life and property.

Strengthening Institutional Capacity: Effective DRR requires strengthening the capacity of national and local institutions, including governments, emergency response agencies, and community-based organizations. Capacity-building ensures that institutions are better equipped to handle disaster preparedness, response, and recovery efforts.

Community Participation and Engagement: Engaging communities in DRR planning and decision-making is essential for successful implementation. Involving local communities ensures that DRR measures are context-specific, culturally appropriate, and respond to the needs and priorities of those at risk.

Infrastructure Resilience: DRR aims to enhance the resilience of critical infrastructure, such as buildings, bridges, and utilities, to withstand disaster events. Designing infrastructure with disaster-resistant features helps reduce damage and disruption during disasters.

Ecosystem-based Approaches: DRR recognizes the role of natural ecosystems in providing essential services and as buffers against hazards. Ecosystem-based approaches involve the conservation and restoration of ecosystems to reduce disaster risks.

Climate Change Adaptation: Given the increasing influence of climate change on disasters, DRR integrates climate change adaptation strategies to address emerging risks. Adaptation measures help communities cope with changing climatic conditions and build resilience.

Education and Awareness: DRR emphasizes the importance of public education and awareness campaigns to promote a culture of safety and preparedness. Knowledgeable and informed communities are better equipped to respond effectively during disasters.

Social Inclusion and Equity: DRR initiatives prioritize the inclusion of vulnerable and marginalized groups, ensuring that they benefit from risk reduction measures. Addressing social disparities reduces the disproportionate impact of disasters on vulnerable populations.

Mainstreaming DRR in Development Planning: DRR is most effective when integrated into all phases of development planning and policy-making. Mainstreaming DRR ensures that risk reduction becomes an integral part of development initiatives, making communities more resilient in the long term.

Data and Information Management: DRR relies on accurate and up-to-date data for risk assessment, early warning systems, and decision-making. Effective data management helps in evidence-based planning and implementation.

International Cooperation and Partnerships: DRR is a global challenge that requires collaborative efforts among countries and stakeholders. International cooperation and partnerships foster the exchange of knowledge, resources, and best practices in disaster risk reduction.

10.1.1 Principles of Disaster Risk Reduction

Disaster Risk Reduction (DRR) is a systematic approach to minimizing the adverse impacts of disasters on communities, economies, and the environment. The principles of DRR guide the development and implementation of strategies and measures to prevent, mitigate, prepare for, respond to, and recover from disasters. These principles emphasize proactive measures and long-term sustainability. Here are the key principles of Disaster Risk Reduction in detail:

Risk Assessment and Understanding: This principle involves understanding the hazards, vulnerabilities, and exposure to risks in a given area. Conducting risk assessments helps identify the specific threats posed by natural or man-made hazards and assess the potential impacts on communities and the environment.

Addressing Root Causes and Drivers of Risk: DRR aims to address the underlying factors that contribute to disaster risk, such as poverty, environmental degradation, inadequate infrastructure, and weak governance. By tackling these root causes, communities become more resilient and better able to cope with hazards.

Building Resilience and Enhancing Adaptive Capacity: Resilience refers to the ability of a community or system to withstand and recover from shocks and stresses. DRR focuses on building resilience by enhancing adaptive capacity, which involves developing the skills, knowledge, and resources needed to cope with changing conditions and emerging risks.

Empowerment and Community Engagement: Local communities are at the forefront of disaster risk reduction efforts, as they possess valuable knowledge and understanding of their environment and vulnerabilities. Empowering communities through involvement in decision-making, planning, and implementation increases the effectiveness and sustainability of DRR measures.

Integration of DRR into Development: DRR should be integrated into development planning and policies to ensure that new infrastructure and investments are risk-informed and contribute to long-term resilience. Development projects that consider potential hazards and climate change impacts are less likely to create new vulnerabilities.

Multi-stakeholder Collaboration and Cooperation: DRR requires collaboration and cooperation among various stakeholders, including governments, non-governmental organizations, private sector, academia, and affected communities. Effective partnerships enhance the sharing of knowledge, resources, and expertise.

Early Warning Systems and Preparedness: Early warning systems play a crucial role in disaster risk reduction by providing timely alerts to communities about impending hazards. Preparedness measures, such as drills and training, help ensure that communities and response agencies are ready to act swiftly during emergencies.

Gender and Social Inclusion: DRR should consider the different vulnerabilities and capacities of various social groups, including women, children, elderly, and people with disabilities. Ensuring the inclusion and participation of all segments of society in DRR efforts promotes equity and enhances resilience.

Sustainable and Eco-friendly Practices: DRR emphasizes the use of sustainable and eco-friendly practices that conserve natural resources and protect the environment. Preserving ecosystems, adopting green infrastructure, and promoting climate-resilient agriculture are examples of sustainable practices.

Learning from Experience and Best Practices: DRR is an iterative process that encourages learning from past disasters, evaluating response efforts, and integrating best practices into future planning. Continuous improvement and knowledge-sharing strengthen DRR initiatives.

The application of these principles in disaster risk reduction contributes to building a more resilient and sustainable society, where communities are better prepared to face future challenges and minimize the impacts of disasters.

10.1.2 Phases in Disaster Management Cycle

The disaster management cycle consists of four main phases, each representing a specific stage in the process of preparing for, responding to, recovering from, and mitigating the impacts of a disaster. These phases form a continuous and iterative cycle that helps in effective disaster management.

1. **Mitigation Phase**: The mitigation phase focuses on reducing the risk and impact of potential disasters. It involves activities aimed at preventing or lessening the effects of disasters before they occur. Key aspects of this phase include:

   Risk Assessment: Identifying and analysing the potential hazards and vulnerabilities that exist in a specific area.

   Planning and Policy Development: Formulating policies and plans to address the identified risks and vulnerabilities.

   Public Awareness and Education: Educating the public and raising awareness about disaster risks, preparedness measures, and safety guidelines.

   Infrastructure Development: Building or retrofitting infrastructure to make it more resilient to disasters.

   Environmental Conservation: Preserving natural resources and ecosystems to act as buffers against certain disasters.

2. **Preparedness Phase**: The preparedness phase involves establishing measures and capacities to respond effectively to disasters when they occur. It focuses on developing plans, building capacity, and ensuring readiness for timely and coordinated response. Key aspects of this phase include:

   Emergency Planning: Developing detailed plans and procedures for responding to specific types of disasters.

   Training and Exercises: Conducting regular training programs and simulation exercises to familiarize responders with their roles and responsibilities during disasters.

   Stockpiling and Pre-positioning of Resources: Ensuring the availability of essential supplies, equipment, and resources needed for immediate response and relief efforts.

   Early Warning Systems: Implementing systems to detect and alert about impending disasters, enabling timely evacuations and response actions.

Communication Systems: Establishing robust communication networks to facilitate coordination among different response agencies.

3. **Response Phase**: The response phase involves the immediate actions taken to address the impacts of a disaster and help affected communities. It focuses on saving lives, minimizing suffering, and ensuring basic needs are met. Key aspects of this phase include:

Search and Rescue: Conducting search and rescue operations to locate and extract trapped or injured individuals.

Medical Assistance: Providing emergency medical care and setting up medical facilities for treating the injured.

Evacuation and Sheltering: Evacuating people from dangerous areas and providing temporary shelters for displaced individuals.

Distribution of Aid: Providing food, water, and other essential supplies to affected communities.

Coordination and Information Management: Ensuring effective coordination among various response agencies and disseminating accurate information to the public.

4. **Recovery Phase**: The recovery phase focuses on restoring and rebuilding affected communities to their pre-disaster state or better. It aims to enhance the resilience of communities and reduce the impact of future disasters. Key aspects of this phase include:

Damage Assessment: Conducting thorough assessments of the damage caused by the disaster to guide recovery efforts.

Infrastructure Rehabilitation: Repairing and rebuilding damaged infrastructure and public facilities.

Livelihood Restoration: Assisting individuals and businesses in recovering their livelihoods and economic activities.

Psychosocial Support: Providing psychological support and counselling to individuals and communities affected by the disaster.

Long-term Planning: Formulating long-term strategies to enhance disaster resilience and reduce vulnerabilities in the future.

The disaster management cycle is a continuous process, as the lessons learned from each phase inform the subsequent phases, improving the overall effectiveness of disaster management efforts. By effectively implementing each phase, disaster management can minimize the impact of disasters, protect lives and property, and promote the long-term resilience of communities.

10.1.3 Mitigation Phase in Disaster Management Cycle

The mitigation phase in the disaster management cycle is the first and most crucial stage, focused on preventing or reducing the impact of potential disasters before they occur. It involves a range of actions aimed at identifying and addressing vulnerabilities, reducing risks, and building resilience within communities and infrastructure. Mitigation efforts are designed to minimize the adverse effects of disasters and lay the foundation for effective disaster response and recovery. Let us delve into the key components and principles of the mitigation phase:

A] **Key Components of Mitigation Phase:**

Risk Assessment and Analysis: This involves identifying and evaluating potential hazards and vulnerabilities in a specific area. Risk assessment helps determine the likelihood and potential impact of various disasters, such as earthquakes, floods, hurricanes, or industrial accidents.

Planning and Policy Development: Based on the risk assessment, authorities formulate policies and plans to address the identified risks and vulnerabilities. This includes land-use planning, building codes and standards, zoning regulations, and environmental protection measures.

Public Awareness and Education: Raising public awareness about disaster risks and preparedness is essential. This includes disseminating information about potential hazards, evacuation routes, and safety guidelines to the general public, schools, and businesses.

Infrastructure Development and Retrofitting: Building and retrofitting infrastructure to make it more resilient to disasters is a key mitigation strategy. This involves using disaster-resistant construction techniques, reinforcing buildings, bridges, and critical facilities to withstand potential impacts.

Environmental Conservation and Ecosystem Restoration: Preserving and restoring natural resources and ecosystems can act as buffers against certain disasters. Wetlands, mangroves, and forests, for example, can help absorb floodwaters and mitigate the impact of storm surges.

B] Principles of Mitigation Phase:

Prevention is Better than Cure: The primary focus of the mitigation phase is to prevent or minimize the occurrence and impact of disasters. Taking preventive measures before disasters strike is more effective and cost-efficient than dealing with the consequences afterward.

Comprehensive Approach: Mitigation efforts should be comprehensive and encompass various aspects of disaster risk reduction. This includes physical measures like infrastructure development, as well as non-structural measures like policy development and community engagement.

Community Participation: Engaging and involving the local community in mitigation efforts is crucial for their success. Community members have valuable knowledge about their local environment and are key stakeholders in implementing mitigation measures.

Adaptive and Sustainable Strategies: Mitigation efforts should be adaptable to changing circumstances and consider long-term sustainability. Integrating climate change projections and future risks ensures that mitigation measures remain effective in the face of evolving hazards.

Inclusivity and Equity: Mitigation should be inclusive and address the needs of all members of society, especially vulnerable populations. Ensuring equitable access to resources and opportunities for disaster risk reduction is essential.

Multi-stakeholder Collaboration: Effective mitigation requires collaboration among various stakeholders, including government agencies, private sector, NGOs, and communities. Coordination and cooperation between these entities enhance the overall effectiveness of mitigation efforts.

Thus, the mitigation phase in the disaster management cycle lays the foundation for disaster risk reduction and resilience-building. By adopting proactive and comprehensive measures, such as risk assessment, planning, public awareness, infrastructure development, and environmental conservation, communities can minimize the impact of potential disasters. The principles of mitigation underscore the importance of prevention, inclusivity, collaboration, and sustainability, ensuring that disaster risk reduction efforts are effective, equitable, and enduring. By investing in mitigation, communities can significantly reduce the human and economic costs of disasters, fostering safer and more resilient societies.

10.1.4 Preparedness Phase in Disaster Management Cycle

The preparedness phase in the disaster management cycle is a critical stage focused on establishing measures and capacities to respond effectively to disasters when they occur. It aims to ensure readiness, coordination, and timely response to mitigate the impact of disasters and save lives. Preparedness efforts are essential in minimizing casualties, injuries, and damage, as well as facilitating a swift and effective recovery. Let us explore the key components and principles of the preparedness phase:

A] Key Components of Preparedness Phase:

Emergency Planning: This involves developing detailed and comprehensive emergency plans that outline the roles, responsibilities, and actions of various stakeholders during a disaster.

Emergency plans address specific types of disasters, evacuation routes, communication protocols, and resource allocation strategies.

Training and Exercises: Regular training and simulation exercises are conducted to familiarize emergency responders, government officials, and community members with their roles and responsibilities in disaster situations. These exercises test the effectiveness of emergency plans and improve the overall response capacity.

Stockpiling and Pre-positioning of Resources: Ensuring the availability of essential supplies, equipment, and resources before a disaster strike is crucial. This includes medical supplies, food, water, emergency shelter materials, and equipment for search and rescue operations.

Early Warning Systems: Implementing effective early warning systems is essential in providing timely alerts to at-risk populations about impending disasters. Early warning systems use various technologies to detect and monitor hazards and trigger warnings to residents in vulnerable areas.

Communication Systems: Establishing reliable communication networks is vital for effective disaster response and coordination. Robust communication systems enable the exchange of information among emergency responders, government agencies, and communities.

B] **Principles of Preparedness Phase:**

Proactive Approach: The preparedness phase follows a proactive approach, emphasizing the need to plan and prepare for disasters before they occur. Being ready to respond in advance increases the chances of a successful and timely response.

Risk-Informed Decision Making: Preparedness efforts are based on risk assessments and analyses, helping decision-makers understand potential hazards and vulnerabilities. This ensures that resources are directed towards addressing the most significant risks.

Interagency Coordination: Effective preparedness requires collaboration and coordination among various agencies, including government departments, emergency services, NGOs, and private sectors. Interagency cooperation enhances the overall response capacity.

Capacity Building: Building the capacity of individuals, organizations, and communities is a key principle of preparedness. Training and exercises enhance the knowledge and skills of responders, improving their ability to handle disaster situations.

Flexibility and Adaptability: Preparedness plans and strategies should be adaptable to various types of disasters and changing circumstances. Flexibility allows for effective response in dynamic and evolving disaster scenarios.

Public Participation: Engaging the public and local communities in preparedness efforts is vital. Public participation enhances awareness, encourages disaster preparedness at the individual level, and strengthens community resilience.

Thus, the preparedness phase in the disaster management cycle plays a crucial role in ensuring effective disaster response and minimizing the impact of disasters on communities. By adhering to the principles of proactive planning, risk-informed decision making, interagency coordination, capacity building, flexibility, and public participation, preparedness efforts become more robust and successful. A well-prepared and coordinated response during disasters saves lives, reduces damage, and paves the way for a quicker recovery and rebuilding process. Investing in preparedness measures is essential to building resilient communities capable of withstanding and recovering from various disaster events.

10.1.5 Response Phase in Disaster Management Cycle

The response phase in the disaster management cycle is the immediate stage following the occurrence of a disaster. It involves the deployment of resources, personnel, and emergency services to save lives, protect property, and help affected individuals and communities. The response phase is crucial in providing timely and effective support to those impacted by the disaster. Let us explore the key components and principles of the response phase:

A] Key Components of Response Phase:

Search and Rescue Operations: One of the primary tasks during the response phase is to conduct search and rescue operations to locate and extract survivors from the disaster-affected areas. Trained personnel, including first responders, firefighters, and medical teams, play a critical role in these operations.

Medical Assistance and Emergency Care: Providing medical assistance and emergency care to the injured is a priority during the response phase. Setting up medical facilities and mobilizing medical personnel are crucial to address the immediate health needs of disaster victims.

Evacuation and Sheltering: Evacuating people from dangerous areas and providing temporary shelters for displaced individuals are essential tasks. Evacuation plans and procedures are implemented to move people to safer locations.

Distribution of Aid and Supplies: The response phase involves distributing essential supplies, such as food, water, blankets, and hygiene kits, to those affected by the disaster. These supplies are critical in meeting the basic needs of survivors.

Communication and Information Management: Effective communication systems are essential in coordinating response efforts. Timely and accurate information is disseminated to the public and responders to ensure efficient decision-making.

B] Principles of Response Phase:

Life-Saving Priority: The primary focus of the response phase is on saving lives. Every effort is made to prioritize search and rescue operations and provide medical assistance to those in critical condition.

Speed and Timeliness: Response actions are time-sensitive, and rapid deployment of resources and personnel is crucial to mitigate the impact of the disaster. Quick response can save lives and prevent further damage.

Coordinated Efforts: The response phase requires coordinated efforts among various agencies, including government departments, emergency services, NGOs, and volunteers. Effective coordination ensures that response efforts are well-organized and efficient.

Situational Awareness: Maintaining situational awareness is essential in understanding the evolving disaster scenario. Continuous monitoring and assessment of the situation help in making informed decisions and adjusting response strategies as needed.

Flexibility and Adaptability: Response actions should be flexible and adaptable to changing circumstances. The nature and scope of the disaster may evolve, requiring responses to be adjusted accordingly.

Community Engagement and Respect for Culture: Engaging with affected communities, respecting their culture and traditions, and involving them in the response efforts is vital for effective response and support.

Thus, the response phase in the disaster management cycle is a critical period where immediate actions are taken to save lives and help those impacted by the disaster. Speed, coordination, and effective communication are key principles that underpin successful response efforts. By adhering to these principles and ensuring timely deployment of resources and services, responders can mitigate the impact of disasters and provide much-needed support to affected individuals and communities. The response phase lays the groundwork for the subsequent recovery phase, where efforts are focused on rebuilding and restoring the affected areas. A well-coordinated and timely response can significantly reduce the human suffering and damages caused by disasters, making it a vital aspect of disaster management.

10.1.6 Recovery Phase in Disaster Management Cycle

The recovery phase in the disaster management cycle is the period following the immediate response to a disaster. It involves activities aimed at rebuilding, restoring, and recovering the affected communities and infrastructure to their pre-disaster state or better. The recovery phase is essential in facilitating the recovery and reconstruction process, promoting resilience, and addressing the long-term impacts of the disaster. Let us explore the key components and principles of the recovery phase:

A] Key Components of Recovery Phase:

Damage Assessment and Needs Analysis: Conducting thorough damage assessments is crucial in understanding the extent of the damage caused by the disaster. This assessment helps identify the needs and priorities for recovery efforts.

Infrastructure Rehabilitation and Reconstruction: Repairing and rebuilding damaged infrastructure and public facilities are essential in restoring normalcy and functionality to the affected areas.

Livelihood Restoration: Assisting individuals and businesses in recovering their livelihoods is critical in ensuring economic recovery. This may involve providing financial assistance, training, or employment opportunities.

Psychosocial Support: Providing psychological support and counselling to individuals and communities affected by the disaster helps address the emotional and mental health impacts of the disaster.

Social and Economic Recovery: Focusing on social and economic recovery measures helps in revitalizing communities and improving their overall well-being.

Long-term Planning and Resilience: Formulating long-term strategies for enhancing disaster resilience and reducing vulnerabilities is crucial to prevent or mitigate the impact of future disasters.

B] Principles of Recovery Phase:

Build Back Better: The recovery phase provides an opportunity to rebuild in a way that reduces future vulnerabilities and enhances resilience. The principle of "Build Back Better" emphasizes the importance of incorporating disaster risk reduction measures into the recovery process.

Inclusivity and Equity: The recovery phase should be inclusive, considering the needs and priorities of all members of the community, especially vulnerable populations. It is essential to address social disparities and ensure equitable access to resources and services.

Community Empowerment: Engaging and empowering affected communities in the recovery process is crucial for successful and sustainable recovery. Community members have valuable insights into their needs and preferences, and their active involvement leads to more effective outcomes.

Coordination and Collaboration: Effective coordination among various stakeholders, including government agencies, NGOs, private sectors, and donors, is essential for a comprehensive and coordinated recovery effort.

Adaptive Planning: Recovery plans should be adaptable and flexible to accommodate changing circumstances and emerging needs during the recovery process.

Sustainability: The recovery phase should focus on sustainable development practices, considering environmental, social, and economic factors to ensure that the recovered communities are resilient in the long term.

Thus, the recovery phase in the disaster management cycle is a critical period where efforts are focused on rebuilding and restoring the affected communities and infrastructure. By adhering to the principles of "Build Back Better," inclusivity, community empowerment, coordination, adaptability, and sustainability, the recovery phase can be more effective and successful. Recovery measures not only restore the pre-disaster conditions but also enhance the resilience of communities to future disasters. Investing in long-term planning and disaster risk reduction during the recovery phase is essential in creating safer and more resilient societies. The recovery phase sets the foundation for building back stronger and ensuring that communities can bounce back from future disasters more effectively.

10.2 Structural and Non-Structural Measures for DRR

Disaster risk reduction (DRR) involves a combination of structural and non-structural measures to minimize the impact of disasters and build resilience in communities. These measures are designed to prevent or mitigate the effects of hazards and enhance the ability of communities to cope with and recover from disasters. Let us explore each type of measure in detail:

1. **Structural Measures**: Structural measures involve physical changes to the environment and infrastructure to reduce the vulnerability to disasters. These measures are tangible and visible and are often essential for protecting lives and property during disasters. Some common structural measures include:

a. **Building Codes and Standards**: Implementing and enforcing building codes and standards is crucial to ensuring that structures are designed and constructed to withstand potential hazards. This includes earthquake-resistant construction, wind-resistant buildings, and flood-proofing measures.

b. **Flood Control Structures**: Building flood control structures such as dams, levees, and embankments can help regulate and redirect floodwaters, reducing the risk of flooding in downstream areas.

c. **Seawalls and Coastal Protection**: Seawalls and coastal protection structures help safeguard coastal areas from storm surges, erosion, and tsunamis.

d. **Retrofitting of Infrastructure**: Strengthening existing infrastructure to make it more resilient to disasters is known as retrofitting. This includes reinforcing bridges, roads, and buildings to withstand seismic events or other hazards.

e. **Diversions and Drainage Systems**: Constructing diversions and drainage systems helps redirect excess water during heavy rainfall, reducing the risk of flooding.

2. **Non-Structural Measures**: Non-structural measures focus on strategies that do not involve physical changes to the environment but rather address social, economic, and environmental aspects to reduce disaster risk. These measures are often complementary to structural measures and include:

a. **Early Warning Systems**: Implementing effective early warning systems is crucial for alerting communities about impending disasters, enabling timely evacuation and preparedness.

b. **Education and Awareness**: Public education and awareness campaigns help raise awareness about disaster risks, preparedness measures, and safety guidelines. Educated communities are better prepared to respond to disasters effectively.

c. **Land Use Planning**: Proper land use planning ensures that vulnerable areas are not developed in high-risk zones, reducing exposure to hazards.

d. **Insurance and Risk Transfer Mechanisms**: Encouraging the adoption of insurance and risk transfer mechanisms helps communities recover financially after disasters.

e. **Community-Based Disaster Risk Management (CBDRM)**: Engaging local communities in disaster risk management and planning empowers them to take ownership of their safety and resilience.

f. **Environmental Conservation**: Preserving natural resources and ecosystems can act as a buffer against certain disasters, such as wetlands mitigating the impact of floods.

g. **Health and Emergency Services**: Strengthening healthcare and emergency services helps address medical needs during disasters and enhances response capabilities.

h. **Research and Innovation**: Investing in research and innovation helps develop new technologies and approaches for disaster risk reduction.

Thus, combining structural and non-structural measures is essential for effective disaster risk reduction. While structural measures provide tangible protection and resilience, non-structural measures address the social, economic, and environmental aspects of disaster risk. An integrated approach that includes a mix of both types of measures is necessary to build disaster-resilient communities and reduce the impact of hazards on lives and livelihoods.

10.3 Vulnerability and Capacity Assessment for DRR

Vulnerability and Capacity Assessment (VCA) is a systematic and participatory approach used in disaster risk reduction (DRR) and disaster management. It is designed to identify the vulnerabilities of communities, households, and individuals to hazards, as well as their capacity to cope with and recover from disasters. VCA helps in understanding the factors that contribute to vulnerability and the resources available to enhance resilience, thereby informing the development of effective DRR strategies. Let us explore the key components and process of Vulnerability and Capacity Assessment in detail:

A] **Key Components of Vulnerability and Capacity Assessment (VCA):**

Understanding Vulnerability: VCA begins with identifying the vulnerabilities of a community or area to different hazards. Vulnerability refers to the characteristics and circumstances of a population that make them more susceptible to the negative impacts of disasters. It includes socio-economic factors, physical exposure to hazards, access to resources, and institutional capacity.

Analysing Capacity: The assessment also involves evaluating the capacity of the community or area to cope with and recover from disasters. Capacity includes the available resources, skills, knowledge, and social networks that can be utilized to reduce disaster risks and enhance resilience.

Participatory Approach: VCA follows a participatory approach, involving the active participation of community members, local authorities, and stakeholders. The involvement of those affected by disasters ensures that their perspectives, needs, and priorities are considered in the assessment process.

Data Collection: Data is collected through various methods, including surveys, interviews, focus group discussions, and observations. Both qualitative and quantitative data are gathered to get a comprehensive understanding of vulnerabilities and capacities.

Risk Assessment: VCA also includes a risk assessment component, where hazards and potential impacts are analysed. This helps identify the most significant risks and their potential consequences on the community.

Mapping and Visual Representation: Visual tools, such as maps, diagrams, and charts, are often used to present the assessment findings in a clear and accessible manner.

B] **Process of Vulnerability and Capacity Assessment (VCA):**

Preparation and Planning: The assessment process begins with planning and organizing the assessment team, defining objectives, and determining the scope of the assessment.

Data Collection: Data is collected through various participatory methods, involving community members, local authorities, and other stakeholders.

Analysis and Synthesis: The collected data is analysed to identify patterns, trends, and key vulnerabilities and capacities. The information is then synthesized to provide a comprehensive understanding of the disaster risks and resilience of the community.

Risk Mapping: Hazard and risk mapping is conducted to visualize the spatial distribution of hazards, vulnerabilities, and capacities.

Findings and Recommendations: The assessment findings are presented to the community and stakeholders in a transparent manner. The report includes recommendations for strengthening capacities and reducing vulnerabilities.

Integration into DRR Strategies: The VCA findings are integrated into the development of DRR strategies and plans. The recommendations help prioritize actions and investments for building resilience and reducing disaster risks.

Thus, Vulnerability and Capacity Assessment is a crucial tool in disaster risk reduction, as it provides valuable insights into the factors that contribute to vulnerability and the resources that can be harnessed for enhancing resilience. By adopting a participatory and data-driven approach, VCA ensures that the needs and perspectives of the affected community are considered in disaster planning and management. Integrating VCA findings into DRR strategies helps in building safer and more resilient communities that can effectively cope with and recover from disasters.

10.4 Post Disaster Environmental Response

Post-disaster environmental response refers to the actions taken after a disaster to address the environmental impacts and restore the natural environment. Disasters, whether natural or human-induced, can have severe consequences on the environment, including pollution, habitat destruction, and ecosystem degradation. Post-disaster environmental response aims to mitigate these impacts, promote ecological recovery, and foster sustainable development. Let us explore the key aspects and measures of post-disaster environmental response in detail:

A] **Key Aspects of Post-Disaster Environmental Response:**

Environmental Damage Assessment: The first step in post-disaster environmental response is conducting a comprehensive assessment of the environmental damage caused by the disaster. This involves evaluating the extent of pollution, habitat loss, water contamination, soil erosion, and other environmental impacts.

Waste Management and Debris Clearance: Disasters often generate a significant amount of waste and debris. Proper waste management and debris clearance are essential to prevent further pollution and environmental degradation.

Contaminated Site Remediation: Disasters may result in the release of hazardous substances and pollutants into the environment. Remediation efforts are required to clean up contaminated sites and prevent the spread of toxins.

Protection of Natural Resources: Post-disaster environmental response includes measures to protect and conserve natural resources, such as forests, wetlands, and marine ecosystems.

Preserving these resources is crucial for ecosystem recovery and maintaining ecological balance.

Reforestation and Habitat Restoration: Restoring vegetation and natural habitats is a key aspect of post-disaster environmental response. Reforestation efforts help prevent soil erosion and promote biodiversity.

Water Quality Management: Ensuring access to safe and clean water is essential for post-disaster recovery. Water quality management involves treating contaminated water sources and implementing measures to prevent further pollution.

B] **Measures for Post-Disaster Environmental Response:**

Emergency Environmental Response Teams: Specialized teams of environmental experts and responders are deployed to assess the environmental damage and coordinate response efforts.

Environmental Impact Assessments (EIAs): Conducting EIAs helps in understanding the extent of the disaster's impact on the environment and prioritizing response actions.

Public Awareness and Education: Educating communities about the importance of environmental protection and sustainable practices is crucial for long-term resilience.

Restoration of Critical Ecosystem Services: Efforts are made to restore critical ecosystem services, such as flood regulation, groundwater recharge, and carbon sequestration.

Use of Environmentally Friendly Technologies: Adopting environmentally friendly and sustainable technologies for reconstruction and recovery helps reduce future environmental risks.

Collaboration with Environmental Organizations: Partnering with environmental organizations and NGOs can enhance the effectiveness of post-disaster environmental response.

C] **Challenges in Post-Disaster Environmental Response:**

Limited Resources: Adequate funding and resources may be challenging to obtain for post-disaster environmental response, especially in developing countries.

Long-Term Monitoring and Restoration: Environmental recovery is often a long-term process, and continuous monitoring and restoration efforts are required.

Coordination and Communication: Effective coordination between different agencies and stakeholders is essential for a successful environmental response.

Conflicting Priorities: Balancing the immediate needs of disaster-affected communities with long-term environmental concerns can be challenging.

Restoration of Biodiversity and Ecosystem Services: Disasters often disrupt natural habitats and lead to biodiversity loss. Post-disaster environmental response includes efforts to restore ecosystems and protect endangered species. Restoring biodiversity is essential for maintaining ecological balance and the provision of ecosystem services like pollination, pest control, and water purification.

Sustainable Reconstruction and Infrastructure Development: After a disaster, there is an opportunity to rebuild infrastructure in a more sustainable and environmentally friendly way. Incorporating green building practices, using renewable energy sources, and considering climate-resilient designs can minimize future environmental impacts and reduce the vulnerability of structures to disasters.

Conservation and Sustainable Use of Resources: Post-disaster environmental response emphasizes the sustainable use of natural resources. Implementing responsible resource management practices, such as regulated logging, fishing quotas, and water conservation measures, helps prevent overexploitation and degradation.

Promoting Green Livelihoods: Encouraging green livelihoods and sustainable economic activities can help disaster-affected communities recover while minimizing negative impacts on the environment. Supporting eco-friendly agriculture, ecotourism, and renewable energy projects can create income-generating opportunities and foster environmental stewardship.

Addressing Climate Change and Disaster Risk Reduction: Post-disaster environmental response acknowledges the link between climate change and the increasing frequency and intensity of disasters. Combining climate change adaptation strategies with disaster risk reduction measures enhances resilience and reduces vulnerability.

Capacity Building and Training: Building the capacity of local communities, government agencies, and environmental organizations is vital for effective post-disaster environmental response. Training programs can empower people to actively participate in environmental protection and restoration efforts.

Establishing Early Warning Systems for Environmental Hazards: Apart from early warning systems for natural disasters, post-disaster environmental response may involve setting up monitoring and alert systems for environmental hazards like chemical spills, air pollution, or water contamination.

Engaging the Private Sector: Involving the private sector, industries, and businesses in post-disaster environmental response can lead to more sustainable practices and corporate social responsibility initiatives that benefit both the environment and communities.

Integration of Indigenous Knowledge: Indigenous communities often possess valuable knowledge and practices for sustainable resource management. Integrating indigenous knowledge into post-disaster environmental response can enhance the effectiveness and cultural appropriateness of interventions.

Monitoring and Evaluation: Regular monitoring and evaluation of post-disaster environmental response initiatives are crucial to assess their effectiveness, identify challenges, and make necessary adjustments for continuous improvement.

Cross-Boundary Collaboration: Many disasters, especially those related to environmental degradation and climate change, have cross-boundary impacts. International cooperation and collaboration are essential for addressing transboundary environmental issues and fostering regional resilience.

Thus, Post-disaster environmental response plays a pivotal role in mitigating the adverse impacts of disasters and fostering sustainable recovery. By focusing on restoring ecosystems, adopting green practices, promoting resilience to climate change, and engaging local communities, post-disaster environmental response ensures that recovery efforts are environmentally responsible and contribute to long-term well-being. Integrating environmental considerations into disaster management strategies is essential for building a safer, more sustainable, and resilient future for communities facing increasing environmental challenges and disaster risks.

Disaster Risk Reduction is not a one-time effort but a continuous process that requires ongoing commitment, investment, and coordination among various stakeholders. By integrating DRR into all aspects of development and fostering a proactive approach, societies can build resilience and reduce the impact of disasters on lives and livelihoods.

10.5 Prevention Measures for DRR

Prevention measures for Disaster Risk Reduction (DRR) focus on actions and strategies aimed at avoiding or minimizing the occurrence of disasters or reducing their potential impacts. These measures are essential for building resilience and creating safer communities. Here are various prevention measures for DRR:

Land Use Planning and Zoning: Implementing appropriate land use planning and zoning regulations helps to control the development of infrastructure and settlements in high-risk areas. Restricting construction in floodplains, seismic zones, and coastal areas reduces exposure to hazards.

Building Codes and Regulations: Enforcing and updating building codes and construction regulations ensure that buildings and infrastructure are designed and constructed to withstand potential hazards. This includes earthquake-resistant structures, flood-resistant foundations, and wind-resistant building designs.

Early Warning Systems: Establishing and maintaining early warning systems enables timely dissemination of alerts to communities and authorities about impending disasters. Early warning systems help in evacuating vulnerable populations and activating disaster response plans.

Infrastructure Resilience: Designing critical infrastructure, such as roads, bridges, and utilities, with resilience features enhances their ability to withstand disasters. Integrating climate-resilient infrastructure helps maintain essential services during and after **disasters.**

Natural Hazard Mitigation: Implementing measures to mitigate natural hazards, such as landslide control, flood embankments, and coastal protection, reduces their impact on communities.

Retrofitting of Existing Structures: Retrofitting existing buildings and infrastructure to meet current safety standards improves their ability to withstand disasters. Strengthening older structures against earthquakes and other hazards enhances their resilience.

Afforestation and Reforestation: Planting trees and restoring forests can mitigate the impacts of disasters like floods and landslides by stabilizing slopes, improving water absorption, and reducing erosion.

Ecosystem-based Approaches: Preserving and restoring natural ecosystems, such as wetlands and mangroves, provide natural buffers against hazards like storms, floods, and coastal erosion.

Disaster Risk Education and Awareness: Conducting public education campaigns and awareness programs on disaster risk and preparedness helps in promoting a culture of safety and resilience. Educating communities on evacuation procedures, hazard awareness, and first-aid skills is crucial.

Emergency Preparedness and Response Plans: Developing and regularly updating emergency preparedness and response plans at the community, local, and national levels ensure effective coordination during disasters. Conducting drills and exercises to test response mechanisms enhances readiness.

Climate Change Adaptation: Integrating climate change adaptation strategies into development planning helps communities cope with the changing climate and emerging risks. Climate-resilient agriculture, water management, and urban planning are examples of adaptation measures.

Social Inclusion and Capacity-building: Ensuring the inclusion of vulnerable and marginalized groups in disaster risk reduction efforts strengthens community resilience. Capacity-building programs equip individuals and organizations with the knowledge and skills needed to respond effectively to disasters.

International Cooperation and Research: Collaborating with international partners and sharing knowledge and best practices improves disaster risk reduction globally. Conducting research on disaster trends and impacts informs evidence-based policies and interventions.

Prevention measures for DRR require multi-stakeholder engagement, commitment, and sustained efforts. By implementing a combination of these measures, communities can significantly reduce the risks associated with disasters and build a safer and more resilient future.

10.6 Mitigation Measures for DRR

Mitigation measures for Disaster Risk Reduction (DRR) focus on reducing the severity and impact of disasters by addressing their root causes and vulnerabilities. These measures aim to minimize the potential damage and losses that disasters can cause. Mitigation strategies are essential for building resilience and enhancing the long-term sustainability of communities. Here are various mitigation measures for DRR:

Building and Infrastructure Resilience: Designing and constructing buildings and critical infrastructure to withstand potential hazards, such as earthquakes, hurricanes, and floods, reduces vulnerability. Retrofitting existing structures to meet safety standards enhances their resilience.

Natural Hazard Mitigation: Implementing measures to mitigate specific natural hazards, such as constructing flood barriers, building retaining walls in landslide-prone areas, and implementing forest fire prevention strategies, can reduce their impact.

Ecosystem-based Approaches: Preserving and restoring natural ecosystems, such as wetlands, mangroves, and forests, can serve as natural buffers against hazards, reducing the risk to communities.

Climate Change Adaptation: Integrating climate change adaptation strategies into development planning helps communities cope with the changing climate and its impacts on disasters. Examples include adopting climate-resilient agricultural practices, water resource management, and urban planning.

Early Warning Systems and Preparedness: Establishing and maintaining early warning systems helps detect and communicate potential disaster events, enabling timely evacuation and preparedness measures. Conducting regular drills and exercises ensures that communities and responders are prepared to act swiftly during emergencies.

Disaster-resistant Infrastructure and Lifeline Systems: Strengthening lifeline systems, such as communication networks, water supply, and energy distribution, helps maintain essential services during and after disasters. Implementing redundancy and backup systems improves their resilience to disruptions.

Land Use Planning and Zoning: Implementing appropriate land use planning and zoning regulations helps direct development away from high-risk areas and reduce exposure to hazards.

Public Education and Awareness: Conducting public education campaigns on disaster risks and preparedness helps in promoting a culture of safety and empowering communities to take proactive measures.

Social Inclusion and Vulnerable Populations: Ensuring the inclusion of vulnerable and marginalized groups in mitigation efforts is crucial to address their specific needs and reduce their exposure to risks.

Investment in Research and Data Collection: Conducting research on disaster trends, vulnerabilities, and impacts helps inform evidence-based policies and interventions. Improving data collection and monitoring systems enhances understanding of disaster risks and allows for informed decision-making.

International Cooperation and Knowledge Sharing: Collaborating with international partners and sharing knowledge, experiences, and best practices enhances global disaster risk reduction efforts.

Mitigation measures are proactive and cost-effective investments that contribute to reducing the impacts of disasters and creating more resilient communities. Integrating these strategies into development planning and policy-making ensures that disaster risk reduction becomes an integral part of sustainable development initiatives. By adopting a comprehensive and multi-stakeholder approach, societies can minimize the risks associated with disasters and work towards a safer and more sustainable future.

10.7 Preparedness Planning For DRR

Preparedness planning for Disaster Risk Reduction (DRR) involves a series of actions and measures taken in advance to ensure that communities, organizations, and governments are ready to respond effectively to potential disasters. Preparedness planning aims to minimize the loss of life, property, and livelihoods during emergencies. Here are various preparedness planning measures for DRR:

Emergency Response Plans: Developing comprehensive emergency response plans at the community, local, and national levels is essential for effective disaster response. These plans outline roles, responsibilities, and coordination mechanisms among different stakeholders during emergencies.

Early Warning Systems: Establishing early warning systems to detect and disseminate information about potential disasters, such as hurricanes, floods, and tsunamis, is crucial for timely evacuation and preparedness. Training communities on how to respond to early warning alerts is an integral part of preparedness planning.

Evacuation and Sheltering Strategies: Developing evacuation plans that identify safe routes and assembly points for communities to evacuate during emergencies. Identifying suitable shelters and capacity-building for shelter management is also part of preparedness planning.

Training and Capacity-building: Conducting regular training and drills for community members, emergency responders, and volunteers on disaster response procedures and protocols. Building the capacity of responders and organizations involved in disaster management enhances their effectiveness during emergencies.

Resource and Equipment Stockpiling: Pre-positioning essential resources, such as food, water, medical supplies, and emergency equipment, in strategic locations ensures a rapid response to disasters. Maintaining stockpiles reduces the time required to mobilize resources during emergencies.

Public Education and Awareness: Conducting public awareness campaigns to educate communities about disaster risks, preparedness measures, and response actions. Raising awareness among the public fosters a culture of safety and encourages proactive measures.

Communication and Information Management: Establishing reliable communication systems to disseminate information and updates during disasters. Developing information management systems to collect, analyse, and share data relevant to disaster preparedness and response.

Coordination and Networking: Strengthening coordination mechanisms among various stakeholders, including government agencies, non-governmental organizations, and private sector partners. Networking and collaboration enhance the effectiveness of preparedness planning and response efforts.

Scenario-based Planning: Conducting scenario-based planning exercises to simulate potential disaster events and test response mechanisms. Evaluating the outcomes of these exercises helps identify gaps and areas for improvement.

Institutional Preparedness: Ensuring that government agencies and organizations responsible for disaster management are adequately prepared to respond to emergencies. Regularly reviewing and updating institutional preparedness plans is critical.

Financial Preparedness: Allocating and securing funds for disaster response and recovery efforts in advance. Building financial reserves or contingency funds helps in rapidly mobilizing resources during emergencies.

Preparedness planning is an ongoing and dynamic process that requires continuous assessment, learning, and improvement. By being proactive and investing in preparedness, communities and organizations can reduce the impacts of disasters and save lives during emergencies.

10.8 Early Warning Systems in India for DRR

India has implemented several Early Warning Systems (EWS) for Disaster Risk Reduction (DRR) to enhance preparedness and response to various natural hazards. These systems aim to detect potential disaster events in advance and disseminate timely alerts to at-risk communities, enabling them to take preventive actions and evacuate if necessary. Here are some of the key Early Warning Systems in India:

India Meteorological Department (IMD) – Cyclone Warning: IMD is responsible for issuing cyclone warnings along India's coastline. The Cyclone Warning Division of IMD monitors cyclone formation and intensification in the Indian Ocean and issues alerts with advance forecasts of cyclone tracks, intensity, and potential landfall locations. Alerts are disseminated through various media channels, including radio, television, and social media.

Cyclone Warning by IMD is Cyclone Fani (2019) located at Odisha, India in May 2019, Cyclone Fani, one of the strongest tropical cyclones to hit India, made landfall in Odisha. The India

Meteorological Department (IMD) issued timely warnings and advisories regarding the cyclone's track, intensity, and potential landfall locations. Due to the early warnings and well-executed preparedness measures, the authorities were able to evacuate millions of people from the coastal areas, saving countless lives and reducing the potential for casualties and damage.

National Disaster Management Authority (NDMA) – Early Warning Dissemination System:

The NDMA has established a centralized communication platform called the Early Warning Dissemination System (EWDS). WDS uses satellite-based technology to disseminate alerts for cyclones, tsunamis, earthquakes, and other hazards to designated authorities and the public. The system includes sirens, text messages, and other means of communication to reach remote areas.

NDMA's Early Warning Dissemination System (EWDS) is a continuous system used to disseminate early warnings for various hazards, including cyclones, earthquakes, floods, and other disasters. The EWDS uses satellite-based technology to communicate alerts to designated authorities and the public through various means, including sirens, text messages, and social media. The EWDS has been instrumental in alerting communities and authorities in advance about potential disasters, enabling timely evacuation, preparedness, and response measures.

Flood Early Warning Systems: Several states in India have implemented flood early warning systems to predict and alert communities about potential flooding. These systems use real-time data from rain gauges, river gauges, and weather stations to monitor rainfall and water levels in rivers and reservoirs. Alerts are sent to local authorities and communities in flood-prone areas to facilitate evacuation and preparedness.

Flood Early Warning Systems is used in Bihar Floods (2020) in 2020, when Bihar experienced severe floods due to heavy monsoon rains and overflowing rivers. The state of Bihar has implemented flood early warning systems that use real-time data from rain gauges and river gauges to monitor rainfall and water levels. The early warning alerts helped local authorities and communities prepare for the floods, evacuate vulnerable populations, and manage relief operations effectively.

Earthquake Early Warning System (EEWS): India is in the process of setting up an Earthquake Early Warning System (EEWS) to detect seismic activity and issue alerts before the onset of strong earthquakes. The system uses a network of seismic sensors to detect the initial waves of an earthquake and provide warnings to high-risk areas.

Earthquake Early Warning System (EEWS) is used when Mild Earthquake in Delhi-NCR in April 2020, with a magnitude of 3.5 struck parts of Delhi-NCR. While the full-fledged Earthquake Early Warning System (EEWS) is still being implemented, seismic sensors detected the earthquake's initial waves and issued alerts to the authorities. The EEWS provided a few seconds of advance warning, allowing people to take cover and evacuate from buildings, reducing the risk of injuries.

Tsunami Warning System: India is part of the Indian Ocean Tsunami Warning and Mitigation System (IOTWMS). The system includes a network of seismic sensors and tide gauges to detect undersea earthquakes and potential tsunamis. Once a potential tsunami is detected, alerts are issued to coastal communities and authorities. Tsunami Warning System is used for Indian Ocean Tsunami (2004) in Coastal areas of India and several other countries bordering the Indian Ocean. On December 26, 2004, a massive undersea earthquake off the coast of Sumatra triggered a devastating tsunami. The Indian Ocean Tsunami Warning and Mitigation System (IOTWMS) had not been fully operational at the time of the 2004 tsunami. The lack of a comprehensive tsunami warning system resulted in a significant loss of life and damage to coastal communities in India and other countries bordering the Indian Ocean.

Heatwave Early Warning System: Some states in India have established heatwave early warning systems to forecast extreme heat events and alert vulnerable populations. These systems use weather data to predict heatwave conditions and issue advisories to the public and healthcare facilities. Heatwave Early Warning System is used in Extreme Heatwave in Rajasthan (2016). In May 2016, Rajasthan experienced an extreme heatwave with temperatures soaring above 50 degrees Celsius. The state of Rajasthan had implemented a heatwave early warning system to forecast and alert about extreme heat events. The early warning system helped authorities and communities prepare for the heatwave, issue health advisories, and take measures to protect vulnerable populations.

Landslide Early Warning System: In hilly regions prone to landslides, local authorities have set up landslide early warning systems. These systems use rainfall data, ground monitoring instruments, and geospatial technologies to detect potential landslides and alert communities. Landslide Early Warning System is used for Landslides in Darjeeling, West Bengal (2020). In August 2020, heavy rainfall triggered landslides in the hilly region of Darjeeling. The region had set up landslide early warning systems that used rainfall data, ground monitoring instruments, and geospatial technologies to detect potential landslides. The early warning system helped alert communities in advance, enabling them to take precautionary measures and avoid high-risk areas during the heavy rainfall period.

The effectiveness of these Early Warning Systems depends on the availability of real-time data, strong communication networks, and the capacity of communities to respond to alerts. Continuous improvements and investments in these systems are essential to enhance disaster preparedness and reduce the impact of disasters on vulnerable communities in India. The examples highlight the importance of Early Warning Systems in India for Disaster Risk Reduction and their significant role in saving lives and reducing the impact of disasters on vulnerable communities.

10.8.1 Early Warning Systems in Other Countries for DRR

Japan – Earthquake Early Warning System (EEW):

Japan Meteorological Agency (JMA): https://www.jma.go.jp/jma/indexe.html

United States – National Weather Service (NWS) Warnings:

National Weather Service (NWS): https://www.weather.gov/

Indonesia – Tsunami Early Warning System:

Indonesian Agency for Meteorology, Climatology, and Geophysics (BMKG): https://www.bmkg.go.id/

Mexico – Sistema de Alerta Sísmica Mexicano (SASMEX):

CENAPRED (National Center for Disaster Prevention): https://www.gob.mx/cenapred

Bangladesh – Cyclone Early Warning System:

Bangladesh Meteorological Department: https://www.bmd.gov.bd/

Philippines – Project NOAH (Nationwide Operational Assessment of Hazards):

Official Project NOAH website: https://www.noah.dost.gov.ph/

Thailand – Disaster Warning and Information System (DWIS):

Thai Meteorological Department: http://www.tmd.go.th/en/

Germany – German Flood Warning Service:

Federal Office of Civil Protection and Disaster Assistance (BBK): https://www.bbk.bund.de/EN/home.html

Kenya – Kenya Meteorological Department (KMD) Warnings:

Kenya Meteorological Department: https://www.meteo.go.ke/

Australia – Bureau of Meteorology Warnings:

Bureau of Meteorology: http://www.bom.gov.au/

10.9 Relief and Response Strategies for DRR

Relief and response strategies for Disaster Risk Reduction (DRR) in India focus on providing immediate assistance and support to affected communities during and after disasters. These strategies aim to address the urgent needs of disaster victims, facilitate recovery, and minimize further loss of life and property. Here are various relief and response strategies for DRR in India:

Search and Rescue Operations: Conducting search and rescue operations to locate and evacuate individuals trapped in collapsed buildings, landslides, or other hazardous situations. Specialized rescue teams, including the National Disaster Response Force (NDRF), are deployed for swift and efficient operations.

Medical Assistance and First Aid: Providing medical assistance and first aid to injured individuals immediately after a disaster strikes. Mobile medical teams and temporary medical camps are set up to treat the injured and prevent the spread of diseases.

Emergency Shelter and Camp Management: Establishing emergency shelters and managing temporary camps to accommodate displaced people. Adequate arrangements are made for food, clean drinking water, sanitation, and essential supplies.

Distribution of Relief Materials: Distributing relief materials, including food, water, clothing, blankets, and hygiene kits, to affected communities. Government agencies, NGOs, and volunteers are involved in relief distribution.

Psychosocial Support: Providing psychosocial support to disaster-affected individuals, including counselling and mental health services. Trauma counselling and emotional support are crucial for helping people cope with the psychological impacts of disasters.

Restoring Basic Services: Restoring disrupted essential services, such as electricity, communication, and transportation, to facilitate relief efforts and recovery.

Damage and Needs Assessment: Conducting rapid damage and needs assessment to identify the extent of damage and the most urgent needs of affected communities. The assessment helps in prioritizing relief efforts and resource allocation.

Community Mobilization: Mobilizing local communities and volunteers to actively participate in relief and response activities. Local knowledge and resources play a significant role in effective disaster response.

Coordination and Information Management: Ensuring effective coordination among various government agencies, NGOs, and international organizations involved in relief efforts. Information management systems facilitate data sharing and coordination.

Rehabilitation and Reconstruction: Planning and implementing rehabilitation and reconstruction efforts for affected infrastructure and communities. Building back better and more resilient structures is a key focus.

Livelihood Restoration: Assisting affected communities in restoring their livelihoods through various measures, such as providing financial support, vocational training, and income-generating activities.

Early Recovery Measures: Initiating early recovery measures to support affected communities in their transition from relief to recovery. These measures aim to promote resilience and ensure a smoother recovery process.

Lessons Learned and Capacity Building: Learning from past disaster response experiences and integrating lessons learned into future planning and preparedness. Capacity-building efforts strengthen the disaster response capabilities of government agencies and local communities.

Relief and response strategies are essential in the immediate aftermath of disasters to save lives, helps those in need, and lay the groundwork for recovery and long-term resilience. Effective coordination, community engagement, and collaboration between different stakeholders are crucial in ensuring a successful response to disasters in India.

10.10 Recovery and Reconstruction Approaches for DRR

Recovery and reconstruction approaches for Disaster Risk Reduction (DRR) in India focus on restoring and rebuilding communities, infrastructure, and livelihoods in the aftermath of a disaster. These approaches aim to promote resilience and long-term sustainability while integrating disaster risk reduction principles into the recovery process. Here are various recovery and reconstruction approaches for DRR in India:

Build Back Better (BBB) Approach: The BBB approach emphasizes constructing infrastructure and buildings that are more resilient to future disasters than their pre-disaster counterparts. Incorporating hazard-resistant and climate-resilient designs helps reduce vulnerability to similar events in the future.

Community-led Recovery: Engaging affected communities in the recovery and reconstruction process ensures that their needs, preferences, and local knowledge are considered. Participatory planning and decision-making empower communities and enhance the ownership of recovery initiatives.

Ecosystem-based Approaches: Integrating ecosystem-based approaches into recovery and reconstruction efforts by restoring and preserving natural ecosystems, such as wetlands and mangroves, can help reduce the impacts of future disasters. Ecosystems act as natural buffers against hazards like floods, storm surges, and landslides.

Livelihood Restoration and Diversification: Supporting affected households in restoring their livelihoods through financial assistance, vocational training, and income-generating activities. Encouraging livelihood diversification reduces dependency on vulnerable sectors and enhances resilience.

Inclusive and Gender-responsive Reconstruction: Ensuring that the needs and priorities of vulnerable and marginalized groups, including women, children, and elderly, are considered in the reconstruction process. Addressing gender-specific needs helps promote equality and social inclusion.

Resilience-based Infrastructure Development: Designing critical infrastructure with a focus on resilience, considering potential hazards and climate change impacts. Incorporating features like raised platforms, flood-resistant foundations, and earthquake-resistant structures enhances infrastructure resilience.

Risk Transfer and Insurance Mechanisms: Exploring risk transfer mechanisms, such as disaster insurance, to protect individuals, businesses, and public assets against future disasters. Insurance can provide a safety net and expedite recovery processes.

Capacity Building and Training: Strengthening the capacity of local governments, organizations, and communities in disaster risk reduction, preparedness, and response. Training programs help build skills and knowledge needed to manage future disaster events effectively.

Sustainable Development and Urban Planning: Integrating disaster risk reduction considerations into urban planning and development to create more resilient and sustainable cities. Proper land use planning and zoning regulations help minimize exposure to hazards.

Adaptive Social Protection: Developing social protection programs that can adapt to disaster impacts and provide support to affected populations. Social safety nets help vulnerable communities recover and cope with the aftermath of disasters.

Public Awareness and Education: Continuing public awareness and education campaigns to promote a culture of safety and resilience. Educating the public about disaster risks, preparedness, and response measures empowers individuals to take proactive actions.

Monitoring and Evaluation: Implementing monitoring and evaluation mechanisms to assess the effectiveness and impact of recovery and reconstruction efforts. Regular evaluations help identify strengths, weaknesses, and areas for improvement.

The success of recovery and reconstruction approaches in India relies on collaboration among government agencies, non-governmental organizations, private sector partners, and local communities. Integrating DRR principles into the recovery process ensures that communities are better equipped to withstand future disasters and thrive in a changing environment.

10.11 Avoiding Epidemics After Flood Disaster

To avoid dangerous epidemics after a flood disaster, several necessary steps should be taken to ensure public health and hygiene are maintained. Floods can lead to water contamination, overcrowding in relief camps, and increased vulnerability to infectious diseases. Implementing the following measures can help prevent the outbreak and spread of epidemics:

a. **Safe Drinking Water Supply**: Ensure access to safe drinking water by setting up water purification systems or distributing clean drinking water. Boiling or treating water with chlorine or other disinfectants can help eliminate harmful pathogens.

b. **Sanitation and Hygiene Promotion**: Promote proper sanitation and hygiene practices among the affected population. Encourage handwashing with soap and clean water, and provide adequate toilet facilities to prevent the contamination of water sources and the spread of waterborne diseases.

c. **Vector Control**: Conduct vector control measures to prevent the breeding of mosquitoes and other disease-carrying insects. This may include fogging, larviciding, and distribution of mosquito nets.

d. **Vaccination and Immunization**: Prioritize vaccination and immunization campaigns, especially for diseases that are endemic in the area. Vaccinations can help prevent the spread of vaccine-preventable diseases in crowded and unsanitary conditions.

e. **Health Surveillance and Early Detection**: Set up health surveillance systems to monitor disease outbreaks and implement early detection measures. Rapid response teams should be deployed to investigate suspected cases and implement containment measures promptly.

f. **Medical Care and Treatment**: Ensure access to medical care and treatment for those affected by injuries or illnesses. Set up medical camps and facilities to provide essential healthcare services.

g. **Education and Communication**: Conduct public awareness campaigns on disease prevention and the importance of sanitation and hygiene practices. Use various communication channels to disseminate health-related information to the affected population.

h. **Environmental Clean-up**: Initiate a comprehensive environmental clean-up to remove debris, stagnant water, and contaminated materials. Proper waste management is crucial to prevent the proliferation of disease vectors and maintain a safe living environment.

i. **Coordination and Collaboration**: Facilitate coordination and collaboration among government agencies, NGOs, healthcare organizations, and other stakeholders involved in disaster response and public health interventions.

j. **Shelter and Camp Management**: Ensure proper management of relief camps and shelters to prevent overcrowding and maintain hygiene standards. Adequate spacing between shelters, provision of basic amenities, and regular cleaning and disinfection are essential.

k. **Mental Health Support**: Recognize the psychological impact of a flood disaster and provide mental health support to those affected. Counselling services and support groups can help individuals cope with trauma and stress.

Thus, by implementing these necessary steps, disaster management authorities can significantly reduce the risk of dangerous epidemics after a flood disaster. Timely action, proper planning, and effective coordination are vital in safeguarding the health and well-being of the affected population and preventing the spread of infectious diseases. A multi-sectoral approach that integrates health, water, sanitation, and hygiene interventions is essential to create a resilient and healthy community in the aftermath of a flood disaster.

10.12 Emergency Plan Rehearsal in Disaster Management

An emergency plan rehearsal, also known as a disaster drill or exercise, is a crucial component of disaster management. It involves simulating a disaster scenario to test the preparedness, response capabilities, and coordination of various stakeholders involved in disaster management. The primary objective of an emergency plan rehearsal is to evaluate the effectiveness of the emergency response plan, identify areas for improvement, and enhance the overall disaster readiness of organizations, communities, and authorities. This essay explores the importance of emergency plan rehearsals in disaster management, the different types of exercises, and the benefits they offer in mitigating the impact of disasters.

A] **Importance of Emergency Plan Rehearsals:**

Assessment of Preparedness: Rehearsing emergency plans provides an opportunity to assess the preparedness of organizations and response teams. It helps identify strengths and weaknesses in planning, resource allocation, and response procedures.

Testing Communication Systems: Communication is critical during disasters. Rehearsals test the efficiency of communication systems and protocols among various stakeholders, ensuring smooth flow of information.

Familiarization with Roles and Responsibilities: Participants in the exercise become familiar with their roles and responsibilities during an emergency. This ensures a coordinated response when a real disaster occurs.

Enhancing Coordination: Emergency plan rehearsals involve multiple organizations and agencies, fostering collaboration and coordination among them. It improves the ability to work together in a unified manner during an actual emergency.

Identifying Gaps and Deficiencies: The exercise highlights any gaps in resources, training, or equipment that may hinder an effective response. These deficiencies can then be addressed to improve overall preparedness.

Building Confidence: Regular rehearsals build confidence in responders and help them develop a better understanding of their roles and the protocols to follow. This confidence can be crucial during high-stress situations.

Learning from Mistakes: Mistakes made during rehearsals provide valuable learning opportunities. Participants can analyse and correct their actions, avoiding similar errors in real-life emergencies.

B] **Types of Emergency Plan Rehearsals:**

Tabletop Exercises: Tabletop exercises involve discussion-based simulations, where participants review and discuss emergency scenarios without deploying resources. This type of rehearsal is valuable for testing plans and procedures in a low-stress environment.

Functional Exercises: Functional exercises involve specific functions or operations within an organization or between multiple agencies. Participants perform their roles and interact with others to test response capabilities.

Drills: Drills focus on practicing specific actions or procedures. For example, fire drills in buildings help occupants understand evacuation procedures and locate emergency exits.

Full-Scale Exercises: Full-scale exercises simulate a complete disaster scenario, involving multiple agencies and resources. These exercises are the most comprehensive and provide a realistic test of disaster response capabilities.

C] **Benefits of Emergency Plan Rehearsals:**

Enhanced Preparedness: Rehearsing emergency plans improves overall preparedness for disasters, ensuring a prompt and effective response.

Improved Decision Making: Regular drills help responders make quick and informed decisions during real emergencies, reducing response time and improving outcomes.

Risk Reduction: Identifying and addressing deficiencies in emergency plans and response procedures minimizes the risk of errors during actual disasters.

Better Resource Allocation: Rehearsals help in allocating resources efficiently and effectively, ensuring their optimal utilization during emergencies.

Public Confidence: Communities and stakeholders gain confidence in the capabilities of responders and disaster management authorities through visible preparedness efforts.

Thus, Emergency plan rehearsals are an indispensable part of disaster management. Through rigorous testing, coordination, and evaluation, these exercises enhance the capabilities of organizations, authorities, and communities to respond effectively to disasters. The valuable insights gained from rehearsals help in refining emergency plans, addressing weaknesses, and improving overall disaster preparedness. By investing in regular emergency plan rehearsals, disaster management efforts become more robust, proactive, and better equipped to protect lives, property, and the environment during times of crisis.

10.13 Important Agencies in India

National Disaster Management Authority (NDMA):

Website: https://ndma.gov.in/

Headquarters: NDMA Bhawan, A-1 Safdarjung Enclave, New Delhi – 110029, India.

Ministry of Home Affairs (MHA):

Website: https://www.mha.gov.in/

Headquarters: North Block, Central Secretariat, New Delhi – 110001, India.

National Disaster Response Force (NDRF):

Website: https://www.ndrf.gov.in/

Headquarters: NDRF HQ, 5th Battalion, Sector-III, RK Puram, New Delhi – 110066, India.

Ministry of Agriculture and Farmers' Welfare:

Website: https://www.agriculture.gov.in/

Headquarters: Krishi Bhawan, Rajendra Prasad Road, New Delhi – 110001, India.

Ministry of Health and Family Welfare:

Website: https://www.mohfw.gov.in/

Headquarters: Nirman Bhawan, Maulana Azad Road, New Delhi – 110011, India.

Ministry of Road Transport and Highways:

Website: https://morth.nic.in/

Headquarters: Transport Bhawan, Parliament Street, New Delhi – 110001, India.

National Institute of Disaster Management (NIDM):

Website: https://nidm.gov.in/

Headquarters: 5-B, IIPA Campus, IP Estate, Mahatma Gandhi Marg, New Delhi – 110002, India.

10.14 Training of Human Resources in (DRR)

A] **Planning at Different Levels**

1. **State Level:** At the state level, training of human resources in DRR planning is critical to ensure effective disaster preparedness and response capabilities. State disaster management authorities conduct various training programs for government officials, disaster response teams, and other stakeholders. The training covers a wide range of topics, including:

   i. Understanding the state's disaster profile, vulnerabilities, and risk assessment.

   ii. Developing and implementing state-level disaster management plans and policies.

   iii. Coordinating with district-level authorities and other stakeholders during disasters.

   iv. Conducting mock drills and exercises to test preparedness and response capabilities.

   v. Training on specific aspects of DRR, such as flood management, earthquake preparedness, etc.

   vi. Building capacity in early warning systems and information dissemination.

2. **District Level**: At the district level, training focuses on enhancing the capacity of local government officials, first responders, and community members. The district administration collaborates with state and national disaster management agencies to conduct these training programs. Key aspects of training at the district level include:

   i. Understanding district-specific hazards, vulnerabilities, and risk mapping.

   ii. Formulating district-level disaster management plans and contingency plans.

   iii. Conducting community-based disaster risk reduction programs and awareness campaigns.

   iv. Training first responders in search and rescue techniques, medical aid, and evacuation procedures.

   v. Capacity building of local NGOs and community organizations in disaster response.

   vi. Training on integrating disaster risk reduction into development planning.

3. **College Level**: In higher education institutions, disaster management is often integrated into academic curricula. Colleges and universities offer specialized courses

and degree programs in disaster management and risk reduction. The training at the college level includes:

i. In-depth study of disaster management principles, policies, and best practices.

ii. Research and analysis of past disasters and their impact on communities.

iii. Field visits and internships to gain practical experience in disaster management.

iv. Training in disaster risk assessment and vulnerability analysis.

v. Learning about the role of technology and innovation in disaster management.

4. **School Level**: At the school level, training focuses on creating a culture of safety and preparedness among students, teachers, and staff. Schools conduct various drills and awareness programs to equip students with basic knowledge of disaster preparedness. The training includes:

i. Conducting regular fire drills and earthquake drills to teach students how to respond during emergencies.

ii. Integrating disaster risk reduction into the school curriculum through subjects like Environmental Studies.

iii. Training students in basic first aid and CPR techniques.

iv. Raising awareness about hazards and risks in the local community and how to address them.

v. Involving students in community-based disaster risk reduction activities.

Thus, Training of human resources in DRR planning at different levels is crucial to build a resilient society that can effectively respond to disasters and reduce their impact. From state-level officials to school children, each level plays a significant role in disaster preparedness and response. By empowering individuals with the knowledge and skills needed to address disasters, a culture of safety and resilience can be fostered, ensuring a safer and more secure future for all.

A] **NGOs working in Assam, Bihar, & West Bengal for Disaster Management work**

Assam:

Assam State Disaster Management Authority (ASDMA): This is the government agency responsible for disaster management in Assam. It works to build disaster resilience, conduct awareness campaigns, and coordinate response and relief efforts.

ActionAid India: ActionAid India works on various social issues, including disaster management and risk reduction in Assam. They provide relief and rehabilitation assistance during disasters and also work on capacity building and community resilience.

Oxfam India: Oxfam India responds to disasters in Assam, providing emergency relief and long-term support for affected communities. They also advocate for better disaster management policies and practices.

Bihar:

Bihar State Disaster Management Authority (BSDMA): Similar to ASDMA, BSDMA is the government body responsible for disaster management in Bihar. It focuses on preparedness, response, and recovery activities.

Caritas India: Caritas India is involved in disaster response and recovery efforts in Bihar. They work on emergency relief, livelihood restoration, and community development.

Concern Worldwide: Concern Worldwide operates in Bihar, helping during disasters, especially in terms of water and sanitation, nutrition, and healthcare.

West Bengal:

West Bengal Disaster Management Authority (WBDMA): WBDMA is the government agency responsible for disaster management in the state. It leads disaster response and relief efforts and focuses on capacity building and community resilience.

Save the Children India: Save the Children India works in West Bengal, providing disaster relief and recovery assistance to affected communities. They also implement programs for child protection and education during disasters.

CARE India: CARE India responds to disasters in West Bengal, offering humanitarian assistance, livelihood support, and rehabilitation services.

It is important to verify the current status and activities of these NGOs, as well as explore other organizations that might be working in disaster management in these states. NGOs often collaborate with government agencies, international organizations, and local communities to effectively address disaster-related challenges.

CHAPTER 11

Institutional Mechanisms for Disaster Management

11.1 Institutional Mechanism for Disaster Management

11.2 Role and Responsibilities of Government Bodies for DM

11.3 Importance of Community Participation in DM

11.4 Role and Responsibilities of Local Bodies in DM

11.5 Crisis Management in Disasters

11.6 Role and Responsibilities of NGOs and Civil Societies in Disaster Response

11.7 Legislation and Policies for Disaster Risk Reduction in India

    11.7.1 Disaster Management Policy for Environment and Local Action

    11.7.2 National Disaster Management Policy (2009):

    11.7.3 National Disaster Management Plan (2016):

    11.7.4 Funding Sources for Disaster Management in India

    11.7.5 Institutional Capacity Building Initiatives in India

11.8 Disaster Management Act 2005

11.9 Role of Red Cross Society during Disaster Management

11.10 Role of UNO during Disaster Management

11.11 Role of European Union during Disaster Management

11.12 Role of World Bank during Disaster Management

11.1 Institutional Mechanism for Disaster Management

Institutional Mechanism for Disaster Management in India refers to the organizational structure and arrangements put in place by the government to manage and respond to disasters effectively.

It involves various ministries, departments, agencies, and bodies at the national, state, and local levels. The institutional mechanism in India follows a multi-tiered approach to ensure a coordinated and comprehensive response to disasters. Here are the key components of the Institutional Mechanism for Disaster Management in India:

National Disaster Management Authority (NDMA): The NDMA is the apex body responsible for formulating national policies, plans, and guidelines for disaster management in India. It is headed by the Prime Minister of India and consists of members from various ministries and experts in the field of disaster management. The NDMA provides overall direction and coordination for disaster risk reduction, preparedness, response, and recovery at the national level.

Ministry of Home Affairs (MHA): The MHA is the nodal ministry for disaster management in India. It oversees the implementation of disaster management policies and programs across various ministries and agencies. The MHA provides financial and logistical support to states during disasters and coordinates international assistance when required.

National Executive Committee (NEC): The NEC is a committee constituted under the Disaster Management Act, 2005, and is chaired by the Secretary of the Ministry of Home Affairs. It assists the NDMA in the coordination of disaster response and relief operations.

National Crisis Management Committee (NCMC): The NCMC is the highest body for crisis management during disasters and emergencies. It is chaired by the Cabinet Secretary of India and includes senior officials from key ministries and departments. The NCMC oversees the overall response and coordination during major disasters.

National Disaster Response Force (NDRF): NDRF is a specialized force under the National Disaster Management Authority. It is responsible for conducting search and rescue operations, providing immediate relief, and assisting in the evacuation of affected communities during disasters.

Ministry of Agriculture and Farmers' Welfare: This ministry addresses agricultural-related aspects of disaster risk reduction. It implements programs and measures to minimize the impact of disasters on agriculture, provide support to farmers, and promote climate-resilient farming practices.

State Disaster Management Authorities (SDMAs): Each state in India has its own SDMA responsible for disaster management within the state. SDMAs coordinate disaster risk reduction, preparedness, response, and recovery efforts within their respective states.

District Disaster Management Authorities (DDMAs): At the district level, DDMAs are responsible for implementing disaster management plans and activities. DDMAs coordinate disaster response and relief operations at the district level, ensuring timely assistance to affected communities.

Local Government Bodies: Municipal corporations, panchayats, and urban local bodies have a significant role in disaster risk reduction at the local level. They are involved in disaster preparedness, early warning dissemination, evacuation, and local-level response during emergencies.

National Institute of Disaster Management (NIDM): NIDM is the premier institute for training, research, and capacity building in disaster management. It conducts training programs for various stakeholders, develops disaster management curriculum, and promotes research and knowledge dissemination in the field of DRR.

The institutional mechanism in India emphasizes the importance of coordination, preparedness, and collaboration among various stakeholders to effectively manage disasters and reduce their impact on communities and the environment. It follows a hierarchical structure with clear roles and responsibilities at each level to ensure a well-coordinated and efficient response during disasters.

11.2 Role and Responsibilities of Government Bodies for DM

Government bodies in India play crucial roles and have specific responsibilities in disaster management to ensure a coordinated and effective response to disasters. These bodies are responsible for various aspects of disaster risk reduction, preparedness, response, and recovery. Here are the key government bodies involved in disaster management in India and their respective roles and responsibilities:

National Disaster Management Authority (NDMA):

Role of NDMA is Formulating national policies, plans, and guidelines for disaster management in India. Responsibilities of NDMA is Providing overall direction and coordination for disaster risk reduction, preparedness, response, and recovery at the national level. Issuing advisories, guidelines, and early warnings to support state and district-level authorities during disasters. Conducting research and promoting capacity-building in disaster management.

Ministry of Home Affairs (MHA):

Role of MHA is Nodal ministry for disaster management in India. Responsibilities of MHA is Overseeing the implementation of disaster management policies and programs across various ministries and agencies. Providing financial and logistical support to states during disasters. Coordinating international assistance when required.

National Executive Committee (NEC):

Role of NEC is Assisting the NDMA in coordinating disaster response and relief operations. Responsibilities of NEC are Advising the NDMA on disaster management policies and measures, Ensuring effective coordination among various ministries and departments during disasters.

National Crisis Management Committee (NCMC):

Role of NCMC – Highest body for crisis management during disasters and emergencies. Responsibilities of NCMC are Overseeing the overall response and coordination during major disasters and taking important decisions on resource mobilization and response strategies.

National Disaster Response Force (NDRF):

Role: Specialized force for disaster response and relief operations. Responsibilities: Conducting search and rescue operations in disaster-affected areas. Providing immediate relief, medical aid, and evacuation assistance to affected communities. Assisting in the management of relief camps and distribution of essential supplies.

Ministry of Agriculture and Farmers' Welfare:

Role: Addressing agricultural-related aspects of disaster risk reduction. Responsibilities: Implementing programs and measures to minimize the impact of disasters on agriculture and farmers. Providing support to farmers during and after disasters. Promoting climate-resilient farming practices.

State Disaster Management Authorities (SDMAs):

Role: Responsible for disaster management within each state. Responsibilities: Formulating and implementing state-level policies and plans for disaster risk reduction, preparedness, response, and recovery. Coordinating disaster response activities in collaboration with various state departments and agencies. Mobilizing resources and requesting central government support when required.

District Disaster Management Authorities (DDMAs):

Role: Implementing disaster management plans and activities at the district level. Responsibilities: Coordinating disaster response and relief operations at the district level. Conducting risk assessments and preparedness activities within the district. Ensuring timely assistance and relief to affected communities.

Local Government Bodies:

Role: Playing a significant role in disaster risk reduction at the local level. Responsibilities: Implementing disaster preparedness measures at the community level. Disseminating early warnings and coordinating evacuations during emergencies. Providing immediate assistance and relief to affected populations.

National Institute of Disaster Management (NIDM):

Role: Premier institute for training, research, and capacity building in disaster management. Responsibilities: Conducting training programs for various stakeholders in disaster management. Developing disaster management curriculum and promoting research and knowledge dissemination. Assisting in the development of disaster management policies and guidelines.

These government bodies work collaboratively to enhance disaster risk reduction measures and build resilience in India. Their collective efforts and coordination are critical in protecting lives, livelihoods, and infrastructure during disasters and in promoting a safer and more disaster-resilient nation.

11.3 Importance of Community Participation in DM

Community participation in disaster management is of paramount importance as it plays a crucial role in enhancing the effectiveness, sustainability, and resilience of disaster response and risk reduction efforts. Here are the key reasons why community participation is essential in disaster management:

Local Knowledge and Understanding: Local communities possess invaluable knowledge about their environment, vulnerabilities, and coping mechanisms. Their understanding of local hazards, risks, and resources can significantly contribute to developing effective disaster management plans and response strategies.

Rapid Response and Immediate Assistance: During the initial stages of a disaster, immediate response and assistance are critical. Local communities are often the first to respond, providing aid and support to affected individuals before external help arrives. Their prompt action can save lives and mitigate the impact of disasters.

Resilience Building: Engaging communities in disaster management fosters resilience by empowering them to be proactive in risk reduction and preparedness. Communities can identify and address their specific vulnerabilities, reducing their exposure to hazards and enhancing their capacity to cope with disasters.

Effective Early Warning Systems: Early warning systems are more effective when local communities are actively involved. They can help disseminate warnings, ensure that information reaches everyone, and facilitate timely evacuations when necessary.

Cultural and Social Context: Disaster management measures must be culturally and socially appropriate to be effective. Local communities can provide insights into community dynamics, traditional practices, and social structures, enabling disaster management efforts to be more contextually relevant.

Community Ownership and Empowerment: When communities actively participate in disaster management, they take ownership of their safety and well-being. This sense of ownership leads to increased empowerment and a greater commitment to implementing and sustaining disaster risk reduction measures.

Resource Mobilization and Allocation: Local communities can mobilize local resources, knowledge, and manpower during disaster response and recovery. Their active participation facilitates effective resource allocation and helps ensure that resources are utilized efficiently.

Effective Communication and Coordination: Community participation facilitates better communication and coordination between local authorities, government agencies, NGOs, and other stakeholders. This leads to more efficient disaster response and reduces duplication of efforts.

Inclusivity and Vulnerable Groups: Community involvement ensures that the needs of vulnerable groups, such as women, children, elderly, and people with disabilities, are considered in disaster planning and response.

Community-Based Risk Reduction Strategies: Engaging communities in risk assessment and planning allows for the development of community-based risk reduction strategies tailored to specific local contexts and needs.

Sustainable Recovery and Reconstruction: Community participation in the recovery and reconstruction process ensures that rebuilding efforts align with the community's priorities and promote long-term sustainability.

Trust and Social Cohesion: Active community involvement fosters trust between the community and response agencies. When communities are engaged in decision-making and response efforts, they feel more confident in the actions taken by authorities and are more likely to cooperate during emergencies. This strengthens social cohesion and solidarity, leading to a more united and supportive community.

Cost-Effectiveness: Community participation in disaster management can lead to cost-effective solutions. Local communities often have a better understanding of low-cost and sustainable mitigation measures that can be implemented using local resources. Their participation can also help identify cost-efficient ways to address specific vulnerabilities and hazards.

Community Resilience and Adaptation: Engaging communities in disaster management encourages them to adopt a proactive approach to resilience. As communities recognize their roles in risk reduction and preparedness, they become more adaptable to changing circumstances and better equipped to face future challenges.

Customized Solutions: Local communities have unique needs and characteristics. Their involvement in disaster management ensures that interventions are tailored to their specific circumstances, rather than relying on generic approaches that may not address the community's unique challenges.

Capacity Building and Training: Involving communities in disaster management provides opportunities for capacity building and training. Through workshops and exercises, communities can develop skills in disaster preparedness, first aid, search and rescue, and other essential response activities.

Participatory Decision-Making: Community participation ensures that disaster management plans and policies are developed with input from those directly affected. It promotes participatory decision-making, democratic governance, and transparency in the disaster management process.

Reduction of Casualties and Losses: Communities that actively engage in disaster management are better prepared to respond promptly and effectively during emergencies. This proactive approach can significantly reduce casualties and property losses.

Sustainable Behavioural Change: Engaging communities in disaster management can foster sustainable behavioural changes related to safety practices and preparedness. For example, communities may adopt safer construction practices or regularly conduct mock drills, reinforcing a culture of safety.

Enhanced Data Collection and Reporting: Local communities can contribute to data collection and reporting during and after disasters. By providing real-time information about damages and needs, communities assist authorities in making informed decisions and allocating resources appropriately.

Disaster Risk Communication: Community participation facilitates effective risk communication. Local residents can help disseminate warnings and information within the community through various communication channels, ensuring that all members receive vital information.

Long-Term Engagement and Sustainability: Community participation is not limited to disaster response alone. It encourages ongoing engagement in risk reduction and resilience-building activities, promoting long-term sustainability and preparedness.

Incorporating community participation in disaster management fosters a sense of collective responsibility and solidarity, leading to a more resilient society. It empowers individuals to actively contribute to their safety and well-being, ultimately reducing the impact of disasters and building a more disaster-resilient community and nation as a whole. Community participation is a fundamental pillar of effective disaster management. Engaging and empowering communities not only strengthens disaster resilience but also fosters a sense of ownership and shared responsibility in safeguarding lives and livelihoods during disasters. Recognizing the importance of communities as key stakeholders in disaster management is vital for building a safer and more resilient society.

11.4 Role and Responsibilities of Local Bodies in DM

Local bodies and authorities play a critical role in disaster management as they are the first responders during emergencies and have a deep understanding of the local context and vulnerabilities. Their proximity to the affected communities allows for quick and efficient disaster response and coordination. Here are the key roles and responsibilities of local bodies and authorities in disaster management:

Preparedness and Planning: Developing and implementing local-level disaster management plans, including risk assessments, hazard mapping, and contingency plans. Identifying vulnerable areas and populations and formulating strategies to address their specific needs during disasters. Conducting mock drills and exercises to enhance preparedness and response capabilities.

Early Warning and Communication: Disseminating early warnings to communities about impending hazards and coordinating evacuation if necessary. Establishing effective communication channels to ensure the timely flow of information to and from the affected areas. Providing timely updates to higher authorities and neighbouring districts about the situation on the ground.

Search and Rescue Operations: Mobilizing local resources and personnel for search and rescue operations immediately after a disaster strikes. Coordinating with neighbouring communities and districts to maximize the search and rescue efforts.

Emergency Relief and Shelter: Providing immediate relief and assistance to affected communities, including food, water, medical aid, and temporary shelter. Coordinating the setup and management of relief camps and distribution centers.

Medical and Health Services: Assessing and addressing medical needs in the aftermath of a disaster. Setting up medical camps and emergency health facilities to provide medical assistance to the affected population. Ensuring the availability of essential medicines and medical supplies.

Public Safety and Law Enforcement: Ensuring public safety and order during and after a disaster. Managing traffic and crowd control to facilitate smooth evacuation and relief operations. Preventing looting and ensuring the safety of relief supplies.

Infrastructure Restoration and Rehabilitation: Assisting in the assessment of infrastructure damage and coordinating the restoration and rehabilitation of essential services such as roads, bridges, water supply, and electricity. Prioritizing the repair and reconstruction of critical infrastructure to enable the resumption of normalcy.

Community Engagement and Mobilization: Engaging with the local community to raise awareness about disaster risk reduction and preparedness. Mobilizing community members to participate in disaster management activities and volunteer for response efforts.

Coordination with Higher Authorities: Providing regular updates and situation reports to higher-level disaster management authorities. Seeking assistance and resources from state and national agencies when local capacities are overwhelmed.

Documentation and Reporting: Maintaining comprehensive records of the disaster's impact, response measures, and relief distribution. Submitting timely reports to higher authorities for documentation and decision-making.

Post-Disaster Assessment and Needs Analysis: Conducting post-disaster assessments to determine the extent of damages and needs for recovery and reconstruction. Identifying long-term rehabilitation and reconstruction requirements.

Capacity Building and Training: Organizing capacity-building programs and training for local officials and volunteers to enhance their knowledge and skills in disaster management.

Community Evacuation and Safe Sheltering: Identifying safe evacuation routes and coordinating the orderly evacuation of at-risk communities to designated shelters or safer locations. Ensuring that evacuation centers are equipped with essential facilities and resources to accommodate the affected population.

Psychosocial Support and Counselling: Providing psychosocial support and counselling to affected individuals and communities to address trauma, anxiety, and emotional distress caused by the disaster. Collaborating with mental health professionals and support organizations to ensure comprehensive psychosocial care.

Protection of Livestock and Pets: Coordinating the evacuation and sheltering of livestock and pets to protect them from harm during disasters. Ensuring that animal welfare needs are addressed during and after the disaster.

Environmental Protection and Conservation: Identifying and managing environmentally sensitive areas and ensuring that disaster response activities do not cause further harm to the environment. Implementing measures to promote environmental conservation and sustainability during recovery and reconstruction.

Data Collection and Damage Assessment: Collecting accurate and timely data on the impact of the disaster, including casualties, damages to infrastructure, and loss of livelihoods. Conducting damage assessments to determine the extent of losses and the resources required for recovery.

Coordination with Non-Governmental Organizations (NGOs) and Volunteers: Collaborating with NGOs, community-based organizations, and volunteers to strengthen disaster response and recovery efforts. Facilitating the integration of external assistance and resources into local response operations.

Public Awareness and Education: Conducting awareness campaigns and educational programs to enhance community understanding of disaster risks, preparedness measures, and safety practices. Engaging schools, colleges, and community centers in disseminating disaster-related information.

Prevention of Secondary Hazards: Taking measures to prevent secondary hazards, such as disease outbreaks or secondary accidents, during the response phase. Ensuring the safe handling and disposal of hazardous materials and debris.

Post-Disaster Rehabilitation and Livelihood Restoration: Developing plans and programs for the rehabilitation of affected communities and the restoration of livelihoods. Implementing livelihood support measures to enable communities to recover and rebuild their economic activities.

Community-Based Monitoring and Feedback Mechanisms: Establishing community-based monitoring and feedback mechanisms to assess the effectiveness of response measures and gather feedback from affected individuals. Using feedback to improve future disaster management strategies and plans.

Integration of Technology and Innovation: Exploring the use of technology, such as early warning systems, drones, and geospatial mapping, to improve disaster preparedness, response, and recovery. Adopting innovative solutions for better data collection, communication, and decision-making.

Local bodies and authorities are the backbone of disaster management at the grassroots level. Their effective and coordinated efforts are crucial in saving lives, protecting property, and promoting community resilience during disasters. As the first line of response, their preparedness, quick action, and community engagement are instrumental in mitigating the impact of disasters and facilitating a smooth recovery process. Local bodies and authorities serve as the frontline responders during disasters and emergencies. Their role is instrumental in reducing the impact of disasters on communities and promoting effective recovery. By involving local communities, building their capacities, and fostering cooperation among various stakeholders, local bodies play a central role in creating a more resilient and disaster-ready society.

11.5 Crisis Management in Disasters

Crisis management refers to the coordinated efforts and processes undertaken to address and overcome a crisis situation effectively.

In the context of disasters, crisis management plays a crucial role in mitigating the impact of the disaster, protecting lives and property, and facilitating a smooth and efficient recovery process. Effective crisis management requires a well-organized and integrated approach involving multiple stakeholders, including government agencies, emergency responders, non-governmental organizations, and the affected communities. Let us delve into the key aspects of crisis management and its principles in the context of disasters.

a. Preparedness: Preparedness is the foundation of effective crisis management. It involves planning, training, and equipping disaster response teams, as well as raising awareness among the public about disaster risks and response protocols. Preparedness activities include developing emergency response plans, conducting drills and exercises, and establishing early warning systems to alert communities about impending disasters.

b. Rapid Response: Timely and coordinated response is essential during a disaster. Crisis management teams must swiftly mobilize resources and personnel to provide emergency assistance, rescue operations, and medical aid. An efficient response can help minimize casualties, prevent further damage, and initiate immediate relief measures.

c. Communication and Information Sharing: Clear and accurate communication is critical during a crisis. Crisis management teams must establish effective communication channels to disseminate vital information to the public, responders, and relevant authorities. Timely and reliable information empowers individuals to make informed decisions and take appropriate actions to safeguard themselves and their communities.

d. Command and Control: A well-defined chain of command and control is crucial in crisis management. Establishing a unified command structure helps streamline decision-making and coordination among various agencies and stakeholders. It ensures that actions are taken in a cohesive and organized manner, avoiding duplication of efforts and confusion.

e. Flexibility and Adaptability: Disasters are dynamic and unpredictable events, often requiring crisis management teams to adapt their strategies and plans rapidly. Flexibility in response allows teams to address emerging challenges and changing circumstances effectively.

f. Resource Management: Optimal utilization of resources is essential during a disaster. Crisis management teams must allocate resources efficiently to where they are most needed, prioritizing life-saving efforts and critical infrastructure protection.

g. Collaboration and Partnerships: Disaster response requires collaboration among various agencies, organizations, and community members. Building strong partnerships between government entities, NGOs, private sector, and community-based organizations fosters a more comprehensive and coordinated response.

h. Continuity and Recovery: Crisis management extends beyond the immediate response phase. It involves developing plans for long-term recovery and continuity of services. Post-disaster recovery efforts focus on rebuilding infrastructure, restoring essential services, and supporting affected communities in their recovery journey.

i. Learning and Improvement: Disasters serve as learning experiences, and crisis management teams must conduct post-event evaluations to identify strengths, weaknesses, and areas for improvement. Regular debriefings, after-action reports, and exercises help enhance future disaster preparedness and response capabilities.

Thus, Crisis management is a multifaceted process that encompasses preparedness, response, recovery, and learning from disaster events. In the context of disasters, effective crisis management requires a well-coordinated, flexible, and adaptable approach, with a strong emphasis on communication, collaboration, and resource management. By implementing these principles, crisis management teams can effectively mitigate the impact of disasters, save lives, and facilitate a swift and successful recovery process.

11.5.1 Difference between Emergency Management and Crisis Management

While both Emergency Management and Crisis Management aim to protect lives and property during challenging situations, they differ in terms of scope, timeframe, and nature of events they address. Emergency Management focuses on preparedness, response, and recovery from various types of emergencies and disasters. On the other hand, Crisis Management primarily deals with unforeseen and rapidly developing events, requiring immediate response and containment to prevent further harm. Both aspects are essential in Disaster Management to ensure a comprehensive and effective approach to handling different scenarios.

Table 11.1 Difference between Emergency Management and Crisis Management.

Aspect	Emergency Management	Crisis Management
Definition	A systematic approach to preparing for, responding to, and recovering from emergencies or disasters.	A set of actions and strategies to manage and mitigate the impact of unexpected and rapidly developing events.
Scope	Focused on various types of emergencies and disasters, both natural and human-made.	Primarily deals with sudden and unexpected events that can have severe consequences.
Timeframe	Generally, covers preparedness, response, and recovery phases of disasters.	Primarily focuses on the immediate response and containment of a crisis.
Nature of Events	Includes both planned events (e.g., drills, exercises) and unplanned emergencies.	Primarily deals with unforeseen events and may not have a pre-determined response plan.

Planning	Involves developing comprehensive emergency plans and procedures for various scenarios.	Often requires real-time decision-making and adapting to evolving situations.
Coordination	Requires coordination among various agencies, stakeholders, and community members.	Often involves rapid coordination and collaboration among crisis management teams and decision-makers.
Response Time	Emphasizes a structured and timely response to mitigate the impact of disasters.	Requires an immediate and decisive response to prevent the crisis from escalating further.
Goal	To protect lives, property, and the environment during emergencies.	To manage and contain the crisis to prevent further harm and restore stability.
Examples	Natural disasters like earthquakes, floods, hurricanes, and human-made disasters like industrial accidents, terrorist attacks.	Hostage situations, terrorist attacks, financial crises, cyberattacks, public health emergencies (e.g., pandemic).

11.6 Role and Responsibilities of NGOs and Civil Societies in Disaster Response

Non-Governmental Organizations (NGOs) and civil society organizations (CSOs) play vital roles in disaster response, complementing the efforts of government agencies and other stakeholders. Their agility, flexibility, and close ties to communities enable them to provide valuable assistance during and after disasters. Here are the key roles and responsibilities of NGOs and civil society organizations in disaster response:

Immediate Relief and Assistance: NGOs and CSOs are often among the first to respond to disasters, providing immediate relief such as food, water, shelter, medical aid, and clothing to affected communities. They conduct rapid assessments to identify urgent needs and prioritize assistance.

Search and Rescue Operations: In coordination with local authorities, some NGOs have specialized search and rescue teams that deploy to disaster-affected areas to assist in locating and rescuing survivors.

Medical Care and Health Services: Many NGOs have medical teams and mobile health clinics that provide medical care to the injured and sick. They offer psychological support and counselling to help individuals cope with trauma and emotional distress.

Distribution of Relief Supplies: NGOs and CSOs manage the efficient distribution of relief supplies to ensure they reach the most vulnerable and underserved communities. They work to prevent hoarding and ensure equitable access to essential resources.

Emergency Shelter and Rehabilitation: NGOs and CSOs are involved in setting up emergency shelters and providing temporary housing solutions for displaced individuals and families. They support the rehabilitation and repair of damaged houses and infrastructure.

Water, Sanitation, and Hygiene (WASH) Interventions: NGOs implement WASH programs to provide clean drinking water, sanitation facilities, and hygiene education to prevent the outbreak of waterborne diseases.

Protection of Vulnerable Groups: NGOs and CSOs prioritize the protection of vulnerable groups such as women, children, elderly individuals, and people with disabilities during disaster response. They address the specific needs and rights of these groups to ensure their safety and well-being.

Livelihood Support and Recovery: NGOs assist in the restoration of livelihoods by providing support to farmers, fishermen, and small businesses affected by disasters. They offer vocational training and income-generating activities to help affected communities recover economically.

Community Mobilization and Empowerment: NGOs and CSOs engage with local communities to empower them in the disaster response process. They involve communities in decision-making, planning, and implementation of recovery projects.

Information Dissemination and Awareness: NGOs play a crucial role in disseminating information about disaster risks, safety measures, and available support services to affected communities. They raise awareness about disaster preparedness and resilience-building measures.

Advocacy and Policy Influence: NGOs and CSOs advocate for policies that promote disaster risk reduction, climate resilience, and social protection for vulnerable communities. They work to ensure that disaster response efforts are inclusive and address the root causes of vulnerability.

Coordination and Collaboration: NGOs and CSOs collaborate with government agencies, UN agencies, and other humanitarian partners to avoid duplication of efforts and ensure a coordinated response. They actively participate in cluster meetings and coordination mechanisms to share information and resources.

Monitoring and Evaluation: NGOs and CSOs monitor the impact and effectiveness of their disaster response efforts to assess the outcomes and adapt their strategies accordingly. They provide feedback to improve future response initiatives.

NGOs and civil society organizations bring a community-driven approach to disaster response, focusing on the specific needs and strengths of the affected population. Their efforts contribute significantly to saving lives, alleviating suffering, and promoting resilience among disaster-affected communities. Their work complements the actions of government agencies and other stakeholders, resulting in a more comprehensive and effective disaster response.

11.6.1 Importance of Taking Help of Ngo and Civil Societies.

The involvement of Non-Governmental Organizations (NGOs) and Civil Society Organizations (CSOs) in disaster response is of utmost importance for several reasons. Their active participation enhances the overall effectiveness and efficiency of disaster management efforts. Here are the key reasons highlighting the importance of seeking help from NGOs and civil society organizations during disaster response:

Rapid and Flexible Response: NGOs and CSOs are known for their agility and quick response capabilities. They can mobilize resources and personnel swiftly to provide immediate assistance and relief to affected communities. Their ability to adapt to rapidly changing situations allows for a more efficient response in the critical early phases of a disaster.

Proximity to Communities: NGOs and CSOs often have well-established connections and networks within the communities they serve. Their close proximity to the affected populations enables them to better understand local needs, cultural sensitivities, and vulnerabilities, resulting in more targeted and appropriate response actions.

Community-Centered Approach: NGOs and CSOs prioritize the needs and perspectives of the affected communities. Their community-centered approach ensures that disaster response efforts are people-centric, inclusive, and respectful of local customs and traditions.

Expertise and Specialization: Many NGOs and CSOs have specialized expertise in specific areas such as health, nutrition, water, sanitation, education, and livelihood support. Their knowledge and experience in these sectors complement the efforts of government agencies and other stakeholders, allowing for a more comprehensive response.

Reach to Vulnerable and Marginalized Groups: NGOs and CSOs often work with marginalized and vulnerable groups that may be overlooked or underrepresented in mainstream disaster response efforts. Their inclusive approach ensures that the needs of these groups are adequately addressed.

Innovation and Adaptability: NGOs and CSOs are often at the forefront of adopting innovative technologies and approaches to address emerging challenges. Their innovative solutions contribute to more effective disaster response and recovery strategies.

Resource Mobilization: NGOs and CSOs have diverse funding sources, including public donations, grants, and partnerships. They can mobilize financial and material resources from multiple stakeholders, facilitating a more robust response even in resource-constrained environments.

Coordination and Collaboration: NGOs and CSOs are active participants in coordination mechanisms like cluster meetings, ensuring better collaboration between humanitarian actors. Their engagement helps avoid duplication of efforts and ensures a coherent response.

Advocacy and Policy Influence: NGOs and CSOs can advocate for policy changes and reforms that address the root causes of vulnerability and enhance disaster risk reduction efforts. Their advocacy work contributes to building a more resilient society in the long run.

Post-Disaster Recovery and Rehabilitation: NGOs and CSOs play a crucial role in long-term recovery and rehabilitation efforts. Their sustained engagement with affected communities ensures continuity in support beyond the immediate response phase.

Accountability and Transparency: NGOs and CSOs are often held to high standards of accountability and transparency in their operations. Their involvement in disaster response ensures that assistance reaches those in need and that resources are used efficiently.

Thus, the involvement of NGOs and civil society organizations during disaster response brings numerous benefits, including speed, adaptability, community-centricity, expertise, and innovation. Their contributions complement the efforts of government agencies and other stakeholders, creating a more comprehensive and compassionate response to disasters. Embracing their expertise and collaboration strengthens disaster resilience and fosters a collective and united approach to disaster management.

11.7 Legislation and Policies for Disaster Risk Reduction in India

In India, several legislations and policies govern disaster risk reduction and management to ensure a systematic and coordinated approach towards disaster preparedness, response, and recovery. Here are the key legislations and policies related to disaster risk reduction in India:

Disaster Management Act, 2005: The Disaster Management Act is the primary legislation that provides a comprehensive framework for disaster management in India. It was enacted to promote a proactive and holistic approach to disaster management and to establish institutional mechanisms for effective coordination and response. The key features of this Act are as follows:

National Disaster Management Authority (NDMA): The Act establishes the NDMA at the national level, responsible for policy formulation, coordination, and implementation of disaster management plans.

State Disaster Management Authorities (SDMAs): Each state and Union Territory in India has a State Disaster Management Authority responsible for disaster management within its jurisdiction.

District Disaster Management Authorities (DDMAs): The Act mandates the establishment of District Disaster Management Authorities at the district level.

National Plan, State Plans, and District Plans: The Act requires the formulation of National Disaster Management Plan, State Disaster Management Plan, and District Disaster Management Plan to ensure an integrated and coordinated response.

National Disaster Response Force (NDRF): The Act provides for the establishment of specialized response forces, known as the National Disaster Response Force (NDRF), to respond to disasters promptly and effectively.

Disaster Management Funds: The Act provides for the creation of National Disaster Response Fund (NDRF) and State Disaster Response Fund (SDRF) to finance disaster response and relief operations.

Disaster Mitigation, Preparedness, and Awareness: The Act emphasizes disaster mitigation, preparedness, and public awareness as crucial components of disaster management.

National Policy on Disaster Management, 2009: The National Policy on Disaster Management outlines the approach and guiding principles for disaster risk reduction and management in India. It aims to build a safer and disaster-resilient India by promoting a culture of prevention, preparedness, and mitigation. The key elements of this policy include:

Mainstreaming Disaster Risk Reduction: The policy emphasizes the integration of disaster risk reduction into development planning and decision-making processes.

Institutional Strengthening: The policy focuses on strengthening institutional capacities at all levels for effective disaster management.

Community Participation: It highlights the importance of involving local communities in disaster risk reduction and response efforts.

Knowledge Management and Research: The policy encourages research and knowledge-sharing to improve disaster management practices.

Risk Assessment and Early Warning Systems: It emphasizes the need for comprehensive risk assessments and the development of effective early warning systems.

National Disaster Response Force (NDRF) Guidelines, 2006: The NDRF Guidelines outline the organization, structure, and deployment protocols for the National Disaster Response Force. The guidelines specify the roles and responsibilities of NDRF teams during different types of disasters.

National Guidelines on School Safety, 2016: The National Guidelines on School Safety provide a framework for ensuring the safety and preparedness of educational institutions to withstand various hazards and disasters. It focuses on building disaster-resilient schools and promoting disaster education among students and staff.

National Guidelines on Urban Earthquake Risk Management, 2010: These guidelines focus on enhancing earthquake preparedness and risk reduction in urban areas. They provide strategies for ensuring the safety of buildings, infrastructure, and communities in earthquake-prone regions.

National Guidelines for Biological Disasters, 2008: The guidelines address preparedness, response, and management strategies for biological disasters, including pandemics and epidemics.

National Policy on Disaster Management – Plan of Action, 2009: The Plan of Action provides a detailed roadmap for the implementation of the National Policy on Disaster Management.

These legislations and policies are essential in guiding disaster risk reduction efforts in India. They establish a legal framework, set guidelines and procedures, and promote a proactive and integrated approach to disaster management. The combined efforts of the government, NGOs, civil society organizations, and local communities, guided by these policies, are crucial in building a more resilient and disaster-ready nation.

11.7.1 Disaster Management Policy for Environment and Local Action

India has adopted various policies and frameworks to address disaster management, including those that focus on the environment and local action. Let us explore in detail the disaster management policies and initiatives in India that emphasize environmental protection and local community participation:

National Disaster Management Policy (2009): The National Disaster Management Policy is a comprehensive framework that outlines India's approach to disaster management. It aims to minimize the adverse impacts of disasters and enhance the resilience of communities and ecosystems. The policy emphasizes the importance of integrating environmental considerations into all phases of disaster management, including mitigation, preparedness, response, and recovery.

A] Key Elements of the National Disaster Management Policy:

Community Participation: The policy recognizes the central role of local communities in disaster management. It promotes community-based disaster risk reduction (CBDRR) approaches, empowering communities to identify risks, develop mitigation strategies, and participate in decision-making processes.

Environment Protection and Conservation: The policy highlights the need to protect and conserve the environment to reduce disaster risks. It encourages measures such as afforestation, wetland preservation, and sustainable land use planning to enhance ecosystem resilience.

Climate Change Adaptation: Recognizing the link between climate change and disasters, the policy advocates for climate change adaptation strategies as part of disaster risk reduction efforts.

Institutional Strengthening: The policy emphasizes strengthening institutions at all levels to effectively manage disasters. It promotes capacity building, research, and knowledge sharing to enhance disaster management capabilities.

Public Awareness and Education: The policy stresses the importance of public awareness and education to create a culture of safety and resilience. It encourages the dissemination of information about disaster risks and preparedness measures to the general public.

National Disaster Management Plan (2016): The National Disaster Management Plan is a comprehensive document that operationalizes the National Disaster Management Policy. It provides guidelines and standard operating procedures for various disaster management activities, including those related to environmental protection and local action.

B] Key Aspects of the National Disaster Management Plan:

Environment and Ecosystem Management: The plan emphasizes the protection and restoration of ecosystems as a crucial aspect of disaster risk reduction. It encourages the promotion of sustainable practices and the integration of environmental considerations into all development projects.

Community-Based Disaster Risk Reduction: The plan emphasizes the importance of involving local communities in disaster risk reduction efforts. It outlines strategies for empowering communities, conducting vulnerability assessments, and promoting community-led initiatives.

Early Warning Systems: The plan stresses the establishment and strengthening of early warning systems to alert communities about impending disasters, including environmental hazards like floods, cyclones, and landslides.

Capacity Building and Training: The plan prioritizes capacity building and training for disaster management personnel and local communities. It aims to enhance the technical skills and knowledge required for effective disaster response and recovery.

Knowledge Management and Research: The plan emphasizes the need for data-driven decision-making and encourages research and data collection on disaster risk, vulnerability, and environmental impacts.

Thus, India's disaster management policies, including the National Disaster Management Policy and National Disaster Management Plan, demonstrate the country's commitment to integrating environmental considerations and local action into disaster management practices. By prioritizing community participation, environment protection, climate change adaptation, and capacity building, India aims to enhance its resilience to disasters and create a safer and more sustainable future for its people and ecosystems. However, continuous efforts and effective implementation of these policies are crucial to ensure successful disaster management outcomes and address the growing challenges posed by environmental risks and climate change impacts.

11.7.2 National Disaster Management Policy (2009):

Disasters are a significant threat to human lives, infrastructure, and the environment. India, being prone to various natural and man-made disasters, recognizes the importance of effective disaster management. The National Disaster Management Policy, formulated in 2009, serves as a comprehensive framework to guide the country's disaster management efforts. The policy emphasizes a proactive approach, community participation, and sustainable practices to build resilience and safeguard lives and assets.

C] **Key Objectives of the National Disaster Management Policy (2009):**

Minimize Vulnerability and Risk: The primary objective of the policy is to reduce vulnerability to disasters and minimize associated risks. It focuses on strengthening the country's capacity to manage potential disasters effectively.

Mainstream Disaster Risk Reduction (DRR): The policy aims to integrate disaster risk reduction into all developmental plans and policies to ensure that disaster considerations are considered during development activities.

Community Participation: The policy recognizes the central role of communities in disaster management. It aims to foster community participation in all phases of disaster management, from planning and preparedness to response and recovery.

Capacity Building and Training: Building the capacity of disaster management agencies, first responders, and communities is a crucial aspect of the policy. It emphasizes continuous training, research, and knowledge dissemination.

Effective Response and Recovery: The policy emphasizes strengthening the country's response and recovery capabilities to minimize the impact of disasters and facilitate speedy recovery.

Institutional Strengthening: The policy focuses on strengthening the institutional framework for disaster management at the national, state, and local levels. It aims to enhance coordination among various agencies and stakeholders involved in disaster management.

D] Key Components of the National Disaster Management Policy (2009):

Disaster Risk Reduction (DRR): The policy highlights the importance of adopting a proactive approach to disaster management. It stresses the need to identify and address underlying risk factors to reduce the likelihood and impact of disasters.

Vulnerability and Risk Assessment: The policy emphasizes the importance of conducting vulnerability and risk assessments to identify high-risk areas and populations. This assessment helps prioritize disaster risk reduction measures.

Community-Based Disaster Management: Recognizing the resilience of local communities, the policy promotes community-based disaster management. It encourages the active involvement of communities in disaster preparedness, response, and recovery.

Early Warning Systems: The policy underscores the establishment of effective early warning systems to alert communities about impending disasters. Timely warnings enable communities to take appropriate preparedness measures.

Capacity Development: Building the capacity of government agencies, first responders, and communities is a key focus of the policy. It advocates continuous training and knowledge sharing to enhance disaster management capabilities.

Coordination and Networking: The policy stresses the need for effective coordination among various stakeholders involved in disaster management. It promotes networking and collaboration to ensure a cohesive response.

E] Implementation of the National Disaster Management Policy (2009):

The successful implementation of the policy requires the active participation and cooperation of various stakeholders, including government agencies, non-governmental organizations (NGOs), civil society, private sector, and communities. To ensure effective implementation, the following measures are essential:

Legislation and Regulatory Framework: Enactment of appropriate laws and regulations related to disaster management is crucial to provide a legal basis for disaster response and recovery.

Capacity Building: Investing in training and capacity building of disaster management personnel is essential to enhance their skills and knowledge.

Public Awareness and Education: Creating awareness among the public about disaster risks and preparedness measures is crucial to foster a culture of safety.

Research and Innovation: Encouraging research and innovation in disaster management helps in developing new technologies and approaches for better response and recovery.

Funding and Resource Allocation: Adequate funding and resource allocation are essential to support disaster management initiatives effectively.

Thus, the National Disaster Management Policy (2009) lays a solid foundation for disaster risk reduction and management in India. By emphasizing a proactive approach, community participation, and capacity building, the policy aims to enhance the country's resilience to disasters and safeguard lives and assets. Continuous efforts and effective implementation of the policy are necessary to address the growing challenges posed by disasters and ensure a safer and more sustainable future for all citizens of India.

11.7.3 National Disaster Management Plan (2016):

Disasters have become a recurring reality in India, posing significant threats to human lives, infrastructure, and the environment. To effectively respond to and mitigate the impact of disasters, the Government of India formulated the National Disaster Management Plan (NDMP) in 2016. The plan is a comprehensive and all-encompassing document that outlines the country's approach to disaster management across all phases of the disaster management cycle.

A] Key Objectives of the National Disaster Management Plan (2016):

Comprehensive Approach: The NDMP aims to provide a holistic and integrated framework for disaster management that addresses the unique challenges posed by various natural and man-made disasters.

Proactive Preparedness: The plan focuses on proactive preparedness measures to reduce the vulnerability of communities and infrastructure to disasters. It aims to strengthen the country's resilience by investing in risk reduction and mitigation efforts.

Community Involvement: Recognizing the importance of community participation in disaster management, the plan emphasizes the involvement of local communities in all stages of disaster management, from planning to response and recovery.

Coordination and Cooperation: The plan promotes effective coordination and cooperation among various stakeholders, including government agencies, non-governmental organizations (NGOs), civil society, private sector, and international organizations.

Building Capacity: Enhancing the capacity of disaster management agencies, first responders, and communities is a key objective of the NDMP. It emphasizes training, knowledge dissemination, and the use of modern technologies for effective response.

Mainstreaming Disaster Risk Reduction (DRR): The plan seeks to integrate disaster risk reduction considerations into all developmental plans and policies to ensure sustainable and resilient development.

A] Key Components of the National Disaster Management Plan (2016):

Prevention and Mitigation: The plan emphasizes the importance of investing in preventive measures and mitigation efforts to reduce the impact of disasters. It includes measures like building codes, land-use planning, and early warning systems.

Risk Assessment and Mapping: Conducting comprehensive risk assessments and hazard mapping is crucial for effective disaster management. The plan outlines guidelines for vulnerability and risk assessment across various sectors.

Community-Based Disaster Management: The NDMP recognizes the role of local communities in disaster management and encourages community-based approaches for preparedness and response.

Capacity Building and Training: Building the capacity of disaster management agencies, first responders, and communities is a key focus of the plan. It includes training programs, simulation exercises, and knowledge sharing initiatives.

Early Warning and Communication: The plan emphasizes the establishment of robust early warning systems and communication networks to disseminate timely information to the public.

Infrastructure and Essential Services: Ensuring the resilience of critical infrastructure and essential services like healthcare, transportation, and utilities is vital for effective disaster response and recovery.

B] Implementation of the National Disaster Management Plan (2016):

The successful implementation of the NDMP requires a multi-pronged approach involving various stakeholders. The following measures are essential for effective implementation:

Policy and Legal Framework: The plan needs to be supported by appropriate policies and legal frameworks that provide the necessary authority and mandate for disaster management activities.

Capacity Building and Training: Investing in training and capacity building of disaster management personnel and community volunteers is crucial for effective response and recovery.

Public Awareness and Education: Creating awareness among the public about disaster risks, preparedness, and response measures is essential for building a culture of safety.

Technology and Innovation: Embracing modern technologies like GIS, remote sensing, and communication tools can significantly enhance disaster management capabilities.

Coordination and Collaboration: Effective coordination among various stakeholders is essential for a cohesive and synchronized disaster response.

Funding and Resource Allocation: Adequate funding and resource allocation are necessary to support disaster management initiatives effectively.

Thus, the National Disaster Management Plan (2016) reflects India's commitment to building a resilient and disaster-ready nation. By adopting a comprehensive approach, involving local communities, and investing in capacity building and technology, the plan aims to enhance India's ability to respond to and mitigate the impact of disasters. Continuous efforts and effective implementation of the NDMP are crucial to address the growing challenges posed by disasters and ensure a safer and more sustainable future for all citizens of India.

11.7.4 Funding Sources for Disaster Management in India

Disaster management in India is funded through various sources, including both government and non-government channels. These funding sources are essential to support disaster response, relief, recovery, and risk reduction efforts. Here are the main funding sources for disaster management in India:

National Disaster Response Fund (NDRF): The National Disaster Response Fund is a dedicated fund established under the Disaster Management Act, 2005. It is managed by the Central Government and is used to finance immediate relief and response operations during major disasters. The fund is supplemented through budgetary allocations from the government and contributions from various sources.

State Disaster Response Fund (SDRF): Similar to the NDRF, each state and Union Territory has a State Disaster Response Fund, which is used to finance disaster response and relief activities at the state level. It is funded through budgetary allocations from the respective state governments and contributions from other sources.

Calamity Relief Fund (CRF): The Calamity Relief Fund is a state-specific fund created to support the immediate response and relief activities during disasters and calamities. It is financed through budgetary allocations from the state government and contributions from other sources.

Corporate Social Responsibility (CSR) Funds: Many private sector companies in India allocate a portion of their profits for Corporate Social Responsibility (CSR) activities. CSR funds are often utilized to support disaster relief and rehabilitation efforts, especially by companies with operations in disaster-prone areas.

International Assistance and Aid: During major disasters, international organizations, foreign governments, and donor agencies often extend financial and material assistance to India. These contributions are used to augment the resources available for disaster management activities.

Public Donations and Contributions: Public donations and contributions from individuals, community organizations, and philanthropic institutions play a significant role in disaster response and relief efforts. Donations can be made directly to government disaster relief funds, NGOs, or other recognized relief agencies.

Bilateral and Multilateral Aid: India also receives financial support from bilateral and multilateral agencies for disaster management initiatives. These funds may be channelled through specific projects aimed at disaster risk reduction, capacity building, and response planning.

National and International NGOs: Non-Governmental Organizations (NGOs) operating in India also mobilize funds from various sources, including domestic and international donors, to support their disaster response and relief activities.

Insurance and Risk Transfer Mechanisms: Insurance companies offer disaster-related insurance products to individuals and businesses to mitigate financial losses caused by disasters.

In some cases, the government may also utilize insurance and risk transfer mechanisms to manage the financial impact of disasters.

Central and State Government Budgetary Allocations: Both the Central Government and state governments allocate funds in their annual budgets for disaster management activities. These allocations are used for capacity building, infrastructure development, awareness campaigns, and other disaster risk reduction measures.

World Bank and International Financial Institution Projects: India also receives funding for disaster risk reduction and management projects from international financial institutions like the World Bank and the Asian Development Bank.

It is essential to have a diverse range of funding sources to ensure that disaster management efforts are adequately resourced and sustainable. A combination of government funding, private sector contributions, international aid, and public donations enables a comprehensive and well-coordinated response to disasters in India.

11.7.5 Institutional Capacity Building Initiatives in India

Institutional capacity building is crucial for enhancing disaster management in India. It involves strengthening the knowledge, skills, and resources of various organizations, agencies, and stakeholders involved in disaster preparedness, response, and recovery. Several initiatives have been undertaken in India to improve institutional capacity in disaster management. Some of the key initiatives include:

National Institute of Disaster Management (NIDM): NIDM is the premier institute in India dedicated to disaster management training, education, research, and capacity building. It offers various training programs, workshops, and courses for government officials, professionals, and community members to enhance their understanding of disaster risk reduction and management.

State Disaster Management Institutes (SDMIs): Several states in India have established State Disaster Management Institutes (SDMIs) to provide training and capacity-building programs at the state level. These institutes offer courses tailored to the specific disaster risks and challenges faced by each state.

District Disaster Management Authorities (DDMAs): District Disaster Management Authorities play a vital role in disaster preparedness and response at the district level. Capacity-building initiatives are often conducted to train district-level officials, first responders, and community members to effectively manage disasters.

National and State Disaster Response Forces (NDRF and SDRF): The NDRF and SDRF are specialized forces responsible for disaster response and rescue operations. Regular training and exercises are conducted to keep these forces prepared for rapid deployment during emergencies.

Community-Based Disaster Management (CBDM) Programs: The government and various NGOs conduct community-based disaster management programs to empower communities with the knowledge and skills to prepare for and respond to disasters effectively. These initiatives promote community resilience and reduce vulnerabilities.

Mock Drills and Exercises: Regular mock drills and simulation exercises are conducted at various levels to test disaster preparedness plans and response capabilities. These drills help identify gaps and improve coordination among different agencies.

Capacity Building for Specific Hazards: Initiatives are undertaken to build specialized capacity for managing specific hazards like earthquakes, floods, cyclones, droughts, chemical accidents, etc. Training and workshops focus on the unique challenges posed by each type of disaster.

International Collaboration and Training Programs: India collaborates with international organizations, such as the United Nations and other countries, for disaster management training and knowledge exchange. These collaborations facilitate the adoption of best practices and global standards.

School Safety Programs: Capacity-building initiatives for school teachers and students focus on school safety and preparedness. These programs are designed to ensure the safety of students during disasters and to promote a culture of disaster awareness in schools.

Public Awareness and Information Dissemination: Capacity building includes raising public awareness about disaster risks and promoting a culture of preparedness. Information dissemination through mass media, social media, and community engagement helps in educating the general public about disaster management.

Training for NGOs and Volunteer Organizations: Capacity-building initiatives also target NGOs and volunteer organizations involved in disaster response and relief efforts. Training programs equip them with the necessary skills to work effectively during emergencies.

By investing in institutional capacity building, India aims to strengthen the entire disaster management ecosystem. Building the knowledge and skills of key stakeholders helps in fostering a culture of safety and preparedness, leading to more effective disaster response and risk reduction.

11.8 Disaster Management Act 2005

Disasters, both natural and man-made, have the potential to cause widespread devastation and disrupt the lives of millions. Recognizing the need for a robust and coordinated approach to disaster management, India enacted the Disaster Management Act, 2005. This comprehensive legislation serves as the foundation for effective disaster risk reduction, preparedness, response, and recovery in the country. The Act establishes institutional mechanisms, delineates the roles and responsibilities of various stakeholders, and emphasizes the importance of community participation and coordination to build a more disaster-resilient nation.

A] **Key Provisions of the Disaster Management Act, 2005:**

Institutional Setup: The Act sets up the National Disaster Management Authority (NDMA) at the national level, State Disaster

Management Authorities (SDMAs) at the state level, and District Disaster Management Authorities (DDMAs) at the district level. These bodies are responsible for formulating policies, plans, and guidelines for disaster management and coordinating response efforts.

National, State, and District Plans: The Act mandates the formulation of the National Disaster Management Plan, State Disaster Management Plan, and District Disaster Management Plan. These plans outline the roles and responsibilities of various authorities and stakeholders, ensuring a coordinated and comprehensive approach to disaster management.

Disaster Management Funds: The Act establishes the National Disaster Response Fund (NDRF) at the national level and the State Disaster Response Fund (SDRF) at the state level. These funds are utilized to finance disaster response and relief operations.

National Disaster Response Force (NDRF): The Act provides for the establishment of the National Disaster Response Force (NDRF), a specialized force responsible for quick and effective search and rescue operations during disasters.

Disaster Mitigation and Preparedness: The Act emphasizes the importance of disaster mitigation and preparedness. It calls for regular mock drills, capacity building programs, and public awareness campaigns to enhance the nation's readiness to face disasters.

B] **Importance and Impacts of the Disaster Management Act, 2005:**

Coordinated Response: The Act's institutional setup ensures a coordinated response to disasters at various levels. The clear distribution of roles and responsibilities among different authorities enhances the efficiency of disaster management efforts.

Proactive Risk Reduction: The Act prioritizes disaster risk reduction and promotes the integration of risk reduction measures into development planning. This proactive approach helps minimize vulnerabilities and potential losses.

Community Participation: The Act recognizes the significance of community participation in disaster management. It encourages the involvement of local communities in preparedness activities, early warning systems, and response measures.

Capacity Building: The Act's focus on capacity building enhances the skills and knowledge of disaster management personnel. Training programs and exercises enable authorities to respond effectively to disasters.

Legal Framework for Relief Measures: The Act provides a legal basis for declaring a disaster and implementing relief measures. This ensures that assistance reaches affected individuals and communities promptly.

C] **Challenges and Way Forward:**

Implementation Gap: Despite the Act's provisions, there may be challenges in its effective implementation, including resource constraints, lack of awareness, and bureaucratic hurdles. Addressing these challenges requires sustained efforts and commitment.

Integration with Development Planning: Integrating disaster risk reduction into development planning remains a challenge. More comprehensive efforts are needed to ensure that development projects consider disaster resilience.

Technology and Data Management: Enhancing the use of technology and data management is critical for improving early warning systems, risk assessments, and information dissemination during disasters.

Thus, The Disaster Management Act, 2005, stands as a landmark legislation that reinforces India's commitment to building disaster resilience and preparedness. By establishing a comprehensive legal framework and institutional setup, the Act enhances the nation's ability to respond to disasters effectively. However, it requires continuous efforts from all stakeholders, including the government, NGOs, private sector, and communities, to ensure its successful implementation. Emphasizing capacity building, community engagement, and proactive risk reduction will pave the way for a more resilient and disaster-ready India in the future.

D] **Provisions of Disaster Management Act 2005**

The Disaster Management Act, 2005 is a comprehensive legislation in India that provides a legal framework for effective disaster management. It aims to ensure a proactive, holistic, and coordinated approach towards disaster preparedness, response, and recovery. The Act empowers various authorities at the national, state, and district levels to carry out disaster management activities. Here are the key provisions of the Disaster Management Act, 2005, explained in detail:

National Disaster Management Authority (NDMA): The Act establishes the National Disaster Management Authority (NDMA) at the national level. The NDMA is the apex body responsible for policy formulation, coordination, and implementation of disaster management plans at the national level. The Prime Minister of India serves as the Chairperson of the NDMA.

State Disaster Management Authorities (SDMAs): Each state and Union Territory in India has a State Disaster Management Authority (SDMA) responsible for disaster management within its jurisdiction. The Chief Minister of the state serves as the Chairperson of the SDMA.

District Disaster Management Authorities (DDMAs): The Act mandates the establishment of District Disaster Management Authorities (DDMAs) at the district level. The District Collector or District Magistrate serves as the Chairperson of the DDMA.

National Plan, State Plans, and District Plans: The Act requires the formulation of the National Disaster Management Plan, State Disaster Management Plan, and District Disaster Management Plan. These plans outline the roles and responsibilities of various authorities, agencies, and stakeholders in disaster management and ensure a coordinated response to disasters.

Disaster Management Funds: The Act provides for the creation of two funds – the National Disaster Response Fund (NDRF) and the State Disaster Response Fund (SDRF). These funds are used to finance disaster response and relief operations. The NDRF is managed by the Central Government, and the SDRF is managed by each state government.

National Disaster Response Force (NDRF): The Act provides for the establishment of specialized response forces called the National Disaster Response Force (NDRF). These forces are responsible for undertaking quick and effective search and rescue operations during disasters.

Responsibilities of Central Ministries and Departments: The Act mandates all central ministries and departments to integrate disaster management into their development plans, projects, and policies. It promotes a whole-of-government approach to disaster risk reduction.

Disaster Mitigation, Preparedness, and Awareness: The Act emphasizes the importance of disaster mitigation, preparedness, and public awareness. It aims to reduce the impact of disasters by taking proactive measures to minimize risks and promote community preparedness.

Disaster Response and Relief Measures: The Act lays down the procedures for declaring a disaster, coordinating disaster response efforts, and providing relief measures to affected individuals and communities.

National Institute of Disaster Management (NIDM): The Act provides for the establishment of the National Institute of Disaster Management (NIDM). NIDM is responsible for training, research, and capacity building in disaster management.

Powers of NDMA, SDMAs, and DDMAs: The Act confers certain powers on NDMA, SDMAs, and DDMAs to issue guidelines, directions, and advisories for disaster management.

Information Management: The Act emphasizes the importance of information management and coordination among different authorities and stakeholders during disaster response.

Cooperation and Coordination: The Act promotes cooperation and coordination among various agencies, departments, and organizations involved in disaster management.

Penalties and Offences: The Act prescribes penalties for obstructing disaster response operations, making false claims for relief, or providing false information during disasters.

National Executive Committee (NEC) and State Executive Committee (SEC): The Act provides for the constitution of the National Executive Committee (NEC) and State Executive Committee (SEC). These committees assist NDMA and SDMAs, respectively, in the implementation of disaster management plans and policies.

Capacity Building and Training: The Act emphasizes the importance of capacity building and training for disaster management personnel at various levels. It encourages the development of specialized skills and knowledge to enhance disaster response and mitigation efforts.

Public Awareness and Education: The Act stresses the need to raise public awareness and education about disaster risks, preparedness, and response measures. It promotes the dissemination of information through media, awareness campaigns, and community engagement.

Preparedness Measures for Different Types of Disasters: The Act recognizes that different types of disasters require tailored preparedness measures. It provides provisions for specific disaster types like chemical disasters, nuclear disasters, biological disasters, and radiological emergencies.

Integration of Disaster Risk Reduction in Development Plans: The Act calls for the integration of disaster risk reduction considerations into development plans and projects. It aims to ensure that development activities are conducted in a manner that reduces disaster vulnerabilities.

Research and Development: The Act encourages research and development in disaster management and risk reduction. It recognizes the importance of continuous learning and innovation to enhance disaster preparedness and response.

International Cooperation: The Act acknowledges the significance of international cooperation in disaster management. It encourages collaboration with foreign countries and international organizations for capacity building, knowledge sharing, and technical assistance.

Special Provisions for Epidemic Diseases: The Act includes special provisions to deal with the management of epidemic diseases, including the declaration of epidemic areas and the implementation of containment measures.

Preparedness of Essential Services: The Act emphasizes the need for ensuring the preparedness of essential services, such as health facilities, water supply, communication networks, and power infrastructure, to maintain their functionality during disasters.

Recovery and Rehabilitation: The Act outlines measures for post-disaster recovery and rehabilitation, focusing on restoring normalcy, rebuilding infrastructure, and supporting affected communities in their recovery efforts.

Institutional Coordination and Information Exchange: The Act promotes institutional coordination and information exchange among various disaster management authorities and stakeholders to ensure a seamless and efficient response.

Disaster Risk Assessment and Vulnerability Analysis: The Act emphasizes the importance of conducting disaster risk assessments and vulnerability analysis to identify potential hazards and areas prone to disasters.

The Disaster Management Act, 2005, is a comprehensive legislation that empowers India's disaster management authorities to take proactive measures in disaster risk reduction, preparedness, response, and recovery. It underscores the significance of a coordinated and integrated approach involving multiple stakeholders to build a resilient and disaster-ready nation. The Act plays a critical role in guiding disaster management efforts in India and serves as a legal framework for addressing the challenges posed by various types of disasters effectively.

11.9 Role of Red Cross Society during Disaster Management

The Red Cross Society, also known as the International Red Cross and Red Crescent Movement, is a global humanitarian organization dedicated to providing aid, relief, and support during emergencies and disasters. Founded in 1863 by Henry Dunant, the Red Cross Society has since grown to become one of the most recognized and respected organizations in disaster management worldwide. Its core principles of humanity, impartiality, neutrality, independence, voluntary service, unity, and universality guide its actions in delivering assistance to those in need.

Preparedness and Early Warning: The Red Cross Society plays a vital role in disaster preparedness and early warning efforts. It collaborates with national and local authorities to develop and implement disaster preparedness plans, ensuring communities are equipped to respond effectively to potential hazards. Red Cross volunteers engage in risk assessments, hazard mapping, and community education, enabling people to understand the risks they face and take proactive measures to mitigate them.

Emergency Response and Relief: When disasters strike, the Red Cross Society responds rapidly with emergency relief efforts. Its trained volunteers and staff work on the ground to provide essential aid, including food, water, shelter, medical care, and psychosocial support to affected communities. The organization's global network ensures a coordinated response, mobilizing resources from various Red Cross and Red Crescent Societies worldwide to provide timely assistance.

Medical Support and First Aid: Red Cross volunteers are often the first responders during emergencies, providing essential medical support and first aid to the injured. Their presence at disaster sites helps stabilize and treat victims until professional medical services can arrive. Additionally, the Red Cross Society runs hospitals, clinics, and mobile medical units to offer healthcare services during disasters.

Psychosocial Support: Disasters can have a profound impact on the mental and emotional well-being of affected individuals. The Red Cross Society offers psychosocial support through trained volunteers, counsellors, and mental health professionals. They provide a safe space for people to express their feelings, cope with trauma, and rebuild their lives.

Water, Sanitation, and Hygiene (WASH) Services: Access to clean water and proper sanitation is crucial during disasters to prevent the spread of diseases. The Red Cross Society sets up WASH facilities, including clean water points, latrines, and hygiene promotion activities, to ensure basic hygiene needs are met in affected areas.

Recovery and Rehabilitation: The Red Cross Society's role does not end with immediate relief efforts. It stays involved in the long-term recovery and rehabilitation process. This includes supporting communities to rebuild homes, livelihoods, and infrastructure, ensuring they regain their self-sufficiency.

Capacity Building and Training: The Red Cross Society places a strong emphasis on capacity building and training. It conducts disaster preparedness and response training programs for volunteers and communities, empowering them to take an active role in disaster management. By strengthening local capacities, the Red Cross Society fosters resilience and self-reliance.

International Cooperation and Advocacy: The Red Cross Society's international network enables it to advocate for disaster-affected communities on a global stage. It works closely with governments, international organizations, and other humanitarian agencies to influence policies, share best practices, and advocate for the needs and rights of affected populations.

Gender and Inclusivity: The Red Cross Society is committed to promoting gender equality and inclusivity in disaster management. It ensures that the specific needs and vulnerabilities of women, children, elderly, and persons with disabilities are addressed during emergencies.

Thus, the Red Cross Society's role during disaster management is indispensable. Its humanitarian principles, global network, and dedicated volunteers make it a powerful force in responding to emergencies and alleviating the suffering of affected communities. By prioritizing preparedness, timely response, and long-term support, the Red Cross Society continues to save lives, restore dignity, and build resilience in the face of disasters worldwide. Its unwavering commitment to humanity and compassion exemplifies the spirit of solidarity and collective responsibility in times of crisis.

11.10 Role of UNO during Disaster Management

Disasters, whether natural or man-made, can cause widespread devastation and impact millions of lives. Recognizing the global nature of disasters and their cross-border implications, the United Nations (UN) plays a crucial role in disaster management. The UN, through various specialized agencies and mechanisms, mobilizes international support, coordinates response efforts, and advocates for disaster risk reduction and resilience-building worldwide.

Coordination and Leadership: The UN serves as a central coordinating body during disaster response and recovery efforts. It brings together various UN agencies, humanitarian organizations, and governments to streamline relief efforts and prevent duplication of resources. The UN Office for the Coordination of Humanitarian Affairs (OCHA) is at the forefront of coordinating emergency response efforts and ensuring effective collaboration among stakeholders.

Early Warning and Preparedness: The UN supports the establishment and enhancement of early warning systems to alert countries and communities about potential disasters. This includes systems for cyclones, tsunamis, floods, and other hazards. The UN provides technical assistance and capacity building to countries to strengthen their preparedness and response mechanisms.

Emergency Humanitarian Assistance: The UN, through agencies like the World Food Programme (WFP), UNICEF, and the World Health Organization (WHO), delivers critical humanitarian assistance to affected populations. This includes food, clean water, shelter, healthcare, and other essential supplies required to sustain life during emergencies.

Protection and Human Rights: The UN prioritizes the protection of vulnerable populations, including women, children, refugees, and internally displaced persons (IDPs) during disasters. It ensures that the human rights of affected communities are respected, and efforts are made to prevent and address issues like human trafficking, violence, and exploitation in crisis situations.

Capacity Building and Training: The UN provides technical support and training to governments and communities in disaster-prone regions to enhance their capacity for disaster risk reduction and management. This includes promoting sustainable development practices, climate change adaptation, and resilience-building measures.

Advocacy for Disaster Risk Reduction: The UN advocates for disaster risk reduction at the global, regional, and national levels. It works to raise awareness about the importance of disaster risk reduction and the need to invest in prevention and preparedness measures.

Climate Change Mitigation and Adaptation: As disasters are increasingly influenced by climate change, the UN takes a proactive approach to climate change mitigation and adaptation. It promotes international agreements and initiatives to reduce greenhouse gas emissions and supports vulnerable countries in adapting to climate impacts.

Peacekeeping and Conflict Resolution: The UN's peacekeeping missions play a crucial role in conflict-affected regions, where disasters can exacerbate existing vulnerabilities. By maintaining peace and stability, peacekeeping operations contribute to creating an environment conducive to effective disaster response and recovery.

International Policy and Legal Framework: The UN has established international policies and legal frameworks to guide disaster response and risk reduction efforts. For example, the Sendai Framework for Disaster Risk Reduction provides a roadmap for reducing disaster risks and building resilience.

Thus, the United Nations plays a pivotal role in disaster management, leveraging its global reach, expertise, and diplomatic influence to support countries and communities in times of crisis. By coordinating emergency response efforts, providing humanitarian assistance, advocating for disaster risk reduction, and addressing the root causes of vulnerability, the UN continues to make significant contributions to global efforts to mitigate the impact of disasters and build resilient societies. As disasters become more frequent and complex, the UN's leadership and commitment to promoting international cooperation remain essential in addressing the challenges posed by disasters and securing a safer and more sustainable future for all.

11.11 Role of European Union during Disaster Management

The European Union (EU) is a regional political and economic union consisting of 27 European countries. While the EU primarily focuses on economic integration and political cooperation, it also plays a significant role in disaster management. With its member states facing various natural and man-made hazards, the EU has developed a comprehensive framework to coordinate disaster response, help, and promote resilience-building measures across its territory.

Coordination and Cooperation: The EU serves as a coordinating body for disaster management efforts among its member states. It facilitates cooperation and information exchange among countries to ensure a coherent and effective response to disasters.

European Emergency Response Coordination Centre (ERCC): The ERCC is the central hub for coordinating EU-wide emergency response efforts. It monitors disasters, mobilizes resources, and deploys EU Civil Protection assets to support affected countries.

Emergency Response and Assistance: Through its Civil Protection Mechanism, the EU provides emergency assistance to member states facing major disasters. This includes deploying specialized teams, equipment, and humanitarian aid to support affected communities.

Solidarity and Financial Assistance: The EU demonstrates solidarity with member states during disasters by providing financial assistance and grants. The EU Solidarity Fund has been instrumental in providing financial support for recovery and reconstruction efforts.

Preparedness and Risk Reduction: The EU emphasizes disaster preparedness and risk reduction measures. It supports member states in developing national disaster risk management strategies, conducting risk assessments, and implementing preventive measures.

Climate Change Adaptation: Recognizing the impact of climate change on disaster frequency and intensity, the EU emphasizes climate change adaptation and mitigation strategies to reduce disaster risks.

Research and Innovation: The EU promotes research and innovation in disaster management technologies and practices. It funds projects that focus on improving disaster resilience and response capabilities.

Cross-Border Cooperation: Disasters often cross national borders, requiring cooperation among neighbouring countries. The EU facilitates cross-border collaboration to enhance regional disaster management efforts.

Humanitarian Aid and Crisis Response: The EU is a significant donor of humanitarian aid globally. It provides funding and resources to support emergency response efforts in non-EU countries affected by disasters.

Disaster Response Exercises: The EU conducts joint disaster response exercises to test its emergency response mechanisms and improve preparedness.

Crisis Communication: The EU plays a role in disseminating timely and accurate information during disasters, ensuring public awareness and facilitating coordination among relevant stakeholders.

Thus, the European Union's role in disaster management is a testament to the power of regional cooperation and solidarity. By coordinating response efforts, providing financial assistance, promoting risk reduction measures, and facilitating cross-border cooperation, the EU contributes to building resilience and reducing the impact of disasters on its member states. In a world facing increasing disaster risks and challenges, the EU's commitment to disaster management and humanitarian assistance is a vital component of its broader mission to promote peace, stability, and prosperity among its members and beyond.

11.12 Role of World Bank during Disaster Management

The World Bank is a multilateral financial institution that provides loans, grants, and technical assistance to developing countries for various development projects. While its primary focus is on poverty reduction and sustainable development, the World Bank also plays a significant role in disaster management. As disasters can have severe economic and social impacts on countries, the World Bank's involvement in disaster management is crucial for supporting affected populations and promoting resilience-building measures.

Emergency Response and Recovery: The World Bank responds swiftly to disasters by providing emergency financial assistance to affected countries. This support helps governments address immediate needs such as infrastructure repair, healthcare, and humanitarian aid for affected communities.

Disaster Risk Financing and Insurance: The World Bank encourages countries to invest in disaster risk financing and insurance mechanisms. It helps governments develop risk financing strategies, including catastrophe bonds and insurance schemes, to better manage the financial burden of disasters.

Risk Assessments and Capacity Building: The World Bank conducts risk assessments and vulnerability analyses in disaster-prone regions to identify potential hazards and vulnerabilities. It then provides technical assistance and capacity-building programs to strengthen countries' disaster preparedness and response capabilities.

Resilience-Building Measures: The World Bank supports projects that aim to enhance resilience and reduce disaster risks. These projects may include infrastructure improvements, climate change adaptation measures, and community-based disaster management initiatives.

Sustainable Recovery and Reconstruction: After disasters, the World Bank supports sustainable recovery and reconstruction efforts. It encourages countries to rebuild infrastructure in a more resilient and environmentally friendly manner, ensuring that reconstruction efforts contribute to long-term development goals.

Public Financial Management: The World Bank assists countries in strengthening their public financial management systems to ensure that funds are effectively used for disaster response and recovery efforts.

Disaster Risk Reduction: The World Bank promotes disaster risk reduction by integrating risk considerations into development planning and investment projects. This ensures that development activities consider potential disaster impacts.

Knowledge Sharing and Best Practices: The World Bank serves as a platform for knowledge sharing and best practices in disaster management. It facilitates information exchange among countries and partners to improve disaster response and risk reduction strategies.

Regional and Global Collaboration: The World Bank collaborates with regional organizations and other international agencies in disaster management efforts. It works closely with the United Nations, the International Monetary Fund (IMF), and other partners to provide a coordinated and effective response to disasters.

Thus, the World Bank's role in disaster management is instrumental in supporting countries in times of crisis and promoting resilience-building measures. Through emergency financial assistance, risk financing strategies, capacity building, and support for sustainable recovery and reconstruction, the World Bank helps countries recover from disasters and reduce their vulnerability to future events. By integrating disaster risk reduction into development planning and sharing knowledge and best practices, the World Bank contributes to building a safer and more sustainable future for vulnerable populations worldwide. As disasters continue to pose challenges to global development, the World Bank's commitment to disaster management remains essential in achieving its mission of poverty reduction and shared prosperity.

CHAPTER 12

Case Studies and Best Practices in India

12.1 National Disaster Management Guidelines in India

Disasters, both natural and human-made, pose significant challenges to societies worldwide. India, being a disaster-prone country, has recognized the importance of effective disaster management to mitigate the impact of such events and protect lives and property. The National Disaster Management Guidelines in India serve as a comprehensive framework to guide disaster preparedness, response, recovery, and risk reduction efforts across the country. This essay delves into the key components of the National Disaster Management Guidelines, their objectives, and the strategies employed to build a resilient and disaster-ready nation.

A] National Disaster Management Guidelines: Objectives

The National Disaster Management Guidelines in India are formulated to achieve the following key objectives:

Comprehensive Planning: The guidelines provide a comprehensive framework for planning and implementing disaster management activities at various levels, from the national to the local level.

Multi-Sectoral Approach: The guidelines emphasize a multi-sectoral and inter-agency approach to disaster management, recognizing that effective response and recovery require collaboration among various government departments, non-governmental organizations, and community stakeholders.

Community Involvement: The guidelines emphasize the active involvement of communities in disaster management. Engaging communities in risk reduction efforts ensures that local knowledge and resources are harnessed effectively.

Capacity Building: Capacity building is a crucial aspect of the guidelines. The focus is on enhancing the capabilities of disaster management authorities, responders, and communities to respond effectively to disasters.

Mainstreaming Disaster Risk Reduction: The guidelines promote the integration of disaster risk reduction into development planning and policies to reduce vulnerability and enhance resilience.

B] Key Components of National Disaster Management Guidelines:

Risk Assessment and Mapping: The guidelines stress the importance of conducting comprehensive risk assessments to identify hazards, vulnerabilities, and exposure in different regions of the country. Risk maps are developed to inform decision-making and resource allocation.

Early Warning Systems: Early warning systems are a critical element of disaster management. The guidelines emphasize the establishment of effective and timely early warning mechanisms for various hazards, including cyclones, floods, earthquakes, and tsunamis.

Disaster Response and Relief: The guidelines provide detailed protocols for disaster response and relief operations. These include pre-positioning of resources, coordination mechanisms, and procedures for conducting search and rescue operations.

Disaster Recovery and Rehabilitation: The guidelines outline strategies for post-disaster recovery and rehabilitation. This includes measures to rebuild infrastructure, restore essential services, and support affected communities in rebuilding their lives.

Capacity Building and Training: Capacity building is integral to disaster management. The guidelines highlight the importance of training responders, government officials, and communities in disaster management techniques and protocols.

Public Awareness and Education: The guidelines stress the need for public awareness and education on disaster risks and preparedness measures. Information dissemination campaigns are conducted to inform the public about safety procedures.

Research and Development: The guidelines promote research and development in the field of disaster management. This includes the use of innovative technologies and best practices to enhance disaster preparedness and response.

Resource Mobilization and Funding: The guidelines address the issue of resource mobilization for disaster management activities. It emphasizes the need for adequate funding and resource allocation to strengthen disaster management capabilities.

Thus, the National Disaster Management Guidelines in India play a crucial role in building a resilient and disaster-ready nation. By providing a comprehensive framework for disaster management, the guidelines ensure that efforts are directed towards risk reduction, preparedness, and effective response. Through capacity building, community involvement, and multi-sectoral coordination, India aims to minimize the impact of disasters and safeguard lives and property. As the country continues to face diverse disaster challenges, the National Disaster Management Guidelines provide a roadmap to build a safer and more resilient future for all its citizens.

12.2 Disaster Management practices at working and residential places

Disaster management practices at working and residential places are essential for ensuring the safety and well-being of individuals during emergencies. Whether it is a workplace, school, residential area, or any other setting, having effective disaster management measures in place can significantly reduce the impact of disasters and save lives. Let us explore in detail the disaster management practices at working and residential places in India:

A] **Disaster Management Practices at Working Places:**

Emergency Response Plan (ERP): Every workplace should have a well-defined Emergency Response Plan that outlines specific actions to be taken in various types of emergencies. The ERP should include evacuation procedures, communication protocols, emergency contact information, and roles and responsibilities of employees during a crisis.

Evacuation Drills: Regular evacuation drills should be conducted to familiarize employees with evacuation routes and assembly points. These drills help identify gaps in the evacuation process and ensure a swift and orderly evacuation during a real emergency.

Emergency Communication: Effective communication is crucial during emergencies. Workplaces should have systems in place to quickly disseminate emergency alerts and instructions to all employees. This may include loudspeakers, PA systems, mobile apps, or text messages.

First Aid and Medical Facilities: Workplaces should have adequately stocked first aid kits and trained personnel to provide immediate medical assistance during emergencies. Additionally, access to medical facilities or tie-ups with nearby hospitals should be arranged for more severe incidents.

Fire Safety Measures: Fire is a common workplace hazard. Adequate fire safety measures, such as fire extinguishers, smoke detectors, fire alarms, and sprinkler systems, should be in place and regularly maintained.

Safety Training and Awareness: Employees should undergo regular safety training and awareness programs to understand various types of hazards and appropriate responses. Training should cover fire safety, earthquake preparedness, handling hazardous materials, and other relevant topics.

Disaster Recovery and Business Continuity Planning: Workplaces should have contingency plans in place to recover quickly after a disaster and ensure business continuity. This includes data backup, alternate work locations, and risk assessments for critical operations.

B] Disaster Management Practices at Residential Places:

Home Emergency Plan: Residents should have a household emergency plan that includes escape routes, a meeting place for family members, and contact information for emergency services and neighbours.

Earthquake Preparedness: India is prone to earthquakes, and residential areas should be earthquake-resistant. Residents should be educated about the "Drop, Cover, and Hold On" technique during earthquakes.

Flood Preparedness: For areas prone to flooding, residents should be aware of evacuation routes and have emergency kits with essentials like food, water, first aid supplies, and important documents.

Cyclone Preparedness: Coastal areas are susceptible to cyclones. Residents should be informed about cyclone shelters, evacuation procedures, and early warning systems.

Fire Safety: Residential buildings should have fire safety measures in place, including smoke detectors, fire extinguishers, and fire exits. Residents should be educated about fire prevention and response.

Waste Management: Proper waste management practices can prevent environmental hazards and reduce the risk of disease outbreaks during disasters.

Community Awareness: Engaging with the local community to raise awareness about disaster preparedness and response can lead to a more resilient neighbourhood.

Thus, Effective disaster management practices at working and residential places play a critical role in safeguarding lives and minimizing damage during emergencies. Awareness, training, and preparedness are key elements that can significantly enhance the ability of individuals and communities to respond to disasters effectively. By incorporating these practices into daily routines and regularly conducting drills and exercises, India can build a safer and more disaster-resilient nation.

12.3 Key Responsibilities of Engineers in Disaster Reduction Techniques

Engineers play a vital role in disaster reduction techniques by applying their technical expertise, problem-solving skills, and innovative thinking to mitigate the impact of disasters and enhance community resilience. Some of the key responsibilities of engineers in disaster reduction techniques include:

Risk Assessment and Hazard Analysis: Engineers conduct risk assessments and hazard analyses to identify potential vulnerabilities and threats in communities. They evaluate the susceptibility of infrastructure, buildings, and critical systems to various hazards like earthquakes, floods, cyclones, and other disasters.

Designing Resilient Infrastructure: Engineers are responsible for designing and constructing resilient infrastructure that can withstand the forces of natural disasters. This includes bridges, buildings, roads, water supply systems, and other essential facilities.

Developing Early Warning Systems: Engineers play a crucial role in developing and implementing early warning systems for different types of disasters. These systems provide timely alerts to communities, allowing them to take necessary precautions and evacuate if needed.

Creating Disaster-Resistant Building Codes: Engineers contribute to the development of building codes and regulations that incorporate disaster-resistant features. These codes ensure that structures are constructed to withstand the impact of disasters and minimize potential damage.

Implementing Retrofitting and Strengthening Measures: Engineers retrofit existing structures and buildings to enhance their resilience to disasters. They recommend and implement strengthening measures to improve the structural integrity of buildings.

Designing Flood Control and Drainage Systems: Engineers design flood control and drainage systems to manage water flow during heavy rains and floods. Proper drainage systems help reduce the risk of flooding and associated damages.

Landslide Mitigation: Engineers develop and implement landslide mitigation strategies, such as slope stabilization, to reduce the risk of landslides in hilly and mountainous regions.

Coordinating Emergency Response Plans: Engineers collaborate with disaster management authorities to develop emergency response plans. They help optimize the allocation of resources and coordinate the deployment of technical teams during disasters.

Developing Sustainable and Eco-Friendly Solutions: Engineers strive to develop sustainable and eco-friendly disaster reduction techniques. They consider environmental factors and the long-term impact of their solutions on the ecosystem.

Public Awareness and Education: Engineers play a role in public awareness and education campaigns, disseminating information about disaster risks, preparedness, and safety measures.

Monitoring and Post-Disaster Assessment: Engineers monitor critical infrastructure during disasters and conduct post-disaster assessments to evaluate damages and identify areas for improvement.

Incorporating Climate Change Considerations: Engineers consider climate change scenarios and its potential impact on disaster risks while designing and implementing disaster reduction techniques.

Research and Innovation: Engineers engage in research and innovation to develop new technologies and techniques for disaster risk reduction, leveraging the latest advancements in science and engineering.

The contributions of engineers are essential in developing comprehensive disaster reduction techniques that save lives, protect property, and build more resilient communities. Their expertise is integral to addressing the challenges posed by disasters and working towards a safer and sustainable future

12.3.1 Role and Responsibilities of Civil Engineer in Disaster Management

Civil engineers play a crucial role in disaster management by applying their specialized skills and knowledge to mitigate the impact of disasters, enhance preparedness, and support recovery efforts. Their role encompasses various responsibilities that contribute to building resilience in communities and infrastructure. Here are the key roles and responsibilities of civil engineers in disaster management:

Risk Assessment and Vulnerability Analysis: Civil engineers assess the vulnerability of infrastructure and communities to different types of disasters. They conduct risk assessments to identify potential hazards and vulnerabilities and develop strategies to reduce risks.

Designing Disaster-Resilient Infrastructure: One of the primary responsibilities of civil engineers is to design and construct disaster-resilient infrastructure. They ensure that buildings, bridges, roads, dams, and other critical structures can withstand the forces of natural disasters, minimizing damages and protecting lives.

Developing Early Warning Systems: Civil engineers contribute to the development and implementation of early warning systems for disasters such as floods, cyclones, and earthquakes. These systems provide timely alerts to communities, enabling them to take necessary precautions.

Implementing Retrofitting and Strengthening Measures: Engineers retrofit existing structures to enhance their resilience to disasters. They recommend and implement strengthening measures to improve the structural integrity of buildings and infrastructure.

Planning and Designing Flood Control Measures: Civil engineers are involved in planning and designing flood control measures, including drainage systems, levees, and embankments, to manage water flow during heavy rainfall and reduce the risk of flooding.

Landslide Mitigation and Slope Stabilization: Engineers develop and implement strategies for landslide mitigation, such as slope stabilization measures, to reduce the risk of landslides in vulnerable areas.

Coordination in Emergency Response: During disasters, civil engineers collaborate with disaster management authorities and other professionals to coordinate emergency response efforts. They help optimize the allocation of resources and provide technical expertise.

Post-Disaster Damage Assessment: After a disaster, civil engineers conduct post-disaster damage assessments to evaluate the condition of infrastructure and identify areas for repair and reconstruction.

Community Awareness and Education: Civil engineers participate in public awareness and education campaigns to disseminate information about disaster risks, preparedness, and safety measures to the public.

Environmental Considerations: Engineers consider environmental factors and ecological impacts while designing and implementing disaster management strategies to ensure sustainable solutions.

Incorporating Climate Change Considerations: Civil engineers consider climate change scenarios and potential impacts while developing disaster management plans and adapting infrastructure for future challenges.

Research and Innovation: Engineers engage in research and innovation to develop new technologies and techniques for disaster risk reduction, leveraging the latest advancements in the field.

Post-Disaster Reconstruction and Recovery: Civil engineers play a vital role in post-disaster reconstruction and recovery efforts. They contribute to rebuilding damaged infrastructure and implementing long-term recovery plans.

By fulfilling these roles and responsibilities, civil engineers contribute significantly to disaster management efforts, ensuring the safety and resilience of communities and infrastructure in the face of natural and man-made disasters.

12.3.2 Role and Responsibilities of Civil Engineer in Disaster Risk Reduction

The role of civil engineers in disaster risk reduction (DRR) is critical for minimizing the impact of disasters on communities and infrastructure. Civil engineers apply their expertise in designing, planning, and implementing measures that reduce vulnerabilities and enhance resilience to various hazards. Their responsibilities in disaster risk reduction encompass a range of activities aimed at building safer and more sustainable environments. Here are the key roles and responsibilities of civil engineers in disaster risk reduction:

Hazard Assessment and Risk Analysis: Civil engineers conduct hazard assessments and risk analyses to identify potential threats and vulnerabilities in a given area. They study geological, hydrological, meteorological, and other factors to understand the likelihood and potential impact of various hazards.

Designing Resilient Infrastructure: One of the primary responsibilities of civil engineers in DRR is to design and construct disaster-resilient infrastructure. This includes buildings, bridges, roads, dams, and other critical facilities that can withstand the forces of natural disasters.

Implementing Building Codes and Standards: Civil engineers ensure that construction projects adhere to building codes and standards that incorporate disaster-resistant features. They play a key role in enforcing regulations to improve the safety of structures.

Retrofitting and Upgrading: Engineers are involved in retrofitting existing structures to enhance their resilience to disasters. They recommend and implement measures to strengthen buildings and infrastructure against potential hazards.

Flood Management and Drainage Systems: Civil engineers plan and design flood management and drainage systems to manage water flow during heavy rainfall and prevent flooding in vulnerable areas.

Slope Stabilization and Landslide Mitigation: Engineers develop strategies for slope stabilization and landslide mitigation to minimize the risk of landslides in hilly and mountainous regions.

Coordinating Early Warning Systems: Civil engineers contribute to the development and coordination of early warning systems that provide timely alerts to communities about approaching hazards.

Community Engagement and Awareness: Engineers play a role in engaging with local communities, raising awareness about disaster risks, and promoting preparedness measures.

Urban Planning and Land Use Management: Civil engineers contribute to urban planning and land use management that considers disaster risk reduction principles. They help in identifying safe areas for development and avoiding high-risk zones.

Environmental Considerations: Engineers take environmental factors into account when designing DRR measures to ensure that solutions are sustainable and do not harm the ecosystem.

Incorporating Climate Change Adaptation: Civil engineers consider climate change scenarios and potential impacts while designing and implementing DRR strategies to ensure resilience to future challenges.

Research and Innovation: Engineers engage in research and innovation to develop new technologies and practices for DRR, leveraging advancements in the field.

Post-Disaster Reconstruction and Recovery: In the aftermath of disasters, civil engineers are involved in post-disaster reconstruction and recovery efforts. They assess damages and participate in rebuilding efforts with a focus on resilient infrastructure.

By fulfilling these roles and responsibilities, civil engineers play a pivotal role in disaster risk reduction, contributing to the safety and sustainability of communities and infrastructure in the face of natural and human-made hazards.

12.4 Medical Preparedness Aspect of Disaster Management

Medical preparedness is a crucial aspect of disaster management that focuses on ensuring the availability of adequate medical resources, facilities, and personnel to respond effectively to health-related challenges during disasters. The goal of medical preparedness is to minimize the impact of disasters on public health by providing timely and appropriate medical care to affected individuals. This aspect involves planning, coordination, training, and resource allocation to address the unique healthcare needs arising from various types of disasters. Here are the key components of medical preparedness in disaster management:

Disaster Healthcare Planning: Medical preparedness begins with comprehensive disaster healthcare planning. This involves identifying potential health risks and challenges specific to the region, assessing the healthcare infrastructure's capacity, and developing strategies to manage increased demand during emergencies.

Prepositioning Medical Supplies: To ensure a rapid response, medical supplies, including medicines, medical equipment, and personal protective equipment (PPE), are prepositioned at strategic locations. This enables immediate access to essential resources in disaster-affected areas.

Emergency Medical Facilities: Medical preparedness includes setting up temporary medical facilities such as field hospitals, mobile clinics, and medical camps near disaster-affected zones. These facilities help in providing medical care to injured individuals and those with health conditions exacerbated by the disaster.

Medical Personnel Training: Healthcare professionals undergo specialized training in disaster medicine and response techniques. This training equips them with the skills to handle the unique challenges of mass casualties, triage patients effectively, and manage limited resources during emergencies.

Emergency Medical Evacuation: Medical preparedness involves developing systems for rapid medical evacuation of critically injured individuals to nearby medical facilities with advanced treatment capabilities.

Communication and Information Management: Establishing effective communication networks is vital for medical preparedness. It enables seamless coordination among medical teams, emergency responders, and healthcare facilities, facilitating efficient patient management.

Public Health Surveillance: Medical preparedness includes implementing public health surveillance systems to monitor disease outbreaks, assess the health status of affected populations, and identify potential health risks in disaster zones.

Psychosocial Support: Medical preparedness considers the mental health and psychosocial needs of disaster survivors. Trained personnel offer counselling and support to address emotional trauma and stress-related issues.

Community Health Education: Preparedness efforts include educating communities about disaster-related health risks, preventive measures, and how to access medical assistance during emergencies.

Interagency Coordination: Effective medical preparedness involves close coordination between various agencies, including healthcare institutions, emergency services, public health departments, and NGOs.

Continuity of Care: Medical preparedness also involves ensuring the continuity of care for individuals with pre-existing medical conditions during and after disasters.

Vulnerable Population Considerations: Special attention is given to vulnerable populations such as children, elderly individuals, pregnant women, and individuals with disabilities, addressing their unique healthcare needs during disasters.

Medical preparedness is an ongoing process that requires collaboration among multiple stakeholders, including healthcare providers, government agencies, non-governmental organizations, and communities. By ensuring a robust medical response during disasters, medical preparedness plays a crucial role in reducing the overall impact on public health and saving lives.

12.4.1 Medical Preparedness in India

Medical preparedness in India is a critical aspect of disaster management, considering the country's vulnerability to a wide range of natural and man-made disasters. India faces various hazards such as earthquakes, floods, cyclones, heatwaves, epidemics, industrial accidents, and terrorist attacks, which can significantly impact public health. As a result, medical preparedness in India encompasses a comprehensive approach to ensure a timely and effective medical response during emergencies. Here are some key aspects of medical preparedness in India:

National and State-level Disaster Healthcare Plans: India has a National Disaster Management Plan and State Disaster Management Plans that include specific provisions for medical preparedness. These plans outline the roles and responsibilities of various healthcare authorities and provide guidelines for medical response during disasters.

National Disaster Medical Response Force (NDRMF): The NDRMF is a specialized force under the National Disaster Response Force (NDRF) responsible for medical response during disasters. It comprises medical professionals and paramedics trained in disaster medicine and emergency response.

Emergency Medical Facilities and Mobile Hospitals: India has provisions for setting up emergency medical facilities, field hospitals, and mobile medical units in disaster-prone areas. These facilities can be quickly deployed to provide medical care to affected communities.

Prepositioning of Medical Supplies: The Central and State governments preposition medical supplies and equipment at strategic locations to ensure a rapid response during emergencies. These supplies include essential medicines, vaccines, surgical equipment, and PPE.

Emergency Medical Evacuation and Transport: India has well-established emergency medical evacuation systems that involve coordination between air, road, and rail transport services to transfer critically injured patients to advanced medical facilities.

Medical Training and Capacity Building: Medical professionals and first responders undergo training in disaster medicine, mass casualty management, and emergency medical services. Regular capacity building programs enhance the skills of healthcare personnel in disaster response.

Public Health Surveillance and Disease Control: Public health authorities in India monitor disease outbreaks and implement disease control measures during disasters. Rapid response teams are deployed to prevent and contain the spread of communicable diseases.

Psychosocial Support Services: Medical preparedness includes providing psychosocial support to disaster survivors, helping them cope with emotional trauma and stress. Mental health professionals offer counselling and support.

Community Health Education and Awareness: Educational campaigns are conducted to raise awareness among communities about disaster-related health risks, preventive measures, and how to access medical assistance during emergencies.

Interagency Coordination and Multi-sectoral Approach: Medical preparedness in India involves coordination among various agencies, including healthcare institutions, emergency services, disaster management authorities, and non-governmental organizations.

Adapting to Climate Change and Environmental Health Risks: India considers the impact of climate change on public health and incorporates climate resilience strategies into medical preparedness planning.

Telemedicine and Technology Integration: Telemedicine and technology play a role in medical preparedness by enabling remote consultations, real-time information exchange, and data management during emergencies.

Medical preparedness in India is a dynamic process that evolves with changing disaster scenarios and emerging challenges. The continuous efforts of the government, healthcare professionals, and various stakeholders contribute to building a resilient healthcare system capable of effectively responding to disasters and safeguarding public health.

12.5 Plans to Counter Threats to Water Supply During Disaster

Counteracting threats to water supply during disasters is essential to ensure access to safe drinking water, maintain sanitation, and support public health in affected areas. Several plans and strategies are implemented to address water supply challenges during disasters. Here are some of the key plans:

Water Supply Contingency Plans: Water supply contingency plans are developed by local authorities, water utilities, and disaster management agencies. These plans outline measures to maintain an uninterrupted water supply during disasters, including identifying alternative water sources, setting up temporary water treatment facilities, and ensuring the availability of water tankers. Water supply contingency plans are comprehensive documents that outline specific actions to be taken in the event of a disaster that disrupts regular water supply. These plans identify potential hazards and vulnerabilities to the water supply system and establish protocols for maintaining water services during emergencies. They include steps to activate backup water sources, prioritize critical facilities for water supply restoration, and coordinate efforts between water utilities and disaster management agencies.

Prepositioning Water and Water Treatment Supplies: Water utilities and disaster management agencies preposition water storage tanks, bottled water, water treatment chemicals, and water purification systems in disaster-prone areas. These supplies can be quickly deployed to meet immediate water needs.

Emergency Water Treatment Facilities: During disasters, emergency water treatment facilities may be established to treat water from available sources like rivers, ponds, and lakes. Mobile water treatment units equipped with filtration and disinfection systems can purify water for distribution.

Water Conservation Measures: Water conservation measures are promoted to reduce water consumption during emergencies. Awareness campaigns encourage communities to use water efficiently and avoid wastage.

Water Quality Monitoring: Regular water quality monitoring is conducted to ensure the safety of drinking water sources. Rapid water testing methods are employed to assess the potability of water during and after disasters.

Alternative Water Sources: In areas where the primary water supply systems are compromised, alternative water sources such as groundwater wells, rainwater harvesting systems, and community ponds may be utilized.

Water Distribution Points: Water distribution points are set up in disaster-affected areas to provide safe drinking water to the population. These points are managed by local authorities and relief agencies.

Water Purification Tablets and Filters: Water purification tablets and filters are distributed to households and communities to treat water at the point of use. These simple interventions can help make water safe for consumption.

Water, Sanitation, and Hygiene (WASH) Programs: Integrated WASH programs are implemented to address water supply, sanitation, and hygiene needs during disasters. These programs focus on ensuring safe water storage, proper sanitation facilities, and hygiene practices to prevent waterborne diseases.

Cross-sectoral Collaboration: Disaster management agencies collaborate with water and sanitation authorities, health departments, and humanitarian organizations to address water supply challenges comprehensively.

Community Participation: Involving the affected communities in water supply planning and decision-making enhances the effectiveness of water supply interventions during disasters.

Adapting to Climate Change Impacts: Considering climate change effects on water resources, disaster management plans incorporate climate resilience strategies to safeguard water supply systems.

These plans and strategies are adapted to specific disaster scenarios and the local context. By proactively addressing threats to water supply, disaster management authorities aim to minimize the impact of water scarcity and ensure the availability of safe drinking water for affected populations. By implementing these measures and integrating them into disaster management frameworks, authorities can better ensure access to safe drinking water and improved sanitation, thereby protecting public health during and after disasters.

12.6 Case Studies of Successful Disaster Management

India has witnessed numerous successful disaster management initiatives that highlight the country's efforts in mitigating the impact of disasters and building resilience. Here are some notable case studies of successful disaster management initiatives in India:

Gujarat Earthquake (2001): The Gujarat earthquake of 2001, measuring 7.7 magnitude, caused widespread destruction in the state. The disaster management response was significant, with the prompt mobilization of rescue teams, medical aid, and relief supplies. The establishment of a control room for coordinating rescue efforts and the use of satellite imagery for damage assessment showcased the use of technology in disaster response. The disaster led to improvements in building codes and disaster preparedness measures in the state.

Highlights of Gujarat Earthquake (2001):

Magnitude: 7.7

Date: January 26, 2001

Affected Population: Over 20 million people in Gujarat

Casualties: Approximately 20,000 people killed, and more than 167,000 injured

Expenditure: The estimated economic loss was around $5.5 billion.

Special Concern: The earthquake severely impacted infrastructure, with buildings, roads, and bridges collapsing. The disaster highlighted the need for earthquake-resistant construction and disaster preparedness in high-risk areas.

Cyclone Phailin (2013) – Odisha: Cyclone Phailin was a severe cyclonic storm that hit the coastal areas of Odisha in 2013. The state authorities, in collaboration with the National Disaster Response Force (NDRF) and other agencies, successfully evacuated around one million people to safe shelters before the cyclone made landfall. The proactive evacuation and preparedness efforts saved numerous lives and minimized casualties.

Highlights of Cyclone Phailin (2013) – Odisha:

Date: October 12, 2013

Affected Population: Approximately 12 million people in Odisha

Casualties: Despite being classified as a Category 4 cyclone, the death toll was around 44, thanks to the successful evacuation efforts.

Expenditure: The estimated economic loss was around $700 million.

Special Concern: Cyclone Phailin's intensity and potential impact prompted the largest evacuation in India's history, showcasing the importance of early warning systems, disaster preparedness, and the involvement of local communities.

Kerala Floods (2018): The state of Kerala experienced devastating floods in 2018 due to heavy monsoon rains. The disaster management response was swift, with coordinated efforts by government agencies, non-governmental organizations (NGOs), and the public. Social media and technology played a significant role in disseminating information and coordinating rescue efforts. The "Compassionate Keralam" initiative saw people coming together to offer assistance and support to those affected.

Highlights of Kerala Floods (2018):

Date: August 2018

Affected Population: Over 5.5 million people in Kerala

Casualties: The floods claimed over 480 lives.

Expenditure: The estimated economic loss was around $2.8 billion.

Special Concern: The Kerala floods highlighted the significance of disaster management in urban areas. Heavy rainfall, inadequate drainage systems, and encroachments on water bodies worsened the situation. It underscored the need for better urban planning and sustainable development practices.

Cyclone Fani (2019) – Odisha: Cyclone Fani was one of the strongest tropical cyclones to hit Odisha in decades. The state government's proactive approach and early preparedness measures, including timely evacuation of vulnerable communities, saved many lives and reduced the impact on infrastructure. The disaster management authorities effectively used technology to track the cyclone's path and intensity, enabling better planning and response.

Highlights of Cyclone Fani (2019) – Odisha:

Date: May 3, 2019

Affected Population: Around 16 million people in Odisha

Casualties: Despite being a severe cyclone, the death toll was limited to 64 due to timely evacuation efforts.

Expenditure: The estimated economic loss was around $1.5 billion.

Special Concern: Cyclone Fani tested the disaster management capabilities of Odisha, which had considerably improved since the 1999 Odisha cyclone. The evacuation of over 1.2 million people showcased the success of early warning systems and community preparedness.

COVID-19 Pandemic (2020): The COVID-19 pandemic posed unprecedented challenges for disaster management in India. The government implemented a nationwide lockdown to contain the spread of the virus. Various initiatives, such as the establishment of COVID-19 care centers, ramping up healthcare infrastructure, and promoting public awareness about preventive measures, showcased the country's resilience in responding to a health emergency of global proportions.

Highlights of COVID-19 Pandemic (2020):

Period: Since March 2020

Affected Population: The entire country of over 1.3 billion people

Casualties: As of September 2021, India reported over 450,000 deaths due to COVID-19.

Expenditure: The economic impact of the pandemic on India has been extensive, with various relief and economic stimulus packages being implemented by the government.

Special Concern: The COVID-19 pandemic presented unique challenges in disaster management, focusing on healthcare infrastructure, testing, contact tracing, and vaccination. The pandemic led to an unprecedented healthcare crisis, requiring a coordinated national response.

Chennai Floods (2015): The city of Chennai experienced severe flooding in 2015 due to heavy rainfall. Disaster management authorities collaborated with the Indian Navy, NDRF, and other agencies to conduct rescue operations and provide relief to affected communities. Social media played a crucial role in disseminating information about emergency services and helplines.

Highlights of Chennai Floods (2015):

Period: December 2015

Affected Population: Over 4 million people in Chennai and surrounding areas

Casualties: The floods claimed around 470 lives.

Expenditure: The economic loss was estimated to be around $3 billion.

Special Concern: The Chennai floods exposed vulnerabilities in urban planning and inadequate stormwater drainage systems. It emphasized the importance of climate-resilient infrastructure and flood mitigation measures in rapidly urbanizing areas.

Bhuj Earthquake (2001): The Bhuj earthquake in Gujarat brought significant lessons in disaster management. The disaster highlighted the importance of building earthquake-resistant structures and strengthening disaster preparedness measures. The earthquake led to a reevaluation of building codes and standards to enhance seismic resilience.

These case studies demonstrate India's progress in disaster management, including preparedness, response, and recovery efforts. Successful initiatives emphasize the importance of early warning systems, technology integration, community participation, cross-sectoral collaboration, and the use of lessons learned from past disasters. The continuous improvement and implementation of best practices contribute to building a more resilient nation in the face of future challenges.

Highlights of Bhuj Earthquake (2001):

Magnitude: 7.7

Date: January 26, 2001

Affected Population: Around 8 million people in Gujarat

Casualties: The earthquake caused over 13,800 deaths and left over 166,000 people injured.

Expenditure: The economic loss was estimated to be around $5.8 billion.

Special Concern: The Bhuj earthquake demonstrated the need for improving seismic resilience in buildings and infrastructure. It spurred the revision of building codes and the promotion of earthquake-resistant construction practices.

Each of these case studies reflects the efforts made by various stakeholders, including government authorities, disaster management agencies, community organizations, and international aid partners, to respond effectively to the respective disasters. While the data and expenditure may vary, the common thread in each case is the importance of preparedness, early warning systems, timely response, and community participation in reducing the impact of disasters and building resilience in India.

12.7 Best Practices and Innovative Approaches

India has adopted several best practices and innovative approaches for disaster management to enhance preparedness, response, and recovery efforts. These practices reflect the country's commitment to building resilience and minimizing the impact of disasters. Here are some notable best practices and innovative approaches in Indian disaster management:

Early Warning Systems (EWS): India has invested in advanced early warning systems for various disasters, such as cyclones, floods, and earthquakes. The India Meteorological Department (IMD) provides timely alerts to vulnerable communities, enabling early evacuation and preparedness measures. The use of technology, including mobile apps and SMS alerts, ensures that warning messages reach even remote areas.

Example: The Cyclone Warning Division of the India Meteorological Department issues cyclone alerts. For instance, during Cyclone Fani (2019), early warnings helped in the evacuation of over 1.2 million people in Odisha.

Expenditure: The cost of early warning systems varies depending on technology, maintenance, and data infrastructure. Funding may come from both government and international sources.

State Involved: The India Meteorological Department (IMD) coordinates EWS at the national level, and state governments play a crucial role in disseminating warnings and managing evacuation efforts.

People Benefited: The entire coastal population and communities residing in disaster-prone regions benefit from timely alerts, which aid in saving lives and minimizing property damage.

Funding Agencies: The Ministry of Earth Sciences, international agencies, and multilateral organizations may provide financial support for establishing and maintaining EWS.

Community-Based Disaster Risk Reduction (CBDRR): Community participation is central to disaster risk reduction in India. The involvement of local communities in disaster planning, preparedness, and response efforts ensures that interventions are tailored to local nccds and vulnerabilities. CBDRR empowers communities to take ownership of their safety and resilience.

Community-Based Disaster Risk Reduction (CBDRR):

Example: The 'Kudumbashree' project in Kerala empowers women's self-help groups to take part in disaster management activities and community-based resilience building.

Expenditure: Funding for CBDRR initiatives may come from government schemes, international donors, and corporate social responsibility (CSR) initiatives.

State Involved: State governments actively promote CBDRR through community organizations, local authorities, and NGOs.

People Benefited: Communities at the grassroots level, especially vulnerable groups, benefit from CBDRR initiatives as they are involved in decision-making, preparedness planning, and response activities.

Funding Agencies: State Disaster Management Authorities, NGOs, United Nations agencies, and international development partners provide financial support for CBDRR programs.

Crisis Communication and Information Dissemination: During disasters, effective communication is crucial. India utilizes various channels, including social media, websites, and mobile apps, to disseminate real-time information about disaster situations, helplines, and relief measures. This approach enhances public awareness and facilitates coordinated response efforts.

Crisis Communication and Information Dissemination:

Example: During the COVID-19 pandemic, the Indian government used various channels, including Aarogya Setu app, social media, and official websites, to provide real-time information on COVID-19 cases, testing centers, and safety guidelines.

Expenditure: The cost of crisis communication depends on technology, outreach methods, and the scale of dissemination. Governments allocate budgets for communication and information dissemination during disasters.

State Involved: State governments and central agencies coordinate communication efforts during disasters.

People Benefited: The entire population benefits from accurate and timely information, enabling them to take necessary precautions and access essential services.

Funding Agencies: The government, international organizations, and donors support crisis communication efforts.

Use of Technology and Geospatial Information: India leverages technology and geospatial information to assess disaster risks, monitor disaster situations, and plan response activities. Satellite imagery, Geographic Information Systems (GIS), and drones are used for damage assessment and resource allocation during disasters.

Example: The National Remote Sensing Centre (NRSC) under the Indian Space Research Organisation (ISRO) uses satellite imagery to assess damage and provide situational analysis during disasters.

Expenditure: The costs of technology and geospatial information may vary depending on data acquisition, processing, and dissemination. Funding comes from government sources, space agencies, and research institutions.

State Involved: ISRO and NRSC play a key role at the national level, while state governments also utilize geospatial information for disaster management.

People Benefited: Disaster management agencies, governments, and relief organizations benefit from real-time data for planning and response activities.

Funding Agencies: The Department of Space, ISRO, and other scientific agencies fund technology and geospatial initiatives.

National Disaster Response Force (NDRF): The NDRF is a specialized force dedicated to disaster response. The force comprises highly trained personnel equipped with modern tools and equipment for search, rescue, and medical assistance during disasters.

Example: NDRF played a critical role during Cyclone Fani (2019) by deploying teams for rescue and relief operations in Odisha.

Expenditure: The budget for NDRF includes equipment, training, and operational costs. Funding comes from the central government.

State Involved: NDRF operates at the national level and can be deployed in any state in response to disasters.

People Benefited: NDRF's specialized teams provide essential search and rescue services, benefiting disaster-affected communities.

Funding Agencies: The central government provides funding for NDRF operations.

Disaster Recovery and Rehabilitation Planning: India emphasizes post-disaster recovery and rehabilitation planning to facilitate the rebuilding of communities and infrastructure. The National Disaster Recovery Framework (NDRF) guides recovery efforts and promotes sustainable reconstruction practices.

Example: After the 2013 Uttarakhand flash floods, the state government initiated the "Build Back Better" approach, incorporating disaster-resilient design and sustainable practices in reconstruction efforts.

Expenditure: The cost of recovery and rehabilitation varies depending on the scale of the disaster. Funding comes from state and central governments, international donors, and multilateral agencies.

State Involved: State governments lead recovery and rehabilitation efforts in coordination with disaster management authorities.

People Benefited: Disaster-affected communities' benefit from sustainable and resilient reconstruction, which minimizes the risk of future disasters.

Funding Agencies: State and central governments, international donors, and development agencies provide funding for recovery and rehabilitation programs.

Capacity Building and Training: Disaster management agencies conduct regular capacity building and training programs for first responders, healthcare professionals, and community volunteers. These programs enhance skills in disaster response, medical aid, and damage assessment.

Example: The National Institute of Disaster Management (NIDM) conducts training programs for first responders, government officials, and community volunteers.

Expenditure: The cost of capacity building programs includes training materials, trainers' fees, and logistics. Governments allocate budgets for training initiatives.

State Involved: State governments and disaster management institutions coordinate capacity building programs.

People Benefited: First responders, healthcare professionals, and volunteers benefit from improved skills and knowledge in disaster response.

Funding Agencies: The central government, state governments, and international organizations provide financial support for capacity building and training programs.

Public-Private Partnerships (PPPs): India encourages public-private partnerships to strengthen disaster management capabilities. Collaboration with private sector organizations enhances resource mobilization, technology integration, and expertise sharing.

Example: The Mumbai Fire Brigade collaborates with private sector companies to conduct joint disaster drills and develop emergency response plans for industrial areas.

Expenditure: The cost of PPPs varies depending on the nature of collaboration and the scale of projects. Funding comes from both public and private sources.

State Involved: State governments facilitate PPPs and encourage private sector involvement in disaster management initiatives.

People Benefited: Communities residing in industrial areas benefit from improved emergency preparedness and coordination between public and private entities.

Funding Agencies: The private sector and government share funding responsibilities for PPP initiatives.

Disaster Insurance and Risk Transfer Mechanisms: India has explored innovative financial instruments like catastrophe bonds and insurance to transfer disaster risks. These mechanisms provide financial support for post-disaster recovery and rebuilding efforts.

Example: Kerala State Disaster Risk Reduction Fund (KSDRRF) implemented a risk transfer mechanism through insurance to provide immediate financial relief to affected communities during the 2018 floods.

Expenditure: The cost of insurance premiums and risk transfer mechanisms varies depending on coverage and risk assessment. Funding comes from state governments, international donors, and insurance agencies.

State Involved: State governments establish risk transfer mechanisms and work with insurance providers.

People Benefited: Disaster-affected individuals and communities receive financial assistance quickly through insurance payouts.

Funding Agencies: State governments and international organizations support disaster insurance and risk transfer initiatives.

Climate Change Adaptation: With the increasing impact of climate change on disasters, India integrates climate change adaptation strategies into disaster management planning. This approach ensures that disaster risk reduction measures account for future climate scenarios.

Example: The 'National Action Plan on Climate Change' includes various adaptation projects to address climate-related vulnerabilities and strengthen resilience.

Expenditure: The cost of climate change adaptation projects varies depending on the scale and nature of interventions. Funding comes from state and central governments, international donors, and climate funds

State Involved: The central government, in coordination with state governments, implements climate change adaptation projects across the country.

People Benefited: Communities vulnerable to climate change impacts, such as coastal regions, farmers, and urban populations, benefit from adaptation measures.

Funding Agencies: Climate funds like the Green Climate Fund (GCF), Global Environment Facility (GEF), and bilateral and multilateral development partners provide financial support for climate change adaptation initiatives.

Institutional Integration and Coordination: India emphasizes the importance of institutional integration and coordination among various agencies involved in disaster management. The National Disaster Management Authority (NDMA) collaborates with state governments, local authorities, and international partners to ensure a unified and effective response.

Institutional Integration and Coordination:

Example: The National Disaster Management Authority (NDMA) collaborates with state disaster management authorities, district administrations, and various ministries to ensure a coordinated response during disasters.

Expenditure: The cost of institutional integration and coordination includes the establishment of• communication channels and the implementation of joint planning efforts. Funding is provided by the central and state governments.

State Involved: Both central and state governments work together to ensure seamless coordination and integration among disaster management entities.

People Benefited: Disaster-affected communities' benefit from a cohesive and well-coordinated response, ensuring timely and effective relief measures.

Funding Agencies: The central and state governments allocate budgets for disaster management coordination and integration.

Public Awareness Campaigns:

Public Awareness Campaigns: India runs public awareness campaigns to educate the public about disaster risks, safety measures, and the importance of preparedness. These campaigns aim to foster a culture of resilience and promote individual responsibility.

Example: The "Swachh Bharat Abhiyan" (Clean India Campaign) includes disaster preparedness messages, promoting cleanliness to reduce the risk of waterborne diseases during floods.

Expenditure: The cost of public awareness campaigns depends on the scale and outreach efforts. Funding comes from government budgets and public service campaigns.

State Involved: State governments, along with central authorities, run public awareness campaigns as part of their disaster risk reduction initiatives.

People Benefited: The general public gains knowledge about disaster risks, safety measures, and the importance of preparedness, making them more resilient during emergencies.

Funding Agencies: The government, through various ministries, allocates funds for public awareness campaigns.

While these examples highlight successful initiatives and approaches, it is essential to recognize that disaster management in India is an ongoing process that evolves with each disaster experience. The effectiveness of these practices may vary based on factors such as the scale of the disaster, geographic location, institutional capacity, and public participation. Continued efforts, funding, and innovation are required to build a robust disaster management system and enhance resilience in the face of evolving disaster challenges. By adopting these best practices and innovative approaches, India continues to enhance its disaster management capabilities, striving to build a safer and more resilient nation in the face of natural and man-made hazards.

12.8 Lessons Learned and Recommendations

Lessons learned from past disaster management practices in India have led to valuable insights and recommendations for the future. Here are some key lessons learned and recommendations for enhancing disaster management practices in India:

Invest in Preparedness and Early Warning Systems:

Lesson Learned: Timely and accurate early warnings are critical for effective disaster management. Past disasters have shown that early warning systems save lives and enable timely evacuation.

Recommendation: Continued investment in state-of-the-art early warning systems, improved forecasting capabilities, and effective communication channels can enhance disaster preparedness and response.

Strengthen Community Participation and Awareness:

Lesson Learned: Community participation and awareness play a pivotal role in disaster resilience. Active involvement of communities can lead to better disaster planning and response.

Recommendation: Engage communities in disaster risk reduction efforts through capacity building, training, and participatory planning. Foster a culture of resilience through public awareness campaigns.

Promote Integrated Risk Management Approach:

Lesson Learned: Disasters often have cascading effects across sectors. An integrated risk management approach that considers multiple hazards, vulnerabilities, and interdependencies is crucial.

Recommendation: Adopt a multi-hazard approach to disaster risk reduction, considering the interlinkages between various hazards and sectors. Strengthen coordination among different agencies and ministries.

Enhance Infrastructure Resilience:

Lesson Learned: Vulnerable infrastructure exacerbates the impact of disasters. Many past disasters have shown the importance of building resilient infrastructure to withstand shocks.

Recommendation: Implement and enforce building codes and standards that consider disaster risk reduction. Invest in retrofitting and constructing resilient infrastructure to minimize damage during disasters.

Foster Interagency Collaboration:

Lesson Learned: Effective disaster management requires seamless coordination among various government agencies, private sector, NGOs, and international partners.

Recommendation: Strengthen interagency collaboration through joint planning, regular exercises, and information sharing. Develop clear roles and responsibilities for each agency during disasters.

Incorporate Climate Change Adaptation:

Lesson Learned: Climate change impacts increase the frequency and intensity of disasters. Integrating climate change adaptation into disaster management is vital for long-term resilience.

Recommendation: Develop and implement climate-resilient strategies in disaster risk reduction planning. Ensure that climate change considerations are mainstreamed in all disaster management policies.

Invest in Research and Innovation:

Lesson Learned: Evolving disaster challenges require constant research and innovation to develop effective solutions.

Recommendation: Allocate resources for research and innovation in disaster management technologies, methodologies, and practices. Foster partnerships between academia, research institutions, and disaster management agencies.

Strengthen Data and Information Systems:

Lesson Learned: Reliable data and information are essential for evidence-based decision-making during disasters.

Recommendation: Enhance data collection, analysis, and sharing mechanisms. Develop robust information systems to support planning and response efforts.

Promote Inclusive Approach:

Lesson Learned: Vulnerable populations are disproportionately affected by disasters. An inclusive approach is necessary to ensure that no one is left behind in disaster response and recovery.

Recommendation: Prioritize the needs of vulnerable groups, including women, children, elderly, differently-abled, and marginalized communities, in disaster planning and response. Ensure their active participation in decision-making processes.

Continuously Learn and Adapt:

Lesson Learned: Each disaster presents unique challenges and lessons. It is essential to continuously learn from past experiences and adapt strategies accordingly.

Recommendation: Institutionalize a culture of learning and evaluation in disaster management practices. Conduct post-disaster reviews and develop action plans to address identified gaps.

By incorporating these lessons learned and implementing the recommended strategies, India can continue to improve its disaster management practices, build resilience, and protect lives and livelihoods during emergencies. Disaster management must remain a dynamic and evolving process to address the ever-changing risk landscape in the country.

12.8.1 Requirement for Effective Public Awareness Campaign

Effective public awareness campaigns about disaster management require careful planning, strategic communication, and active engagement with the target audience. Here are some essential requirements for conducting successful public awareness campaigns:

Clear Objectives and Target Audience Identification:

Define clear and measurable objectives for the awareness campaign, such as promoting preparedness, safety measures, or specific behaviours during disasters.

Identify the target audience based on demographics, geographic location, and vulnerability to specific hazards. Tailor the campaign messages to resonate with the audience's needs and preferences.

Engaging Messaging and Communication Channels:

Craft clear, concise, and engaging messages that convey the campaign's key information effectively. Use simple language and visuals to enhance understanding.

Utilize various communication channels to reach a broader audience, including television, radio, social media, print media, posters, and community meetings.

Partnerships and Collaborations:

Collaborate with government agencies, NGOs, community-based organizations, educational institutions, and media partners to amplify the campaign's reach and impact.

Engage local influencers, celebrities, and community leaders to endorse the campaign and encourage active participation.

Cultural Sensitivity and Inclusivity:

Consider cultural nuances and local context when designing campaign materials and messages to ensure they are relevant and respectful to diverse communities.

Emphasize inclusivity by addressing the needs of vulnerable populations, including women, children, elderly, differently-abled individuals, and marginalized communities.

Use of Technology and Innovation:

Leverage technology, such as mobile apps, interactive websites, and social media platforms, to engage a tech-savvy audience and encourage two-way communication.

Incorporate innovative approaches like gamification, virtual reality, or augmented reality to create immersive experiences and increase message retention.

Consistent and Repetitive Messaging:

Repeat key messages consistently throughout the campaign to reinforce the information and increase retention.

Use repetition across multiple channels to reach individuals who may not have been exposed to the message initially.

Monitoring and Evaluation:

Regularly monitor the reach and impact of the campaign through metrics such as audience engagement, website traffic, or social media interactions.

Conduct post-campaign evaluations to assess the effectiveness of the messaging and identify areas for improvement.

Community Involvement and Empowerment:

Involve local communities in the campaign's development and implementation to ensure that messages are culturally relevant and resonate with their experiences.

Empower communities by providing them with actionable information and resources to take charge of their own safety and preparedness.

Timely and Responsive Communication:

Ensure that the campaign responds promptly to emerging disaster situations by providing real-time updates and guidance.

Deliver timely messages before, during, and after disasters to prepare communities and aid in recovery efforts.

Long-Term Sustainability:

Plan for the long-term sustainability of the campaign by integrating disaster management education into school curriculums, community programs, and workplace training.

Secure funding and support to continue awareness campaigns in the long run, considering that disaster preparedness is an ongoing process.

By fulfilling these requirements, public awareness campaigns about disaster management can effectively engage communities, improve understanding, and encourage proactive behaviours that contribute to disaster resilience and reduced vulnerability.

12.8.2 Requirements for Effective Early Warning Systems

Effective Early Warning Systems (EWS) are crucial for disaster management, as they enable timely response and preparedness, ultimately saving lives and minimizing damages. To ensure their effectiveness, Early Warning Systems must meet several key requirements:

Reliable Data and Monitoring:

Early Warning Systems should rely on accurate and up-to-date data from various sources, such as meteorological agencies, seismic monitoring stations, hydrological sensors, and satellite observations.

Continuous monitoring of potential hazards, including weather patterns, seismic activities, river levels, and other indicators, is essential for providing timely warnings.

Forecasting and Predictive Models:

EWS should employ advanced forecasting and predictive models that can analyse data and predict potential disasters with a high degree of accuracy.

Models should consider various factors that contribute to disaster risks, such as climate patterns, geological conditions, and human activities.

Clear and Timely Communication:

Warnings should be communicated clearly, using language and formats easily understood by the target audience, including local communities and authorities.

Timeliness is critical; warnings must be issued promptly to allow enough time for preparedness and evacuation.

Multiple Communication Channels:

EWS should utilize multiple communication channels, such as text messages, radio broadcasts, sirens, social media, and mobile apps, to reach as many people as possible, including those in remote areas.

Localized and Context-Specific Warnings:

EWS should be able to provide warnings at a localized level, considering the unique characteristics of each area and the specific hazards they are prone to.

Context-specific warnings help to avoid unnecessary panic and enhance community understanding and response.

Accessibility and Inclusivity:

EWS should be accessible to all members of the community, including people with disabilities, the elderly, and those who may face language barriers.

Efforts should be made to ensure that warnings are inclusive and reach vulnerable populations effectively.

Testing and Simulation Exercises:

Regular testing and simulation exercises of the EWS are essential to evaluate its effectiveness and identify any weaknesses or gaps.

Exercises also familiarize communities with the warning signals and response protocols.

Interagency Coordination:

EWS requires close coordination among various government agencies, meteorological departments, disaster management authorities, and other relevant stakeholders.

Clear roles and responsibilities should be defined for each agency to ensure a seamless response during emergencies.

Public Awareness and Education:

Educating the public about the EWS, its purpose, and how to respond to warnings is critical for its success.

Public awareness campaigns help build trust in the system and encourage prompt action during disasters.

Continuous Monitoring and Improvement:

Early Warning Systems should be continuously monitored and evaluated for effectiveness and relevance.

Feedback from users and stakeholders should be used to make necessary improvements and updates to the system.

Sustainability and Funding:

Early Warning Systems require long-term sustainability, including adequate funding and support from governments, international organizations, and donors.

Ensuring funding continuity is vital to maintain and upgrade the system over time.

By fulfilling these requirements, Early Warning Systems can effectively serve their purpose in disaster management, ensuring that timely warnings reach the right people, enabling communities to take appropriate actions to safeguard lives and property.

12.9 Population Growth, Urbanization and Disaster Risk

Increased population and high growth in urbanization have significant implications for disaster risk in India. As more people migrate to urban areas in search of better opportunities, the urban population is expanding rapidly, leading to various challenges that contribute to increased disaster risk.

Overcrowding and Pressure on Infrastructure: Urban areas often become overcrowded due to the influx of people. This puts immense pressure on existing infrastructure, including housing, transportation, water supply, and waste management systems. Overburdened infrastructure is more susceptible to failure during disasters, leading to disruptions and exacerbating the impact of calamities.

Unplanned Urbanization: High rates of urbanization sometimes lead to unplanned and haphazard growth. Informal settlements and slums emerge without adequate infrastructure and disaster-resilient construction practices. Such areas are at greater risk during disasters like floods, landslides, or earthquakes.

Environmental Degradation: Rapid urbanization often results in deforestation, land degradation, and loss of wetlands, reducing the natural barriers that once protected against disasters like floods, storms, and coastal erosion.

Increased Vulnerability to Climate Change: Urban areas are particularly vulnerable to the effects of climate change, such as rising temperatures, heatwaves, and extreme weather events. Urban heat islands exacerbate heat-related health issues, while climate-induced disasters like floods and storms become more intense and frequent.

Water Management Challenges: Urbanization leads to increased demand for water, straining already limited resources. Inadequate water management can lead to water scarcity, compromising firefighting capabilities during disasters and hindering relief efforts.

Sanitation and Waste Management Issues: Urban areas face challenges in maintaining proper sanitation and waste management. Poor waste disposal can clog drainage systems, leading to flooding during heavy rains.

Social Vulnerability: Urbanization can result in disparities in access to resources and services, leaving certain population groups more vulnerable to disasters. The poor, marginalized communities, and migrants often reside in informal settlements with inadequate infrastructure and limited access to disaster preparedness measures.

High Population Density: Urban areas' high population density increases the number of people exposed to disaster risks. In the event of a disaster, evacuations and response efforts become more complex due to the large number of people needing assistance.

Urban Heat Island Effect: As urban areas have more impervious surfaces, they tend to trap heat, leading to the urban heat island effect. Heatwaves pose a severe threat to the health of urban populations, especially vulnerable groups like the elderly and children.

Infrastructure Vulnerability: Urban areas often have critical infrastructure, such as power plants, hospitals, and transportation hubs, that are at risk during disasters. Disruptions in such infrastructure can severely hamper disaster response and recovery efforts.

Thus, the rapid increase in population and urbanization in India has created both challenges and opportunities for disaster risk reduction. Addressing these challenges requires comprehensive urban planning, resilient infrastructure development, and a focus on social equity. Incorporating disaster risk reduction strategies into urban planning can help mitigate the impact of disasters and build more resilient cities capable of safeguarding the lives and livelihoods of their inhabitants.

CHAPTER 13

Technologies for Disaster Management

13.1 Technologies Useful During Disaster Management

13.2 Remote Sensing and GIS Technology for Disaster Management

13.3 Drones and Unmanned Aerial Vehicles (UAVs) Technology for DM

13.4 Artificial Intelligence (AI) and Machine Learning (ML) Technology for DM

13.5 Internet of Things (IoT) Technology for DM

13.6 Virtual Reality (VR) and Augmented Reality (AR) Technology for DM

13.7 Robotics Technology for DM

13.8 Early Warning Systems & Advance Communication Technology for DM

13.9 Big Data Analytics and Blockchain Technology in DM

13.10 Technology for Control & Management of Urban Disasters due to Climate Change

13.11 Top of FormPopulation Growth, Urbanization and Disaster Risk

13.1 Technologies Useful During Disaster Management

Various technologies play a crucial role in enhancing disaster management efforts, enabling better preparedness, response, and recovery. Here are some of the key technologies that are useful during disaster management:

Remote Sensing and GIS (Geographic Information Systems):

Remote sensing technologies, such as satellite imagery and aerial surveys, provide real-time data on disaster-affected areas, helping assess the extent of damage and plan response efforts.

GIS allows the integration and analysis of geospatial data, facilitating better decision-making, resource allocation, and identification of vulnerable areas.

Early Warning Systems (EWS):

EWS use various technologies, including weather radars, seismic sensors, and river gauges, to detect potential hazards and issue timely warnings to at-risk communities.

Modern EWS utilize advanced communication technologies to disseminate warnings through text messages, mobile apps, social media, and sirens.

Communication Technologies:

During disasters, communication infrastructure is often disrupted. Technologies like satellite phones, mesh networks, and deployable communication towers help restore communication and coordination among responders.

Drones and Unmanned Aerial Vehicles (UAVs):

Drones are deployed for rapid damage assessment, search and rescue operations, and delivery of essential supplies to remote or inaccessible areas during disasters.

UAVs equipped with sensors can collect valuable data for post-disaster analysis and planning.

Artificial Intelligence (AI) and Machine Learning (ML):

AI and ML technologies can analyse vast amounts of data to detect patterns, predict disaster impacts, and optimize resource allocation for effective response.

AI-powered chatbots and virtual assistants are used for providing real-time information and answering queries during disasters.

Internet of Things (IoT):

IoT devices, such as environmental sensors and smart meters, collect real-time data on various parameters like temperature, humidity, and water levels, enabling better monitoring and early detection of anomalies.

Big Data Analytics:

Big data analytics processes large datasets generated during disasters to extract valuable insights, identify trends, and aid in decision-making for response and recovery efforts.

Social Media and Crowdsourcing:

Social media platforms serve as valuable sources of real-time information during disasters. They facilitate crowdsourcing of data, helping locate missing persons and identify areas needing immediate assistance.

Virtual Reality (VR) and Augmented Reality (AR):

VR and AR technologies are used for training responders in simulated disaster scenarios, enhancing their preparedness and decision-making skills.

AR can also overlay critical information onto real-world environments, aiding responders during operations.

Blockchain Technology:

Blockchain ensures secure and transparent data sharing, which is beneficial for managing relief distribution, financial transactions, and verifying the authenticity of aid recipients.

Biometric Identification:

Biometric systems help in rapid and accurate identification of disaster victims, streamlining relief efforts and reuniting families.

Robotics:

Robots are utilized for tasks in hazardous environments, such as search and rescue in collapsed buildings or hazardous material handling.

These technologies continue to evolve and transform disaster management practices, enabling faster and more efficient responses, better risk assessment, and improved coordination among various stakeholders. Integration of these technologies into disaster management strategies can significantly enhance overall disaster resilience and reduce the impact of natural and human-made disasters.

13.2 Remote Sensing and GIS Technology for Disaster Management

Remote Sensing and Geographic Information Systems (GIS) play vital roles in disaster management, offering valuable data and spatial analysis capabilities that aid in various phases of disaster risk reduction.

A] Use of Remote Sensing & GIS Technology

Remote Sensing in Disaster Management: Remote sensing involves the use of satellite or aerial imagery to gather information about the Earth's surface. It provides real-time and near-real-time data, allowing for quick assessment and monitoring during disasters. Some applications of remote sensing in disaster management include:

Damage Assessment: Remote sensing allows for rapid and accurate assessment of the extent of damage caused by disasters like earthquakes, floods, and wildfires. This information helps prioritize response efforts and resource allocation.

Early Warning Systems: Satellite imagery and sensors can detect early warning signs of disasters such as cyclones, tsunamis, and droughts, enabling authorities to issue timely warnings to vulnerable communities.

Monitoring Hazards: Remote sensing helps monitor natural hazards like volcanic eruptions, landslides, and forest fires, providing crucial data for disaster preparedness and response.

GIS in Disaster Management: Geographic Information Systems (GIS) capture, store, analyse, and display spatial data, making it a powerful tool for disaster management. Some applications of GIS in disaster management include:

Vulnerability Mapping: GIS can be used to create vulnerability maps that identify areas prone to various hazards, helping planners develop targeted risk reduction strategies.

Evacuation Planning: GIS-based evacuation plans consider factors like population density, infrastructure, and escape routes, optimizing evacuation efforts during disasters.

Resource Management: GIS helps manage and track resources during response operations, ensuring efficient distribution of aid and relief supplies.

B] **Advantages of Remote Sensing and GIS Integration for Disaster Risk Reduction:**

Timely and Accurate Information: Remote sensing and GIS provide real-time data and spatial analysis, enabling authorities to make informed decisions quickly during disasters.

Enhanced Preparedness: By identifying vulnerable areas and mapping hazards, remote sensing and GIS help authorities develop targeted disaster preparedness and mitigation strategies.

Improved Response and Recovery Efforts: Remote sensing and GIS aid in damage assessment and resource allocation, facilitating more effective response and recovery operations.

Data Visualization: GIS provides interactive and visual representations of data, making complex information easier to understand and communicate to stakeholders.

C] **Disadvantages of Remote Sensing and GIS Integration for Disaster Risk Reduction:**

Cost and Technical Expertise: The integration of remote sensing and GIS technology can be expensive, requiring specialized equipment and trained personnel.

Data Limitations: Remote sensing data may be affected by weather conditions, cloud cover, or image resolution, which can limit its availability during certain disasters.

Data Privacy and Security: Handling spatial data requires careful consideration of privacy and security issues, especially when dealing with sensitive information during disasters.

Reliance on Infrastructure: Remote sensing relies on satellites and ground-based infrastructure, making it vulnerable to damage during disasters, potentially disrupting data availability.

Despite these challenges, the integration of remote sensing and GIS technology remains essential for effective disaster risk reduction. The benefits of timely and accurate information, improved preparedness, and enhanced response efforts outweigh the disadvantages, making remote sensing and GIS valuable tools in building disaster-resilient communities.

13.3 Drones and Unmanned Aerial Vehicles (UAVs) Technology for DM

Drones and Unmanned Aerial Vehicles (UAVs) have emerged as valuable tools in disaster management, offering a wide range of applications that enhance disaster response and risk reduction efforts.

A] Use of Drones & UAVs:

Use of Drones and UAVs in Disaster Management: Drones and UAVs are equipped with cameras, sensors, and GPS technology, enabling them to collect valuable data and imagery from the air. Some key applications of drones and UAVs in disaster management include:

Damage Assessment: Drones can rapidly survey disaster-affected areas, providing high-resolution imagery that aids in damage assessment and helps prioritize response efforts.

Search and Rescue Operations: UAVs equipped with thermal cameras can locate survivors in debris, hazardous terrains, or hard-to-reach areas, assisting search and rescue teams.

Surveillance and Monitoring: Drones can monitor disaster events in real-time, providing valuable situational awareness to responders and decision-makers.

Mapping and Surveying: UAVs can create detailed 3D maps and topographic models, aiding in pre – and post-disaster planning and infrastructure assessment.

Delivery of Aid and Supplies: Drones can transport essential supplies, medical equipment, and communication devices to disaster-affected regions, especially when conventional access routes are disrupted.

B] **Advantages of Drones and UAVs Integration for Disaster Risk Reduction:**

Rapid Response and Deployment: Drones can be quickly deployed, providing real-time data and imagery for immediate situational analysis, guiding response efforts promptly.

Cost-Effective Data Collection: Drones offer a cost-effective alternative to manned aerial surveys, reducing the expenses associated with data acquisition.

Enhanced Safety for First Responders: By assisting in search and rescue operations, drones reduce the risk to human responders in hazardous environments.

Aerial Coverage and Accessibility: Drones can access areas that are difficult or dangerous for ground teams to reach, providing a comprehensive view of the disaster's impact.

Efficient Mapping and Planning: UAVs help create accurate and up-to-date maps, enabling better disaster preparedness, response, and long-term recovery planning.

C] **Disadvantages of Drones and UAVs Integration for Disaster Risk Reduction:**

Regulatory and Legal Challenges: Drone operations are subject to various regulations, and obtaining necessary permissions for deployment can be time-consuming.

Limited Flight Time and Range: Drones have limited flight times and ranges, requiring careful planning to ensure adequate coverage during large-scale disasters.

Weather Sensitivity: Adverse weather conditions, such as strong winds or heavy rain, can impact drone operations and data collection.

Data Processing and Analysis: Processing and analysing large datasets collected by drones require specialized skills and computing resources.

Privacy Concerns: Drone surveillance may raise privacy concerns among affected populations, necessitating transparent and ethical data use.

Despite these challenges, the integration of drones and UAVs in disaster management continues to evolve, and technological advancements address some limitations. When used effectively, drones can significantly contribute to disaster risk reduction, helping to save lives, optimize response efforts, and improve overall disaster resilience.

13.4 Artificial Intelligence (AI) and Machine Learning (ML) Technology for DM

Artificial Intelligence (AI) and Machine Learning (ML) technologies have the potential to revolutionize disaster management by providing advanced data analysis, predictive modelling, and decision-making capabilities. These technologies offer several applications that enhance disaster management efforts:

A]   Use of AI and ML in Disaster Management:

Data Analysis and Pattern Recognition: AI and ML algorithms can analyse vast amounts of data from various sources, such as satellite imagery, social media, and sensor networks. They identify patterns and trends, aiding in early detection and forecasting of disasters.

Predictive Modelling: AI and ML can develop predictive models based on historical data and current environmental conditions. These models help forecast the magnitude and impact of disasters, enabling authorities to make informed decisions.

Natural Language Processing (NLP): NLP allows AI systems to process and understand human language. During disasters, NLP helps in sentiment analysis of social media posts to assess public perception and detect emerging issues.

Robots and Autonomous Systems: AI-powered robots can assist in search and rescue operations, hazardous material handling, and infrastructure inspection in disaster-affected areas.

Decision Support Systems: AI can support decision-making by providing real-time information, recommending optimal response strategies, and simulating disaster scenarios.

Damage Assessment and Response Optimization: AI and ML technologies aid in rapid damage assessment by analysing aerial imagery and sensor data. They optimize resource allocation and response strategies based on real-time data and changing conditions.

B] **Advantages of AI and ML Integration for Disaster Risk Reduction:**

Data-Driven Decision-Making: AI and ML enable evidence-based decision-making, leading to more effective and efficient disaster response and risk reduction strategies.

Early Detection and Warning: Predictive models can identify early warning signs, allowing authorities to issue timely alerts and warnings to vulnerable communities.

Automated Data Processing: AI and ML automate data analysis, processing vast datasets quickly, which would be time-consuming or practically impossible for human operators.

Improved Situational Awareness: AI systems provide real-time situational awareness, helping decision-makers understand the evolving dynamics of disasters.

Efficient Resource Allocation: AI optimizes resource allocation, ensuring that aid and relief supplies are directed to the areas most in need.

C] **Disadvantages of AI and ML Integration for Disaster Risk Reduction:**

Data Quality and Bias: AI and ML models are only as good as the data they are trained on. Biased or inaccurate data can lead to flawed predictions and decisions.

Limited Human Judgment: AI systems lack human judgment and may not account for nuanced factors that human responders consider during complex situations.

Complexity and Skill Requirements: Implementing AI and ML solutions require specialized skills, expertise, and infrastructure, which may be challenging for some organizations.

Ethical Considerations: AI applications in disaster management raise ethical questions related to privacy, data security, and transparency.

Cost and Accessibility: AI and ML technologies can be expensive to implement and maintain, making them less accessible to smaller organizations or developing regions.

By addressing these challenges and leveraging the advantages of AI and ML technologies, disaster management can benefit from data-driven insights, improved decision-making, and enhanced response capabilities, ultimately contributing to more effective disaster risk reduction and resilience building.

13.5 Internet of Things (IoT) Technology for DM

The Internet of Things (IoT) technology has significant applications in disaster management, providing valuable data collection, real-time monitoring, and enhanced situational awareness. IoT's interconnected network of devices enables seamless communication, data sharing, and automation, making it a powerful tool in disaster risk reduction.

A]   **Use of IoT in Disaster Management:**

Environmental Monitoring: IoT sensors can continuously monitor environmental conditions, such as temperature, humidity, air quality, and water levels, enabling early detection of potential hazards like wildfires, floods, or landslides.

Infrastructure Monitoring: IoT devices can monitor the structural health of critical infrastructure, such as bridges and buildings, detecting potential weaknesses or damages caused by disasters.

Early Warning Systems: IoT-enabled sensors and devices can detect seismic activities, extreme weather patterns, or rising water levels, triggering early warning systems to alert at-risk communities.

Real-Time Data Collection: IoT devices provide real-time data during disasters, helping responders and decision-makers make informed and timely decisions.

Search and Rescue Support: IoT technologies can be integrated into wearable devices and equipment used by search and rescue teams to improve their effectiveness and safety.

Supply Chain Management: IoT can enhance supply chain visibility, tracking the movement of relief supplies and ensuring their timely delivery to affected areas.

B] **Advantages of IoT Integration for Disaster Risk Reduction:**

Real-Time Monitoring: IoT provides real-time data, enhancing situational awareness and enabling rapid response during disasters.

Early Detection and Warning: IoT sensors can detect and transmit early warning signs, allowing authorities to issue timely alerts and mitigate potential impacts.

Remote Sensing: IoT devices can be deployed in remote and inaccessible areas, providing critical data without the need for human presence.

Data-Driven Decision-Making: IoT data analytics enable data-driven decision-making, optimizing resource allocation and response efforts.

Efficient Resource Management: IoT helps in the efficient management of resources and assets during disaster response and recovery operations.

C] **Disadvantages of IoT Integration for Disaster Risk Reduction:**

Cost and Infrastructure: Implementing IoT infrastructure and deploying sensors can be expensive, especially in remote or underdeveloped regions.

Data Security and Privacy Concerns: IoT devices collect vast amounts of sensitive data, raising concerns about data security and privacy.

Reliability and Connectivity Issues: IoT devices rely on stable connectivity, which can be challenging in disaster-affected areas with damaged communication networks.

Complexity and Skill Requirements: Implementing and maintaining IoT solutions require specialized skills and technical expertise.

Power Dependency: IoT devices are reliant on power sources, and power disruptions during disasters can affect their functionality.

By addressing the challenges and leveraging the advantages of IoT technology, disaster management can harness its potential to improve preparedness, response, and recovery efforts. Integrating IoT into disaster risk reduction strategies can lead to better data collection, enhanced early warning systems, and more efficient resource management, ultimately increasing community resilience to disasters.

13.6 Virtual Reality (VR) and Augmented Reality (AR) Technology for DM

Virtual Reality (VR) and Augmented Reality (AR) technologies offer immersive and interactive experiences that have valuable applications in disaster management, enhancing training, planning, and response efforts.

A] **Use of VR and AR in Disaster Management:**

Training and Simulation: VR and AR are used to train responders in realistic disaster scenarios, enabling them to practice decision-making, search and rescue techniques, and evacuation procedures in a safe and controlled environment.

Preparedness and Planning: VR and AR tools help visualize disaster scenarios and assess potential risks, allowing authorities to develop effective preparedness and response strategies.

Damage Assessment and Situational Awareness: AR overlays real-time data onto the user's view, providing responders with critical information about the disaster scene, such as structural damage and hazardous conditions.

Communication and Coordination: AR can facilitate communication and coordination among responders by providing real-time information and visual cues, improving teamwork and collaboration during disaster operations.

Public Awareness and Education: VR and AR technologies can be utilized to create engaging and interactive educational materials for the public, raising awareness about disaster risks and preparedness measures.

B] **Advantages of VR and AR Integration for Disaster Risk Reduction:**

Realistic Training: VR and AR simulations offer lifelike training experiences, better preparing responders for actual disaster scenarios.

Enhanced Visualization: VR and AR provide a visual understanding of disaster impacts, aiding decision-making and resource allocation.

Improved Situational Awareness: AR overlays relevant data onto the user's surroundings, enhancing situational awareness for responders.

Safe and Controlled Environment: VR training allows responders to practice in a controlled setting, reducing the risks associated with live exercises.

Engaging Public Awareness: VR and AR can capture the public's attention, making disaster preparedness and education efforts more effective.

C] **Disadvantages of VR and AR Integration for Disaster Risk Reduction:**

Cost and Technical Requirements: Implementing VR and AR solutions can be expensive, requiring specialized hardware and software.

Training and Familiarity: Responders may need time to adapt to VR and AR technologies, potentially affecting the efficiency of their initial use.

Potential Distractions: AR overlays can be distracting in high-pressure disaster situations, requiring users to manage information effectively.

Limited Real-Time Data: AR relies on real-time data availability, which may be impacted by communication disruptions during disasters.

Dependency on Power and Connectivity: VR and AR devices rely on power sources and stable connectivity, which may be challenging during disasters.

By addressing these challenges and maximizing the advantages, VR and AR technologies can significantly enhance disaster risk reduction efforts. The immersive and interactive nature of these technologies can improve responder training, situational awareness, and decision-making, ultimately contributing to more effective disaster management and community resilience.

13.7 Robotics Technology for DM

Robotics technology has shown immense promise in disaster management, providing capabilities that enhance search and rescue operations, hazardous material handling, and remote monitoring during disasters.

A] Use of Robotics Technology in Disaster Management:

Search and Rescue: Robots equipped with cameras, sensors, and robotic arms can navigate through hazardous environments, such as collapsed buildings or areas with toxic substances, to search for survivors and assess damage.

Remote Monitoring: Unmanned robots and drones can be deployed in disaster-affected regions to gather real-time data and imagery, providing situational awareness to responders and decision-makers.

Hazardous Material Handling: Robots can handle dangerous substances or radioactive materials during industrial accidents or nuclear disasters, minimizing the risk to human responders.

Infrastructure Inspection: Robots can inspect critical infrastructure, such as bridges and pipelines, for damage assessment and post-disaster safety evaluations.

Communication and Connectivity: Robots can act as communication relays in areas with disrupted or limited connectivity, helping establish communication links with responders and affected communities.

B] **Advantages of Robotics Integration for Disaster Risk Reduction:**

Safety and Efficiency: Robots can access hazardous environments that are dangerous for human responders, increasing safety and efficiency during search and rescue operations.

Continuous Operations: Robots do not tire or require rest, enabling them to work continuously for extended periods, unlike human responders.

Real-Time Data Collection: Robots provide real-time data and imagery, enhancing situational awareness and supporting data-driven decision-making.

Remote Access: Robots can access remote and difficult-to-reach areas, expanding the scope of disaster assessment and response.

Versatility: Robotics technology can be adapted for various disaster scenarios, offering a wide range of applications in disaster management.

C] **Disadvantages of Robotics Integration for Disaster Risk Reduction:**

Complexity and Skill Requirements: Implementing and operating robotics systems require specialized training and technical expertise.

Cost and Maintenance: Robotics technology can be expensive to acquire and maintain, making it challenging for some organizations or regions to adopt.

Limited Autonomy: Current robotics technology may have limited autonomy, requiring human operators to control them remotely.

Terrain Limitations: Some robots may face challenges in navigating complex or unstable terrains, affecting their efficiency in certain disaster scenarios.

Power Dependency: Robots are reliant on power sources, which may be limited or unavailable in disaster-affected areas.

Despite these challenges, robotics technology continues to advance and shows great potential in improving disaster management practices. By addressing the limitations and maximizing the advantages, the integration of robotics in disaster risk reduction can lead to more effective search and rescue operations, better situational awareness, and improved overall disaster response capabilities.

13.8 Early Warning Systems & Advance Communication Technology for DM

Early Warning Systems (EWS) and advanced communication technology are crucial components of disaster management, enabling timely and effective responses to potential threats and disasters.

A] Use of Early Warning Systems & ACT in Disaster Management:

Early Detection and Warning: Early Warning Systems use various sensors and monitoring devices to detect hazards like earthquakes, tsunamis, floods, cyclones, and wildfires. They trigger alarms and notifications to authorities and at-risk communities, providing advance notice to take preventive measures or evacuate.

Rapid Information Dissemination: Advanced communication technology, such as mobile apps, social media, SMS alerts, and sirens, helps disseminate warning messages to a large number of people swiftly. This rapid information flow allows for faster response coordination and public awareness.

Remote Monitoring: EWS and communication technology enable remote monitoring of disaster-affected areas, providing real-time updates to emergency responders and decision makers.

Automated Alerts and Notifications: EWS can be automated, reducing response time and the need for human intervention, ensuring that warnings reach the right authorities and communities promptly.

Integration with Disaster Response: Early Warning Systems are integrated into disaster response plans, guiding preparedness, resource allocation, and response strategies.

B] Advantages of EWS & ACT for Disaster Risk Reduction:

Improved Preparedness: Early warning messages prompt communities to be better prepared for potential disasters, reducing vulnerability and enhancing resilience.

Timely Response: Quick dissemination of warnings allows people to take immediate action, leading to reduced loss of life and property during disasters.

Enhanced Coordination: Advanced communication technology enables better coordination among various response agencies, enhancing the efficiency of disaster response operations.

Widespread Reach: Communication technology reaches a broad audience, including remote and isolated areas, ensuring that even marginalized communities receive warnings.

Real-Time Data: EWS provides real-time data, enabling decision-makers to make informed choices based on the most current information available.

C] Disadvantages of EWS & ACT for Disaster Risk Reduction:

False Alarms: EWS can sometimes generate false alarms, leading to complacency and decreased trust in future warnings.

Technology Dependency: Advanced communication technology relies on stable and functioning networks, which can be disrupted during disasters.

Limited Accessibility: In regions with limited infrastructure or technological access, some communities may not receive early warnings.

Language and Cultural Barriers: Ensuring that warnings are comprehensible and culturally appropriate to diverse communities can be challenging.

Technological Failure: Technical issues or power outages may impact the functioning of communication systems, affecting timely warning delivery.

To maximize the benefits of Early Warning Systems and advanced communication technology, addressing these challenges is essential. Efforts to increase the resilience of communication infrastructure, improve accessibility to remote areas, and conduct regular public awareness campaigns are necessary for more effective disaster risk reduction. The integration of EWS and advanced communication technology plays a crucial role in reducing disaster risks, enhancing preparedness, and saving lives during emergencies.

13.9 Big Data Analytics and Blockchain Technology in DM

Big Data Analytics and Blockchain Technology have significant applications in disaster management, offering advanced data processing, secure information sharing, and improved transparency during disaster response and risk reduction efforts.

A] **Use of Big Data Analytics and Blockchain in Disaster Management:**

Big Data Analytics:

Data Processing: Big Data Analytics can process and analyse vast amounts of data from various sources, such as social media, satellite imagery, and sensor networks, providing valuable insights for disaster response and preparedness.

Predictive Modelling: Big Data Analytics can develop predictive models based on historical data and real-time information, aiding in forecasting disaster impacts and identifying vulnerable areas.

Situational Awareness: Real-time data analysis enhances situational awareness, enabling decision-makers to make informed choices during disaster response.

Blockchain Technology:

Data Security: Blockchain provides a decentralized and secure way to store and share disaster-related data, safeguarding sensitive information from tampering and unauthorized access.

Transparent Transactions: Blockchain's immutable nature ensures transparency in the flow of resources, aid, and donations during disaster response, minimizing the risk of corruption and fraud.

Decentralized Coordination: Blockchain facilitates peer-to-peer communication and coordination among various response agencies, optimizing resource allocation and response efforts.

B] **Advantages of Big Data Analytics and Blockchain Integration for Disaster Risk Reduction:**

Data-Driven Decision-Making: Big Data Analytics enables evidence-based decision-making, leading to more efficient resource allocation and response strategies.

Real-Time Information: Big Data Analytics provides real-time insights, enhancing situational awareness during disasters and enabling faster response coordination.

Data Security and Integrity: Blockchain ensures the security and integrity of disaster-related data, reducing the risk of data breaches and manipulation.

Efficient Resource Management: Blockchain's transparent and decentralized nature facilitates efficient resource management and distribution during disaster response.

Improved Accountability: Blockchain's immutable ledger enhances accountability and traceability of resources, aid, and donations, ensuring they reach intended beneficiaries.

C] **Disadvantages of Big Data Analytics and Blockchain Integration for Disaster Risk Reduction:**

Data Privacy Concerns: The use of Big Data Analytics raises concerns about the privacy and confidentiality of personal information collected during disaster response.

Technical Complexity: Implementing Big Data Analytics and Blockchain solutions requires specialized skills and technical expertise.

Cost: Integrating Big Data Analytics and Blockchain can be expensive, especially for smaller organizations or regions with limited resources.

Power and Connectivity Dependency: Disaster-affected areas may experience power outages and communication disruptions, affecting data collection and Blockchain transactions.

Regulatory Challenges: Blockchain technology may face regulatory hurdles, particularly in terms of data governance and cross-border transactions.

By addressing these challenges and leveraging the advantages, the integration of Big Data Analytics and Blockchain in disaster management can lead to more effective and transparent disaster response and risk reduction efforts. Embracing these technologies can enhance data-driven decision-making, improve situational awareness, and strengthen the overall resilience of communities to disasters.

13.10 Technology for Control & Management of Urban Disasters due to Climate Change

Climate change is one of the most significant challenges facing the world today, with urban areas particularly vulnerable to its impacts. As global temperatures rise, extreme weather events such as floods, storms, heatwaves, and sea-level rise pose a severe threat to urban communities. The increasing frequency and intensity of these disasters necessitate the adoption of advanced technologies for their control and management. This essay delves into the role of technology in mitigating the effects of urban disasters caused by climate change and the advantages it brings in enhancing disaster control and management.

A] **Use of Technology for Control & Management**

Early Warning Systems and Predictive Analytics: Early warning systems (EWS) are crucial in alerting urban residents and authorities about impending disasters. Advanced technologies such as big data analytics, machine learning, and artificial intelligence can process vast amounts of data from multiple sources, including weather satellites, sensors, and social media, to predict potential disaster events. This allows for timely evacuations and resource mobilization, reducing the impact of disasters on urban populations.

Remote Sensing and GIS Technology: Remote sensing and Geographic Information System (GIS) technology play a significant role in disaster management. Satellite imagery and drones provide real-time data on disaster-affected areas, enabling rapid damage assessment and identification of critical infrastructure vulnerabilities. GIS technology aids in mapping disaster-prone zones, facilitating effective urban planning and land use policies to reduce exposure to risks.

Internet of Things (IoT) for Urban Resilience: IoT technology is instrumental in enhancing urban resilience to climate change-induced disasters. Smart sensors and connected devices in buildings and infrastructure monitor real-time conditions such as temperature, humidity, and structural integrity. This data helps in early detection of weaknesses and allows for preventive maintenance, ensuring the safety of urban structures during extreme weather events.

Smart Urban Infrastructure and Resilient Buildings: Technological advancements enable the construction of smart and resilient urban infrastructure. Self-healing materials, energy-efficient buildings, and green roofs contribute to disaster risk reduction by minimizing damage and resource consumption during disasters. Additionally, advanced materials and construction methods are employed to withstand the impact of extreme weather events.

Mobile Apps and Communication Systems: Mobile applications and advanced communication systems facilitate efficient disaster response and management. Citizens can receive real-time alerts, evacuation routes, and safety guidelines through mobile apps. Moreover, communication networks ensure seamless coordination among first responders and emergency management agencies, improving response time and overall effectiveness during disasters.

Blockchain for Transparent Disaster Relief: Blockchain technology ensures transparent and tamper-proof distribution of disaster relief resources. Smart contracts facilitate automated and secure aid distribution to affected communities, minimizing corruption and ensuring resources reach those in need swiftly. Blockchain also enables the traceability of funds and resources, promoting accountability among stakeholders.

Climate Data and Simulation Models: Sophisticated climate data analysis and simulation models help urban planners and policymakers anticipate the long-term effects of climate change on urban areas. This allows for the formulation of robust adaptation and mitigation strategies, ensuring urban communities are better prepared to face future climate-induced disasters.

B] **Advantages of Technology Integration:**

Timely and Accurate Information: Advanced technologies provide real-time and accurate information, enabling swift and informed decision-making during disasters.

Enhanced Preparedness and Response: Early warning systems and predictive analytics increase preparedness levels, allowing authorities to mobilize resources and evacuate residents proactively.

Reduced Loss of Life and Property: Improved disaster management technologies lead to reduced casualties and minimal damage to urban infrastructure.

Efficient Resource Allocation: Technology streamlines resource allocation, ensuring aid and relief efforts are directed where they are most needed.

Public Awareness and Education: Technology-driven communication systems raise public awareness about disaster risks and encourage proactive measures for disaster preparedness.

C] **Disadvantages and Challenges:**

Cost and Infrastructure: Implementing advanced technologies may be expensive, especially for resource-constrained urban areas.

Data Privacy and Security: Managing sensitive data and ensuring its security is a challenge for technology-based disaster management systems.

Digital Divide: Unequal access to technology can lead to disparities in disaster preparedness and response capabilities among different urban communities.

Thus, the integration of technology in disaster management is essential for enhancing urban resilience to the impacts of climate change. Early warning systems, remote sensing, IoT, and blockchain technology are invaluable tools in reducing disaster risks and improving disaster response. By leveraging the potential of these technologies, urban areas can become better equipped to face the challenges posed by climate change and create safer, more resilient communities for the future. However, it is crucial to address the challenges of affordability, data security, and equitable access to technology to ensure that all urban residents benefit from these advancements in disaster control and management.

References

1. "Disaster Management and Preparedness" by Rajib Shaw
2. "Disaster Management: A Disaster Manager's Handbook" by the National Institute of Disaster Management (NIDM)
3. "Disaster Management: Enabling Resilience" by Harsh K. Gupta and S. P. Harsha Vardhan
4. "Disaster Resilience: An Integrated Approach" by Douglas Paton and David Johnston
5. "Disaster Risk Reduction: Approaches and Case Studies" by Cuny Institute for Sustainable Cities
6. "Handbook of Disaster Research" by Havidán Rodríguez, William Donner, and Joseph E. Trainor
7. "Introduction to Disaster Management" by Dr. Anil Kumar Sinha
8. "Introduction to International Disaster Management" by Damon P. Coppola
9. "Principles of Emergency Management and Emergency Operations Centers (EOC)" by Michael J. Fagel
10. "The International Handbook of Social Impact Assessment: Conceptual and Methodological Advances" edited by Frank Vanclay and Ana Maria Esteves
11. Central Water Commission (CWC): Website: https://cwc.gov.in/
12. Disaster Administration and Management, Text & Case studies – SL Goel-Deep and Deep Publications
13. Disaster management – S. K. Singh, S.C. Kundu, Shobha Singh A – 119, William Publications, New Delhi. ·
14. Disaster Management – Vinod K Sharma IIPA, New Delhi,1995
15. Disaster Management Division, Ministry of Home Affairs:
16. Website: https://www.ndmindia.nic.in/

17. Disaster Management – G.K Ghosh-A.P.H. Publishing Corporation ·

18. Disaster Risk Management Profile, Mumbai, India. http:// emi.pdc.org/ cities/CP-Mumbai-09-05.pdf

19. Disaster Risk Reduction Portal, India: Website: https:// disasterportal.nic.in/

20. Gujarat Disaster Management Authority, Ghandinagar. www.gsdma.org.

21. Indian Meteorological Department (IMD): Website: http:// www.imd.gov.in/

22. Indian National Centre for Ocean Information Services (INCOIS):

23. Website: https://www.incois.gov.in/

24. Indian Red Cross Society (IRCS): Website: https:// indianredcross.org/

25. Ministry of Home Affairs (MHA), Government of India:

26. Website: https://www.mha.gov.in/

27. National Cyclone Risk Mitigation Project (NCRMP): Website: https://ncrmp.gov.in/

28. National Disaster Database (NIDM): Website: http://nidm.gov.in/ndb/

29. National Disaster Management Authorities, Government of India. www.ndma.gov.in

30. National Disaster Management Authority (NDMA): Website: https://ndma.gov.in/

31. National Disaster Response Force (NDRF): Website: https://ndrf.ndma.gov.in/

32. National Institute of Disaster Management (NIDM): Website: https://nidm.gov.in/

33. National Remote Sensing Centre (NRSC): Website: https:// www.nrsc.gov.in/

34. Pinkowski, J. (Ed.). (2008). Disaster Management Handbook (1st ed.). CRC Press. https://doi.org/10.1201/9781420058635

35. Sasikumar K., Dhirendra Bhargava, Disaster Management Plan for GIR: IGNFA, Dehradun.

36. Sidhu K.S., Tsunami Rehabilitation Program, Planning Commission, March 18, 2005, Manila.

37. United Nations Office for Disaster Risk Reduction (UNDRR) – India: Website: https://www.undrr.org/country/india

38. World Health Organization (WHO) India – Emergency Preparedness and Response: Website: https://www.who.int/india/emergencies

About the Author

Prof. Er. Pravin Khandve

B.E. Civil, M. Tech, PG.D.B.M., PG.D.I.D., PG.D.I.T., PG.D.I.J., PG.D.O.A.F.A., B.A. Soc.

M.I.E.I., M.I.S.C.A., M.I.W.W.A., M.I.S.E.T., M.I.S.T.E, M.E.C.I., M.I.C.I., M.A.C.C.E.

Current Position held:

- Vice Principal, Prof Ram Meghe College of Engineering & Management, Badnera – Amravati
- Head of Department, Civil Engineering, PRMCEAM, Badnera
- Mentor, Atal Tinkering Lab, Atal Innovation Mission, MHRD-GOI, New Delhi
- Dean – Infrastructure, PRMCEAM, Badnera
- Cell Member – Internal Quality Assurance Cell, PRMCEAM, Badnera
- Spiritual and Motivational Trainer – Mission IAS Foundation, Amravati
- Founder Director – Proven Victory Knowledge Techniques, Student Development Unit, Amravati
- Founder Secretary – Ekatmik Paryavaran Mitra Sanstha, Amravati
- Executor Editor – International Journal of Chemical & Physical Sciences, Amravati
- Member – Board of Studies – Civil Engineering – Prof Ram Meghe Institute of Technology and Research, Badnera – Amravati

- ➢ Secretary, Association of Civil Engineers, Amravati Centre, Amravati

- ➢ Treasurer, Indian Concrete Institute, ICI Amravati Centre, Amravati

- ➢ Executive Member – Indian Water Works Association, Amravati Chapter, Amravati

- ➢ Executive Member – College Development Council – Radhabai Sarda Arts, Science & Commerce College, Anjangaon Surji.

Other Books by Prof. Er. Pravin Khandve

1. Chikhaldara Tourist Guide, April 1993 (Marathi)   Rs. 50/-
2. Employability Skills Part-I, July 2012 (Marathi)   Rs. 100/-
3. Employability Skills Part-II, July 2013 (Marathi)   Rs. 100/-
4. Rain Water Harvesting – Need of Hour (Marathi)   Rs. 200/-
5. Become an Environment Friend (Marathi)   Rs. 200/-
6. Hazardous Waste Management (English)   Rs. 599/-
7. Municipal Solid Waste Management (English)   Rs. 799/-

Fourth coming Books of Prof. Er. Pravin Khandve

1. Effective Study Techniques (Marathi)   Rs. 300/-
2. Importance of Indian Festival in Modern Life (Marathi)   Rs. 200/-
3. Prove Yourself (Marathi)   Rs. 300/-
4. Basic Civil Engineering (Marathi)   Rs. 450/-
5. Successful Student Characteristics (Marathi)   Rs. 300/-
6. Rain Water Harvesting (English)   Rs. 399/-

Udemy Online Courses by Authore		
Basic Land Surveying	Geomatics & Advance Surveying	Quantity Estimating & Costing for Building
https://www.udemy.com/course/basic-land-surveying/	https://www.udemy.com/course/geomatics-advance-surveying/	https://www.udemy.com/course/quantity-estimating-costing-for-building/

Learn Online with Prof. Er. Pravin Khandve

Download: **PVKT School App** from 

Mob.- 8275732298 Contact Email – pvkexams@gmail.com

 YouTube Channel – @pvkt

LinkedIn – https://www.linkedin.com/in/pravinkhandve/

Author Researcher-ID: B-2509-2016

Author Orcid-ID: 0000-0002-5986-5805

Author Vidwan-ID : 364427

Author Google Scholar-ID: IdntbEYfsNMBgC

www.ingramcontent.com/pod-product-compliance
Lightning Source LLC
Chambersburg PA
CBHW021332150726
47989CB00005B/1959